Navigating the Research-Policy Relationship

Drawing on studies in environmental and sustainability education, this book brings together new work that has explored the research-policy interface in varied contexts and from diverse perspectives.

The relationship between research and policy has become an increasing focus for theoretical inquiry, empirical investigation, and practical development across many different fields. This volume highlights new empirical insights, theoretical ideas, practical examples, and methodological approaches for understanding, navigating, and developing more productive research-policy relationships.

This book will be beneficial to anyone who is interested in understanding the interface between research and policy. The chapters in this book were originally published in the journal *Environmental Education Research*.

Mark Rickinson is Associate Professor in the Faculty of Education at Monash University, Melbourne, Australia. His work is focused on understanding and improving the use of research in education policy and practice.

Marcia McKenzie is Professor and Associate Dean Sustainability in the Faculty of Education at the University of Melbourne, Melbourne, Australia. Her research focuses on critical policy studies, including in relation to sustainability and climate change education.

Navigating the Research-Policy Relationship

Studies in Environmental and Sustainability Education

**Edited by
Mark Rickinson and Marcia McKenzie**

LONDON AND NEW YORK

First published 2024
by Routledge
4 Park Square, Milton Park, Abingdon, Oxon, OX14 4RN

and by Routledge
605 Third Avenue, New York, NY 10158

Routledge is an imprint of the Taylor & Francis Group, an informa business

© 2024 Taylor & Francis

All rights reserved. No part of this book may be reprinted or reproduced or utilised in any form or by any electronic, mechanical, or other means, now known or hereafter invented, including photocopying and recording, or in any information storage or retrieval system, without permission in writing from the publishers.

Trademark notice: Product or corporate names may be trademarks or registered trademarks, and are used only for identification and explanation without intent to infringe.

British Library Cataloguing-in-Publication Data
A catalogue record for this book is available from the British Library

ISBN13: 978-1-032-52320-0 (hbk)
ISBN13: 978-1-032-52323-1 (pbk)
ISBN13: 978-1-003-40612-9 (ebk)

DOI: 10.4324/9781003406129

Typeset in Myriad Pro
by codeMantra

Publisher's Note
The publisher accepts responsibility for any inconsistencies that may have arisen during the conversion of this book from journal articles to book chapters, namely the inclusion of journal terminology.

Disclaimer
Every effort has been made to contact copyright holders for their permission to reprint material in this book. The publishers would be grateful to hear from any copyright holder who is not here acknowledged and will undertake to rectify any errors or omissions in future editions of this book.

Contents

Citation Information vii
Notes on Contributors ix

1 Introducing the complexities of the research-policy relationship 1
   Mark Rickinson and Marcia McKenzie

2 Understanding the research-policy relationship: insights from the critical policy and evidence use literatures 16
   Mark Rickinson and Marcia McKenzie

3 The changing and complex entanglements of research and policy making in education: issues for environmental and sustainability education 34
   Bob Lingard

4 A reflection on the relational aspects of research policy interfaces 49
   Anne Edwards

5 Understanding policymakers' perspectives on evidence use as a mechanism for improving research-policy relationships 54
   Louise Shaxson and Annette Boaz

6 Environment and sustainability education research as policy engagement: (re-)invigorating 'politics as *potentia*' in South Africa 61
   Heila Lotz-Sisitka, Eureta Rosenberg, and Presha Ramsarup

7 Reflections on the science–policy interface within education for sustainable development in Germany 90
   Mandy Singer-Brodowski, Antje Brock, Julius Grund, and Gerhard de Haan

8 Colombia's national policy of environmental education: a critical discourse analysis 107
   María Angélica Mejía-Cáceres, Alejandra Huérfano, Alan Reid and Laísa María Freire

9 Improving policy through research-practice partnerships: Reflections and analysis from New York City 131
Oren Pizmony-Levy, Meredith McDermott, and Thaddeus T. Copeland

10 Sustainability education research and policy in Cyprus: an investigation into their roles and relationships 150
Aravella Zachariou and Konstantinos Korfiatis

Index 167

Citation Information

The chapters in this book were originally published in the journal of *Environmental Education Research*, volume 27, issue 4 (2021). When citing this material, please use the original page numbering for each article, as follows:

Chapter 1
The research-policy relationship in environmental and sustainability education
Mark Rickinson and Marcia McKenzie
Environmental Education Research, volume 27, issue 4 (2021) pp. 465–479

Chapter 2
Understanding the research-policy relationship in ESE: insights from the critical policy and evidence use literatures
Mark Rickinson and Marcia McKenzie
Environmental Education Research, volume 27, issue 4 (2021) pp. 480–497

Chapter 3
The changing and complex entanglements of research and policy making in education: issues for environmental and sustainability education
Bob Lingard
Environmental Education Research, volume 27, issue 4 (2021) pp. 498–512

Chapter 4
A reflection on the relational aspects of research policy interfaces
Anne Edwards
Environmental Education Research, volume 27, issue 4 (2021) pp. 513–517

Chapter 5
Understanding policymakers' perspectives on evidence use as a mechanism for improving research-policy relationships
Louise Shaxson and Annette Boaz
Environmental Education Research, volume 27, issue 4 (2021) pp. 518–524

Chapter 6
Environment and sustainability education research as policy engagement: (re-)invigorating 'politics as potentia' in South Africa
Heila Lotz-Sisitka, Eureta Rosenberg and Presha Ramsarup
Environmental Education Research, volume 27, issue 4 (2021) pp. 525–553

Chapter 7
Reflections on the science–policy interface within education for sustainable development in Germany
Mandy Singer-Brodowski, Antje Brock, Julius Grund and Gerhard de Haan
Environmental Education Research, volume 27, issue 4 (2021) pp. 554–570

Chapter 8
Colombia's national policy of environmental education: a critical discourse analysis
María Angélica Mejía-Cáceres, Alejandra Huérfano, Alan Reid and Laísa María Freire
Environmental Education Research, volume 27, issue 4 (2021) pp. 571–594

Chapter 9
Improving ESE policy through research-practice partnerships: Reflections and analysis from New York City
Oren Pizmony-Levy, Meredith McDermott, and Thaddeus T. Copeland
Environmental Education Research, volume 27, issue 4 (2021) pp. 595–613

Chapter 10
Sustainability education research and policy in Cyprus: an investigation into their roles and relationships
Aravella Zachariou and Konstantinos Korfiatis
Environmental Education Research, volume 27, issue 4 (2021) pp. 614–629

For any permission-related enquiries please visit:
http://www.tandfonline.com/page/help/permissions

Notes on Contributors

Annette Boaz is Professor at the Centre for Health Care and Social Research at the Faculty of Health, Social Care and Education at Kingston University, London, UK. She has more than 25 years of experience in supporting the use of evidence across a range of policy domains. She was Founding Editor of the international journal *Evidence & Policy*.

Antje Brock works as Research Associate at the department of the scientific advisor of the German implementation structures of the UNESCO programme 'ESD for 2030'. Her main research interests are monitoring approaches for education for sustainable development (ESD) and the links between ESD and the concepts of social and environmental justice.

Thaddeus T. Copeland is Director of Sustainability at the Department of Education, USA. His specialities include Program Design and Management, Communications, Environmental Education, Program Evaluation, Strategic Planning, and Partnership Development.

Gerhard de Haan is Professor of educational futures studies; the scientific director of the master's program Future Studies; and an expert in educational futures studies, sustainable development, and education for sustainable development (ESD). From 2005 to 2014, he was the chairman of the German National Committee of the UN Decade of ESD. From 2015 to 2019, he was the scientific advisor of the German implementation of the UNESCO Global Action Programme on ESD, and since 2020, he has been the scientific advisor of the new UNESCO programme 'ESD for 2030'. His research interests are education for sustainable development, citizenship education, future science, knowledge society, and theories and models of education.

Anne Edwards is former Director of the Department of Education at the University of Oxford, UK, and former President of the British Educational Research Association, UK. She holds degrees honoris causa from the Universities of Helsinki and Oslo in recognition of her work on relational expertise and collaboration across practice boundaries. Her research, which draws on Vygotskian understandings of learning and culture, has largely been in the field of professional learning in the caring professions. She has also had a long-standing commitment to ensuring that social research engages with the communities with which it is working in ways that benefit both the communities and the research.

Laísa María Freire is Professor at the Institute of Biology at the Department of Ecology at the Federal University of Rio de Janeiro, Brazil. Her research focuses on environmental education in the teacher science degree and environmental management.

Julius Grund also works as Research Associate at the Department of the scientific advisor of the German implementation structures of the UNESCO programme 'ESD for 2030'. He also works as Lecturer at the Freie Universitat Berlin, Germany. His main research interests are quantitative monitoring approaches for education for sustainable development (ESD), the role of emotions in ESD, and the broader psycho-social context of ESD, such as its link to individual well-being.

Alejandra Huérfano holds a master's in environmental sciences and conservation at the Institute of Biodiversity and Sustainability (NUPEM) at the Federal University of Rio de Janeiro, Brazil. The author has contributed to research in topic, Neoliberalism (international relations) & Policy analysis.

Konstantinos Korfiatis is Professor at the Department of Education at the University of Cyprus, Nicosia, Cyprus. He is, since 2016, a member of the Academic Committee of ERIDOB (European Researchers in Didactics of Biology). His research interests expand to the areas of environmental education, ecology, and sustainability education.

Bob Lingard is Professorial Fellow at the Institute for Learning Sciences & Teacher Education at Australian Catholic University, Australia. He has published widely in the sociology of education and policy sociology in education. His most recent co-authored book is *Globalizing Educational Accountabilities*, 2016.

Heila Lotz-Sisitka holds Tier 1 South African National Research Foundation Chair in Global Change and Social Learning Systems and is Distinguished Professor at Rhodes University, South Africa. The current focus of research is transformative social learning and green skills learning pathways in areas of biodiversity, water food nexus, climate change, social and environmental justice, and just sustainability transitions.

Meredith McDermott is Director of Sustainability at the Department of Education, New York, USA. She is passionate about advancing leadership in sustainability and bridging the gap between science, education, career preparation, and youth.

Marcia McKenzie is Professor and Associate Dean Sustainability in the Faculty of Education at the University of Melbourne, Melbourne, Australia. Her research focuses on critical policy studies, including in relation to sustainability and climate change education.

María Angélica Mejía-Cáceres holds a PhD in Sciences and Health Education. She is currently a member of the research group "Languages and Media in Science & Health Education" at the Federal University of Rio de Janeiro, Brazil, and "Science, Education and Diversity" at Universidad del Valle, Colombia, USA.

Oren Pizmony-Levy is Associate Professor of International and Comparative Education at Teachers College at Columbia University, USA. He is interested in the emergence of movements that challenge schools and education systems worldwide, the role of both transnational and domestic actors in the development of these movements, and the intended and unintended consequences of movements.

NOTES ON CONTRIBUTORS

Presha Ramsarup is Director of the Centre for Researching Education and Labour at the University of the Witwatersrand, South Africa. She is Senior Research Associate at the Environmental Learning Research Centre at Rhodes University, South Africa, and Honorary Associate Professor at the University of Nottingham, UK. Her research work focuses on learning pathways for sustainable development and sustainability, and her work is focused on skills for a just transition.

Alan Reid is Professor at the Faculty of Education at Monash University, Melbourne, Australia. He edits the international research journal, *Environmental Education Research*, and publishes regularly on environmental and sustainability education (ESE) and their research. His interests in research and service focus on growing traditions, capacities, and the impact of ESE research.

Mark Rickinson is Associate Professor in the Faculty of Education at Monash University, Melbourne, Australia. His work is focused on understanding and improving the use of research in education policy and practice.

Eureta Rosenberg is Professor and Chair of Environment and Sustainability Education at Rhodes University, South Africa. Her other scholarly interests include evaluation that supports organisational learning; strategic planning; research ethics suitable for a diversity of research traditions; skills for sustainability; and green work and learning.

Louise Shaxson is Doctoral Candidate at the Centre for Health Care and Social Research at the Faculty of Health, Social Care and Education at Kingston University, London, UK. She is currently Associate Editor of *Development Policy Review* and is on the Boards of two important organisations: INASP, Oxford, UK, and Cenfri, Cape Town, South Africa.

Mandy Singer-Brodowski coordinates the monitoring of education for sustainable development (ESD) at the department of the German scientific advisor of the UNESCO programme on ESD at Institut Futur at the Freie Universitat Berlin, Germany. She worked at the Wuppertal Institute for Climate, Environment and Energy and as the scientific coordinator of the Centre for Transformation Research and Sustainability at the University of Wuppertal, Germany. Her main research interests are ESD, transformative research, and transformative learning.

Aravella Zachariou is Chair of the Unit of Education for Environment and Sustainable Development at Cyprus Pedagogical Institute, Nicosia, Cyprus. Since 2009, she is Visiting Assistant Professor in EE/ESD (environmental education/education for sustainable development) at Frederick University, Cyprus. Her research involves the integration of education for environment and sustainable development in formal and non-formal education and in teacher education.

Introducing the complexities of the research-policy relationship

Mark Rickinson and Marcia McKenzie

ABSTRACT
Within the field of environmental and sustainability education (ESE), the interaction between ESE research and ESE policy has received limited attention. Beyond ESE, however, the research-policy relationship has become an increasing focus for theoretical inquiry, empirical investigation and practical development. Against this backdrop, this article introduces a Special Issue that brings together new work from both within and beyond ESE that has explored the research-policy interface in varied contexts and from diverse perspectives. As a collection, it serves to highlight empirical insights, theoretical ideas, conceptual resources, practical examples, and methodological approaches for understanding, navigating and developing research-policy relationships within and beyond ESE.

The aim of this special issue is to focus attention on an area of environmental and sustainability education (ESE) research that has received limited attention to date—namely, the relationship between ESE research and ESE policy. This is a focus that encompasses topics such as: the varied roles of research in relation to policy practice, and of policy in relation to research practice; the contributions of researchers to ESE policy processes, and conversely of policy makers to ESE research; the nature, dynamics and distinctiveness of research-policy relations within ESE as compared with other areas of public policy and social science; and the theoretical, methodological and relational tools that might contribute to improved understanding and negotiation of the research-policy interface towards advancing ESE.

These issues are important because they are central to the contribution that research can make to the development of environmental and sustainability education in response to the urgent social and environmental issues we face globally. As Bill Scott (2009, p. 163) posed in this journal over 10 years ago, 'Given all the difficulties the world now faces in relation to development and the environment—and the importance of education in addressing such challenges—what insights does environmental education research provide that will help us?'. This challenge for researchers to do more to 'be of use' (Fine and Bererras 2001; McKenzie 2009), to not be 'content to be large fish in a small pond' of fellow researchers but to have the 'ambition to take a greater risk, make a greater impact' (Ardoin, Clark, and Kelsey 2013, p. 17), has been a recurring theme in this journal and beyond.

In considering how ESE research can be of use, this special issue focuses specifically on the interface between ESE research and ESE policy making. Related questions concerning the relationships between ESE research and ESE practice, and ESE policy and ESE practice, are also important to advancing the contributions of ESE. However, as policy researchers, we are particularly attuned to the potential for intergovernmental, national, sub-national, and organisational or institutional policy to impact ESE prioritisation and resources and thus to enable what is possible in practice. In addition, against the backdrop of an increasing policy focus on climate and sustainability in education through the Sustainable Development Goals and other global monitoring processes, a specific emphasis on the interplay of research and policy in ESE is timely and needed.

The issue then brings together the work of researchers and policy makers within and beyond ESE who have explored the relationship between research and policy making in varied contexts and from diverse perspectives. Aiming to provide insights into current research-policy relationships within ESE, the issue also highlights possibilities for future development as informed by ideas from beyond ESE. As discussed later in more detail, the different papers within the collection feature:

- empirical insights into the interactions between ESE research and ESE policy;
- sources of complexity and dynamism in ESE research-policy relationships over time;
- theoretical perspectives for understanding ESE research-policy relationships;
- ways of approaching and engaging with the research-policy interface in ESE;
- ways of investigating ESE research-policy relationships;
- ways of reflecting on experiences of working at the ESE research-policy interface; and
- future needs and opportunities in relation to ESE research-policy relationships.

Before considering the content and contribution of this special issue, though, it is important to understand its context (Figure 1). In striving to stimulate new and more purposeful conversations about ESE research-policy relationships, this collection draws and builds on three prior developments: the long-standing interest in policy and policy research within the ESE field; the increasing body of work on the research-policy relationship in fields beyond ESE; and the work of researchers in ESE who have started to bring these two developments into conversation.

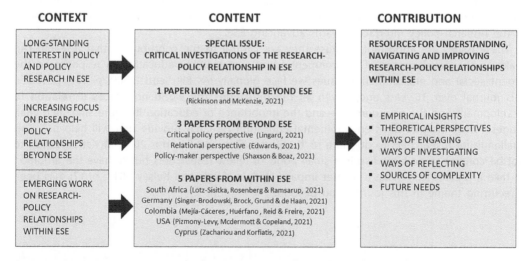

Figure 1. Overview of the context, content and contribution of this Special Issue.

Policy and policy research within ESE

Growing interest in policy and policy research within ESE can be seen in a number of places. The field's first international research handbook included a section looking specifically at 'Analyses of Environmental Education Discourses and Policies' (Stevenson et al. 2013). Positioned within the part of the handbook concerned with 'Conceptualizing Environmental Education as a Field of Enquiry', it highlighted the centrality of politics and policy to the development of ESE as a research field, and included several chapters specifically on policy. More recently, two of the major ESE journals have published special issue collections focused on policy: *'ESE Policy Research'* (Lysgaard, Reid, and Van Poeck 2016) and *'The Politics of Policy in ESD'* (Payne 2016). There has also been a number of syntheses and reviews of ESE policy research (Aikens, McKenzie, and Vaughter 2016; Cheeseman et al. 2019; Lysgaard, Reid, and Van Poeck 2016) that have highlighted not only the growing prominence of such work but also its thematic and methodological tendencies. In addition to some earlier contributions on ESE policy research (e.g. Fien 1991; Gough 1992; Gruenewald and Manteaw 2007; Stevenson 2006, 2007), these recent developments have generated helpful insights into the nature and dynamics of policy, policy making and policy research within ESE.

However, much of the ESE policy research to date has tended to take the form of textual analysis or commentary, versus empirical research on broader policy processes, including on the roles of, and relationships between, researchers and policy makers (Rickinson and McKenzie 2021; Aikens, McKenzie, and Vaughter 2016). For example, neither of the previous policy special issues mentioned above (Lysgaard, Reid, and Van Poeck 2016; Payne 2016), had a dual emphasis on research *and* policy and their inter-relationships. Questions of whether and how ESE research can contribute to ESE policy making and implementation, have largely been left unexamined. With a clear focus on the dynamics of the ESE research-policy interface, this special issue is thus seeking to address this gap, and in a way that builds on existing research insights into the dynamics of ESE policy.

The research-policy relationship beyond ESE

Looking beyond ESE, the relationship between research and policy has become a growing focus for theoretical inquiry, empirical investigation, and practical development across many different fields. An important factor in this growth has been the increased emphasis globally on evidence-based and evidence-informed approaches since the 1990s. The development of ideas, debates and initiatives around this evidence agenda has been very clearly illustrated by specific edited collections (Davies, Nutley, and Smith 2000; Nutley, Walter, and Davies 2007; Boaz et al. 2019) and dedicated journals (e.g. *Evidence and Policy*) that have brought together work from varied sectors and countries in order to consider the use of evidence and research in policy processes. Connected to these kinds of developments has been an increasing emphasis on impact 'as a component of research value' within research assessment processes (Oancea 2019, p. 8). Impact expectations in relation to policy can be seen to have influenced research-policy interactions by promoting more applied and less curiosity-driven policy research (Lingard 2013), and by encouraging researchers to focus on 'how to increase the impact of their own outputs, rather than on understanding the processes behind policy change' (Oliver, Lorenc, and Innvaer 2014, p. 3). Other trajectories of work have highlighted the politics of evidence, advocating attention to the biases and values implicit in research use in policy making (e.g. Lather 2010; Lingard 2013; Parkhurst 2017).

This range of work has shown that the research-policy relationship is a critical focus of inquiry, including across many different fields. For example, in the environmental and sustainability area, there has been work on advancing evidence-informed sustainable development policies (Martunizzi and Scholl 2016), the role of evidence in climate change (Pearce 2014) and conservation (Elgert 2014) policy, and the interactions between social science and environmental policy (Parry and Murphy 2013). In health, a systematic review of evidence-based policy research identified over 145 studies published between 2000 and 2012 on factors affecting the use of evidence by health-related policy makers (Oliver, Lorenc, and Innvaer 2014). In social policy, there are examples of work on the role of expert knowledge in immigration policy (Boswell 2009; Boswell, Geddes, and Scholten 2011) and child protection and illicit drug policy (van Toorn and Dowse 2016). Similarly, within education, there has been work on the research-policy relationship (e.g. Burns and Schuller 2007; Saunders 2007; Lingard 2013) and the role of research evidence in policy processes, both from laudatory and concerned perspectives (e.g. Asen et al. 2013; Clarke 2014; Cochran-Smith and College, 2009; Finnigan and Daly 2014; Lingard 2011; Rickinson et al. 2019).

An important observation, however, is that ESE has not made significant contributions to this interdisciplinary literature to date. There are discussions about research in relation to environmental and sustainability policy (e.g. Reed and Meagher 2019) but little work in relation to environmental and sustainability *education* policy. There are also critiques of the role research in education policy (e.g. Lingard 2013) but few explicit discussions in the domain of *environmental and sustainability* education policy. There have also been no papers focused on environmental and sustainability education within journals such as *Evidence and Policy* that publish studies of the research-policy relationship in varied fields and disciplines. This special issue is therefore motivated by a desire to see not only the research-policy relationship explored more within the ESE field, but also to see ESE further featured within wider literature on the research-policy relationship.

The research-policy relationship and ESE

At present, there are some rich insights into policy within the ESE literature, but little information about the dynamics of the ESE research-policy interface. There are important exceptions, though, where attention has been drawn to ESE policy and ESE research in combination, and we highlight some of those examples here.

Laessøe, Feinstein, and Blum's (2013) paper, for example, looked specifically at 'how [...] scholars of Environmental Education (EE), Education for Sustainable Development (ESD) and Climate Change Education (CCE) might relate to the policy processes in the field' (p. 231). Reflecting on their own experiences of an international project on climate change education as well as wider changes in knowledge production and policy development, they point to a need for more ESE policy research 'that documents what is actually going on in different contexts and on different levels'. They also call for ESE policy researchers to work in 'engaged and interactive' ways with policy makers as critical friends as distinct from critical outsiders (ibid., p. 237). At a similar time, Stevenson's (2013) analysis of how ESE policy statements are shaped by policy processes and discourses also touched on the research-policy relationship. Connecting the idea of 'civically-engaged scholarship' with the goal of 'democratising policy processes', he highlighted how changing the relationship between ESE research and policy needs to link with changing the relationship between ESE policy and practice.

Related to this, prior work (McKenzie 2012; McKenzie, Bieler, and McNeil 2015) suggested ways in which ESE research can critically inform ESE policy. For example, by generating deeper understandings of when and how ESE policies 'emerge, travel and are adapted in particular national or regional contexts', ESE research can 'offer more critical and imaginative interventions in how sustainability is mobilized in education' (McKenzie, Bieler, and McNeil 2015, p. 333). In addition, rather than using evidence to mobilise policy more broadly, local data and contextual specifics can provide opportunities to develop ESE policy in locally appropriate ways. For example, McKenzie (2012, p. 172) outlined: 'Rather than top-down approaches to policy implementation, we are interested in how we can gather "bottom-up" data to help inform understandings', in this case, of quality ESE policy development for diverse communities of Indigenous, newcomer, and settler youth.

Van Poeck and Lysgaard's (2016) introduction to a virtual special issue on ESE policy research is another example of work that has highlighted issues related to ESE research and policy. They refer to the need for ESE researchers 'to be able to defend ourselves, the field and research institutions from too simplistic policy-driven demands for magic bullets' (p. 311). They also point to the value of 'space for critical reflection and dialogue between policy makers, researchers and practitioners' (p. 312), and the importance of 'letting ESE researchers be *researchers* instead of forcing them to take up the role of *expert*' (p. 315, original emphasis). More recently, Stratford and Wals (2020) reflect on their own experiences with evidence-based policy as researchers involved respectively in education policy and evaluation in New Zealand and the evaluation of the Decade for Education for Sustainable Development internationally. Reporting examples of how critical messages can be watered down or removed during the policy process, they argue for 'a more political understanding of knowledge and more healthy policy ecologies […] where …] relations and interactions are relatively open and transparent' (pp. 2–3). A key concern for these authors is that 'evidence-based policy can be a tool for maintaining the political status quo' (p. 5).

The above authors, then, have all drawn attention to the relationship between research and policy as a valuable point of focus within ESE. This special issue seeks to build on this past work and extend consideration of issues, questions and ideas on the ESE research-policy interface through its contributing authors. With that in mind, we now turn to introducing the special issue and the insights it provides into the research-policy relationship in ESE.

Framing the special issue and its contribution

In assembling this special issue, we sought out submissions from both beyond and within ESE. Recognising that investigation of the research-policy interface was not well established within ESE, we wanted to include some scholars from beyond the field whose work might help inform discussions going forward. We thus invited three outsider perspectives, asking them to make connections between their research-policy insights and the ESE field. In addition, through an open call, we secured five contributions from a range of researchers within the ESE field including established research teams and emerging scholars. All the papers in the issue went through peer review, and were additionally contributed to by a host of appreciated reviewers. Our own collaboration on this focus built over a number of years including through co-facilitating a National Policy Forum hosted by the Sustainability and Education Policy Network (SEPN) in Canada in 2016, and workshopping the idea for the special issue with colleagues over several days at a team meeting in that same year. We are grateful for those conversations that helped advance this issue.

We have chosen to organise the papers by first offering a synthesis paper by the guest editors that overviews key aspects of work on the research-policy relationship from beyond and within ESE (Rickinson and McKenzie 2021). This is followed by the three contributions from scholars beyond ESE, which approach the research-policy interface from a critical policy perspective (Lingard 2021), a relational perspective (Edwards 2021) and a policy-maker perspective (Shaxson and Boaz 2021). Next follow five papers by researchers from within ESE who have examined research-policy dynamics in different national or regional contexts, including South Africa (Lotz-Sisitka, Rosenberg, and Ramsarup 2021), Germany (Singer-Brodowski et al. 2021), Colombia (Mejía-Cáceres, Huérfano, Reid and Freire 2021), the US (Pizmony-Levy, Mcdermott, and Copeland 2021), and Cyprus (Zachariou and Korfiatis 2021). Each of these five papers connects in differing ways to the beyond-ESE literatures on evidence use and critical policy studies.

Taken together, we see these papers as providing the ESE field with a range of helpful insights and resources for understanding, navigating and strengthening the relationships between ESE research and policy in different contexts. More specifically, the different contributions in combination help to highlight: (1) *empirical insights* into the interactions between ESE research and ESE policy; (2) *sources of complexity* and dynamism in ESE research-policy relationships over time; (3) *theoretical perspectives* for understanding ESE research-policy relationships; (4) *ways of engaging* with the research-policy interface in ESE; (5) *ways of investigating* ESE research-policy relationships; (6) *ways of reflecting* on experiences of working at the ESE research-policy interface; and (7) *future needs and opportunities* in relation to ESE research-policy relationships.

Empirical insights

One contribution provided by this special issue is empirical insights into the nature and interactions between ESE research and ESE policy. Some papers highlight **ways in which ESE research findings can inform ESE policy**. For example, ESE research findings changing local policy makers' perceptions of and funding for school sustainability coordinators in New York City (Pizmony-Levy, Mcdermott, and Copeland 2021), or influencing the emphasis on informal education and teacher professional development within national ESD policy in Cyprus (Zachariou and Korfiatis 2021). Other papers focus more on how **ESE research *processes* can contribute to ESE policy outcomes**. Lotz-Sisitka, Rosenberg, and Ramsarup (2021), for example, show how relational processes connected to ESE research and evaluation, such as multi-stakeholder policy forums and professional learning networks, were important in building the capacity of government and its social partners to develop, review and implement ESE in South Africa. There are also indications of how **ESE policy can inform ESE research**—for example, in the Cyriot study where ESD policy illuminated shortcoming and gaps in ESD research (Zachariou and Korfiatis 2021). Another area of empirical insight concerns **ESE research and policy being shaped by wider global influences, often in ways that present challenges for research-policy relationships**. In the context of ESD implementation in Germany, for example, Singer-Brodowski et al. (2021) discuss how standardisation agendas have given rise to conflicting expectations between researchers and policy partners around ESD monitoring. That **ESE research-policy relationships can be characterised by absences and gaps as well as presences and connections** is another area of insight. Mejía-Cáceres, Huérfano, Reid and Freire (2021), for example, show how the discourses of certain Colombian researchers are notably absent (or 'disidentified') within the national environmental education policy. Another important insight concerns **the distinctiveness of ESE as an area of policy and research**. Rickinson and McKenzie (2021), for example, highlight the particularity of ESE policy in terms of its multiplicity of *scales*, *breadth* of content, context and participants, and its inherent *contestation* in terms of values, ideologies and discourses. Similar points are made by others, particularly in relation to the 'political complexity' of ESE as a field (Lotz-Sisitka, Rosenberg, and Ramsarup 2021, p. 525).

Sources of complexity

This collection also highlights sources of complexity and dynamism in ESE research-policy relationships over time. One source of complexity is how interactions between research and policy are framed and influenced by **big picture trends affecting policy and governance internationally**. Lingard's (2021) paper discusses the significance of a range of major global influences on research and policy, while other contributors provide ESE-specific examples (e.g. Singer-Brodowski et al. 2021). Another source of complexity is **shifting priorities and**

trajectories in national-level policy over time. The clearest illustration of this comes in Lotz-Sisitka, Rosenberg, and Ramsarup (2021) analysis of ESE research and policy interactions through phases of policy preparation, policy proliferation, policy failures and then policy inconsistencies in post-apartheid South Africa. There is also **complexity in the day-to-day work of policy practitioners**—for example, in terms of the diverse ways in which research and other kinds of evidence can be used within the development of policy narratives (Rickinson and McKenzie 2021; Shaxson and Boaz 2021). The **diversity of different actors and stakeholders involved in ESE research and policy processes and the potential blurring of roles between researchers, policy makers and practitioners** represents another source of complexity. This factor was noted as significant in relation to the ESE research-policy relationship in Germany (Singer-Brodowski et al. 2021), South Africa (Lotz-Sisitka, Rosenberg, and Ramsarup 2021) and Cyprus (Zachariou and Korfiatis 2021).

Theoretical perspectives

Alongside these empirical insights and sources of complexity, this special issue also draws attention to a number of theoretical perspectives for understanding the interactions between ESE research and ESE policy. Some contributors show how insights from **critical policy studies** can illuminate the ways in which ESE research-policy relationships are part of, and shaped by, major changes affecting policy production globally (Lingard 2021; Rickinson and McKenzie 2021). Others highlight the potential of ideas from **evidence use studies** to inform and deepen investigations into the role of research knowledge in ESE policy processes (Pizmony-Levy, Mcdermott, and Copeland 2021; Rickinson and McKenzie 2021; Shaxson and Boaz 2021; Zachariou and Korfiatis 2021). There are also papers that illustrate the value of **political theory** for understanding the interplay between the power of community (or potentia) and the power of institutions (or potestas) in ESE research and policy engagement (Lotz-Sisitka, Rosenberg, and Ramsarup 2021), and **critical discourse analysis** for deciphering whether and how research/researcher discourses are reflected in ESE policy texts (Mejía-Cáceres, Huérfano, Reid and Freire 2021). Furthermore, the scholarship on **science-policy interfaces** can support probing into the roles of ESE researchers within ESD policy implementation and evaluation (Singer-Brodowski et al. 2021), and **cultural-historical activity theory** can help with making sense of the relational aspects of ESE research-policy interfaces as sites of intersecting practices (Edwards 2021).

Ways of engaging

As well as illuminating different theoretical lenses, the papers in this special issue also highlight different ways of engaging with the research-policy interface in ESE. Singer-Brodowski et al.'s (2021) paper, for example, probes into the work of **ESE researchers as scientific advisors** within ESD policy implementation and evaluation processes in Germany. A different form of engagement is considered by Pizmony-Levy, Mcdermott, and Copeland (2021) in their analysis of working together as a researcher and two policy makers within an **ESE research-practice partnership** between the city sustainability office and a local university in New York City. Zachariou and Korfiatis (2021) point to the possibilities enabled by **individuals being *both* researchers and policy makers**, as enabled or required in small countries such as Cyprus. Alongside these fairly structured forms of policy collaboration, Lotz-Sisitka, Rosenberg, and Ramsarup's (2021) work in the South African context elaborates on the unfolding of their **ESE research as policy engagement** within conditions of policy flux over several decades. Key to their approach was recognising the relational nature of research and policy, being willing to undertake multiple modes of research (intensive, extensive, synthesis, and theoretical), and incorporate capacity building and professional learning processes with policy makers and other actors.

Ways of investigating

The collection of papers also provides examples of different ways of empirically investigating research-policy interactions. One approach is to focus on **ESE research and ESE policy as text**, and use critical discourse analysis to identify which researchers' discourses do (and do not) feature within specific policy texts and how they are used (Mejía-Cáceres, Huérfano, Reid and Freire 2021). Another way is to focus on **policy processes** rather than on policy texts, in order to examine through interviews, observations and documentary analysis, the ways in which research evidence is (and is not) used by policy makers in their policy development work (Rickinson and McKenzie 2021; Pizmony-Levy, Mcdermott, and Copeland 2021; Shaxson and Boaz 2021). An alternative to both of these strategies is to investigate **research-policy interactions as an experience** to reflect on as researchers and/or policy makers (see Ways of reflecting section below).

Ways of reflecting

Three of the papers within the collection feature examples of ESE researchers (and, in some cases, policy makers) investigating their own experiences of research-policy interaction. These papers illustrate different ways to reflect on and make sense of experiences of working at the research-policy interface. Singer-Brodowski et al. (2021), for example, use **intersubjective group discussions informed by analytic autoethnography** as a way to surface and analyse challenges within their work as scientific advisors for ESD implementation and evaluation in Germany. Lotz-Sisitka, Rosenberg, and Ramsarup (2021), meanwhile, use a **reflexive meta-review of 30+ years of their ESE research** to identify four trajectories in their work and its policy engagement within the rapidly transforming South African context. Another example is provided by Pizmony-Levy, Mcdermott, and Copeland (2021) who come together as a researcher and two policy makers to make sense of their five-year ongoing research-practice partnership through **qualitative documentary analysis** of varied partnership documents and artifacts. Along similar lines, Zachariou and Korfiatis (2021), in turn, discuss being in both the roles of researcher and policy maker in Cypriot ESD policy development over a number of decades.

Future needs and opportunities

Finally, this special issue helps to signal a number of future needs and opportunities in relation to research-policy relationships within ESE. One clear message is the **general need for more empirical study** on this topic. Rickinson and McKenzie (2021, p. 480), for example, point out how 'current scholarly writing on the research-policy interface in ESE tends to be editorial or commentary in nature as opposed to empirical'. More specifically, there are calls for **local-level studies in more varied locations** in order to understand 'the specificities of the work at the local level' (Mejía-Cáceres, Huérfano, Reid and Freire 2021, p. 571) and to examine 'the interplay of ESD research and policy in national contexts beyond Western Europe and North America' (Zachariou and Korfiatis 2021, p. 614). Another suggested opportunity is for **studies of research-policy interaction in real time**. Singer-Brodowski et al. (2021, p. 554), for example, make clear that 'we would encourage other ESD researchers working in similar [policy] situations to build in systematic observation of, and reflection on, their work and interactions with others' during the process. By contrast, others see a need for **retrospective studies of research-policy interactions over an extended duration**. Noting that many countries now have 30+ years of ESE policy making and policy-research relations, Lotz-Sisitka, Rosenberg, and Ramsarup (2021, p. 525) suggest that 'it may be interesting to conduct similar [meta-review] studies to trace how diverse contexts of policy flux influence the emergence of policy-research relationships and approaches over time'. Several contributors emphasise the importance of **studies that engage with the perspectives of policy makers and other stakeholders**. Singer-Brodowski et al. (2021), for example, note how their work could have been richer if they had involved 'the perspective of other groups of actors' beyond researchers, and Shaxson and Boaz (2021, p. 518) argue that ESE would benefit from 'analysing policymakers' perspectives on evidence use'. Connected to these arguments, there is also recognition of the need for **studies that generate outputs that speak to the needs of ESE policy makers as well as ESE researchers**. Drawing on ideas from evidence use research beyond ESE, Rickinson and McKenzie (2021, p. 480) emphasise the importance of 'striving to generate insights, ideas, frameworks and resources that are not only informative and useful for ESE researchers but also instructive and helpful for ESE policy makers'. There are also calls for **studies that focus on the relational dimensions of policy and research as practices**. Edwards' (2021, p. 513) paper discusses how to understand research-policy interfaces as 'relational engagements […] where different expert practices meet', while Lotz-Sisitka, Rosenberg, and Ramsarup (2021, p. 525) underline the 'relationality between research, policy processes, learning and networking' in their concept of research *as* policy engagement. Finally, the need for **studies that recognise and probe into the role of power** is another theme in the special issue. Mejía-Cáceres, Huérfano, Reid and Freire (2021, p. 571), for example, see promise in 'reflecting further on questions of power and strategies of imposition, emancipation and participation within and across scales', and Brodowski, Brock, Grund and de Haan (2021, p. 554) highlight the need for 'stronger consideration of the role of power' in science-policy interfaces within ESD. Meanwhile, Lingard (2021) points to the challenges of inquiring into and informing the politics of education in post-truth contexts.

The contributions to the special issue

With the above cross-cutting insights from the special issue as a whole in mind, we now elaborate on the main arguments of the individual papers that make up the collection.

In the paper that begins the issue, **Rickinson and McKenzie** explore how the ESE field's capacity to both understand and navigate the research-policy relationship might be expanded. We do so by overviewing two key trajectories of work beyond ESE that have already engaged extensively with this nexus, namely, critical policy studies and evidence use studies. From our positions within these respective fields as well as within ESE, we draw out three key features of the research-policy relationship: what counts as evidence in policy decision-making; what influences policy processes beyond evidence; and what roles research can play in relation to policy making. We discuss how attending further to these considerations could help advance research and policy in ESE. We argue that ESE policy is distinctive in its scale, breadth and contestation, and that there is a need for more diverse work in relation to the ESE research-policy interface. This includes recommendations for more empirical (as opposed to conceptual) work, more studies at national and regional (as opposed to international and local) scales, and more focus on policy processes (as opposed to policy texts). We also suggest the need for more ESE research not only *of* policy, but also for more engagement by researchers with policy makers of all types *for* policy. In this way, the article concludes, we can better understand not only ESE policy, but also how ESE researchers and policy makers together can inform and advance climate action and sustainability through education.

As the first of three papers from beyond ESE, **Lingard**'s paper argues that the complex entanglements of research and policy in education and in ESE need to be understood against the backdrop of major changes affecting contemporary policy production globally. He discusses the influence of state restructuring through new public management and network governance, the globalisation of policy discourses and the cosmopolitanization of policy actors, and the increasing mobility of fast policy and fast policy making. He also highlights the significance of post-truth politics and science denial, and the role of affect and emotions, for ESE research and policy and the relationships between them. In relation to research, he argues that evidence-*informed* (rather than evidence-*based*) policy ought to be the aspiration, that research *for* policy needs to be matched by research *of* policy, and that the roles of private consultancies and think tanks and big data need to be considered critically alongside the roles of universities and research evidence. He sees a particular need for more ESE researchers taking an activist, public intellectual stance and recognising the potential for research to be utilised by those inside and outside the state to contest policies towards more socially just and environmentally sound ends.

In discussing how research and policy can be generatively connected, **Edwards** shares three concepts from her cultural-historical research on interprofessional collaboration in the caring professions: relational expertise, common knowledge and relational agency. The first of these, relational expertise, can be understood as the capacity to draw out what matters for other professionals through conversation, as well as being explicit about what matters for oneself. Common knowledge consists of the motives of the professionals interacting at the research-policy interface, while relational agency is the joint action that can unfold from this common knowledge when working on a common problem. Drawing on a study of university researchers with strong records of policy collaboration and impact, Edwards shows how these concepts can help elucidate successful engagements at the research-policy interface, where success is defined as bringing benefits to both research and policy. She argues that the work of researchers and policy practitioners benefits from their relational engagements at an interface which is recognised as a place where different expert practices meet and where people are open about what matters for them professionally. Seeing potential links to the urgencies of environmental and sustainability issues, Edwards suggests that the ESE field may be able to mobilise these three relational concepts in building capacity for joint action at the research-policy interface in ESE.

As the final paper from beyond ESE, **Shaxson and Boaz** provide an overview of key considerations from prior work on evidence use in policy. They do so by highlighting three studies that gathered detailed information about the interactions between evidence and policy making in different geographical locations (UK, Australia, and USA) and policy areas (health, education and public management). They show how government-based policymakers develop 'policy narratives' which influence their evidence use. They also illustrate how government departmental systems and processes lead policymakers to develop 'evidence narratives' which help them make sense of what evidence to use and how to use it in the policy development process. They suggest that this process involves negotiating three normative considerations: fidelity to science, democratic representation, and cost-effective use of public money. As a result, Shaxson and Boaz suggest that where policy and evidence narratives interact is a key site for empirical research on policy making processes. As they see it, this kind of work within ESE would help ESE researchers better understand how policymakers' demands for evidence are shaped and what this implies for how researchers (and other providers of evidence) can engage more productively with policy makers in relation to ESE.

As the first of five papers from within ESE, **Lotz-Sisitka, Rosenberg and Ramsarup** examine ESE research and policy in South Africa. With a 30+ year time span (1990–2020), these authors chart the evolution of ESE research *as policy engagement* within the context of policy formation and flux. Using a meta-review approach drawing on some 150 studies of South African ESE, they seek to synthesise this body of work in terms of four trajectories in the research-policy relationship over time. These trajectories highlight: (i) the development of ESE research and ESE policy outcomes despite shift in the wider policy context towards neo-liberal logics and ideals; (ii) the role of ESE research in building the capacity of government and its social partners to develop, review and implement ESE; (iii) the importance of new theoretical perspectives for understanding and negotiating research-policy relations, and (iv) the value of fostering diverse or multi-model forms of research and evaluation that encompass the macro and the micro, and future options as well as present challenges. Key to their approach is a theory of politics informed by Dussel's (2008) notion of 'Politics as Potentia', that asserts the primacy of the power of the political community or people (potentia) relative to the exercise of power through institutions, policies and representatives (potestas). They argue for an ongoing re-thinking of the ESE research-policy interface as co-engaged processes of research-and-policy engagement with potential to reduce the negative consequences of the ontological split between community (potentia) and institutions (potestas).

The second ESE paper comes from **Singer-Brodowski, Brock, Grund and de Haan**, who explore the research-policy relationship within scientific advisory and monitoring work related to ESD in Germany. Using the concept of science-policy interfaces (SPIs), they analyse their experiences of working as researchers within this context through an autoethnographic approach. Their analysis and the insights that emerge relate to three main issues for researchers working at the SPI. The first concerns how to deal with different expectations of 'measuring' ESD, and highlights the need for ESE researchers to be mindful of, and proactive in relation to, broader tensions associated with global trends such as evidence-informed education and standardisation. The second relates to how to deal with and support different ways of using evidence at the SPI, and emphasises the importance of recognising and responding to the distinctive needs and interests of different actors, and the potential of designing and conducting research and evaluation in a transdisciplinary way. The third issue concerns how to deal with different kinds of power at the SPI, and underline the need to move beyond power dynamics as a blind spot in order to better understand the role of power within ESE governance. The authors conclude by encouraging other ESD researchers working in similar kinds of situations to build in systematic observation of, and reflection on, their work and interactions with others at the science-policy interface. To this end, they provide a series of reflection questions for use by other groups of researchers and policy makers.

In the next paper by **Mejía-Cáceres, Huérfano, Reid and Freire**, the focus shifts to an analysis of national environmental education policy in Colombia to look for the presence or absence of specific research discourses. Understanding education policy as an ideological tool and policy texts as products of compromises and power struggles, this study uses critical discourse analysis to identify which Colombian researchers' discourses are expressed within policy and how they are mobilized. Key considerations in this analysis are: the frequency of particular researchers' discourses; intertextuality in terms of references from researchers' texts incorporated into the policy text; and interdiscursivity in terms of how particular genres and discourses are blended and articulated. The findings show that while researcher discourses did feature within policy, references to legislative guidelines and international policy discourses were much more prominent. There were also important differences in terms of which researchers' ideas were and were not included—in short, the policy obscured or omitted certain discourses, particularly those offering critical and alternative perspectives. In this way, the authors argue, the work of certain local Colombian scholars has been *disidentified* within the policy text—a situation at odds with historical expectations of collaborative policy development in Colombia. The authors highlight the importance of 'questions of power' and 'the specificities of work at the local level' for future studies of research-policy relationships in the ESE field (p. 518).

The fourth ESE paper by **Pizmony-Levy, Mcdermott and Copeland** examines research and policy in the context of efforts to improve sustainability education within New York City. It is written by a researcher and two policy makers who are part of a five-year ongoing research-practice partnership between the city education department's sustainability office and a local university. Using concepts and ideas from wider literatures on improvement science, research-practice partnerships and research use, the authors reflect on the evolution of the partnership and its influences on the use of evidence to improve ESE in schools. Through qualitative analysis of documentary artifacts from the partnership, they highlight the importance of building mutual trust through repeated, successful and respectful interactions, and of working over time towards a shared understanding of environmental and sustainability education. They also show how research findings and recommendations emerging from the partnership have been used in varied ways, such as instrumentally (e.g. to change funding for school sustainability coordinators) and conceptually (e.g. to challenge misconceptions about the backgrounds of coordinators). In conclusion, the authors argue that this case study highlights one potential role that higher education institutions can play in helping to combat global climate change—that is, partnering with local government agencies to support and enrich ESE policy and practice on a wide scale.

The final paper in the issue is by **Zachariou and Korfiatis**, who discuss the development of ESD in Cyprus as a case study of the 'how, what, when and why' of research and policy interactions. Through thematic documentary analysis of all Cypriot ESD research publications and policy documents, they identify and highlight certain features of the research-policy relationship in that context. They show how ESD policy development processes have involved inputs from researchers, policy makers and practitioners as co-producers and co-modifiers of ESD policy. They highlight ways in which research on specific topics, such as the significance of informal education and the training needs of teachers, informed and transformed the direction of national ESD policy. Conversely, they also document examples where policy has helped to illuminate shortcomings (such as too many similar studies of the role of local community in ESD school projects) and gaps (such as too little work on the implementation of ESD in school- and classroom-level practice) in ESD research. In conclusion, the authors argue that the study of the development and interplay of ESD research and policy in specific local contexts can contribute to new and more diverse routes for ESD policy and research.

Concluding remarks

A recurring theme across the contributions to this special issue is the concept of 'use'. For example, to what extent can or should research be useful for policy, in supporting or critiquing its ends; and conversely how useful is policy for research, in advancing fields of inquiry, careers, collaboration, key questions, or other aspects. While recognising the value of 'blue sky' or basic research 'of' policy, which advances understanding without the expectation or aspiration of its usefulness, we suggest that in the case of ESE research, there is typically also an applied aim of contributing to advancing some aspect of ESE, in other words, research 'for' and with policy. Within this, we recognize the varied forms that research can take to 'be of use' in relation to policy (Fine and Barreras 2001), and that sometimes this is working alongside policy making, and sometimes in opposition, or sometimes in the grey area in between.

In a recent genealogy of the term, Ahmed (2019) highlights the potential that is inherent in the word 'use'. It is 'stubby, plain, workmanlike', but also radiates sturdy practicality in achieving something worthwhile (Felski 2013, cited on p. 5). Ahmed suggests that the requirement to be useful, while often presented generally, tends to fall upon some more than others, often those considered most 'useless' (for example, as we've seen with the COVID-19 crisis, those fulfilling the most essential services are those whose work is too often undervalued and underpaid). This begs the question of whether the requirement or responsibility of useful ESE research or policy falls on some more than others, perhaps in too many cases those most affected by lack of action—countries already hard hit by climate change, communities who have experienced decades or centuries of land-based environmental and colonial injustice.

Ahmed (2019) also alerts us to the value of 'queer uses', or those that reverse or challenge how things are usually approached (p. 75); pointing to the possible value of orientations to the research-policy relationship that are atypical, or against the grain of the usual ways of orienting research to policy and vice versa. This brings to mind, for example, that while policy decision-makers tended to position the school climate strikes of the last few years as at odds with the aims of schooling, in some cases these research-informed strikes (IPCC 2018) have been better policy change levers than the policy and research mechanisms usually thought most useful (University of Saskatchewan 2020).

Another point from Ahmed's meditation on use is to beware of use as a technique of power, such as ESE research-policy work which keeps us busy, but in fact maintains or even perpetuates the status quo. Ahmed also warns that *'Policies that are not in use can still be used as evidence of what does not exist'* (p. 177, italics in original). For example, research-informed ESE policies can be pointed to as indications that adequate action has been taken, even if there are cases where policies are not being enacted due to various barriers of time, resources, commitment, ideology or other factors. This issue of policy non-use can also be relevant in situations where policies are consciously not implemented such as schools resisting or ignoring policy agendas that serve to narrow the curriculum or limit out of school learning or marginalise ESE.

Despite these caveats on the challenges and surprises of 'use', we hope that this special issue can be a platform from which to build more productive relationships between ESE research and policy. By this, we mean relationships characterised by: genuine appreciation for the practices of doing research and developing policy; in-depth understanding of the strengths and weaknesses of research and the realities and dilemmas of policy making; keen awareness of the personal, political and relational challenges of research-policy work; and real commitment to developing powerful policy alternatives for systemic improvement and change.

However, we also remain attuned to the complexities of actually making change in education systems, whether as researchers, policy makers, or both. We recognize that education policy is constituted through institutional histories and habits, policy maker ideology and commitments, as well as the distributed and implicit influences of profit and non-profit providers of textbooks, technology, and schooling (Gulson and Sellar 2019; Lubienski, Brewer, and La Londe 2016; Pitton and McKenzie 2020). Research and other forms of evidence are only some of the many inputs into the making and uptake of policy. And perhaps our research too often works with a limited view of what can or needs to be changed, not questioning enough the forms or procedures of education (Ball 2020). As we walk the lines of doing 'useful' policy research through different kinds of partnerships and collaborations, we also risk becoming part of the infrastructures that support policy that is less than it needs to be for people and the planet. Nonetheless, we hope that this special issue is generative in contributing to discussion of these issues and, more importantly, to education that better responds to the challenges of these times by helping to enact a more sustainable and equitable future.

Disclosure statement

No potential conflict of interest was reported by the authors.

ORCID

Mark Rickinson http://orcid.org/0000-0001-5760-6458
Marcia McKenzie http://orcid.org/0000-0002-8037-8059

References

Ahmed, S. 2019. *What's the Use?* Durham, CA: Duke University Press.
Aikens, K., M. McKenzie, and P. Vaughter. 2016. "Environmental and Sustainability Education Policy Research: A Systematic Review of Methodological and Thematic Trends." *Environmental Education Research* 22 (3): 333–359. doi:10.1080/13504622.2015.1135418.
Ardoin, N. M., C. Clark, and E. Kelsey. 2013. "An Exploration of Future Trends in Environmental Education Research." *Environmental Education Research* 19 (4): 499–520. doi:10.1080/13504622.2012.709823.
Asen, R. D., P. Gurke, R. Conners, R. Solomon, and E. Gumm. 2013. "Research Evidence and School-Board Deliberations: Lessons from Three Wisconsin School Districts." *Educational Policy* 27 (1): 33–63. doi:10.1177/0895904811429291.
Ball, S. J. 2020. "The Errors of Redemptive Sociology or Giving up on Hope and Despair." *British Journal of Sociology of Education* 41 (6): 870–880. doi:10.1080/01425692.2020.1755230.

Boaz, A., G. H. Davies, A. Fraser, and S. Nutley, eds. 2019. *What Works Now? Evidence-Informed Policy and Practice Revisited*. Bristol: Policy Press.
Boswell, C. 2009. *The Political Uses of Expert Knowledge*. Cambridge: Cambridge University Press.
Boswell, C., A. Geddes, and P. Scholten. 2011. "The Role of Narratives in Migration Policy-Making: A Research Framework." *The British Journal of Politics and International Relations* 13 (1): 1–11. doi:10.1111/j.1467-856X.2010.00435.x.
Burns, T., and T. Schuller, eds. 2007. *Evidence in Education: Linking Research and Policy*. Paris: OECD.
Cheeseman, A., T. Wright, J. Murray, and M. McKenzie. 2019. "Taking Stock of Sustainability in Higher Education: A Review of the Policy Literature." *Environmental Education Research* 25 (12): 1697–1712. doi:10.1080/1350462 2.2019.1616164.
Clarke, M. 2014. "The Sublime Objects of Education Policy: Quality, Equity and Ideology." *Discourse: Studies in the Cultural Politics of Education* 34 (4): 584–598.
Cochran-Smith, M., and B. College. 2009. "'Re-Culturin' Teacher Education: Inquiry, Evidence, and Action." *Journal of Teacher Education* 60 (5): 458–468. doi:10.1177/0022487109347206.
Davies, H. T. O., S. M. Nutley, and P. C. Smith, eds. 2000. *What Works: Evidence-Based Policy and Practice in Public Services*. Bristol: Policy Press.
Edwards, A. 2021. "A Reflection on the Relational Aspects of Research Policy Interfaces." *Environmental Education Research* 27 (4): 518–524. doi:10.1080/13504622.2020.1739229.
Elgert, L. 2014. "Governing Portable Conservation and Development Landscapes: Reconsidering Evidence in the Context of the Mbaracayú Biosphere Reserve." *Evidence & Policy: A Journal of Research, Debate and Practice* 10 (2): 205–222. doi:10.1332/174426514X13990327720607.
Felski, R. 2013. "'Introduction.' in 'Use,' Special Issues." *New Literary History* 44 (4): v–xii. doi:10.1353/nlh.2013.0034.
Fien, J. 1991. "Towards School-Level Curriculum Inquiry in Environmental Education." *Australian Journal of Environmental Education* 7: 17–29. doi:10.1017/S081406260000183X.
Fine, M., and R. Barreras. 2001. "To Be of Use." *Analyses of Social Issues and Public Policy* 1 (1): 175–182. doi:10.1111/1530-2415.00012.
Finnigan, K., and A. Daly, eds. 2014. *Using Research Evidence in Education*. New York: Springer.
Gough, A. G. 1992. "Sustaining Development of Environmental Education in National Political and Curriculum Priorities." *Australian Journal of Environmental Education* 8: 115–131. doi:10.1017/S0814062600003335.
Gruenewald, D. A., and B. O. Manteaw. 2007. "Oil and Water Still: How No Child Left behind Limits and Distorts Environmental Education in US Schools." *Environmental Education Research* 13 (2): 171–188. doi:10.1080/13504620701284944.
Gulson, K., and S. Sellar. 2019. "Emerging Data Infrastructures and the New Topologies of Education Policy." *Discourse* 37 (2): 350–366.
IPCC. 2018. Global warming of 1.5C. An IPCC special report. IPCC: Geneva, Switzerland.
Laessøe, J., N. W. Feinstein, and N. Blum. 2013. "Environmental Education Policy Research – Challenges and Ways Research Might Cope with Them." *Environmental Education Research* 19 (2): 231–242. doi:10.1080/13504622.20 13.778230.
Lather, P. 2010. *Engaging (Social) Science: Policy from the Side of the Messy*. New York, NY: Peter Lang.
Lingard, B. 2011. "Policy as Numbers: Ac/Counting for Educational Research." *The Australian Educational Researcher* 38 (4): 355–382. doi:10.1007/s13384-011-0041-9.
Lingard, B. 2013. "The Impact of Research on Education Policy in an Era of Evidence-Based Policy." *Critical Studies in Education* 54 (2): 113–131. doi:10.1080/17508487.2013.781515.
Lingard, B. 2021. "The Changing and Complex Entanglements of Research and Policy Making in Education: Issues for Environmental and Sustainability Education." *Environmental Education Research* 27 (4): 498–512. doi:10.108 0/13504622.2020.1752625.
Lotz-Sisitka, H., H. Rosenberg, and P. Ramsarup. 2020. "Environment and Sustainability Education Research as Policy Engagement: (Re-) Invigorating 'Politics as Potentia.'" *South Africa, Environmental Education Research*. doi:10.108 0/13504622.2020.1759511.
Lubienski, C., J. Brewer, and P. G. La Londe. 2016. "Orchestrating Policy Ideas: Philanthropies and Think Tanks in US Education Policy Advocacy Networks." *The Australian Educational Researcher* 43 (1): 55–73. doi:10.1007/s13384-015-0187-y.
Lysgaard, J. A., A. Reid, and K. Van Poeck. 2016. "The Roots and Routes of Environmental and Sustainability Education Policy Research: An Introduction to a Virtual Special Issue." *Environmental Education Research* 22 (3): 319–332. doi:10.1080/13504622.2015.1108392.
Martinuzzi, A. and G. Scholl. 2016. "Advancing Evidence-Informed Sustainable Development Policies." *Evidence & Policy: A Journal of Research, Debate and Practice* 12 (3): 311–319. doi:10.1332/174426416X14712603178988
Mejía-Cáceres, M. A., A. Huérfano, A. Reid and L. M. Freire. 2021. "Colombia's National Policy of Environmental Education: A Critical Discourse Analysis." *Environmental Education Research* 27 (4): 571–594. doi: 10.1080/13504622.2020.1800594
McKenzie, M. 2009. "Scholarship as Intervention: Critique, Collaboration and the Research Imagination." *Environmental Education Research* 15 (2): 217–226. doi:10.1080/13504620902807576.
McKenzie, M. 2012. "Education for Y'all: Global Neoliberalism and the Case for a Politics of Scale in Sustainability Education Policy." *Policy Futures in Education* 10 (2): 165–177. doi:10.2304/pfie.2012.10.2.165.

McKenzie, M., A. Bieler, and R. McNeil. 2015. "Education Policy Mobility: Reimagining Sustainability in Neoliberal Times." *Environmental Education Research* 23 (3): 319–337.

Nutley, S., I. Walter, and H. T. O. Davies. 2007. *Using Evidence: How Research Can Inform Public Services*. Bristol: Policy Press.

Oancea, A. 2019. "Research Governance and the Future(s) of Research Assessment." *Palgrave Communications* 5 (1): 1–12. doi:10.1057/s41599-018-0213-6.

Oliver, Kathryn, Theo Lorenc, and Simon Innvaer. 2014. "New Directions in Evidence-Based Policy Research: A Critical Analysis of the Literature." *Health Research Policy and Systems* 12 (1): 1–11. doi:10.1186/1478-4505-12-34.

Parkhurst, J. 2017. *The Politics of Evidence*. London: Routledge

Parry, S., and J. Murphy. 2013. "Towards a Framework for Analysing Interactions between Social Science and Environmental Policy." *Evidence & Policy: A Journal of Research, Debate and Practice* 9 (4): 531–546. doi:10.1332/174426413X13836455133196.

Payne, P. G. 2016. "The Politics of Environmental Education. Critical Inquiry and Education for Sustainable Development." *The Journal of Environmental Education* 47 (2): 69–76. doi:10.1080/00958964.2015.1127200.

Pearce, W. 2014. "Scientific Data and Its Limits: Rethinking the Use of Evidence in Local Climate Change Policy." *Evidence & Policy: A Journal of Research, Debate and Practice* 10 (2): 187–203. doi:10.1332/174426514X13990326347801.

Pitton, V., and M. McKenzie. 2020. "What Moves us Also Moves Policy: The Role of Affect in Mobilizing Education Policy on Sustainability." *Journal of Education Policy*. doi:10.1080/02680939.2020.1852605.

Pizmony-Levy, O., M. Mcdermott, and T. Copeland. 2021. "Improving ESE Policy through Research-Practice Partnerships: Reflections and Analysis from New York City." *Environmental Education Research*.

Reed, M., and L. Meagher, In 2019. "Using Evidence in Environmental and Sustainability Issues." In *What Works Now? Evidence-Informed Policy and Practice Revisited*, edited by A. Boaz, H. Davies, A. Fraser, and S. Nutley, 151–170. Bristol: Policy Press.

Rickinson, M., and M. McKenzie. 2021. "Understanding the Research-Policy Relationship in ESE: Key Insights from Critical Policy and Evidence Use Literatures." *Environmental Education Research* 27 (4): 480–497. doi:10.1080/13504622.2020.1804531.

Rickinson, M., L. Walsh, C. de Bruin, and M. Hall. 2019. "Understanding Evidence Use within Education Policy: A Policy Narrative Perspective." *Evidence & Policy: A Journal of Research, Debate and Practice* 15 (2): 235–252. doi: 10.1332/174426418X15172393826277.

Saunders, L., ed. 2007. *Educational Research and Policy-Making*. London: Routledge.

Scott, W. 2009. "Environmental Education Research: 30 Years on from Tbilisi." *Environmental Education Research* 15 (2): 155–164. doi:10.1080/13504620902814804.

Shaxson, L., and A. Boaz. 2021. "'Understanding Policymakers' Perspectives on Evidence Use as a Mechanism for Improving Research-Policy Relationships." *Environmental Education Research* 27 (4): 518–524. doi:10.1080/13504622.2020.1764505.

Singer-Brodowski, M., A. Brock, J. Grund, and G. de Haan. 2020. "Reflections on the Science-Policy Interface within Education for Sustainable Development in Germany." *Environmental Education Research* 27 (4): 554–570. doi:10.1080/13504622.2020.1813691.

Stevenson, R. B. 2006. "Tensions and Transitions in Policy Discourse: Recontextualizing a Decontextualized EE/ESD Debate." *Environmental Education Research* 12 (3–4): 277–290. doi:10.1080/13504620600799026.

Stevenson, R. B. 2007. "Schooling and Environmental/Sustainability Education: From Discourses of Policy and Practices to Discourses of Professional Learning." *Environmental Education Research* 13 (2): 265–285. doi:10.1080/13504620701295650.

Stevenson, R. B. 2013. "Researching Tensions and Pretensions in Environmental/Sustainability Education Policies: From Critical to Civically Engaged Policy Scholarship." In *International Handbook of Research on Environmental Education*, edited by R. B. Stevenson, M. Brody, J. Dillon, and A. E. J. Wals, 147–155. New York: Routledge/American Educational Research Association.

Stevenson, R., M. Brody, J. Dillon, and A. Wals, eds. 2013. *International Handbook of Research on Environmental Education*. New York: Routledge/American Educational Research Association.

Stratford, R., and A. Wals. 2020. "In Search of Healthy Policy Ecologies for Education in Relation to Sustainability: Beyond Evidence-Based Policy and Post-Truth Politics." *Policy Futures in Education* 18 (8): 976–994. doi:10.1177/1478210320906656.

University of Saskatchewan. 2020. *New agreement supports enhanced environmental education in schools*. https://news.usask.ca/articles/colleges/2020/new-agreement-supports-enhanced-environmental-education-in-public-schools.php.

Van Poeck, K., and J. A. Lysgaard. 2016. "The Roots and Routes of Environmental and Sustainability Education Policy Research." *Environmental Education Research* 22 (3): 305–318. doi:10.1080/13504622.2015.1108393.

van Toorn, L., and L. Dowse. 2016. "Policy Claims and Problem Frames: A Cross-Case Comparison of Evidence-Based Policy in an Australian Context." *Evidence & Policy: A Journal of Research, Debate and Practice* 12 (1): 9–24. doi:10.1332/174426415X14253873124330.

Zachariou, A., and K. Korfiatis. 2021. "Sustainability Education Research and Policy in Cyprus: An Investigation into Their Roles and Relationships." *Environmental Education Research* 27 (4): 614–629. doi:10.1080/13504622.2020.1863919.

Understanding the research-policy relationship: insights from the critical policy and evidence use literatures

Mark Rickinson and Marcia McKenzie

ABSTRACT
This paper looks beyond the environmental and sustainability education (ESE) field for ideas on understanding the research-policy relationship. It examines two specific bodies of literature that have analysed the interplay of research and policy in different ways – critical policy studies and evidence use studies. Bringing these two literatures into conversation, we draw out insights in relation to: what counts as evidence in policy decision-making, what influences policy processes beyond evidence, and what roles research can play in relation to policy making. We then consider how these issues from beyond the field might advance research and policy in ESE. We argue that ESE policy is distinctive in its scale, breadth and contestation, and that there is a need for more diverse work in relation to the ESE research-policy interface.

Introduction

Historically there has been a steady though minority interest in the nature and significance of policy in the environmental and sustainability education (ESE) field (see reviews, Stevenson et al. 2013; Aikens, McKenzie, and Vaughter 2016). In recent years, though, the focus on policy research in ESE has been increasing. Two of the field's main journals have featured special issue collections focused on '*ESE Policy Research*' (Lysgaard, Reid, and Van Poeck 2016) and '*The Politics of Policy in ESD*' (Payne 2016). The first major *International Handbook of Research on Environmental Education* (Stevenson et al. 2013) included a section looking specifically at 'Analyses of Environmental Education Discourses and Policies'. There have also been research reviews or edited collections that have explored the nature and character of ESE policy research, highlighting not only its increasing prominence but also its methodological diversification (Aikens, McKenzie, and Vaughter 2016; Van Poeck, Lysgaard, and Reid 2018; Cheeseman et al. 2019).

These developments have generated insights into the nature and dynamics of policy, policy making and policy research within ESE. Their contribution to understanding the relationship *between* research and policy, however, has been more limited. This is because ESE policy studies have tended not to focus specifically on the role of ESE research in ESE policy processes or on the nature of interactions between ESE policy makers and ESE researchers. With a few exceptions (e.g., Laessøe,

Feinstein, and Blum 2013; Van Poeck and Lysgaard 2016), little has been written about the dynamics of the ESE research-policy interface.

ESE as a field is not alone, though, in experiencing limited empirical or conceptual understanding of the research-policy relationship. Similar issues, for example, have been raised in relation to work in health (Oliver, Lorenc, et al. 2014), social work (Gal and Gal 2017), and science (Cairney 2016). These analyses suggest that productive understanding and negotiation of the research-policy interface can be held back, in part, by the ways in which researchers have tended to engage with policy. One issue has been a tendency for researchers to focus on analyzing policy texts rather than investigating broader policy processes (Freeman, Griggs, and Boaz 2011). When policy processes are researched, historically they were often assumed to be linear (i.e., from policy development to implementation), rather than cyclical, multi-directional, or messy (Bowe, Ball, and Gold 1992; Heimans 2012). Another issue has been a tendency for social science researchers to work more readily and closely with practice- and community-based professionals, as compared with more powerful groups such as decision-makers and policy officials (Brewer 2013). In addition, there has been concern about researchers tending to view and make sense of policy in terms of either 'the idealism of "evidence-driven policy making" (where evidence sets the agenda and drives policy choices) [...] or the pessimism of "policy-based evidence" (where evidence is sought simply to legitimise pre-set policies)' Cairney (2019, 21).

The ESE research field shows signs of similar tendencies. Analyses of ESE policy research have highlighted a propensity for analysis of policy texts rather than broader investigation of policy processes. Stevenson et al. (2013, 148) called for work on 'not only the content of EE/ESD/EfS policy statements but also the processes and factors influencing the content of these statements', and Aikens, McKenzie, and Vaughter (2016, 352) proposed 'increased empirical engagement with policy origins and enactment'. The ESE field is also one that has a strong record of collaborative work with practitioners and community groups, but fewer examples of those kinds of approaches being used with policy makers (Laessøe et al., 2013). Indeed, Cheeseman et al.'s (2019, 1707) review of ESE policy research in higher education calls for more 'scholars to connect with local policy makers throughout the research process'. The ESE research field has less commonly demonstrated assumptions about the role of evidence in policy making, though with some emphasis on providing evidence that ESE can increase academic achievement in order to influence policy making (Bartosh et al. 2006; Lieberman 2013). These and other trends have contributed to a relative lack of broader contextual, collaborative, and nuanced approaches to work on the ESE research-policy interface.

In this paper we explore how the ESE field's capacity to understand and navigate the research-policy relationship might be extended. We approach this task by looking at two bodies of research beyond the ESE research field that have each examined the interplay of research and policy – critical policy studies and evidence use studies – and then bringing those into conversation with ESE policy. We start by providing a brief introduction to each of the external bodies of literature, and then consider how our analysis of these fields highlights three key features of the research-policy relationship: what counts as evidence, complex policy processes, and varied roles of research. We then discuss considerations in the ESE policy field, as a way of examining how these three themes intersect with the ESE field and what their implications might be for understanding and advancing the ESE research-policy relationship.

Two views of research and policy: critical policy studies and evidence use studies

Critical policy studies and evidence use studies have both generated insights into the interplay between research and policy in varied settings and across diverse policy fields. However, they have typically each approached and analysed the research-policy relationship in different ways – critical policy studies have tended to focus on macro concerns informed by a critical lens, while evidence use studies have tended to focus on micro processes, often from the perspective of policy makers. Despite this, they are areas of work that may well have potential to complement each other – for example, a recent review of evidence use research noted specifically that critical perspectives were 'notably missing' and would be important to integrate in order to 'attend to the underlying social structure, implicit social inequality, and ways in which inequality is reproduced.' (Gitomer and Crouse 2019, 76). On the other hand, despite its critical orientation to social issues, in some cases critical policy studies can remain quite theoretical in focus and thus detached from the commitments and realities of policy makers; and perhaps could benefit from further collaboration on policy practices (Simons, Olssen, and Peters 2009). As these are research areas that we have each worked with in sustained ways over recent years (e.g., Rickinson et al. 2016; 2017; 2019; McKenzie, Bieler, and McNeil 2015; McKenzie 2017), we are able to bring together our respective experiences and perspectives on their potential relevance to ESE policy research.

Within critical policy studies, 'policy' can be considered a manifestation of the values and priorities that inform decision-making (Easton 1953). It can be understood to extend beyond policy texts themselves, to all authoritative statements which seek to frame or shape educational practices, such as mission statements, guiding documents, or building design; as well as the processes involved in their production and enactment in practice (Ozga 2000; Taylor et al. 1997; Ball, Maguire and Braun, 2012). Policy is in part determined by, as Lingard and Ozga (2007) point out following Dye (1972), 'non-decision making,' or what policy makers do *not* do in education because of structural and relational influences on what they consider to be important (Simons, Olssen, and Peters 2009). Critical policy studies, or 'policy sociology' (e.g. Ball 1997), is a varied field of research which aims to highlight these politics of policy, asking questions about the influences on, and impacts of, policy that might not be asked otherwise (Simons, Olssen, and Peters 2009, xi).

While previously education policy was more localized and specific to regional or national governments, increased globalization over the past half century has led to strong 'topological' or transcalar influences on policy and its mobilization, such as transnational corporations, traveling policy consultants, and the general more rapid spread of policy models through technological and social mobility (Ball 2012; Lewis, Sellar, and Lingard 2016; McKenzie, Bieler, and McNeil 2015; Peck and Theodore 2015; Savage 2020). Thus, increasingly education policy and decision-making are understood to be shaped by the politics of global governance, as well as being under the remit of local and national governments (Dale 2005; Rizvi and Lingard 2010; Sellar and Lingard, 2013). Critical policy studies typically undertake the empirical analysis of such policy considerations in a given setting or comparatively across settings, often through methods of interviews, observation, and textual analysis, in combination with contextual discussion of relevant historical and political factors.

The field of 'evidence use research', on the other hand, is concerned more with the application of social science methods to the understanding of the specific interactions between 'evidence (knowledge, research, expertise) and policy and practice' (Boaz et al. 2016, 6). Such work draws and builds on an older body of literature on 'knowledge utilisation', which focuses on 'increasing the use of knowledge to solve human problems' and stems back to the early 1920s (Backer 1993, 217). A prime example of knowledge utilisation research in the policy area would be Weiss' (1978, 1979) research on conceptualising and investigating the links between social science research and public policy in the US.

Over the last 15–20 years, there has been a significant re-emergence of such work as developments and debates around evidence-based approaches have grown internationally. New journals, such as *Evidence & Policy*, and edited volumes on *What Works* (Davies, Nutley, and Smith 2000), *Using Evidence* (Nutley, Walter, and Davies 2007) and *What Works Now?* (Boaz et al. 2019), have highlighted the extensive literature that now exists on evidence use. Work in this area has generated varied insights into the roles and uses of evidence across many different professional contexts, policy areas and research fields.

In order to consider the potential implications for ESE, it is helpful to start by thinking about how the ideas emerging from the two above external fields of work highlight the significance of certain aspects of the research-policy relationship. While definitely distinct fields of work, there are a number of ways in which these fields offer connected and potentially complementary insights into related areas of concern that may be useful to consider further in ESE policy making and research. These include: what counts as evidence in policy; complex policy processes; and the varied roles of research. We identified these areas of concern through our close reading of each of these literatures, and then made connections across the two bodies of research on related points of focus. In what follows, we elaborate on these three key areas of concern as informed by our analysis of the two external bodies of research. We close the paper by discussing specificities of the ESE policy field and how these three areas of concern may be helpful in advancing understanding and practices at the research-policy interface in ESE.

What counts as evidence in policy decision-making

One common theme addressed in different ways by both critical policy studies and evidence use studies is what counts as evidence in informing policy decision-making. The two literatures come at this topic from distinct angles, with critical policy studies critiquing a growing emphasis on numerical data in the governing of education, while the evidence use literature points out that in many cases what is used as 'evidence' in decision-making does extend beyond numbers and other forms of research-based data to also include sources of information such as case studies, opinion polls, and reports. As we detail below, in both cases, these literatures attend to the kinds of evidence used or mobilized in policy decisions, either explicitly or implicitly, including considerations for educational practice.

Critical policy studies: 'evidence' governing decision-making

Recent critical policy research on 'policy by numbers' highlights a re-emergence of focus on numbers as a central governing mechanism over the past several decades. As Lingard (2011) points out, 'numbers, statistics, rankings, comparisons, data etc. have been central to state functioning since the rise of the nation-state in the eighteenth century' in making countries '"legible" for governing' (Scott 1998 in Lingard 2011, p. 356). However, governance by numbers has exponentially increased in recent decades as a result of neoliberal policy influences such as dominance of an audit culture with a focus on performance measures; as well as new technologies of distance that have enabled audit practices such as developing indicators, large-scale assessments, or 'big data' sets in informing decisions or applying social pressure (Gorur 2017a; Kelley and Simmons 2015; Ozga 2009; Williamson, 2017). Rather than being neutral, such 'social quantification' is political, with prior assumptions and values shaping decisions on what will be measured and how evidence will be used (Rose 1999). Data can thus be considered 'inscription devices' that solidify the domains they represent (e.g., reifying social categories of 'race' or 'intelligence' through the collection and presentation of particular data), and at the same time are often assumed to be and presented as neutral 'technical mechanisms for making judgements' (Rose 1999, 98; Lingard 2011).

In education policy studies, this lens of critical analysis has in particular been brought to bear on international large scale assessments (ILSA) in K-12 education, such as the methodologies and impacts of the Programme for International Student Assessment (PISA) (OECD nd), as well as similar standardized large-scale assessment measures at the national level (e.g., NAPLAN in Australia). Such assessment practices have been found to alter curriculum and to reconfigure the purposes of schooling through the emphasis on competitive appraisal in international rankings and their financial and affective implications (Engel and Frizzell 2015; Finn 2016; Gorur 2017a). This extensive literature documents, for example, how lower SES and otherwise already marginalized student populations are further disadvantaged by large scale assessment results, or the 'PISA-shock' documented when PISA results misalign with a nation's prior self-perception of the quality of their education system, leading to country-wide educational change (Savage and Lingard 2018; Thompson and Cook 2015). Increasing work is also focusing on the creation and use of data within classrooms and schools as 'real-time policy instruments', such as through online applications that seek to regulate student classroom behavior (Gulson and Sellar 2019; Williamson 2016, 2017).

For our discussions in this paper, a key point to draw from this and other critical policy work is the ways that education is increasingly being governed by and through data. These conditions of 'digital education governance' (Williamson, 2016) are a result of decisions by policy makers, often with datasets built and managed through collaboration with academics or other researchers. The emphasis in these developments is not so much on data as inputs to policy decision-making, but as outputs, 'measured by performance indicators, data, numbers and targets' and their role in implementing policy or driving lower-level policy change through 'soft governance' (Lingard 2013, 370; Kelley and Simmons 2015). This is the case, for example, when PISA results lead to particular types of national level policy decisions. Increasingly critical education policy scholars are focusing on the collection of student behavioural data via 'personalized learning' software developed by private sector providers which opens up 'human emotion and behaviour to constant monitoring, quantification, classification, and manipulation' (Williamson 2019). Through this range of contexts, critical education scholars argue that often the numbers are being used to justify or implement policy decision-making, rather than to inform it.

Evidence use studies: varieties of evidence

Despite this emphasis on numerical data in some policy making spheres, when evidence use researchers have looked carefully at the information that policy makers use in their work, they have tended to conclude that there is variety rather than uniformity in the type of evidence used in decision-making. For example, Stevens' (2011, 237) ethnographic study of social policy development in the UK, talks about an 'oversaturation of evidence' where different forms of evidence 'jostle for attention'. Based on six months of participant observation and follow-up interviews in a government department, Stevens identified 15 types of evidence in use. These included: 'internally collected government data and externally produced academic analysis, opinion polls, reports by thinktanks and management consultancies, previous policy papers, independent inquiries, reports of the inspectorates of police and prisons, internal and externally commissioned evaluations of policy initiatives, various kinds of reports from abroad, press reports, television programmes, personal experience and opinion' (ibid., 240).

A similar picture emerges from work on policy making in education. A US study of decision-making processes in local school boards, for example, highlighted six different types of evidence being used: research, experience, testimony, data, example and law/policy (Asen et al. 2013, 40). Likewise, a study of policy development within an Australian state education department found examples of at least twelve different types of evidence that had been used (Rickinson et al. 2017; 2019). These included: sources that were internal to the department and ones that were external; information in the form of publications and information in the form of people; evidence that had been commissioned by the department and evidence that was publicly available from other organisations; and evidence in the form of data, in the form of research, and in the form of testimony.

Key to each of these studies is what they suggest about understanding the research-policy relationship. All underline the need for researchers' interest in the role and use of research to be broadened to interest in the role and use of evidence in all its forms. This may sound simplistic or straightforward but there can be a tendency for researchers to be focused almost exclusively on the uptake of research evidence in isolation. As Oliver, Lorenc, et al.'s (2014, 6) analysis of evidence-based policy research in health reported: 'Most research in the area studies the use of research evidence by policymakers, not what knowledge or information policymakers use'. The difference between the former and the latter is significant in terms of the kinds of understandings about evidence and policy that studies can generate. For, as others have argued (Tseng 2012; Cairney 2016), users of evidence tend to be working with much broader conceptions of evidence than those of researchers.

Bringing critical policy and evidence use studies into conversation, we can consider both how numbers have come to dominate and/or justify decision-making in some national and regional settings, as well as the reality that operating alongside such numerical data are a host of other forms of evidence. Evidence taken from reports, opinion polls, personal experience, and so on, may align with and support the use of data as justification for educational policy making, or in other cases may be juxtaposed and provide opportunities for ensuring a broader and richer evidence base for decision-making.

'Research' is itself a diverse form of evidence, and can span numerical and quantitative studies as well as qualitative and conceptual insights into policy processes. As we consider such diverse research efforts in relation to policy making, these literatures suggest both concerns about quantitative research and other numerical data being used to drive or justify policy decisions, as well as the research-informed understanding that in reality, not only numerical data are being used to shape policy making because policy makers are influenced by a range of materials and knowledge. Both literatures point to the importance of considering what counts as evidence in policy making, to whom, why, and with what impacts; and indeed, as we will see further below, the potential role of policy research in helping to answer those questions.

Complex policy processes

Building on this emphasis on what influences policy decision-making, a second shared area of concern we identified between the critical policy and evidence use literatures is a focus on the complexity of policy processes. For critical policy studies, this includes a recognition that it is not only evidence that informs decision-making, but a host of other more subtle and implicit influences such as personal relationships, persuasive graphics, and global trends. This field has taken this up through a more bird's eye view of the sources, flows, and impacts of these influences as they pass between people and places. For evidence use studies, recognizing the complexity of policy processes has meant a deep dive into the policy practices of specific policy makers – researching how they engage with evidence and those around them to make decisions in practice.

Critical policy studies: Policy influences beyond 'evidence'

The critical policy studies literature has a significant focus on broader pressures influencing policy making, including the effects of other policies (elsewhere or locally), the roles of policy actors and networks both globally and more regionally, and the impacts of meetings and data infrastructures. Studies of these influences on policy development and uptake in critical education policy research have been informed by broader work on policy borrowing, transfer, and more recently, mobility (e.g., Ball 2012; Dale 1999; Rizvi and Lingard 2010; Gulson et al. 2017; McKenzie, Bieler, and McNeil 2015).

In terms of the influences of other policies on policy development or uptake, this can include the transfer or mobility of particular education policy initiatives from elsewhere, such as introducing the use of PISA in an increasing number of countries and with parallel types of educational effects (e.g., Engel and Frizzell 2015). It can also include the effects of other policies within a given setting, such as Indigenous knowledge laws influencing the development of land-based requirements in education policy in the Canadian territory of Nunavut. The 'policy mobilities' lens introduced from economic geography into education offers a way to view the often partial and complex means through which policies move globally (e.g., Peck and Theodore 2010; McCann 2011). That policy trends and specifics are often shared amongst particular regions and countries, as well as more globally (e.g., Western education expectations and practices), suggests the influences of existing policy on 'new' policy decision-making.

A related and growing area of education policy research is the impacts of particular individual or organizational policy makers or networks in shaping policy. In particular, new research has examined the financing of educational initiatives through a focus on 'edu-business' such as organisations like Pearson (Hogan 2016; Hogan, Sellar, and Lingard 2016; Hursch, 2015; Sellar and Lingard, 2013), and national or global networks of actors and organisations promoting particular orientations to education (e.g., work on network governance and education in India, Ball 2012, 2016). Central to such analyses are the roles played by individual policy actors as 'policy entrepreneurs,' 'policy advocates,' or 'boundary spanners' who themselves are globally mobile and facilitate the spread and uptake of particular policy orientations or activities (Ball 2016; Larner and Laurie 2010; Peck and Theodore 2010). The relationalities of these and other policy actors and networks are supported through face-to-face meetings and conferences, as well as electronic communications such as email, blogs, or Twitter. Not only entailing the verbal sharing of ideas and collaborations, these venues also disperse and use key artifacts and policy tools, such as powerpoints, flyers, league tables, models, and programmatic ideas (Ball 2016; Dale 1992; Osborne 2004; Temenos and McCann 2013).

Key to these discussions of influences on the mobility and uptake of policy is the impacts of globalization and the ease with which certain policy actors and ideas now flow or connect across country boundaries in what have been termed, topological (e.g. Lewis, Sellar, and Lingard 2016), or nonscalar ways. This is a shift from the prior dominance of national and regional influences on policy making. Other researchers have called attention to the 'immobilities' of policy, or when particular policy initiatives or trends are not taken up in some settings due to other priorities, key actors, or other forms of policy resistance and non-adoption (Cohen 2017; Jacobs 2012; McLean and Borén 2015; Robinson 2015). A related body of critical education policy research on 'policy enactment' offers analysis of what happens on the ground when policy is resisted, changed or influenced at the intended site of 'implementation' (Ball, Maguire, and Braun 2012). Taking up these research frames can provide insight into why some policy ideas are engaged, promoted, received or resisted, and by whom, regardless of the availability of 'evidence;' and how a better understanding of this complexity of factors can and should be engaged in education policy making, and in research that takes policy as its focus.

Evidence use studies: evidence use and policy development as practices

A related contribution from the evidence use literature on the complexity of policy processes is in understanding both evidence use and policy development as practices. Farley-Ripple et al. (2018, 236), for example, describe how 'little attention has been paid to the practice of evidence use' within education, with the result that 'what practitioners actually do and use when engaging with research' is not well understood. They call for studies that 'seek to explain what activities, routines, roles or tools are employed' during the course of evidence use (ibid., 237). Similar arguments have been made in relation to studies looking at policy. In their editorial for a journal special issue on *The Practice of Policy Making*, for example, Freeman, Griggs, and Boaz (2011, 128) describe how: 'We know surprisingly little of what those we call 'policy makers' actually do when they are doing their job'. In contrast, they argue, 'practice-based inquiries' of policy processes can 'draw our attention back to the complex "messiness" of policy making, of the twists and turns by which policy is ultimately produced and performed' (ibid., 130).

Two studies that have sought to examine the use of evidence in policy through such a practice-orientated lens are Lomas and Brown's (2009) study of provincial health policy makers in Canada, and Rickinson et al.'s (2017; 2019) study of state education policy makers in Australia. Lomas and Brown (2009, 914) set out to challenge the fact that most models of research use in policy 'address the role of the researcher trying to get his or her research used more than that of the civil servant trying to do the using'. Instead they developed 'an insider framework' of evidence use in the policy world, which aimed to provide 'functional guidance to the evidence-orientated civil servant or politician' (Lomas and Brown 2009, 917, 920).

Along similar lines, Rickinson et al. (2017, 175-6) sought to build up 'a rich picture of the nature and dynamics of evidence use within policy processes' by approaching 'policy making as a kind of practice and policy makers as a type of practitioner'. This work framed evidence use in policy using 'a policy narrative perspective', which showed that evidence was involved not only in *constructing* a policy narrative but also in *testing* the narrative with key players, and *communicating* the narrative to key audiences (Rickinson et al. 2019). The policy narrative perspective was helpful for understanding evidence use in policy because it: emphasised the language and practices of policy makers, engaged with the audience-specific nature of policy development, examined the dynamics and mobility of policy developments over time and space, and embraced the political nature of policy making.

Taken together, critical policy studies and evidence use studies offer both a micro look at the nuances of policy practice and decision-making, as well as at broader macro factors beyond evidence that influence policy development and enactment – suggesting the layers of complexity in what influences the day-to-day practices of policy processes and implications for research.

Different roles of research

Finally, both critical policy studies and evidence use studies can also be seen to have generated insights into the different roles of research in relation to policy. Critical policy studies have distinguished between research *of* policy and research *for* policy, and have provided examples of more collaborative ways of seeking to investigate and influence policy by working closely and strategically with groups marginalized by existing policy practices. Evidence use studies, meanwhile, have flagged up the varied ways in which research can be used by policy makers. While there has long been conceptual recognition for research playing varied roles (e.g., Weiss 1978), more recent empirical work with policy makers has illustrated just how varied the uses of research can be.

Critical policy studies: Research 'of' and 'for policy'

Critical policy studies can involve critical analysis *of* the policy process, and/or research *for and in* the policy process (Gordon, Lewis, and Young 1977). In this typology, research *of* policy can be considered research for research's sake as a contribution to knowledge, while research *for* policy aims to contribute to the production and impacts of policy, for example in the case of commissioned or partnership 'problem-solving' research (Lingard 2013). However, as various education policy scholars have pointed out, it is misleading to portray this as a binary, but better perhaps as a 'of/for' continuum (Cibulka 1994; Lingard 2013), or even as mutually compatible aims of critical education policy research (Simons, Olssen, and Peters 2009, 9).

Critically-oriented *for* policy studies are generally different from studies that would take the policy problem as given and seek instrumental solutions that can leave unexamined a power laden and inequitable status quo. They can include analyses of policy processes which inform reports, consultations, presentations, and other engagements with policy audiences. In other cases, collaboration may be with those on the receiving end of policy. For example, Tuck (2012) worked with urban youth in New York state in participatory action research (PAR) focused on their experiences of being pushed out of school and into a general credential program, with research interactions with policy makers aimed at influencing policy reform. Fine and Barreras (2001) have written about the potential for diverse research processes and outputs that 'can be of use' in affecting policy change. This involves researchers producing or performing the type of evidence or activity which will be most useful for the target audience, from quantitative policy studies to testifying in court, authoring media op-eds or facilitating public art projects. This type of public scholarship or 'public science' is often collaborative and methodologically strategic, in that it takes the form most useful to informing just policy change (McKenzie 2009; Tuck and McKenzie 2015).

Evidence use studies: complexity of research use

Relatedly, the evidence use field differentiates between an interest in research *impact* and an interest in research *use*. The subtle but important distinction between these two was highlighted by Weiss in the late 1970s. She argued that social scientists tend to ask 'how can we increase the use of research in decision making?' rather than 'how can we make wiser decisions, and to what extent, in what ways, and under what conditions, can social research help?' (Weiss 1978, 78). The former is more about seeking research impact, while the latter is more about understanding, and potentially improving, research use.

A similar point is made in Oliver, Lorenc, et al.'s (2014) critical analysis of evidence-based policy research in the health field. Based on a systematic review of 145 empirical studies (Oliver, Innvar, et al. 2014), they concluded that there is a clear preoccupation with research impact as opposed to research use. As they describe: 'Researchers have directed their attention at how to increase the impact of their own outputs, rather than on understanding the processes behind policy change' (Oliver, Lorenc, et al. 2014, 3). In other words, 'the agenda of "getting evidence into policy" has side-lined the empirical description and analysis of how research and policy actually interact in vivo.' (ibid., 1).

The shortcoming of this preoccupation with impact rather than use is that it leaves unexplored the complex ways in which research can be used within the policy process. Where studies have taken the time to examine policy processes in detail, they have shown that research can be used in many and varied ways. Lomas and Brown's (2009) interview-based study of senior civil servants in a provincial health ministry in Canada, for example, identified three different areas of policy activity in which research was playing a role: setting agendas, developing new policies and monitoring and modifying existing policies (Lomas and Brown 2009). Furthermore, within each of these areas of activity, research was fulfilling a range of different functions. In setting agendas, research 'may signal an emerging or neglected area for attention' or 'help screen the validity of interest groups' competing claims on the agenda' (Lomas and Brown 2009, 918). In developing new policies, research can 'reduce uncertainty', 'increase confidence', 'prevent duplication' or 'give external validation for recommendation' (ibid., 918). In monitoring and modifying existing policies, research can 'provide basis for ongoing program improvement' or 'create currency of accountability' (ibid., 918).

A similar diversity of roles for research evidence is seen in a later study of state legislators in the US (Bogenschneider, Day, and Parrott 2019), which identified 14 different uses of research. What was significant was that several of these 14 different research uses went well beyond those that would be predicted by prominent theories of knowledge utilisation. For example, research being used to educate others; to enhance debate, dialogue, collaboration and compromise; to earn the trust of colleagues; and to ask important questions for policy or political purposes.

These considerations from both critical policy and evidence use studies underline the importance of taking seriously and being open to the complex and varied roles that research (and researchers) can play in relation to policy, with resulting impacts on the research-policy relationship.

Connections to and implications for ESE

We now turn our attention to ESE policy, and consider what connections there might be between the ideas discussed above and developments within ESE. We start by discussing what characterises ESE policy, before then exploring the research-policy relationship in ESE in terms of the three areas of concern identified above. We finish by highlighting what we see as implications for better understanding and negotiating the ESE research-policy interface in the future.

Characteristics of ESE as an area of policy and research

While some have cautioned against an overemphasis on the uniqueness of different policy areas in relation to the use of evidence (e.g., Davies et al. 2019), others have highlighted the importance of recognising the distinctiveness of individual policy areas (e.g., Boswell, 2009). In line with the latter, Reed and Meagher (2019, 151) argue that 'environmental and sustainability issues present particular challenges for evidence-informed policy and practice'. Likewise, it seems important to consider what characterises ESE as an area of policy and research to inform how or to what extent it is helpful to further consider the identified three areas of concern in relation to research-policy relationships in the ESE field.

Drawing on previous accounts and analyses of ESE policy and policy research (Laessøe et al., 2013; Stevenson et al. 2013; Van Poeck and Lysgaard 2016; Van Poeck, Lysgaard, and Reid 2018; Cheeseman et al. 2019; Glackin and King 2020), we see a number of features that recur as distinctive to ESE policy. These concern issues of *scale* (ESE policy involves a range of overlapping geographical scopes or levels), *breadth* (ESE policy involves diverse learning areas, contexts, outcomes and participants), and *contestation* (ESE policy involves varied and often competing values, ideologies and discourses).

In relation to scale, firstly, the particular importance of developments at the international level is a point that has been underlined repeatedly in relation to ESE policy. Stevenson et al. (2013, 147) for example, describes how 'international organisations (e.g., UNESCO, IUCN) and intergovernmental conferences have played a major role' in ESE policy development for over 50 years. This, he argues, is in contrast to educational policies more generally, which 'traditionally emanated from national or sub-national governments and their agencies' and only more recently have become 'under the forces of globalisation' (ibid., 147). In other words, ESE policy has had a strong international dimension through the influence of intergovernmental agencies from very early on in its development, and this continues to be an important feature of its policy landscape (e.g., Kolleck et al. 2017). Alongside this international influence is a range of other levels of policy making that are also important to on the ground ESE policy and practice. Glackin and King's (2020, 308) recent analysis of environmental education policy in England, for example, identified and examined developments 'at all levels of authority' – including national policy documents, local authority or school network policies, and individual school planning documents. Other analyses or accounts of ESE-related policy have underlined the impact of policy at a variety of levels or scale. A review of research on sustainability policies in higher education, for example, notes research indicating the impact of international policy programs, but also of initiatives at the national, regional and institutional levels (Cheeseman et al. 2019).

In relation to breadth, ESE is a policy area that encompasses a wide diversity of potential topics, pedagogical approaches, contexts, educational aims and learner types. Drawing on features of the field highlighted in the *International Handbook of Research on Environmental Education*, this breadth is reflective of the way in which ESE encompasses formal and informal education ('education and learning that not only takes place within formal institutional settings but also within non-formal or informal public domain settings'); interdisciplinary considerations (due to 'the inter-disciplinary nature of people-society-environment relationships'); and action-orientated outcomes ('concerned not only with knowledge and understanding, and attitudes and values, but also includes developing the agency of learners in participation and taking action') (Stevenson et al. 2013, 2). As a result, ESE policy can take as its focus a range of potential 'topics, missions, strategies, approaches, and outcomes' (Clark et al. 2020, 382), that span and connect with many different aspects of education, environment, and sustainability. This breadth of perspectives in ESE also relates to how 'evidence' may be engaged in ESE policy and research: from assumptions of the neutrality of evidence in science-based domains, to more critical orientations that assume a value orientation in what is provided as evidence and to how the evidence may be engaged in policy decision-making (Reed and Meagher 2019).

Finally, in relation to contestation, ESE is a field whose origins and development have been characterised by debates between competing perspectives, values, discourses and ideologies. There has, for example, been long-standing debate about the role and purpose of ESE policy. As Van Poeck and Lysgaard (2016, 308) describe, 'two vital topics of disagreement [...] are: environmental education (EE) versus education for the environment (EfE) – a discussion about the purpose of education; and environmental education versus ESD – a discussion centred on the field's subject matter and focus'. Along similar lines, Stevenson et al. (2013, 149) note how ESE policy has been characterised and shaped by 'tensions and struggles between different ideological interests' both in the relation to the environment and sustainability and in relation to education. In addition, ESE policy research has been described as 'a contentious and politically sensitive field' (Van Poeck and Lysgaard 2016, 307) with researchers who are often interested 'not only in creating descriptive accounts or theoretical contributions, but also fostering critical engagement and social change' (Laessøe et al., 2013, 233).

Implications for ESE research and policy in the future

With characteristics of the ESE policy field in mind, we conclude by revisiting the three areas of concern identified earlier from the critical policy and evidence use literatures in order to suggest future direction for advancing the research-policy relationship in ESE. As will become clear, we see aspects of how ESE policy research is already engaging with the three identified areas of concern, but also suggest the possibilities for further work on the ESE research-policy interface.

In terms of the first identified area of concern of *'what counts as evidence in policy'*, there has been some related discussion in the ESE policy field. Considerations of policy by numbers and international performativity and data-based governance from critical policy studies, for example, are strongly reflected in developments within ESE such as eco-certification schemes and indicator monitoring, including in relation to the Agenda 2030 Sustainable Development Goals (SDGs) (UN, 2015). These kinds of initiatives to develop ESE 'evidence' aim to advance ESE quantity and quality through monitoring, evaluation and assessment efforts. They can also frame the research-policy relationship in particular ways, such as through collaborations between policy makers and researchers on monitoring initiatives, or in using data to incentivize policy (Benavot 2018; Davis, Kingsbury, and Merry 2012; Finn 2016; Gorur 2017b). The ESE field has also seen 'increased calls for scholars to participate in international empirical studies, evaluations and projects focused on the development of recommendations and guidance for many levels of policy development' (Laessøe et al., 2013, 232; Stern, Powell, and Hill 2014; Zint 2013). This can create dilemmas for researchers about whether and/or how to engage, for example, 'Should we reject the invitation to participate in the construction of these (often narrow) policy agendas, or should we accept it and use it as an opportunity to try to expand the dialogue between researchers and policy makers?' (Laessøe et al., 2013, 233). While some have suggested that 'our research field must create time and space for more reflexive retrospection rather than for monitoring and evaluating pre-defined indicators' (Van Poeck and Lysgaard 2016, 311), there are also potential gains in working with policy makers to mobilize monitoring mechanisms to motivate new targets in national and local policy making.

There are also connections between reports from the evidence use field about different kinds of evidence being used in policy making and calls within ESE for the democratisation of policy processes. Evidence use studies have highlighted 'a greater degree of inclusivity around the types of knowledge admitted to debates about policy' (Davies et al. 2019, 376) – a point that resonates with arguments in ESE policy research. Stevenson et al. (2013, 154), for example, argue for evidence-informed (as opposed to evidence-based) policy in ESE because it 'recognises the place of professional knowledge and values alongside research-generated knowledge or evidence to inform decision making'.

For the second identified area of concern of *'complex policy processes'*, there are also links between the wider literatures examined and ESE policy. One example is the role of individual policy actors or 'policy entrepreneurs' highlighted by critical policy studies that has certainly been evident in the ESE area. The outputs of early international conferences, such as the 1975 Belgrade Workshop which articulated a goal and guiding principles of environmental education, were reportedly influenced by the commitments and perspectives of key researchers such as Professor Bill Stapp, the first director of the UNESCO-UNEP International Environmental Education Program. As Stevenson et al. (2013, 149) describe, the inclusion of an action component within the goal of environmental education 'reflected the ideological commitment of Stapp and many others [...] to foster citizen participation in natural resource management and the resolution of environmental issues'. More recently, Lysgaard, Reid, and Van Poeck (2016, 321), suggest that 'during the UN Decade of ESD, Professors Arjen Wals, John Fien, Chuck Hopkins and Daniella Tilbury' played similar kinds of policy entrepreneurial roles. These same authors also note how 'researchers draw on personal contacts and interactions to shape perceptions and understandings of policy production and critique, using social media, conferences and campaigns to try to influence policy, practice or change' (ibid., 322).

Parallels can also be seen between arguments in the evidence use field about the practice of policy being overlooked by researchers and calls in ESE policy research for studies to better understand the realities of policy processes in real time. Laessøe et al. (2013, 234), for example, suggest the need for 'documentary policy research [...] that documents what is actually going on in different contexts and on different levels', and Cheeseman et al. (2019, 1706-7) call for more work on 'the nuances of policy development and enactment'. Along similar lines, Stevenson et al. (2013, 154) argue that 'policy practices could also be treated as a learning process – just as sustainability itself should be viewed as a learning process'.

In the third identified area of concern of *'different roles of research'*, there are again links between ideas in the wider literatures and the ESE policy field. Work in critical policy studies draws distinctions, or envisions a continuum, between research *of* policy and research *for* and *in* policy, which resonates with ideas surfacing in ESE policy research. A number of ESE policy researchers acknowledge similar kinds of distinctions or tensions, and propose new ways of navigating or integrating them. Laessøe et al. (2013,233-4), for example, talk about 'the troubling dichotomy between an analytical approach towards theory development and an empirically-focused approach which meets the needs of policy makers'. In response, these authors argue for more ESE researchers to undertake what they call 'engaged and interactive policy research' (ibid.,

237). This is work that happens close to the practices of policy making, and involves meaningful relationships between researchers and the different actors involved in the policy process. A slightly different perspective is provided by 'civically-engaged policy research' or 'public scholarship' in ESE (McKenzie 2009; Stevenson et al. 2013). Here there is a similar emphasis on moving beyond a singular goal of knowledge production, but a stronger orientation towards democratising ESE policy processes through research and researchers helping to broaden public dialogue and action. This is about changing not only the relationship between ESE research and policy but also the relationship between ESE policy and practice.

Overall, then, we see points of connection between the key areas of concern we identified across critical policy studies and evidence use studies and prior discussions in ESE policy research. However, what prior work has been done on the research-policy interface in ESE is spread thinly across the ranges in geographic scale and breadth of focus, as well as contestation in perspectives and approaches that typify this field. For example, 'what counts as evidence' has been considered somewhat in relation to the intergovernmental sphere, and at the local level (e.g., eco-schools data), but not extensively across national or regional scales. In addition, conceptual work in the ESE policy field has focused extensively on issues of contestation (such as conceptual critiques of the UN framing of Education for Sustainable Development) (e.g., Jickling and Wals 2008) but far less on the details of the influences on, and enactment of, policy programs (e.g. Bengtsson 2016; Nomura and Osamu 2009). The existing scholarly writing on the research-policy interface in ESE tends to be editorial or commentary in nature (i.e., those cited above of Cheeseman et al. 2019; Laessøe et al., 2013; Lysgaard, Reid, and Van Poeck 2016; Stevenson et al. 2013) as opposed to empirical. Across ESE policy research more broadly the focus has been on discussion of policy texts or framings rather than on understanding other aspects of the policy process through empirical research. In general, we see a shortage of empirical research *of* and *for* ESE policy relative to other important aspects of ESE such as student learning, pedagogy, curriculum and program evaluation.

From the perspective of critical policy and evidence use studies, we thus see an urgent need to develop and encourage a more diverse range of work in relation to ESE policy processes, and on the research-policy interface in particular. In particular, we see a need for:

- not only examining ESE policy texts but also ESE policy development and enactment more broadly, and the roles and uses of research and evidence within and across these policy processes;
- attending to the roles of varied policy actors, intermediaries and infrastructures in the development and movement of policy ideas and initiatives across locations globally and locally;
- researching ESE policy not only as an abstract phenomenon but also as an embodied and enacted practice with particular kinds of actors, actions, norms and knowledge in multiple, evolving contexts;
- developing and exploring different kinds of collaborative frameworks and processes for collaboration with ESE policy makers on policy-relevant problems;
- striving to generate insights, ideas, frameworks and resources that are not only informative and useful for ESE researchers but also instructive and helpful for ESE policy makers;
- reflecting seriously on the differences between seeking to increase the use of ESE research in policy decision-making and seeking to understand how and when research can help in making better decisions; and
- communicating research for different kinds of use by policy makers, including conceptual use (raising questions), strategic use (supporting action) and instrumental use (providing answers).

In conclusion, this paper set out to explore how the ESE field's capacity to understand and navigate the research-policy relationship might be extended by drawing on ideas from two bodies of research from beyond the field. We have suggested key areas of concern regarding the research-policy interface that are highlighted by prior work in those two fields, and how these could be a stimulus for further deepening and expanding ESE policy research.

In exploring the potential of insights from beyond the field, though, it is important to stress that we also see rich possibilities for learning in the other direction. That is, we feel strongly that ESE can offer unique insights to the growing interdisciplinary literature on the research-policy nexus, particularly based on ESE being concerned with a different kind of policy issue than is often the case in education policy studies. For example, while large-scale assessments are generally seen as problematic in the education policy literature due to their effects on policy and student learning and equity, ESE global indicators or eco certification processes can be tools strategically mobilized to work within 'policy by numbers' environments to advance critical ends, such as climate and sustainability action. Thus, it is also important that future efforts to understand and negotiate the research-policy relationship in ESE are shared beyond the ESE policy field. Likewise, ESE research suggests that what often motivates educational change in relation to ESE are not competitive or economic mandates, but rather the environmental passion and advocacy of policy makers, teachers, and students, and their collaboration (Aikens 2019).

We thus advocate for more ESE research on policy, but also for more engagement by researchers with policy makers of all types *for* policy. Through more extensive and targeted research, we can better understand ESE policy, but also how ESE researchers and policy makers together can inform and advance efforts to advance climate action and sustainability through education.

Disclosure statement

No potential conflict of interest was reported by the authors.

ORCID

Mark Rickinson http://orcid.org/0000-0001-5760-6458
Marcia McKenzie http://orcid.org/0000-0002-8037-8059

References

Aikens, K. 2019. "A Critical Policy Analysis of Environmental and Sustainability Education in Canada." University of Saskatchewan PhD thesis. https://harvest.usask.ca/handle/10388/12251.

Aikens, K., M. McKenzie, and P. Vaughter. 2016. "Environmental and Sustainability Education Policy Research: A Systematic Review of Methodological and Thematic Trends." *Environmental Education Research* 22 (3): 333–359. doi:10.1080/13504622.2015.1135418.

Asen, R. D., P. Gurke, R. Conners, R. Solomon, and E. Gumm. 2013. "Research Evidence and School-Board Deliberations: Lessons from Three Wisconsin School Districts." *Educational Policy* 27 (1): 33–63. doi:10.1177/0895904811429291.

Backer, T. E. 1993. "Information Alchemy: Transforming Information through Knowledge Utilization." *Journal of the American Society for Information Science* 44 (4): 217–221. doi:10.1002/(SICI)1097-4571(199305)44:4<217::AID-ASI9>3.0.CO;2-D.

Ball, S. J. 1997. "Policy Sociology and Critical Social Research: A Personal Review of Recent Education Policy and Policy Research." *British Educational Research Journal* 23 (3): 257–274. doi:10.1080/0141192970230302.

Ball, S. J. 2012. *Global Education Inc.* London: Routledge.

Ball, S. J. 2016. "Following Policy: Networks, Network Ethnography and Education Policy Mobilities." *Journal of Education Policy* 31 (5): 549–566. doi:10.1080/02680939.2015.1122232.

Ball, S. J., M. Maguire, and A. Braun. 2012. *How Schools Do Policy: Policy Enactments in Secondary Schools*. London: Routledge.

Bartosh, B.,. M. Tudor, L. Ferguson, and C. Taylor. 2006. "Improving Test Scores through Environmental Education: Is It Possible?." *Applied Environmental Education & Communication* 5 (3): 161–169. doi:10.1080/15330150600912937.

Benavot, A. 2018. *Will SDG4 Achieve Environmental Sustainability? Some Thoughts and Suggestions*. Arizona: Centre for Advanced Studies in Global Education.

Bengtsson, S. L. 2016. "Hegemony and the Politics of Policy Making for Education for Sustainable Development: A Case Study of Vietnam." *The Journal of Environmental Education* 47 (2): 77–90. doi:10.1080/00958964.2015.1021291.

Boaz, A., C. Coburn, D. Gough, L. Palinkas, J. Molas-Gallart, J. Mortimer, S. Morton, et al. 2016. "The Future of Evidence & Policy: Moving Forward from Valencia." *Evidence & Policy: A Journal of Research, Debate and Practice* 12 (1): 3–8. doi:10.1332/174426416X14531221882404.

Boaz, A., G. H. Davies, A. Fraser, and S. Nutley, eds 2019. *What Works Now? Evidence-Informed Policy and Practice Revisited*. Bristol: Policy Press.

Bogenschneider, K., E. Day, and E. Parrott. 2019. "Revisiting Theory on Research Use: Turning to Policymakers for Fresh Insights." *The American Psychologist* 74 (7): 778–793. Advance online publication. http://dx.doi.org/. doi:10.1037/amp0000460.

Boswell, C. 2009. *The Political Uses of Expert Knowledge*, Cambridge: Cambridge University Press.

Bowe, R., S. J. Ball, and A. Gold. 1992. *Reforming Education and Changing Schools*. London: Routledge.

Brewer, J. D. 2013. *The Public Value of the Social Sciences: An Interpretive Essay*. London: Bloomsbury.

Cairney, P. 2016. *The Politics of Evidence-Based Policymaking*." London: Palgrave Macmillan.

Cairney, P. 2019. "Evidence and Policy-Making." In *What Works Now? Evidence-Informed Policy and Practice Revisited*, edited by A Boaz, H Davies, A Fraser and S. Nutley, 21–40. Bristol: Policy Press.

Cheeseman, A., T. Wright, J. Murray, and M. McKenzie. 2019. "Taking Stock of Sustainability in Higher Education: A Review of the Policy Literature." *Environmental Education Research* 25 (12): 1697–1712. doi:10.1080/13504622.2019.1616164.

Cibulka, J. G. 1994. "Policy Analysis and the Study of Education." *Journal of Education Policy* 9 (5): 105–125. doi:10.1080/0268093940090511.

Clark, C. R., J. E. Heimlich, N. M. Ardoin, and J. Braus. 2020. "Using a Delphi Study to Clarify the Landscape and Core Outcomes in Environmental Education." *Environmental Education Research* 26 (3): 381–399. doi:10.1080/13504622.2020.1727859.

Cohen, D. 2017. "Market Mobilities/Immobilities: Mutation, Path-Dependency, and the Spread of Charter School Policies in the United States." *Critical Studies in Education* 58 (2): 168–186. doi:10.1080/17508487.2016.1242507.

Dale, R. 1992. "Recovering from a Pyrrhic Victory? Quality, Relevance and Impact in the Sociology of Education." In *Voicing Concerns: Sociological Perspectives on Contemporary Education Reforms*, edited by M. Arnot and L. Barton, 201–207. Wallingford: Trianglen Books.

Dale, R. 1999. "Specifying Globalization Effects on National Policy: A Focus on the Mechanisms." *Journal of Education Policy* 14 (1): 1–17. doi:10.1080/026809399286468.

Dale, R. 2005. "Globalisation, Knowledge Economy and Comparative Education." *Comparative Education* 41 (2): 117–149.

Davies, H., A. Boaz, S. Nutley, and A. Fraser. 2019. "Conclusions: Lessons from the past, Prospects for the Future." In *What Works Now? Evidence-Informed Policy and Practice Revisited*, edited by A Boaz, H Davies, A Fraser and S. Nutley, 359–382. Bristol: Policy Press.

Davies, H. T. O, S. M. Nutley, and P. C. Smith, eds. 2000. *What Works: Evidence-Based Policy and Practice in Public Services*. Bristol: Policy Press.

Davis, K. E., B. Kingsbury, and S. E. Merry. 2012. "Indicators as a Technology of Global Governance." *Law & Society Review* 46 (1): 71–104. doi:10.1111/j.1540-5893.2012.00473.x.

Dye, T. R. 1972. *Understanding Public Policy*. Englewood Cliffs: Prentice-Hall.
Easton, D. 1953. *The Political System*. New York: Knopf.
Engel, L. C., and M. O. Frizzell. 2015. "Competitive Comparison and PISA Bragging Rights: Sub-National Uses of the OECD's PISA in Canada and the USA." *Discourse: Studies in the Cultural Politics of Education* 36 (5): 665–682. doi: 10.1080/01596306.2015.1017446.
Farley-Ripple, E., H. May, A. Karpyn, K. Tilley, and K. McDonough. 2018. "Rethinking Connections between Research and Practice in Education: A Conceptual Framework." *Educational Researcher* 47 (4): 235–245. doi:10.3102/0013189X18761042.
Fine, M., and R. Barreras. 2001. "To Be of Use." *Analyses of Social Issues and Public Policy* 1 (1): 175–182.
Finn, M. 2016. "Atmospheres of Progress in a Data-Based School." *Cultural Geographies* 23 (1): 29–49. doi:10.1177/1474474015575473.
Freeman, R., S. Griggs, and A. Boaz. 2011. "The Practice of Policy Making." *Evidence & Policy: A Journal of Research, Debate and Practice* 7 (2): 127–136. doi:10.1332/174426411X579180.
Gal, J., and I. W. Gal. 2017. *Where Academia and Policy Meet: Cross-National Perspectives on the Involvement of Social Work Academics in Social Policy*. New York: Policy Press.
Gitomer, D. R., and K. Crouse. 2019. *Studying the Use of Research Evidence: A Review of Methods*. New York, NY: William T. Grant Foundation.
Glackin, M., and H. King. 2020. "Taking Stock of Environmental Education Policy in England – the What, the Where and the Why." *Environmental Education Research* 26 (3): 305–323. doi:10.1080/13504622.2019.1707513.
Gordon, I., J. Lewis, and R. Young. 1977. "Perspectives on Policy Analysis." *Public Administration Bulletin* 25: 26–35.
Gorur, R. 2017a. "Towards Productive Critique of Large-Scale Comparisons in Education." *Critical Studies in Education* 58 (3): 341–355. doi:10.1080/17508487.2017.1327876.
Gorur, R. 2017b. "Statistics and Statecraft: Exploring the Potentials, Politics and Practices of International Educational Assessment." *Critical Studies in Education* 58 (3): 261–265. doi:10.1080/17508487.2017.1353271.
Gulson, K. N., S. Lewis, B. Lingard, C. Lubienski, K. Takayama, and P. T. Webb. 2017. "Policy Mobilities and Methodology: A Proposition for Inventive Methods in Education Policy Studies." *Critical Studies in Education* 58 (2): 224–241. doi:10.1080/17508487.2017.1288150.
Gulson, K., and S. Sellar. 2019. "Emerging Data Infrastructures and the New Topologies of Education Policy." *Environment and Planning D: Society and Space* 37 (2): 350–366. doi:10.1177/0263775818813144.
Heimans, S. 2012. "Coming to Matter in Practice: Enacting Education Policy." *Discourse: Studies in the Cultural Politics of Education* 33 (2): 313–326. doi:10.1080/01596306.2012.666083.
Hogan, A. 2016. "NAPLAN and the Role of Edu-Business: New Governance, New Privatisations and New Partnerships in Australian Education Policy." *The Australian Educational Researcher* 43 (1): 93–110. doi:10.1007/s13384-014-0162-z.
Hogan, A., S. Sellar, and B. Lingard. 2016. "Commercialising Comparison: Pearson Puts the TLC in Soft Capitalism." *Journal of Education Policy* 31 (3): 243–258. doi:10.1080/02680939.2015.1112922.
Hursch, D. 2015. *The End of Public Schools: The Corporate Reform Agenda to Privatize Education*. London: Routledge.
Jacobs, J. M. 2012. "Urban Geographies I: Still Thinking Cities Relationally." *Progress in Human Geography* 36 (3): 412–422. doi:10.1177/0309132511421715.
Jickling, B., and A. Wals. 2008. "Globalization and Environmental Education: Looking beyond Sustainable Development." *Journal of Curriculum Studies* 40 (1): 1–21. doi:10.1080/00220270701684667.
Kelley, J. G., and B. A. Simmons. 2015. "Politics by Number: Indicators as Social Pressure in International Relations." *American Journal of Political Science* 59 (1): 55–70. doi:10.1111/ajps.12119.
Kolleck, N., M. Well, S. Sperzel, and H. Jörgens. 2017. "The Power of Social Networks: How the UNFCCC Secretariat Creates Momentum for Climate Education." *Global Environmental Politics* 17 (4): 106–126. doi:10.1162/GLEP_a_00428.
Laessøe, J., N. W. Feinstein, and N. Blum. 2013. "Environmental Education Policy Research – Challenges and Ways Research Might Cope with Them." *Environmental Education Research* 19 (2): 231–242. doi:10.1080/13504622.2013.778230.
Larner, W., and N. Laurie. 2010. "Travelling Technocrats, Embodied Knowledges: Globalising Privatisation in Telecoms and Water." *Geoforum* 41 (2): 218–226. doi:10.1016/j.geoforum.2009.11.005.
Lieberman, G. A. 2013. *Education and the Environment: Creating Standards-Based Programs in Schools and Districts*. Boston: Harvard Education Press.
Lewis, S., S. Sellar, and B. Lingard. 2016. "PISA for Schools: Topological Rationality and New Spaces of the OECD's Global Educational Governance." *Comparative Education Review* 60 (1): 27–57. doi:10.1086/684458.
Lingard, B. 2011. "Policy as Numbers: Ac/Counting for Educational Research." *The Australian Educational Researcher* 38 (4): 355–382. doi:10.1007/s13384-011-0041-9.
Lingard, B. 2013. "The Impact of Research on Education Policy in an Era of Evidence-Based Policy." *Critical Studies in Education* 54 (2): 113–131. doi:10.1080/17508487.2013.781515.
Lingard, B., and J. Ozga, eds. 2007. *The RoutledgeFalmer Reader in Education Policy and Politics*. New York: Routledge.

Lomas, J., and A. D. Brown. 2009. "Research and Advice Giving: A Functional View of evidence-informed policy advice in a Canadian Ministry of Health." *The Milbank Quarterly* 87 (4): 903–926. doi:10.1111/j.1468-0009.2009.00583.x.

Lysgaard, J. A., A. Reid, and K. Van Poeck. 2016. "The Roots and Routes of Environmental and Sustainability Education Policy Research: An Introduction to a Virtual Special Issue." *Environmental Education Research* 22 (3): 319–332. doi:10.1080/13504622.2015.1108392.

McCann, E. J. 2011. "Urban Policy Mobilities and Global Circuits of Knowledge: Toward a Research Agenda." *Annals of the Association of American Geographers* 101 (1): 107–130. doi:10.1080/00045608.2010.520219.

McKenzie, M. 2009. "*Scholarship as Intervention: Critique, Collaboration and the Research Imagination.*" *Environmental Education Research* 15 (2): 217–226. doi:10.1080/13504620902807576.

McKenzie, M. 2017. "Affect Theory and Policy Mobility: Challenges and Possibilities for Critical Policy Research." *Critical Studies in Education* 58 (2): 187–204. doi:10.1080/17508487.2017.1308875.

McKenzie, M., A. Bieler, and R. McNeil. 2015. "Education Policy Mobility: Reimagining Sustainability in Neoliberal Times." *Environmental Education Research* 23 (3): 319–337.

McLean, B. L., and T. Borén. 2015. "Barriers to Implementing Sustainability Locally: A Case Study of Policy Immobilities." *Local Environment* 20 (12): 1489–1506. doi:10.1080/13549839.2014.909798.

Nomura, K., and A. Osamu. 2009. "The Education for Sustainable Development Movement in Japan: A Political Perspective." *Environmental Education Research* 15 (4): 483–496. doi:10.1080/13504620903056355.

Nutley, S., I. Walter, and H. T. O. Davies. 2007. *Using Evidence: How Research Can Inform Public Services*. Bristol: Policy Press.

OECD. nd. "Programme for International Student Assessment." https://www.oecd.org/pisa/publications/

Oliver, K., S. Innvar, T. Lorenc, J. Woodman, and J. Thomas. 2014. "A Systematic Review of Barriers to and Facilitators of the Use of Evidence by Policymakers." *BMC Health Services Research* 14 (2): 2–12. doi:10.1186/1472-6963-14-2.

Oliver, K., T. Lorenc, and S. Innvaer. 2014. "New Directions in Evidence-Based Policy Research: A Critical Analysis of the Literature." *Health Research Policy and Systems* 12 (34): 34–11. doi:10.1186/1478-4505-12-34.

Osborne, T. 2004. "On Mediators: Intellectuals and the Ideas Trade in the Knowledge Society." *Economy and Society* 33 (4): 430–447. doi:10.1080/0308514042000285224.

Ozga, J. 2000. *Policy Research in Educational Settings: Contested Terrain*. Buckingham: Open University Press.

Ozga, J. 2009. "Governing Education through Data in England: From Regulation to Self-Evaluation." *Journal of Education Policy* 24 (2): 149–162. doi:10.1080/02680930902733121.

Payne, P. G. 2016. "The Politics of Environmental Education. Critical Inquiry and Education for Sustainable Development." *The Journal of Environmental Education* 47 (2): 69–76. doi:10.1080/00958964.2015.1127200.

Peck, J., and N. Theodore. 2010. "Mobilizing Policy: Models, Methods, and Mutations." *Geoforum* 41 (2): 169–174. doi:10.1016/j.geoforum.2010.01.002.

Peck, J., and N. Theodore. 2015. *Fast Policy: Experimental Statecraft at the Thresholds of Neoliberalism*. Minneapolis, MI: University of Minnesota Press.

Reed, M., and L. Meagher. 2019. "Using Evidence in Environmental and Sustainability Issues." In *What Works Now? Evidence-Informed Policy and Practice Revisited*, edited by A. Boaz, H. Davies, A. Fraser and S. Nutley, 151–170. Bristol: Policy Press.

Rickinson, M., C. de Bruin, L. Walsh, and M. Hall. 2016. *The Use of Evidence in Education Policy: A Pilot Study in Victoria*. Melbourne, Victoria: Final report for the Department of Education and Training.

Rickinson, M., C. de Bruin, L. Walsh, and M. Hall. 2017. "What Can Evidence-Use in Practice Learn from Evidence-Use in Policy?" *Educational Research* 59 (2): 173–189. doi:10.1080/00131881.2017.1304306.

Rickinson, M., L. Walsh, C. de Bruin, and M. Hall. 2019. "Understanding Evidence Use within Education Policy: A Policy Narrative Perspective." *Evidence & Policy: A Journal of Research, Debate and Practice* 15 (2): 235–252. doi:10.1332/174426418X15172393826277.

Rizvi, F., and B. Lingard. 2010. *Globalizing Education Policy*. London: Routledge.

Robinson, J. 2015. "Arriving At' Urban Policies: The Topological Spaces of Urban Policy Mobility." *International Journal of Urban and Regional Research* 39 (4): 831–834. doi:10.1111/1468-2427.12255.

Rose, N. 1999. *Powers of Freedom: Reframing Political Thought*. Cambridge: Cambridge University Press.

Savage, G. 2020. "What is Policy Assemblage?" *Territory, Politics, Governance* 8 (3): 319–335. doi:10.1080/21622671.2018.1559760.

Savage, G., and B. Lingard. 2018. "Changing Modes of Governance in Australian Teacher Education Policy." In *Navigating the Common Good in Teacher Education Policy: Critical and International Perspectives*, edited by N. Hobbel and B. L. Bales, 64–80. New York: Routledge.

Sellar, S., and B. Lingard. 2013. "The OECD and Global Governance in Education." *Journal of Education Policy* 28 (5): 710–725. doi:10.1080/02680939.2013.779791

Scott, J. C. 1998. *Seeing like a State: How Certain Schemes to Improve the Human Condition Have Failed*. New Haven: Yale University Press.

Simons, M., M. Olssen, and M. A. Peters. 2009. *Re-Reading Education Policies: A Handbook Studying the Policy Agenda of the 21st Century.*" Rotterdam, NL: Sense Publishers.

Stern, M. J., R. B. Powell, and D. Hill. 2014. "Environmental Education Program Evaluation in the New Millennium: What Do we Measure and What Have we Learned?" *Environmental Education Research* 20 (5): 581–611. doi:10.1080/13504622.2013.838749.

Stevens, A. 2011. "Telling Policy Stories: An Ethnographic Study of the Use of Evidence in Policymaking in the UK." *Journal of Social Policy* 40 (2): 237–255. doi:10.1017/S0047279410000723.

Stevenson, R. B., A. E. J. Wals, J. Dillon, and M. Brody. 2013. "Introduction: An Orientation to Environmental Education and the Handbook." In *International Handbook of Research on Environmental Education*, edited by R. B. Stevenson, M. Brody, J. Dillon, and A. E. J. Wals, 1–6. New York: Routledge, American Educational Research Association.

Stevenson, R. B., Brody, M., Dillon, J., and A. E. J. Wals, eds. 2013. *International Handbook of Research on Environmental Education.* New York: Routledge.

Stevenson, R. B. 2013. "Researching Tensions and Pretensions in Environmental/Sustainability Education Policies: From Critical to Civically Engaged Policy Scholarship." In *International Handbook of Research on Environmental Education*, edited by R. B. Stevenson, M. Brody, J. Dillon, and A. E. J. Wals, 147–155. New York: Routledge, American Educational Research Association.

Taylor, S., Rizvi, F. B. Lingard, B., and M. Henry. 1997. *Educational Policy and the Politics of Change.* London: Routledge.

Temenos, C., and E. McCann. 2013. "Geographies of Policy Mobilities." *Geography Compass* 7 (5): 344–357. doi:10.1111/gec3.12063.

Thompson, G., and I. Cook. 2015. "Becoming—Topologies of Education: Deformations, Networks and the Database Effect." *Discourse: The Cultural Politics of Education, 36(5): 732-748.*

Tseng, V. 2012. "The Uses of Research in Policy and Practice." *Social Policy Report* 26 (2): 1–23. doi:10.1002/j.2379-3988.2012.tb00071.x.

Tuck, E. 2012. *Urban Youth and School Pushout: Gateways, Get-Aways, and the GED.* New York: Routledge.

Tuck, E., and M. McKenzie. 2015. *Place in Research: Theory, Methodology, and Methods.* London: Routledge.

Van Poeck, K., and K. J. Lysgaard. 2016. "The Roots and Routes of Environmental and Sustainability Education Policy Research." *Environmental Education Research* 22 (3): 305–318. doi:10.1080/13504622.2015.1108393.

Van Poeck, K., J. Lysgaard, and A. Reid, eds. 2018. "*Environmental and Sustainability Education Policy: International Trends, Priorities and Challenges.*" London: Routledge.

Weiss, C. H. 1978. "Improving the Linkage between Social Research and Public Policy." Chap 3 in *Knowledge and Policy: The Uncertain Connection*, edited by L. E. Lynn, 23–81. Washington, DC: National Academy Press.

Weiss, C. H. 1979. "The Many Meanings of Research Utilization." *Public Administration Review* 39 (5): 426–431. doi:10.2307/3109916.

Williamson, B. 2016. "Digital Education Governance: Data Visualization, Predictive Analytics, and 'Real-Time' Policy Instruments." *Journal of Education Policy* 31 (2): 123–141. doi:10.1080/02680939.2015.1035758.

Williamson, B. 2017. *Big Data in Education: The Digital Future of Learning, Policy and Practice.*London: Sage.

Williamson, B. 2019. "Psychodata: Disassembling the Psychological, Economic, and Statistical Infrastructure of 'Social-Emotional Learning." *Journal of Education Policy* : 1–26. doi:10.1080/02680939.2019.1672895.

Zint, M. 2013. "Advancing Environmental Education Program Evaluation: Insights from a Review of Behavioural Outcome Evaluations." In *International Handbook of Research on Environmental Education*, edited by R. B. Stevenson, M. Brody, J. Dillon, and A. E. J. Wals, 298–309. New York: Routledge, American Educational Research Association.

The changing and complex entanglements of research and policy making in education: issues for environmental and sustainability education

Bob Lingard

ABSTRACT
This paper focuses on the complex, entangled relationships between research and policy and suggests this is a very important topic in the contemporary era of so-called, 'evidence-based' or 'research-based' policy in education. The paper argues that we can only ever have 'evidence-informed' and 'research-informed' policy because all policy is an admixture of facts (research), politics (discourses, values, ideologies) and professional knowledges, a position readily apparent in respect of ESE and broader climate policy. The paper also argues that post-truth contexts and the politics of affect provide a significant backdrop to research/policy relationships with specific salience in respect of environmental and sustainability education (ESE) research and policy, given the conflictual politics surrounding this domain. The distinction between research *for* and *of* policy is used analytically in the paper. While research *for* policy, often conducted by private consultancies, might have a more direct and immediate impact on policy, it is suggested that research *of* policy, often conducted by academic researchers, and indeed research of a critical kind, potentially can have long-term impact, affecting the assumptive worlds of policy makers, often in unacknowledged ways. Globalization has resulted in the global circulation of policy ideas and thus research can affect policy at varying levels in contemporary policy processes of the restructured/rescaled state. Some consideration is also given to the rise of big data and policy as numbers. The paper discusses implications of such developments for considerations of research/policy relationships, particularly in relation to ESE. The paper concludes by suggesting the current climate emergency demands activist research and researchers in the ESE domain and also activist teachers and students.

Introduction

'Entanglements' adroitly grasps the denotations and connotations of the multiple, complex and competing relationships and uses, misuses, neglect and denial of research knowledge in public policy making, including in education (Lingard 2011, 2020). This depiction is amplified somewhat when one is contemplating the relationships between environmental and sustainability education (ESE) research and education policy in that domain because of the conflictual politics that surround policy issues to do with climate change and sustainability (Lysgaard, Reid and Van Poeck, 2016). The question has been asked in respect of the research/policy relationships or entanglements in regard to ESE research and policy, whether they resemble, 'a dance macabre, an intimate tango, a ballet rehearsal, or more of a mosh pit frenzy' (Lysgaard et al, 2016, 323). This question and these metaphors deftly address the complexity of the desired, actual and possible relationships between ESE research and policy and practice in education. These descriptors proffered by Lysgaard and colleagues are even more applicable when one contemplates straightforward public environmental policies in the context of the current climate emergency and potential moves towards an 'uninhabitable earth' (Wallace-Wells 2019). The relationships between research and policy making in education then - both actual and desired – are complex, entangled and of pressing importance in the context of the realpolitik of contemporary policy making in education. This is particularly so in respect of ESE research and policy in the context of the current climate emergency and the related dire warnings of the UN's Intergovernmental Panel on Climate Change (IPCC). Finalising this paper during the devastating bushfires in Australia serves to drive home further the emergency we are facing right now.

Today there is a great deal of talk about the necessity of 'evidence-based policy' and the usage of 'what works' – in other words, support for research of a utilitarian kind undertaken to directly inform education policy and practice. This language suggests an engineering relationship between evidence and both policy and practice and assumes an oversimplified construction of both policy and professional practice and what informs them (Head 2008). 'Evidence-based policy' and 'what works' have become mantras, almost. The argument here will be that we need to deconstruct debates and discussions about these matters in contemporary educational policy production, including in ESE. Both practices of research and policy are complex and contested, as is the relationship between them. Defining ESE is even more complex, as is research in that domain and its entanglements with policies of various kinds. Think, for example, of the concepts of sustainability and sustainable development that have circulated globally in broad policy and in education and how these sit with, and are constrained by, the meta-policy framing of neoliberalism (McKenzie et al. 2015).

The focus in this paper will largely be on policy production, that is, the production of policy in state structures, not on policy implementation or more accurately, policy enactment (Ball, Maguire, and Braun 2012). Over the past thirty or forty years, state bureaucracies have been restructured under new public management and more recently through what has been called 'network governance' (Ball and Junemann 2012). New public management has seen a thinned-out bureaucracy that sets broad aims and devolves implementation and steers it through performance indicators, while network governance has seen non-state actors (e.g.businesses, philanthropists, consultancy firms) become networked into policy processes inside the state (Koppenjan and Klijn 2004). Both modes are complementary to neo-liberal approaches of marketization, privatization and commercialization in education, yet different from them with their own rationales, for example, trying to speed up policy processes against the perceived sclerotic traditional bureaucratic approaches. Both modes also have witnessed a rescaling of the state and new modes of statecraft with implications for policy and policy processes with significance for the place of evidence in these new policy production processes. These changes and rescalings have complexified further the research/policy relationship. Some have argued that fast global flows of policy models have even 'foreshortened' research and development stages of policy production with much mimicry within national policy making of these global models and thus no productive use of vernacular research knowledge (Peck and Theodore 2015). Of course, in relation to ESE research and policy, the question is the worth and quality of the models being mimicked.

In the contemporary moment, consideration of the concept of evidence-based policy also needs to be situated in the context of globalization, which has reframed policy making at national and sub-national levels (Rizvi and Lingard 2010; Ball 2012; Lingard, Martino, Rezai-Rashti, and Sellar 2016). And, of course, climate change and environmental degradation are issues that have to be confronted globally, regionally, nationally and locally. Additionally, the UN Decade for ESD beginning in 2005 was illustrative in a sense of a global meta-policy, as is the work of the UN's IPCC and the various global agreements on emissions reduction (e.g.Kyoto, Paris). Globalization has witnessed actual and necessary 'debordering' of policy imaginaries (Peck and Theodore 2015, p. xv), intimately linked to emergent global policy fields and policy mobilities. Yet, policy enactment 'remains a stubbornly localized, context-specific process' (Peck and Theodore 2015, p. xvi) that is mediated by local contexts, including in our case by teachers' understandings and commitments to ESE and the character of the actual curriculum in action (Ball, Maguire, and Braun 2012). As noted above, 'sustainability' has become a 'vehicular idea' in policy (Temenos and McCann, 2012) that has circulated globally with real impact on both ESD and ESE and been taken up in vernacular ways locally (McKenzie et al. 2015).

Consideration of evidence-based policy also needs to be set in the context of the rise of so-called 'post-truth' politics, most evident in the virulent attacks on notions of expertise, and where according to the Oxford Dictionary, 'objective facts are less influential in shaping public opinion than appeals to emotion and personal beliefs'. Related has been the rise of 'science denial' (McIntyre, 2018), perhaps best evidenced in attacks on the science of climate change as backdrop to the controversies surrounding ESE. Climate science deniers are evident in many conservative governments around the globe. Their influence is evident, for example, in President Trump's rolling back of President Obama's environmental protection laws and in the failure of the Morrison government in Australia to change tack on their climate policy and increase carbon emissions targets despite devastating bushfires in late 2019, early 2020. (See Booker Prize winning Australian novelist, Richard Flanagan's (2020) two devastating opinion pieces in the *New York Times* arguing Australia is committing 'climate suicide'.)

In a complementary way, critical policy analysis has also recently given attention to the significance of affect in policy processes (McKenzie 2017), acknowledging Berlant's (2011, p.226) prescient observation that public spheres (including politics and thus policies) are always 'affect worlds'. Furthermore, data and complementary datafication of the social world, facilitated by data infrastructures, enhanced computational capacities and algorithmic governance (Williamson 2017), also now increasingly frame policy production and practice in education. This raises interesting questions in relation to research/policy relationships: is the use of such data and data analysis an example of the use of research in policy making? If the response to that question is affirmative, then research in that case is reduced to data. There is also the interesting contradiction between the enhanced usage of big data in policy production and the politics of post-truth, science denial and the significance of affect in policy production and practice. These matters almost seem to function in an intensified way when one considers matters to do with ESE.

In what follows, initially the focus will be on how we should understand policy and what impact globalization has had on the text production phase of policy production, including in relation to the role of research. The underpinning premise here is that an understanding of policy is necessary to comprehending research/policy relationships in all their myriad forms. Next consideration will be given to how we might think about research and its complex and multifarious relationships with policy. The potentially disjunctive cultures between research and policy will be traversed, before the paper draws to a close through a contextualising of considerations of research/policy relationships and critical issues about these relationships for both research and policy, including the emergence of policy as numbers and policy being underpinned by state data, while at the same time being challenged in a post-truth political environment. Where appropriate, references will be made to the specificities of the ESE research/education policy relationships throughout and these matters will also be returned to in the conclusion.

Policy in a global context

A classic (old but still useful) definition of public policy proffered by the American political scientist, David Easton (1953), was that policy is 'the authoritative allocation of values'. Gale and Densmore (2003) argue that he was actually talking about politics and political systems, rather than explicitly referencing policy. Thus I would reword his definition so that we see policy as the authoritative allocation of values framed by politics and mediated by the logics of practice of the state. This is the space of the relationship between politicians and public service policy makers, where the political meets state logics. The logics of practice of the state, according to Bourdieu (1998), claim the right to stipulate and apply the universal ('the monopoly of the universal'), that is, for example, policy applies in all schools in a system putatively in the same way. This monopoly of the universal in education policy comes up against the idiosyncratic specificities of the contingent logics of school and classroom practices; thus proffering a Bourdieusian account of inevitable infidelities in policy implementation or enactment. In contemporary parlance, policy has a 'one size fits all' character, despite almost inevitable infidelities in policy implementation or enactment. While there is an isomorphism between all schools in a system, each school also has its contingent 'thisness' and specific contexts mediating policy enactment. With state restructurings, firstly under new public management, and more recently under network governance, new actors are involved in state policy production, including edu-business personnel and non-educational professionals, ensuring a broader range of perspectives and values, including non-educational ones, are involved in education policy production with significant implications for policy enactment. This involvement also has implications for the values being allocated in respect of policy and this is especially so in respect of ESE with the concept of sustainable development cohering the dominant manifestation of ESE with neo-liberal capitalism (McKenzie et al. 2015).

Easton developed his definition some time ago now; much has changed since the 1950s; for example, policy is now not the sole prerogative of the nation state with many policy effects stemming from global and regional agreements. Thus we need to deconstruct each element of the Easton-derived definition, namely, authority, allocation and values, in the context of the effects of globalization on state structures and statecraft. In classic Weberian sociology, authority is the legitimate right to exercise power. This is an important aspect of public policy, including education and ESE policy; the state can and does legitimately produce and implement policies. Allocation refers to state structures and how the policy cycle of influence, text production and practice/implementation/enactment (Ball 1994; Ball, Maguire, and Braun 2012; Ball 2015), and sometimes, evaluation, works. Values in Easton's classic definition can be read as ideology, politics, discourse, depending on theoretical orientation. On policy as discourse, Ball (1994) argued that policy is both discourse and text, with the former in a Foucauldian sense framing what can be said in the actual policy text. Today, dominant discourses regarding appropriate education policy circulate globally. In the context of globalization then, there has been a 'transnationalization of policy discourses' and a related 'cosmopolitanization of policy actors' (Peck and Theodore 2015, p.224). Transnationalization references the global flows of policy ideas, while cosmopolitanization references the global dispositions of policy makers. This is particularly so in respect of broad environmental policy and also in relation to ESE policy (McKenzie et al. 2015). Yet we need to recognise that these realities of contemporary policy production rub up against post-truth politics and the role of emotion in politics, both of which affect policy production and enactment.

Elsewhere Rizvi and Lingard (2010) have argued that the contemporary conditions of globalization have challenged all elements of the Easton definition as defined above. Easton's 1953 definition assumed that the social was homologous with the nation-state and related, that all education policy making basically occurred within the nation and at subnational levels. Each element of Easton's definition has also been affected by contemporary processes of globalization, including what Appadurai (1996) described as the global, yet disjunctive, flows of ideas, images, people and finance across national borders. However, this is not to accept that the nation-state is no longer important. Rather, it is to acknowledge that the nation-state now works in different ways in the context of multiple processes of globalization that have flowed since the end of the Cold War in the late 1980s and consequent on the emergence of a global economy and the dominance of neo-liberal dispositions amongst policy makers globally. New spatialities have accompanied globalization with implications for governance, for example, new regionalisms, supranational governance and global policy fields. Furthermore, this reworking of the nation-state is also mediated by political structure, for example a unitary form of government as in New Zealand, as opposed to a federal form as in Canada, Australia, Germany and the USA. We have mediations within nations of both centralising and decentralising tendencies in governance.

Additionally, I would argue that the globalization of the economy that flowed after the end of the Cold War and politics around its effects have actually undergone various changes since then; think of the significance of September 11, the Global Financial Crisis, Brexit, the election of President Trump and 'America First', the articulation of new ethno-nationalism, the rise of the Far Right politically in various parts of the globe (France, Germany, Austria, Hungary, the Philippines for example), and also think of left progressive mobilisations against neo-liberal globalization and related rise of green politics in opposition to this, manifested *inter alia* in the idea of the Green New Deal in the USA, in global demonstrations regarding the climate crisis and the work of Greta Thunberg. The relevant point here is the significance of the rise of these new nationalisms and ethnonationalism for effectively confronting a global problem such as the climate emergency.

In respect of authority: while the nation-state (and sub-national governments) remains centrally important in policy production, this nation-based authority has been complemented by authority resulting from the enhanced significance of international organisations in education (e.g.the OECD), specifically international large scale assessments (ILSAs) such as PISA and TIMSS and PIRLS, and also authority resulting from regional and sometimes supranational agreements and political structures (e.g.ASEAN and the EU). Furthermore, with network governance national and global businesses and philanthropies also affect policy production within the state. We might speak here of a rescaled networked state. Contemporary education policy has been reframed at the meta-level as the production of requisite human capital thought necessary to ensure the competitiveness globally of the putative national economy. That economistic framing carries implications for ESE and also for the relationships between ESE research and policy; for example, in an articulation of sustainability which is compatible with neoliberal global capitalism (McKenzie et al. 2015). However, in the context of globalization nations have also stressed the role of schooling in respect of national citizenship, and also emphasised global citizenship goals for schooling, goals which were evidenced in the school student climate strikes around the world in 2019.

Allocation processes have also been affected in the move to network governance with networks now stretched beyond state and other nationally-based players. There are, for example, important global policy networks in education, with policy actors in nations and in international organisations such as the OECD occupying similar epistemic positions and adopting aligned policy dispositions (Lingard, Sellar, and Baroutsis 2015). Here, Ball (2012, p. 93) has observed, 'education policy analysis can no longer sensibly be limited to within the nation-state – the fallacy of methodological territorialism'. He adds that 'policy analysis must also extend its purview beyond the state and the role of multilateral agencies and NGOs to include transnational businesses practices' (p.93). There are implications here for doing education policy analysis today and for considering the research/policy relationship and especially in the domain of ESE research, given the significance of both national and global action in relation to effectively confronting global change and the place of ESE in relation to these matters. Clearly a global approach is needed in relation to climate policy and to address the current climate emergency. ESE here also needs to be linked to the focus in schools on national and global citizenship. In the ESE domain, there is likely to be a situation where the policy is at times ahead of teacher understandings and commitments, or indeed where the latter are well ahead of policy frames, particularly evident in the work of activist teachers. Private sector involvement in the policy cycle potentially affects research/policy relationships in that increasingly there is much policy usage of consultancy firm commissioned research for policy, rather than the use of more academic, critical research. Such research *for* policy takes the status quo for granted and works within it and thus will support a certain version of ESE over more radical visions.

Values, politics and discourses in education policy have also been reframed in the context of globalization by the epistemic communities that conjoin policy makers in nations and international organizations and at times those in edu-businesses. There is now emergent global education policy and an emergent global education policy field (Lingard and Rawolle 2011) that sees the flows of global 'policyscapes' (Ball 1998; Carney 2009), 'vehicular ideas' (Temenos and McCann, 2013), and some convergence in respect of policy discourses in education in nations around the globe. I would stress though, the ongoing significance of the ways in which 'path dependence' still works in the global/national effects in education policy; here in relation to globalized policy discourses and the global education policy field. National history, culture and politics still mediate these pressures in policy and so what we see are always vernacular expressions of these policy discourses (Appadurai 1996; Takayama 2015). On this point, Cohen (2017), for example, speaks of relationality between globally circulating mobile policy ideas and 'local struggles over their shape within the same frame'. In this observation, we also get the sense of policy mobilities, also picked up in the ideas of policyscapes and vehicular policy ideas. Such policy mobilities and scapes also carry implications for doing education policy analysis at this time (Gulson et al. 2017) and also for contemplating research/policy relationships of all kinds in education, including in ESE.

In relation to policy mobilities and policyscapes, Peck and Theodore (2016) have spoken about fast policy and fast policy making to encapsulate the fast flows of policy models and ideas today around the globe. Peck and Theodore (2016, p.xvii) observe that fast policy references 'those social practices and infrastructures that enable and sustain policy 'mobility', which enable the complex folding of policy lessons derived from one place into reformed and transformed arrangements elsewhere'. Here they note both the motion and fixity of contemporary policy processes and while fast policies flow around the globe, as noted above, policy enactment still 'remains a stubbornly localized, context-specific process' (p. xvi). They also assert that fast policy making has implications for the place and role of research in policy production, a point that will be returned to later in the paper.

So, I have considered the way we now need to think of defining policy in education in the context of globalization. There are also other matters to consider in relation to defining policy. We also must understand the component parts that constitute policy. On this issue, Head (2008) is very helpful in arguing that all policy is a complex admixture of facts (research/evidence), values (politics, ideologies, discourses) and professional knowledges. The latter are involved in policy enactment and mediate the achievement of policy aspirations. As well, often such professional knowledges also mediate policy production, say as in Japan, where outstanding pedagogues become policy makers in the three layers of educational bureaucracy (instructional advisers) (Takayama and Lingard 2019).

The important point to note here then, is that we can thus never accurately speak of evidence-based policy. Research evidence, for example, is only ever one component part of any education policy or indeed of any public policy, including ESE policy. The extent of the research base is different for different policies, given varying political conditions for the production of the policy and varying timeframes. Different types of research work in and with different temporalities, as do various varieties of educational policy, with implications for research/policy relationships.

So this is one imperative in thinking about research-policy relationships: we need to accept that at best we only ever have research-informed policy, evidence-informed policy. Research-based policy would be indicative of an undemocratic technocracy, rather than a democratic way of producing policy. Values thus of necessity drive policy; the question of course is which and whose values? Nonetheless, politicians often seek legitimacy for their actions in research, statistics and data, and deflect responsibility and accountability elsewhere. State restructuring, especially devolution and greater school autonomy, can also deflect responsibility from the Minister and Ministry to schools and teachers and ensure a unilateral top-down approach to accountability often based on test data. The use of big-data to determine policy can also function in undemocratic ways and also potentially simply reproduce the past rather than seeking to work in new ways to meet new challenges.

Burn and Schuller (2007, p.16), who wrote a report for the OECD on research and policy in education, argued that policy-making in education is neither rational nor clinical and as such, they speak, instead of 'the use of research to foster evidence-informed policy', which leaves quite open the extent of actual usage of research in education policy making. I have real sympathy with their construction of the research/policy relationship and giving credence to the significance of values in framing policy.

While acknowledging the insights from Head's (2008) account of policy as an admixture of facts, values and professional knowledges, we also have to think of the place of affect and emotion in relation to both the setting of policy agendas and in respect of policy reception. Here Ahmed's (2014) idea of a 'national mood', almost a national 'structure of feeling' to use Raymond Williams' evocative phrase, is significant in both agenda setting and reception of policies, say in education or specifically in relation to ESE, a policy domain particularly susceptible to the affective in politics and policy. McKenzie (2017), using Anderson (2014, pp.3-5), speaks of affect in terms of politics and policy as an object of power, individual capacities derived from encounters, and a collective condition, which can be compared with Williams' structure of feeling and Ahmed's national mood. As McKenzie (2017, p. 2) notes, 'what moves us collectively and individually is also important for what moves policy'. This would seem to be particularly the case in relation to environmental policy that seeks to effectively limit climate change and to ESE policy. One element of activist politics around the climate emergency must work at this level of the affective to change hearts and minds.

Huntley (2020) reports US research from the Yale Program on Climate Change Communication which measures the US public's beliefs, attitudes and policy preferences and which categorises the population into six segments regarding attitudes to climate change: the alarmed (31%), the concerned (26%), the cautious (16%), the disengaged (7%), the doubtful (10%) and dismissive (10%). Huntley also asserts that her research shows that these categories would seem to apply in the Australian context, and that attitudes about climate change are much more informed by world views than by the science, suggesting the important role of affect in changing attitudes and ensuring effective national and global environmental policies. Indeed, it is in such policies that we actually see the veracity of Head's (2008) argument that all policy is a varying admixture of research evidence, values and professional knowledges, and that values and affect come into play as much as the research evidence, when policy makers seek to balance competing pressures and construct broad climate change/emergency policy. Indeed, usage by different politicians of different nomenclature, for example change or emergency, and in commitments to different levels of emissions reduction, reflect the place of values/ideology in policy-making as against the science as a basis for policy.

Furthermore, mediatization of policy is a significant related factor here in respect of the mobilisation of affect. Today as well, we might speak of 'deep mediatization' (Hepp and Hasebrink 2018) to signify the importance of social media in relation to multiple publics and multiple affect worlds, which play out in politics and policy and also in the echo effect that works in relation to post-truth politics, which will be picked up later in this paper. Today we probably also need to speak of the 'social mediatization' of policy with the use of social media for consultation and dissemination (Baroutsis and Lingard 2019).

Research

A distinction was made some time ago now between research *for/of* policy (Gordon, Lewis, and Young 1977), with the former more akin to commissioned research and seeking to inform policy directly and the latter more academically oriented and seeking to enhance knowledge and understanding of a phenomenon. However, real caution is needed in respect of this binary and an oversimplified reading of it. Sometime ago now, the central foundational figure in research on research utilisation, Carol Weiss (1979) provided an account of the multiple kinds of social science research impact on policy, documenting seven types of research/policy relationships; namely, knowledge-driven (research *for* policy), problem–solving (research *for* policy), interactive approaches (involving researchers on relevant committees and advisory groups), political (research as legitimation for policy), tactical (used to delay), enlightenment over a lengthy period, and intellectual enterprise (both research and policy are affected by the dominant ideas of a given period [Foucault's 'regime of truth'] and by the 'national mood'). The point needs to be made that, despite the contemporary demand for evidence-based policy making, there is limited research on the utilisation of research in actual policy making, but the situation is improving. This demand has also precipitated new academic interest in the topic and the emergence of journals such as *Evidence & Policy: A Journal of Research, Debate and Practice*.

On the surface at least, it appears to be the case that research *for* policy probably has a more direct impact on policy. Research *of* policy is of an academic kind and thus impact in respect of such research is usually measured in terms of citations, what we might see as academic impact. Recently, though, in a number of nations there has been a real push for academic research to have broader impact, including on politics and policy. It is worth noting here that impact is a complex concept and that the effects of research on policy are often mediated and long-term. Research for policy probably is more likely to have direct and quick, in a temporal sense, effects on policy. Sometimes there is a very short timeframe for the production of such research for policy, reflecting what Peck and Theodore (2015) refer to as the contemporary condition of fast policy making. Yet, Weiss's research also argued an enlightenment or 'percolation' impact of more academic research on policy. This is the long-term policy effect of research and often not recognised as such. On this very point, Orland (2009, p.115) has observed, 'research-based knowledge affects policy gradually by shaping how decision makers understand and frame a problem and decode potential solutions'. This is the long-term impact of research (including research *of* policy) on the assumptive worlds of policy makers, on the habitus of policy makers, often unacknowledged by them.

As suggested in the Introduction, there is a way in which today under the changing conditions of globalization that there has been something of a cosmopolitanization of the dispositions of policy makers around the globe with research for policy reports by consultancy firms often underpinning these globally mobile policy models (Peck and Theodore 2015). (As an aside, such cosmopolitanization of policy actors' disposition should be positive for confronting globally the current climate emergency.) Peck and Theodore (2015) argue in respect of fast policy making and policy mobilities circulating around the globe, that the research and development phase of such policies is foreshortened. Specifically they argue that, 'Enabled by the rise of global models and the increased availability/visibility of information and advice on policy innovations and experiments in extralocal locations; compressed R & D is a consequence and cause of compressed turnover time in policy designs' (p.224). Here the R & D phase might also be eviscerated when the global policy model touches down in a local site. They also make a similar argument regarding research utilisation in policy processes about the effects of the 'what works' performance pragmatism. Again there is shortening of the R & D phase or no use of research explicitly, when extant working policy models are adopted and adapted and 'what works' approaches often utilise systematic reviews that also circulate globally.

The apparently disjunctive cultures between research, at least of the more academic kind, and policy have been alluded to already. Evidence of this cultural disjunction is picked up on in talk of 'knowledge translation' to refer to enhancing the impact of research on both policy and practice. Many universities around the globe have established senior positions to oversee knowledge translation as governments push for more direct impact of university research under pressures from an instrumental mode of research accountability. Yet again, though, we should be wary of seeing the two cultures as hermetically sealed, disjunctive, non-intersecting sets. Think of the numbers of senior policy makers with research degrees, career movements across the university/public sector divide, and of the educational levels of the professionals that make and enact policy. Think as well of the long-term impact of academic research on the assumptive worlds of policy makers as argued by Weiss.

Orland (2009, p.117) has documented five features of research that limit to some extent the usage of research (directly) in policy production. These are really cultural disjunctions, which Orland refers to as 'separate orbits': 'original contribution versus replication/refinement', 'understanding versus fixing problems', different communication conventions, 'disciplinary' versus 'interdisciplinary', 'collaborative approaches' and 'different time frames', with the latter very evident in the research of/for policy distinction. Orland also adds the importance of different reward structures for academics and policy makers in respect of research, a distinction also linked to the different meanings of impact dealt with above. Communication differences are important here: academics communicate with other academics in academic journals and through conference presentations, often in arcane language. Research for policy directly communicates with policy makers and is written in ways that enable this. It is worth thinking about the research work of Think Tanks here, whose research is also communicated in more direct, yet idiosyncratic ways distinct from research communication in academic journals. Usually the language of Think Tank reports seeks to directly affect policy makers and the media and thus is written in a particular language (sometimes mediatized) and from a specific normative stance. Both research for policy and Think Tank research take as given the policy problem as constituted by politicians and policy makers. This is a problem-solving approach to research/policy relationships. In contrast, critical policy research often takes deconstruction of the problem construction work of a policy as the first step in critical policy analysis. This is because all policies construct discursively the problems to which the policy offers a putative solution (Bacchi 2009). In the context of the horrendous, catastrophic bushfires in Australia in late 2019/early 2020, the Morrison conservative federal government's policy response has basically been to accept climate change (deny there is a climate emergency), reject increasing emission reduction goals and instead simply stress resilience and adaptation to these frightening changing conditions. Their policy (or lack of effective policy as I see it) has constructed the problem in a particular (non-science-based) way. At one level, this is to appease climate science deniers in the government and also their fossil fuel industry backers. Peter Renshaw (2019) described the Morrison government's stance here in and outside of parliament as a 'festival of denial and inaction'. At another level, it is unequivocal evidence that research, here climate science, is only one factor determining public policy.

Public policy more recently has also attempted to valorise certain types of social science research with randomised controlled experiments being regarded as the 'gold standard'. Related has been the rise of (big) data and metrics in new modes of governance, in which context Lather (2013) speaks of metric mania and a new neo-positivism. Luke and Hogan (2006) suggest an intimate linkage between this new mode of governance and educational research and observe, 'the centrality of data and numbers to contemporary modes of governance mean that current debates over what counts as evidence in state policy formation are indeed debates over what counts as educational research' (p.170). Research for policy usually demands the use of quantitative data[1], while research of policy often utilises mixed method approaches.

Lysgaard et al. (2016) suggest these matters are even more fraught in terms of ESE research and policy making, given the common stance of many ESE researchers as activists. Activists often see their research work as best aimed at changing broad public opinion or the national mood as a way to move policy forward, rather than be directly involved in actual policy making, which necessarily involves compromises of various kinds. This is acknowledgement of the significance of affect in garnering support for effective policy making more broadly in relation to the climate emergency and also in respect of ESE. One would hope in terms of the affective in politics that the devastating and catastrophic bushfires in Australia will have precipitated a significant change of national mood, a change in the structure of feeling, regarding global warming in this era of the Anthropocene and enhanced public demand for more to be done in public policy.

I would acknowledge the significance of critical research offering critiques of policy developments in ESE: a pluralism of research types is necessary in democratic open societies and research that critiques rather than informs policy (directly at least) is necessary and must also be defended. This will become more necessary as a reductive definition of research impact takes hold of research policy framings within nations. The research/policy situation is complicated further by the policy positioning of ESE, say in curricula (science and social science), in cross-curricula, in broad exhortations, or even in relation to citizenship education policy including foci on both national and global citizenship. Yet, encouragingly, Lysgaard and colleagues argue that the friction between the research field of ESE and policy and policy production might be productive. Here they effectively use the work of Nutley, Walter, and Davies (2007) concerning 'a number of barriers and enablers to the use of research in policy', namely, the nature of the research, the characteristics of the researchers and potential research users, links between research and users, and the context for the use of research (pp.325-326), the latter would include the national mood or broader structure of feeling. In terms of the nature of research, it is significant that 'uncontested findings' is a factor in utilisation of research in policy production, which comes up against the tentativeness of (social) scientific findings and these are always open to critique, development and change. Importantly, this is a common difference between Think Tank Research, and also that conducted by consultancies, and academic research, with the former both expressing their research findings in policy relevant, plain language, often in unequivocal ways, often bowdlerising research findings in the field.

In supporting a pluralism of research types in relation to ESE, in the current policy moment of a climate emergency, I would stress, though, that there is a need for more activist research and more ESE researchers taking an activist, 'citizen-scholar-activist', public intellectual stance (McKenzie 2009). As McKenzie (2009, p. 218) notes, 'This means going beyond tinkering with the status quo: beyond creating, offering or evaluating programs and policies which indeed get people outside, or get them learning about places or environmental issues, and yet leave their, and our larger assumptions and practices unturned'. This is clearly a different construction of research impact from that driving public policy moves for publicly funded to research to have more impact through translation into practice (McKenzie 2009).

Contexts and conclusions

The argument proffered here has been that understanding the changing nature of policy processes and policy content in contemporary times, including understanding new practices of rescaled statecraft, are necessary for understanding how and in what ways which types of research have real effects on policy processes and on policy content. Research enters the policy cycle now at various points from the global through to local policy enactment and there are actors involved now beyond researchers employed in state agencies and universities, including those in large private consultancies and Think Tanks, with big data also as a driver of and informing policy. And of course, we need to acknowledge that research also reaches teachers and principals in schools in ways other than through policy and its effects in policy enactment. Research affects professional practice in education in other mediated ways through teacher education and professional development and also more directly through further study and direct research relationships with schools (Figgis et al. 2000; McMeniman et al. 2000). Presumably the changing national mood that has been mentioned also has an impact on teacher dispositions in ways that are positive for ESE and in respect of climate policy more broadly. Critical ESE research, and public intellectual work of activist ESE researchers, can also contribute to the production of activist teachers and to changes in the national mood, which in turn affect both policy and practice.

Brief allusions have been made throughout about the place of science denial, post-truth and affect in policy and policy processes. Some commentary will be provided here on the relevance of these aspects of the contexts of contemporary policy agenda setting and policy reception, especially in the ESE domain. Earlier, the Oxford Dictionary definition of post-truth was documented. The prefix 'post' here does not mean after truth, but rather refers to the fact that 'appeals to emotion and personal beliefs' can be in some cases more significant in policy and politics than facts, and in our case research. As McIntyre (2018, p. 11) asserts, 'somethings are true irrespective of how we feel about them'. Yet one need only think of the political *modus operandi* of President Trump to understand this post-truth context. For example, his opinion and feelings regarding anthropogenic climate change are more significant drivers of climate policy in contemporary USA than is a scientific research consensus about such matters, evidenced in one way in his petulant, nationalistic intention to withdraw the USA from the 2016 Paris agreement (*Paris Agreement under the United Nations Framework Convention on Climate Change*) to take effect in November, 2020. This is not to argue that Trump created the post-truth context; rather, he is more a symptom of that context. It appears to have taken the bushfire crisis in Australia to have pushed the conservative Morrison government in Australia to at least acknowledge the contribution of climate change to this situation, yet their policies in a limiting way stress adaptation and resilience rather than confronting the climate emergency.

Regarding post-truth: the position adopted in this paper, of course, is that facts, 'truth' and research evidence should still matter and actually still do. The placing of truth in quote marks is to acknowledge that there is no such thing as epistemological innocence and yet the necessity to avoid collapsing into epistemological relativism, while accepting that a reading of a non-nuanced and overly simplified postmodernist version of knowledge might have been a precursor to post-truth, as argued by McIntyre (2018). Van Poeck (2019) utilising the perspective of science and technology studies, specifically the work of Latour and Jasanoff, acknowledges the social construction of all knowledge, including climate science, but offers a stance that does not collapse into a relativist 'anything goes' epistemological position, which fuels post-truth, by stressing *inter alia* the quality of the constructedness of the science. There are also significant implications here as well for the enactment of ESE in classrooms, but which are beyond the concerns of this paper.

McIntyre (2018), in an informative treatise on post-truth, argues its major origins lie in the emergence of science denial, first evidenced in respect of the political and ideological work of tobacco companies to deny research demonstrating causal links between smoking and lung cancer, and then honed in respect of climate change. McIntyre (2018, p. 21) suggests that through this strategy of science denial 'the public has been hoodwinked into thinking that there is a great scientific controversy' over climate change, when there is actually a scientific consensus. Media coverage, which grants equal time to climate change deniers as to scientific accounts, works with false equivalences (the equivalence of non-equivalences), an achievement of the political work of the science deniers and an important contributing factor, according to McIntyre, to the rise of the politics of post-truth. He opines, 'Global warming is perhaps the most egregious case of modern science denial', which disputes 'the compelling scientific evidence for anthropogenic climate change' (p. 27), adding, 'In a world where ideology trumps science, post-truth is the inevitable next step' (p. 34).

The post-truth context, though challenged by many, is part of the contemporary backdrop to ESE, ESE research, ESE policy and the relationships between them and links to the impact of affect in policy and policy production in ESE. The rise of ethno-nationalism in the US and xenophobic 'America First' also challenges the work of international multilateral organisations and the production of global meta-policies and also severely limits our capacities to address the pressing matters of global warming and climate change, matters which demand a multilateral global response, as with the Kyoto and Paris protocols. This muddies the broader context of ESE and yet also sees some educational approaches to ESE connecting with moves for global citizenship education.

It has been argued throughout that the relationships between research and policy are complex and entangled and even more so in the relationships between ESE research and various cognate policies. Related, it has been strongly asserted that we can never have research-based policy, only ever research-informed policy. This is so because all policies in a democracy are an interesting and variable admixture of facts (research), politics (ideologies, discourses) and professional knowledges, with both policy agendas and policy reception being affected by the national mood. This is as it should be: politicians are elected to govern, not researchers.

We thus need to accept the reality of research-informed policy in a democracy. Furthermore, in a democracy not all research in the academy ought to be of the *for* policy kind; rather and to reiterate, the open pursuit of knowledge and understanding means that the democratic demands research *of* policy as well as research *for* policy. Of course, educational research without a specific focus on policy can also have real policy effects. Additionally, public policy in a democracy ought to support blue skies research, where the researcher sets the research questions, and such policy should also enable a space for critical policy research and critical research more broadly. The enhancement of understanding is important to productive policy development and we know that such research often has long term impact on the assumptive worlds of politicians and other policy makers. Think here of research on climate change and research in respect of ESE. However, it appears to be the case that research is most often used to legitimate policy, rather than inform it in productive ways. Here some have cynically spoken of policy-informed research, rather than research-informed policy. Globalization and the resulting rescaled state also mean research informs policy production at various global scales, as mobile vehicular policy ideas circulate globally and mutate as they touch down nationally and locally.

Research for policy is sometimes seen as synonymous with problem-solving research. Critical policy approaches stress that the first step in critical policy analysis is to analyse and deconstruct the way the policy in question constructs the public or educational problem to which it is a putative solution (Bacchi 2009). This is akin to the distinction often talked about in the social sciences between the *taking* and *making* of research problems. It is also probably incumbent on critical policy researchers who 'make' their research foci to rearticulate their research 'findings' in a language suitable for broader public dissemination beyond academic journals and conferences as a contribution to civil society and political debates. Critical research, including critical policy research, might also be utilised by activists both inside and outside the state (and activist teachers) to contest policies (processes and content) in a democratic way toward more socially just and environmentally sound ends. Teacher Unions today often commission research as part of their strategies to engage with and contest state policy processes and policy content. Critical policy research can potentially affect the national mood, the structure of feeling, as well as the assumptive worlds of policy makers in the longer term, at the same time as it is affected by these.

Critical policy research becomes even more important at a time when we are witnessing both the mediatization and social mediatization of education policy (Adhikary, Lingard and Hardy

2018; Baroutsis and Lingard 2019) in a post-truth context, where strength of emotional conviction can drive policy production and where expertise is sometimes disregarded, even disparaged. There are important implications for relationships between ESE research and policy in this context. Such research can also be aimed at the national mood as a way to affect policy agendas in education. Furthermore, as alluded to in the introduction, the datafication of the social world and imminent rise of big data in school systems will likely witness another neo-positivist framing of education policy, research *for* policy in another manifestation. Research *of* these policy developments will also be important and indeed the contemporary moment of the 'evidence-based policy' mantra demands more research on research utilisation in policy production in all public policies. This is especially so in respect of ESE and ESE research usage or neglect in policy.

Finalising this paper during the catastrophic bushfire season in Australia and the government's most inept, indeed delinquent, policy responses has suggested to me that this is probably the moment when activist research and researchers in the ESE domain are more necessary than ever before, as is the activism of teachers and students. This is, however, risky business. The Australian Prime Minister's response to the school student climate strikes in 2019 was that we need more learning and less activism in schools. Quality ESE research and quality ESE will have long term positive effects, no doubt. The current stage of the climate emergency carries significant implication for both; for example, in respect of educational research there is a pressing need to challenge the Enlightenment assumption of infinite resources and think instead of the 'finiteness of global resources' (Rappleye and Komatsu 2020). An urgent question right now, however, is: 'Do we have time to wait for quality research to constitute quality ESE and for this to have long term effects?'. The answer is clear. At this moment, activist research, indeed climate activism, must be a component part of changing the national mood so that better policy responses are demanded by the people and delivered by governments and the people.

Note

1. Recently, I have been part of a team that conducted research for a government in Australia, which included both quantitative survey data and qualitative data from interviews and focus groups. In an oral presentation to the department senior leaders about the research 'findings', a senior policy maker stressed they really only wanted to know what the hard data said (that is, the survey) and were not so interested in what we saw as the very informative qualitative data.

Disclosure statement

No potential conflict of interest was reported by the author(s).

References

Adhikary, R. W., B. Lingard, and I. Hardy, 2018. "A Critical Examination of *Teach for Bangladesh's* Facebook Page: 'Social Mediatisation' of Global Education Reforms in the Post-Truth Era." *Journal of Education Policy* 33 (5): 632–267. doi:10.1080/02680939.2018.1445294.
Ahmed, S. 2014. "Not in the Mood." *New Formations* 82 (82): 13–28. doi:10.3898/NeWF.82.01.2014.
Anderson, B. 2014. *Encountering Affect: Capacities, Apparatuses, Conditions*. Burlington, VT: Ashgate.
Appadurai, A. 1996. *Modernity at Large*. Minneapolis: University of Minnesota Press.
Bacchi, C. 2009. *Analysing Policy: What's the Problem Represented to Be?* Sydney: Pearson.
Ball, S. J. 1994. *Education Reform: A Critical and Poststructural Approach*. Buckingham: Open University Press.

Ball, S. J. 1998. "Big Policies/Small World: An Introduction to International Perspectives in Education Policy." *Comparative Education* 34 (2): 119–130. doi:10.1080/03050069828225.

Ball, S. J. 2012. *Global Education Inc.: New Policy Networks and the No-Liberal Imaginary*. London: Routledge.

Ball, S. J. 2015. "What is Policy? 21 Years Later: Reflections on the Possibilities of Policy Research." *Discourse: Studies in the Cultural Politics of Education* 36 (3): 306–566. doi:10.1080/01596306.2015.1015279.

Ball, S. J., and C. Junemann. 2012. *Networks, New Governance and Education*. Bristol: Policy Press.

Ball, S. J., M. Maguire, and A. Braun. 2012. *How Schools Do Policy: Policy Enactment in Secondary Schools*. London: Routledge.

Baroutsis, A., and B. Lingard. 2019. "Headlines an Hashtags Herald New 'Damaging Effects' in Education Policy? Media Commentary on Australia's Declining PISA Performance." In *Education Research and Media*, edited by A. Baroutsis, S. Riddle and P. Thomson. London: Routledge.

Berlant, L. 2011. *Cruel Optimism*. Durham, NC: Duke University Press.

Bourdieu, P. 1998. *Practical Reason*. Cambridge, UK: Polity Press.

Burns, T., and Schuller, T. 2007. "The Evidence Agenda." In *Evidence in Education Linking Research and Practice*, edited by OECD, 15–32. Paris: OECD.

Carney, S. 2009. "Negotiating Policy in an Age of Globalization: Exploring Educational 'Policyscapes' in Denmark, Nepal, and China." *Comparative Education Review* 53 (1): 63–88. doi:10.1086/593152.

Cohen, D. 2017. "Market Mobilities/Immobilities: Mutation, Path Dependency, and the Spread of Charter Schools in the United States." *Critical Studies in Education* 58 (2): 168–186. doi:10.1080/17508487.2016.1242507.

Easton, D. 1953. *The Political System*. New York: Knopf.

Figgis, J., A. Zubrick, A. Butorac, and A. Alderson. 2000. "Backtracking Practice and Policies to Research." In *The Impact of Educational Research*, edited by Department of Education, Training & Youth Affairs, 279–373. Canberra: The Commonwealth of Australia.

Flanagan, R. 2020. "Opinion: Australia is Committing Climate Suicide." New York Times, 3 January.

Flanagan, R. 2020. "Opinion: How Does Nation Adapt to Its Own Murder?" New York Times, 25 January.

Gale, T., and K. Densmore. 2003. *Engaging Teachers: Towards a Radical Democratic Agenda for Schooling*. Buckingham: Open University Press.

Gordon, I., J. Lewis, and R. Young. 1977. "Perspectives on Policy Analysis." *Public Administration Bulletin* 25: 26–35.

Gulson, K., Lewis, S. Lingard, B. Lubienski, C. Takayama, K. and P. Taylor Webb. 2017. "Policy Mobilities and Methodology: A Proposition for Inventive Methods in Education Policy Studies." *Critical Studies in Education* 58 (2): 224–241. doi:10.1080/17508487.2017.1288150.

Head, B. 2008. "Three Lenses of Evidence-Based Policy." *Australian Journal of Public Administration* 67 (1): 1–11. doi:10.1111/j.1467-8500.2007.00564.x.

Hepp, A., and U. Hasebrink. 2018. "Researching Transforming Communications in Times of Deep Mediatization: A Figurational Approach." In *Communicative Configurations: Tranforming Communications in Times of Deep Mediatization*, edited by A. Hepp, A. Breiter and U. Hasebrink, 15–48. Gewerbestrasse, Switzerland: Palgrave MacMillan.

Huntley, R. 2020. "Climate Change Splits the Public into Six Groups: Understanding Them Is Key to Future Action." *Big Ideas, ABC Radio National*, January 29.

Koppenjan, J., and E. Klijn. 2004. *Managing Uncertainties in Networks: Public Private Controversies*. London: Routledge.

Lather, P. 2013. "Methodology – 21: What Do we in the Afterward?" *International* Journal of Qualitative Studies in Education 26 (6): 634–645. doi:10.1080/09518398.2013.788753.

Lingard, B. 2011. "Policy as Number: Ac/Counting for Educational Research." *The Australian Educational Researcher* 38 (4): 355–382. doi:10.1007/s13384-011-0041-9.

Lingard, B. 2019. "The Global Education Industry, Data Infrastructures, and Restructuring of Government School Systems." In *Researching the Global Education Industry*, edited by M. Parreira do Amaral, G. Steiner-Khamsi, & C. Thompson, 135–155. Gewerbestrasse, Switzerland: Palgrave Macmillan.

Lingard, B. 2020. "The Policy Sociology of Geoff Whitty: Current and Emergent Issues regarding Education Research in Use." In *Knowledge, Policy and Practice in Education and the Struggles for Social Justice: Essays Inspired by the Work of Geoff Whitty*, edited by A. Brown and E. Wisby, 165–178. London: UCL Press.

Lingard, B., and S. Rawolle. 2011. "New Scalar Politics: Implications for Education Policy." *Comparative Education* 47 (4): 489–502. doi:10.1080/03050068.2011.555941.

Lingard, B., S. Sellar, and A. Baroutsis. 2015. "Researchng the Habitus of Global Policy Actors in Education." *Cambridge Journal of Education* 45 (1): 25–42. doi:10.1080/0305764X.2014.988686.

Lingard, B., W. Martino, G. Rezai-Rashti, and S. Sellar. 2016. *Globalizing Educational Accountabilities*. New York: Routledge.

Luke, A., and D. Hogan. 2006. "Redesigning What Counts as Evidence in Educational Policy: The Singapore Model." In *World Yearbook of Education 2006: Educational Research and Policy: Steering the Knowledge-Based Economy*, edited by J. Ozga, T. Seddon and T. Popkewitz, 170–184. London: Routledge.

Lysgaard, J., Reid, A. and Van Poeck, K. 2016. "The Roots and Routes of Environmental and Sustainability Education Policy Research - an Introduction to a Virtual Special issue." *Environmental Education Research* 22 (3): 319–332.

McIntyre, L. 2018. Post-Truth. Cambridge, MA: MIT Press.

McKenzie, M. 2009. "Scholarship as Intervention: Critique, Collaboration and the Research Imagination." *Environmental Education Research* 15 (2): 217–226. doi:10.1080/13504620902807576.

McKenzie, M. 2017. "Affect Theory and Policy Mobility: Challenges and Possibilities for Critical Policy Research." *Critical Studies in Education* 58 (2): 187–204. doi:10.1080/17508487.2017.1308875.

McKenzie, M., A. Bieler, and R. McNeil. 2015. "Education Policy Mobility: Reimagining Sustainability in Neoliberal Times." *Environmental Education Research* 21 (3): 319–337. doi:10.1080/13504622.2014.993934.

McMeniman, M., Cumming, J., Wilson, J., Stevenson, J. Sim. C. 2000. Teacher knowledge in action In *The Impact of Educational Research*, edited by Department of Education, Training & Youth Affairs, 385–549. Canberra: The Commonwealth of Australia.

Nutley, S., I. Walter, and H. Davies. 2007. *Using Evidence: How Research Can Inform Public Service*. Bristol: The Policy Press.

Orland, M. 2009. "Separate Orbits: The Distinctive Worlds of Educational Research and Policy Making." In *Handbook of Educational Policy Research*, edited by G. Sykes, B. Schneider, D. Plank and T. Ford, 113–128. New York: Routledge.

Peck, J., and N. Theodore. 2015. *Fast Policy: Experimental Statecraft at the Thresholds of Neoliberalism*. Minneapolis: University of Minnesota Press.

Rappleye, J., and H. Komatsu. (2020). "Towards (Comparative) Educational Research for a Finite Future." *Comparative Education*. doi:10.1080/03050068.2020.1741197

Renshaw, P. 2019. "Feeling for the Anthropocene: Education Futures and the Place of Living Justice." In *Radford Memorial Lecture, AARE Conference, QUT*.

Rizvi, F., and B. Lingard. 2010. *Globalizing Education Policy*. London: Routledge.

Takayama, K. 2015. "Provincialising the World Culture Theory Debate: Critical Insights from a Margin." *Globalisation, Societies and Education* 13 (1): 34–57. doi:10.1080/14767724.2014.967485.

Takayama, K., and B. Lingard. 2019. "Datafication of Schooling in Japan: An Epistemic Critique through the 'Problem of Japanese Education." *Journal of Education Policy* 34 (4): 449–469. doi:10.1080/02680939.2018.1518542.

Temenos, C. and McCann, E. 2012. "The Local Politics of Policy Mobility: Learning, Persuasion, and the Production of a Municipal Sustainability Fix." *Environment and Planning A: Economy and Space*. 44 (6): 1389–1406. doi:10.1068/a44314

Van Poeck, K. 2019. "Environmental and Sustainability Education in a Post-Truth Era: An Exploration of Epistemology and Didactics beyond the Objectivism-Relativism Dualism." *Environmental Education Research* 25 (4): 472–491. doi:10.1080/13504622.2018.1496404.

Wallace-Wells, D. 2019. *The Uninhabitable Earth: A Story of the Future*. Great Britain: Penguin Books.

Weiss, C. 1979. "The Many Meanings of Research Utilisation." *Public Administration Review* 39 (5): 426–431. doi:10.2307/3109916.

Williamson, B. 2017. *Big Data in Education: The Digital Future of Learning Policy and Practice*. London: Sage.

A reflection on the relational aspects of research policy interfaces

Anne Edwards

ABSTRACT
In this short reflection on how research and policy can connect fruitfully, I briefly outline three key concepts that have arisen in my work on inter-professional collaboration in the caring professions: relational expertise, common knowledge and relational agency. I have argued that these concepts describe the work that is done at sites of intersecting practices to enable quick and meaningful collaboration on complex problems. I also, however, point to the dangers of omitting the intentions of citizens from these exchanges. Describing the research-policy interface as a site of intersecting practices, I draw on a recent study undertaken at a UK University to show how these concepts can explain successful relational engagements at the research-policy interface that benefit both research and policy and highlight the moral purposes of this kind of engagement in relation to environmental and sustainability education.

Why is a focus on the relational aspects of the interface important?

> The public policy context of many OECD countries can be described as financially austere, organisationally complex and characterised by decentralised decision making. While several commentators argue that under these conditions the need for timely, accessible and reliable evidence is becoming ever more important, our existing models and maps for connecting evidence, policy and practice often seem ill-suited to the task. (Nutley 2012)

Nutley's statement reminds us that when austerity dominates economic strategies the effects are felt throughout national and local systems, whether smart cities, transport, health, education or welfare. My argument, echoing Nutley, is that research-policy connections can operate nationally and locally to enable the devolved decision-making that is necessary for timely and informed responses to national and local imperatives in environmental and sustainability education policies. When these connections are successful they recognise and deploy the resources that are available nationally and locally at every level in these systems.

Consequently experts, in environmental and sustainability education research and in related policy work respectively, can gain from seeing the interface as a site of intersecting practices: where the specialist practices of research and the specialist practices of policy-making and implementation meet. Once their interactions are seen in this way we can identify the expertise that ensures that relevant knowledge flows between these sets of practices, to the benefit of both.

Expertise is needed. Nowotny, weary of how research-public interfaces were characterised merely by flows of information, argued that 'Experts must now extend their knowledge, not simply to be an extension of what they know in their specialist field, but to consist of building links and trying to integrate what they know with what others want to, or should know and do.' (Nowotny 2003, 155). This is the challenge I address here; while arguing that specialist expertise lies not only in the practices of environmental and sustainability education research, but also in the practices of policy-making and policy implementation, and in the daily lives of citizens. There is a danger that emphasising the research-policy interface that the lifeworlds of citizens are not represented directly. Yet, particularly in the area of environmental and sustainability politics citizens are becoming increasingly active in attempts at shaping policy agenda, from the Thunberg effect on the future electorate to the impassioned desperation of Extinction Rebellion.

Consequently multi-directional knowledge flows, where policy-makers engage seriously with the informed concerns of citizens, as well as with researchers, are crucial. I therefore use the term knowledge exchange in preference to research impact. There is a moral purpose behind this decision, which is mirrored by Nutley's concern with connecting research and policy for societal good.

Relational expertise for knowledge exchange

While I have long been committed to the ethical aspects of sharing interim findings with research participants and involving them in critiquing our interpretations of their lives (Rickinson and Sebba 2011), it was not until I researched inter-professional working in the welfare professions (Edwards 2010; Edwards et al. 2009) that I recognised parallels between my attempts at reflexivity between fields of study and research projects and how inter-professional collaborations were accomplished. I therefore briefly outline the key ideas from analyses of these collaborations, before considering their relevance for research-policy interfaces.

My cultural-historical approach to research means that I conceptualise practices as inhabited, historically shaped, knowledge-laden, freighted by emotion and given direction by values (Edwards 2010). In the professions, whether research or policy work, practices are where knowledge accrues, identities are formed and where values and priorities are shared. Moving knowledge across practice boundaries is therefore difficult. Nonetheless, my observations of successful inter-professional collaborations indicated that they are sustained by understanding each others' professional values and priorities. This understanding is built in meetings where problems are discussed and time given to issues of values and priorities so that the understandings can be used to co-ordinate problem-solving actions.

I recognised that meetings, where social workers and mental health workers or teachers met for one or two hours, were similar to the meetings where research teams took findings from projects to policy-makers. We researchers needed to understand what mattered for the civil servants and the ministers to whom they were accountable. We then tailored our project feedback as the studies progressed to connect to their concerns. We also helped civil servants to recognise what mattered to us as researchers, such as where we could and couldn't compromise on research design and method. We also worked regionally and locally with those involved in policy-implementation to meet local needs and met separately with those delivering policies in daily interactions with service users and the same processes were evident. Importantly, we left all these meetings with clearer ideas of where the national policy agenda was moving and the regional and local demands being faced in different parts of England, helping us interpret our data in ways that made findings relevant. Equally we hoped that the other participants left with reasonable expectations of the projects. Toomey has made similar points in her account of encounters between environmental scientists and local people in a project based in a Bolivian National Park, concluding that researchers need to think relationally when in the field and recognise that impact works both ways (Toomey 2016).

The expertise that was exercised in these meetings was similar to the expertise and related concepts I had identified in our analyses at the sites of intersecting practices where diverse professions collaborated (Edwards 2010, 2011, 2012). The expertise is 'relational expertise', a capacity to elicit what matters for the other professionals in the conversation and to be explicit about what matters professionally for oneself. Exercising relational expertise can lead to the building of 'common knowledge'. Common knowledge consists of what matters for the other professionals, what are their professional motives. Common knowledge, made up of the motives of the participating professionals, can then mediate later exchanges, whether in meetings or in the fleeting conversations about actions that need to be taken quickly. The third concept is 'relational agency' which can unfold in joint action on a problem. The joint actions bring to bear the different specialist expertise of participants, to expand the problem so that more of its facets are revealed. Professional expertises can then be co-ordinated to tackle this broader interpretation of the problem. Common knowledge plays a critical role in both the expansion of and responses to the problem, allowing participants to construct elaborated views of the focal issue and to recognise the different contributions that can be made by different professions and calibrate their responses.

Relational work at the interfaces

These relational concepts are relevant to interdisciplinary research and research where practitioners are continuously involved in informing the research process. In these cases the project itself becomes a site of intersecting practices. A nice example of such is the UK Health Alliance on Climate Change (BMJ 2019). The Alliance brings together the concerns of medical practitioners, nurses and other health professionals, calling for actions which will combat climate change and its impact on health and communicate those messages to government.

Here I instead focus on short-lived sites of intersecting practices at the boundaries between research and policy-making and implementation, the opportunities that can be seized to ensure informed knowledge flows. To do so I draw on data from a small-scale study of successful knowledge exchange achieved by social-scientists at one UK university (Edwards 2017).

The study comprised interviews with 13 social scientists, selected by their university for the high social impact of their research. The university knew of their work because of preparation for the 2014 UK Research Excellence Framework exercise, where 20% of a department's profile rested on the societal impact of its research. The interviews focused on what the researchers did to accomplish impact and why they did it. At the time of the interviews the idea of relationship-building in pathways to impact had become accepted by the (ESRC) Economic and Social Research Council: 'Impact can be immediate or realised over the longer term, but is most effective where social scientists are supported to build relationships with relevant stakeholders from the earliest stages of the research process' (ESRC. 2015, 2). It was therefore unsurprising that the 13 high impact narratives all involved relationships across practice boundaries.

The transcribed interviews were interrogated employing the relational concepts, to reveal how they might be enacted during knowledge exchange. The analysis identified two stages, which were often repeated over the duration of a project. The first was exercising relational expertise in eliciting what mattered to stakeholders and being very clear about what was important for the research team. This created common knowledge, an understanding of the motives in each practice, which could be used as a resource in the second stage. The second stage comprised strong iterations between the research team and the others, whether the process was co-construction of new knowledge or simply interim reporting and gathering feedback.

Two leaders of Research Centres revealed how Centres can sustain relationships with policy communities. First a criminologist discusses her research relationship with a senior police-officer and how they build common knowledge and collaborate on the Centre's research agenda. '[Name] and I get together once a year and work out what research is new and up-coming in the Centre, and what new things are happening in their area and we design a programme together.'

Next an educational researcher describes her regular meetings with a government team focusing on children's welfare, showing how common knowledge is built. 'I meet the [name of team] every two months... and I tell them what projects we are doing at the moment... the latest findings... and implications... and they talk about what problems they need research to address.'

Another researcher, not in a Research Centre, discussed how she built relational work into the design of her geography projects. In one study the team placed a facilitator in the field who was '... trying to make sure that everyone was drawn in' and another person who modelled the ideas so that '... the next time we met everyone could play around with their idea on the same screen as everyone else's idea.' This process was called 'levelling' and '... whether the ideas came from social and natural scientists, or from people from the locality, all of them got tested in the same way.' These models held the common knowledge that moved the project forward. The identification of what matters for different stakeholders, building common knowledge, seemed key for many interviewees, '... we look for common points'. The outcomes were enriched interpretations and responses resonating of relational agency '... many of the ideas, I couldn't tell you who thought of them first, we had them as part of the discussion.'

Here one participant describes knowledge exchange, echoing the ESRC and returning us to the moral aspects of knowledge exchange. 'So I would define knowledge exchange as working in partnership with an organisation or agency outside the academy in order to develop research, do research, to share and disseminate research... with a view really to making a difference in the system.'

The moral purpose of a relational approach knowledge exchange at the interfaces

The moral purpose of knowledge exchange surfaced across the interviews, and may become an unanticipated benefit of emphases on impact. We have had earlier reminders about the moral responsibilities of researchers. Thirty years ago Giddens argued that '... new knowledge (concepts, theories, findings) does not simply render the social world more transparent, but alters its nature, spinning off in novel directions.' (Giddens 1990, 153). Chaiklin made a similar point 'Social science research has the potential to illuminate and clarify the practices we are studying as well as the possibility to be incorporated into the very practices being investigated.' (Chaiklin 1993, 394). Both argue against unsustainable claims for the neutrality of social researchers and for moral responsibility towards citizens and their lifeworlds: social research is often relational.

The relational style of the interviewees and their responsible attention to knowledge exchange at all levels of the systems they were examining seemed to mitigate the concerns of Giddens and Chaiklin. Aiming to make a difference in the systems they studied, the 13 high impact researchers employed the three relational concepts, relational expertise, common knowledge and relational agency, to both enrich their studies with insights from a wide range of stakeholders and to negotiate their findings at different policy interfaces.

These three concepts are largely interdependent as relational expertise is needed to build common knowledge and common knowledge is necessary for the exercise of relational agency. Nonetheless, the most important concept is perhaps common knowledge i.e. an understanding of what matters in each practice: the criteria for good research employed by the researchers and the policy priorities of the policy specialists.

My argument during this reflection is therefore that the work of researchers and policy practitioners benefits from their relational engagements at an interface which is recognised as a place where different expert practices meet and where people are open about what matters for them professionally. But we should not forget the personal. The success of engaged amateurs in keeping climate change in the headlines points to how well-placed environmental and sustainability education research is for revealing and weaving the motives and intentions of citizens into their research. For early feminists "the personal is political" was a much-used and successful mantra. It is perhaps worth reviving in environmental and sustainability education research.

These benefits of working across these practice boundaries can be observed throughout the research process. First the problems to be studied can be expanded to capture as many relevant elements as possible in the design of the study; when studies are underway, it can ensure that the research is sensitive to changing policy and local environments and these environments are sensitive to unanticipated findings from the research and; when analyses are completed it can help with the negotiation of findings into policy and the life-worlds of participants.

Disclosure statement

No potential conflict of interest was reported by the author(s).

ORCID

Anne Edwards http://orcid.org/0000-0002-4608-716X

References

BMJ. 2019. The UK Health Alliance on Climate Change. Accessed 9 December 2019. https://www.bmj.com/campaign/climate-change

Chaiklin, S. 1993. "Understanding the Social Scientific Practice of Understanding Practice." In *Understanding Practice: Perspectives on Activity and Context*, edited by Chaiklin, S., and J. Lave Cambridge: Cambridge University Press, pp. 377–401.

Edwards, A. 2010. *Being an Expert Professional Practitioner: The Relational Turn in Expertise*. Dordrecht: Springer.

Edwards, A. 2011. "Building Common Knowledge at Boundaries Between Professional Practices." *International Journal of Educational Research* 50 (1): 33–39.

Edwards, A. 2012. "The Role of Common Knowledge in Achieving Collaboration across Practices." *Learning, Culture and Social Interaction* 1 (1): 22–32.

Edwards, A. 2017. "Relational Approaches to Knowledge Exchange." In *Working Relationally in and across Practices: cultural-Historical Approaches to Collaboration*, edited by Author ed. New York: Cambridge University Press.

Edwards, A., H. Daniels, T. Gallagher, J. Leadbetter and P. Warmington. 2009. Improving Inter-Professional Collaborations: Multi-agency Working for Children's Wellbeing. London: Routledge.

ESRC. 2015. ESRC strategic plan. http://www.esrc.ac.uk/_images/Strategic_Plan_2015_tcm8-33418.pdf22.2.15.

Giddens, A. 1990. *The Consequences of Modernity*. Bristol: Polity Press.

Nowotny, H. 2003. "Democratising Expertise and Socially Robust Knowledge." *Science and Public Policy* 30 (3): 151–156. doi:10.3152/147154303781780461.

Nutley, S. 2012. "Connecting Evidence, Policy and Practice in an Era of Austerity, Complexity and Decentralised Decision Making." Opening Plenary at the Campbell Collaboration Colloquium – Copenhagen. http://www.sfi.dk/Default.aspx?ID=10712 22. 2. 2015.

Rickinson, M., and J. Sebba. 2011. *Improving User-Engagement in Educational Research*. London: Routledge.

Toomey, A. 2016. "What Happens at the Gap between Knowledge and Practice? Spaces of Encounter and Misencounter between Environmental Scientists and Local People." *Ecology and Society* 21 (2): 279–297. doi:10.5751/ES-08409-210228.

Understanding policymakers' perspectives on evidence use as a mechanism for improving research-policy relationships

Louise Shaxson and Annette Boaz

ABSTRACT
This special issue examines how relationships between research and policy in environmental and sustainability education (ESE) can be strengthened. Our contribution draws on three cases from outside the ESE space to analyse policymakers' perspectives on using evidence to inform decision-making, and to show that government-based policymakers develop 'policy narratives' which influence their evidence use. We also illustrate how government departmental systems and processes lead policymakers to develop 'evidence narratives' which help them make sense of what evidence to use and how to use it in the policy development process. At its core, such work involves negotiating three normative positions around evidence, concerning: fidelity to science, democratic representation, and cost-effective use of public money. In light of this, we suggest that where policy narratives and evidence narratives interact should be interpreted as a key site for empirically investigating evidence-informed policymaking activities. Developing a detailed awareness of what policymakers do on a daily basis, and discerning how organisational systems and processes influence particular demands for evidence and how it is used, will foster a better understanding of the relationships between research and policy.

Introduction

In 2018, a review of international trends, priorities and challenges in environmental and sustainability education (ESE) examined ongoing debates about how to link research to policy in the field of ESE (van Poeck, Lysgaard, and Reid 2018). The authors noted that ESE researchers mainly acted either as independent expert advisers to policymakers, or as solvers of discrete environmental sustainability problems. In their opinion, separating these two functions risks reinforcing a demarcation between the science and politics of ESE, which would be unhelpful for such a sensitive and contentious field. This current Special Issue builds on these concerns to ask how research-policy relationships in ESE can be made more productive by ensuring that ESE research can be better informed by an understanding of ESE policy and vice versa.

van Poeck, Lysgaard and Reid echoed Laessøe, Feinstein, and Blum's (2013) call to improve the 'documentary role' of policy research for ESE; uncovering and recording what happens during the policymaking process to explore the detail of its complex, contested and social nature (Laessøe, Feinstein, and Blum 2013; Aikens, McKenzie, and Vaughter 2016). The argument for examining the details of ESE policy processes reflects calls from outside the ESE space to improve our understanding of how research and policy can be linked, by focussing on policymakers' perspectives on evidence use (Oliver, Lorenc, and Innvaer 2014). In this article we briefly review three studies from outside the ESE field—in health policy, education policy and public management—that each use a documentary approach to investigate these perspectives. Together, they suggest that investigating how policymakers develop 'policy narratives' and 'evidence narratives'—and how these narratives interact with each other—could offer researchers a new approach for exploring how evidence is used in public policymaking for ESE and how this shapes the demand for ESE research.

Studying the relationship between evidence and policy

There is a broad literature on evidence-informed decision-making in government, reflecting a long-standing interest in the relationships between academic research, public policymaking and professional practice (Nutley, Walter, and Davies 2007; Head 2008). Much of the literature stems from two concerns. The first is to use evidence to challenge or critique existing or planned policies (Cairney 2019). The second is to improve the role of robust evidence in policy and practice decisions to improve good governance in public policymaking (Stone 2002; Parkhurst 2017). As in van Poeck, Lysgaard, and Reid's (2018) review, these concerns are linked to debates about how researchers can engage effectively with research users to improve the relevance and quality of research, to enhance its impact and to connect with other processes of knowledge generation (Rickinson, Sebba, and Edwards 2011; Gagliardi et al. 2015). Researchers have studied the mechanics of how evidence is used to inform policy decisions (Edwards 2020) and how it is translated, exchanged and brokered between evidence producers and evidence users (Oliver, Lorenc, and Innvaer 2014; Ward 2016). Different schools of thought such as evaluation (Weiss 1979), science and technology studies (Jasanoff 2005), policy studies (Cairney 2019) and implementation science (Nilsen 2015)—while unconnected to each other—have brought nuance to these debates.

The idea that policymaking is a series of bounded rational decisions (Botterill and Hindmoor 2012) is critiqued by authors such as Cairney and colleagues, who emphasise the political, negotiated nature of policy processes and the need to formulate arguments and take decisions based on limited, uncertain and ambiguous evidence (Cairney 2019; Cairney, Oliver, and Wellstead 2016). However, most explorations of how evidence is negotiated and used in specific policy areas have tended to be for the purpose of critiquing the ways decisions have ultimately been made. Oliver, Lorenc, and Innvaer (2014) note that there has been little documentation of what policymakers actually do on a day-to-day basis and how their daily 'work practices' (Schatzki, Knorr Cetina, and von Savigny 2001; see also Edwards 2020) influence how they use evidence. Without this empirical understanding, researchers will be challenged to analyse policymakers' perspectives on evidence use and to help civil servants develop more effective practices (Hallsworth, Parker, and Rutter 2011).

To gain this understanding we identified three recent studies which gathered detailed information about the interactions between evidence and policymaking in three different geographies and policy areas. In the UK, Maybin (2016) conducted in-depth interviews with policymakers from the Department of Health between 2009 and 2011, analysing documents and observing a range of meetings at which aspects of health policy were discussed. She investigated how mid-ranking civil servants used evidence to get up to speed on new issues, drill into the detail of a topic or conceptualise policy challenges in order to make decisions themselves or to recommend the decisions that others should take. In Australia, Rickinson et al. (2017, 2019) used document analysis, interviews and observational work to examine how educational policymakers used evidence in the policy development process. The research focussed on three policy initiatives within the Department of Education and Training in the State of Victoria. It explored what types of evidence were used, who was involved in the process, what drove and hindered the effective use of evidence, and what could be done to improve it. (Shaxson 2019) used document analysis to examine the work practices (systems and processes) put in place by a range of departments in the UK and USA to support evidence use in policy development. Referring to Parkhurst's (2017) principles of the good governance of evidence the research analysed whether, in aggregate, these practices contributed to a holistic approach to evidence-informed policymaking.

The three studies examine how policymakers find and use evidence from different perspectives. Analysing all three together highlights two broad findings of interest to ESE researchers. These are described in more detail in the next two sections. The first is that as policymakers work with their colleagues to inform decision making processes, they develop 'policy narratives' which influence—and are influenced by—their own perspectives on evidence. The second is that department-wide systems and processes help policymakers negotiate different normative positions on evidence. We suggest that this results in the creation of 'evidence narratives' which similarly influence their perspectives on how evidence could and should be used.

Policymakers use evidence to shape policy narratives

Policymakers' daily work practices (Schatzki, Knorr Cetina, and von Savigny 2001) include developing documents, overseeing ongoing programmes of work, advising ministers, responding to ad-hoc enquiries including questions in Parliament and supporting the work of expert committees (Maybin 2016). These help define what the problem is, keep issues on the agenda, identify drivers of change, challenge assumptions and design and select interventions (Rickinson et al. 2017). In performing the practices policymakers must negotiate different problem frames, interests and perspectives on key issues (Head 2016). They use a range of techniques to do this—making complex phenomena more manageable by visualising, conceptualising, defining and categorising what policies aim to do and who they aim to benefit. Policymakers also develop and test out ideas and proposals on colleagues and external advisers; using evidence tactically to persuade others of the validity of ideas, to mobilise support or to provide an independent voice in order to defuse conflicts over policy proposals (Maybin 2016).

Maybin and Rickinson et al both found that the aim of policymakers' practices is not to define what is correct but to build, test and communicate a coherent policy 'narrative': a storyline about the policy issue that helps communicate a particular perspective on which aspects of the issue are important and an appreciation of why they are important (Monaghan 2011). Policy narratives help people make sense of, organise and transmit information about the past, present and possible future of the issue; shaping the decisions that are subsequently taken (Wilkinson 2011). A critical consideration for Maybin's health policymakers was to create narratives that could be defended against internal and external critiques including from colleagues in other departments, stakeholder groups, Parliament and the media. But policy narratives and the ideas they contain are malleable (Smith 2014) as policymakers seek to keep key issues on the table while simultaneously responding to critiques and attempting to align these narratives with other policy agendas. How effective policymakers are at this process of alignment depends on their 'policy know-how' (Maybin 2016, 136): the technical, organisational and networking skills they need to do their jobs effectively and the rules, procedures and historical context from which each issue has arisen (Howlett and Wellstead 2011).

Different types of evidence are used to inform the detail of policy narratives. The studies by Maybin and Rickinson et al. both note the use of evidence from programme evaluations; internal and external stakeholder consultations; data from state, national and international assessments; meetings with frontline staff; reports from consultants and advisors and evidence from researchers who are considered by policymakers to be particularly authoritative. These different types of evidence are combined to shape the narrative, test ideas and challenge the internal coherence of emerging proposals. Rickinson et al. found that the range of evidence sources used by education policymakers was wider during the policy development phase than in subsequent phases where policymakers placed more emphasis on testing and communicating the narrative with stakeholders. This observation supports Maybin's finding that when policymakers began to communicate with key stakeholders to negotiate their buy-in to a particular policy proposal, having robust evidence became less important than having a coherent narrative.

Department-wide systems and processes also influence how evidence is used

Most government departments have broad remits and will be developing policy narratives for many different issues simultaneously. While policymakers often have latitude to develop their own relationships around evidence, researchers working on public sector reform agree that changing departmental processes and structures can help improve government effectiveness (Pollitt 2013). In the third study analysed here, Shaxson (2019) examined how various practices developed to strengthen the use of evidence in several government departments in the UK and USA. Seven practices were identified: appointing senior officials with mandates to oversee the use of evidence, setting up independent expert advisory committees, devising quality frameworks, formulating strategy documents that took a forward look at what evidence was likely to be needed in future, creating working groups, building analytical toolboxes, and writing guidelines and standards for evidence quality. As well as contributing evidence to developing individual policy narratives, policy officials also supported department-wide activities such as risk planning, effective budget management, and stimulating innovation.

The seven practices were found to serve different purposes: advising political representatives, strengthening decision-making, demonstrating achievement of outcomes, managing budgets effectively, building partnerships, raising evidence quality, and maintaining and developing capacity and capability for evidence use. A single practice could serve multiple purposes: for example, a senior official may be simultaneously responsible for using evidence to advise politicians, managing human and financial resources and demonstrating how well departmental goals are being achieved. At the same time, other policymakers could be working to understand whether outcomes are being delivered effectively, using quality frameworks to help them decide which sources of evidence could be considered robust in different implementing contexts.

There are two main findings from the Shaxson (2019) study. First, there appears to be broad agreement within the departments studied on the need for formal work practices (such as structures, processes and appointments to senior positions) to support the use of evidence inside government departments. However, there is considerable variability in what those practices look like, how they are combined and how extensively they cover the different aspects of evidence use. Second, the analysis highlighted that designing these practices to be effective required negotiating three normative positions around evidence. The first is 'fidelity to science' or the need to ensure that any evidence put forward for decision making is of high technical quality (Parkhurst, 2017). The second is 'democratic representation', or the need to recognise that policy-making is both a political and a technical endeavour and to incorporate public understandings into the evidence base for decisions, not simply technical advice (Parkhurst, 2017). The third is 'effective resource management', or the need to manage the human and financial resources available to the department to deliver value for money in pursuit of the policy goals. Policymakers' perspectives on evidence use may therefore develop somewhat separately from policy narratives. They are influenced by how the three normative positions on evidence are negotiated and how those negotiation processes are mediated by each department's work practices.

Drawing together these three studies leads us to suggest a new concept that could encapsulate the results of these mediated negotiations. Just as policy narratives help policymakers make sense of, organise and transmit information about the policy issue, we propose that policymakers may simultaneously be developing 'evidence narratives' to help them make sense of, organise and transmit information about what evidence they are using to inform decision-making and why. We suggest that one interpretation of the research-policy relationship (and of the wider process of evidence-informed policymaking) could be as the site of interaction between evidence narratives and policy narratives. While a policy narrative provides a perspective on which aspects of the policy issues are important and why, an evidence narrative provides a perspective on the robustness and utility of the evidence base that underpins the policy narrative. Evidence narratives could therefore play an important role in shaping the plausibility of policy narratives and vice versa, with shifting policy narratives highlighting strengths and weaknesses in the evidence base. Examining how policy narratives and evidence narratives develop, align, reinforce and conflict with one another, and whether this changes with different audiences, could provide detailed insights into the research-policy relationship.

Understanding policymakers' perspectives on evidence use: suggestions for ESE research

In the call for proposals for this Special Issue, the editors quote the appeal from Lingard (2013, 113) to 'reconsider … the actual and desired nature of research-policy relationships in education'. Lessons from outside the ESE space suggest that one fruitful avenue for enquiry is to analyse policymakers' perspectives on evidence use by developing an empirical understanding of what policymakers do on a daily basis; how policy narratives and evidence narratives develop and the organisational systems and processes that shape how evidence is used in the policy process. Further work on this would help ESE researchers better understand how policymakers' demands for evidence are shaped and what this implies for how researchers (and other providers of evidence) can engage more productively with policymakers in relation to ESE.

The three studies referenced in this article cover different policy environments (Australia, the UK and the USA) and policy areas (health, environment and education); suggesting that their findings may be more widely applicable. But the proposed concept of an 'evidence narrative' needs further examination: how do policymakers negotiate various normative positions on evidence? How do organisational systems shape these negotiation processes? Where and how do evidence narratives interact with policy narratives and to what effect? What does this imply for the roles that ESE researchers and/or policymakers could play in strengthening research-policy relationships?

The studies worked in a 'documentary' role, examining the policy process in detail and *in situ* to gain detailed insights into policymakers work practices. ESE researchers working in this vein could help address van Poeck, Lysgaard, and Reid's (2018) suggestion to reduce the demarcation between the science and the politics of environmental and sustainability education. Any insights gained through further research in this area would not be limited to ESE alone. By helping us understand policymakers' perspectives on the use of policy and evidence narratives, ESE researchers could also make a significant contribution to the wider literatures on evidence-informed policymaking and research-policy relationships.

Acknowledgements

Annette Boaz, Kingston University and St George's University of London, is supported by the National Institute for Health Research (NIHR) Applied Research Collaboration South London (NIHR ARC South London) at King's College Hospital NHS Foundation Trust. The views expressed are those of the authors and not necessarily those of the NIHR or the Department of Health and Social Care.

Disclosure statement

No potential conflict of interest was reported by the author(s).

ORCID

Louise Shaxson http://orcid.org/0000-0001-8558-1024
Annette Boaz http://orcid.org/0000-0003-0557-1294

References

Aikens, Kathleen, Marcia McKenzie, and Philip Vaughter. 2016. "Environmental and Sustainability Education Policy Research: A Systematic Review of Methodological and Thematic Trends." *Environmental Education Research* 22 (3): 333–359. doi:10.1080/13504622.2015.1135418.
Botterill, Linda Courtenay, and Andrew Hindmoor. 2012. "Turtles All the Way Down: Bounded Rationality in an Evidence-Based Age." *Policy Studies* 33 (5): 367–379. doi:10.1080/01442872.2011.626315.
Cairney, Paul. 2019. "The UK Government's Imaginative Use of Evidence to Make Policy." *British Politics* 14 (1): 1–22. doi:10.1057/s41293-017-0068-2..
Cairney, Paul, Kathryn Oliver, and Adam Wellstead. 2016. "To Bridge the Divide between Evidence and Policy: Reduce Ambiguity as Much as Uncertainty." *Public Administration Review* 76 (3): 399–402. doi:10.1111/puar.12555.
Edwards, Anne. 2020. "A Reflection on the Relational Aspects of Research Policy Interfaces." *Environmental Education Research* 1–5. doi:10.1080/13504622.2020.1739229.
Gagliardi, Anna R., Whitney Berta, Anita Kothari, Jennifer Boyko, and Robin Urquhart. 2015. "Integrated Knowledge Translation (IKT) in Health Care: A Scoping Review." *Implementation Science* 11 (1): 1–12. doi:10.1186/s13012-016-0399-1.
Hallsworth, Michael, Simon Parker, and Jill Rutter. 2011. "Policymaking in the Real World." London. https://www.instituteforgovernment.org.uk/sites/default/files/publications/Policymakingintherealworld.pdf. Accessed 3 April 2020.
Head, Brian W. 2008. "Three Lenses of Evidence-Based Policy." *Australian Journal of Public Administration* 67 (1): 1–11. doi:10.1111/j.1467-8500.2007.00564.x.
Head, Brian W. 2016. "Toward More 'Evidence-Informed' Policy Making?" *Public Administration Review* 76 (3): 472–484. doi:10.1111/puar.12475.
Howlett, Michael, and Adam Wellstead. 2011. "Policy Analysts in the Bureaucracy Revisited: The Nature of Professional Policy Work in Contemporary Government." *Politics & Policy* 39 (4): 613–633. doi:10.1111/j.1747-1346.2011.00306.x.
Jasanoff, Sheila. 2005. *Designs on Nature: Science and Democracy in Europe and the United States*. Princeton, NJ: Princeton University Press.
Laessøe, Jeppe, Noah Weeth Feinstein, and Nicole Blum. 2013. "Environmental Education Policy Research— Challenges and Ways Research Might Cope with Them." *Environmental Education Research* 19 (2): 231–242. doi:10.1080/13504622.2013.778230.
Lingard, Bob. 2013. "The Impact of Research on Education Policy in an Era of Evidence-Based Policy." *Critical Studies in Education* 54 (2): 113–131. doi:10.1080/17508487.2013.781515.
Maybin, Jo. 2016. *Producing Health Policy: Knowledge and Knowing in Government Policy Work*. Basingstoke: Palgrave Macmillan.
Monaghan, Mark. 2011. *Evidence versus Politics: Exploiting Research in UK Drug Policy Making?* Bristol: Policy Press.
Nilsen, Per. 2015. "Making Sense of Implementation Theories, Models and Frameworks." *Implementation Science* 10 (1): 53. doi:10.1186/s13012-015-0242-0.
Nutley, Sandra, Isabel Walter, and Huw Davies. 2007. *Using Evidence: How Research Can Inform Public Services*. Bristol: Policy Press.
Oliver, Kathryn, Theo Lorenc, and Simon Innvaer. 2014. "New Directions in Evidence-Based Policy Research: A Critical Analysis of the Literature." *Health Research Policy and Systems* 12 (1): 34. doi:10.1186/1478-4505-12-34.
Parkhurst, Justin. 2017. *The Politics of Evidence: From Evidence-Based Policy to the Good Governance of Evidence*. Abingdon, UK: Taylor & Francis.
Pollitt, Christopher. 2013. "The Evolving Narratives of Public Management Reform." *Public Management Review* 15 (6): 899–922. doi:10.1080/14719037.2012.725761.
Rickinson, Mark, Kate de Bruin, Lucas Walsh, and Matthew Hall. 2017. "What Can Evidence-Use in Practice Learn from Evidence-Use in Policy?" *Educational Research* 59 (2): 173–189. doi:10.1080/00131881.2017.1304306.

Rickinson, Mark, Judy Sebba, and Anne Edwards. 2011. *Improving Research through User Engagement*. Abingdon: Routledge. https://research.monash.edu/en/publications/improving-research-through-user-engagement.

Rickinson, Mark, Lucas Walsh, Kate de Bruin, and Matthew Hall. 2019. "Understanding Evidence Use within Education Policy: A Policy Narrative Perspective." *Evidence & Policy* 15 (2): 235–218. doi:10.1332/174426418X15172393826277.

Schatzki, Theodore R., Karin Knorr Cetina, and Eike von Savigny. 2001. *The Practice Turn in Contemporary Theory*. London: Routledge.

Shaxson, Louise. 2019. "Uncovering the Practices of Evidence-Informed Policymaking." *Public Money & Management* 39 (1): 46–60. doi:10.1080/09540962.2019.1537705.

Smith, Katherine E. 2014. "The Politics of Ideas: The Complex Interplay of Health Inequalities Research and Policy." *Science and Public Policy* 41 (5): 561–574. doi:10.1093/scipol/sct085.

Stone, Deborah. 2002. *Policy Paradox: The Art of Political Decision-Making*. 2nd revised. New York: W. W. Norton & Company.

van Poeck, Katrien, Jonas A. Lysgaard, and Alan Reid. 2018. *Environmental and Sustainability Education Policy: International Trends, Priorities and Challenges*. London: Routledge/Taylor & Francis. https://www.worldcat.org/title/environmental-and-sustainability-education-policy-international-trends-priorities-and-challenges/oclc/991645018?referer=di&ht=edition

Ward, Vicky. 2016. "Why, Whose, What and How? A Framework for Knowledge Mobilisers." *Evidence & Policy*. doi:10.1332/174426416X14634763278725.

Weiss, C. H. 1979. "The Many Meanings of Research Utilization." *Public Administration Review* 39 (5): 426–431. doi:10.2307/3109916.

Wilkinson, Katy. 2011. "Organised Chaos: An Interpretive Approach to Evidence-Based Policy Making in Defra." *Political Studies* 59 (4): 959–977. doi:10.1111/j.1467-9248.2010.00866.x.

Environment and sustainability education research as policy engagement: (re-)invigorating 'politics as *potentia*' in South Africa

Heila Lotz-Sisitka, Eureta Rosenberg and Presha Ramsarup

ABSTRACT
Using a meta-review approach organized historically in relation to critical policy incidents, this paper critically reviews the process of developing and (re) invigorating Environment and Sustainability Education (ESE) (policy) research *as ESE policy engagement* over a 30+ year period in a rapidly transforming society, South Africa. It offers an example of long term policy-research meta-review in a context of policy flux. It adds to a body of international ESE policy studies that are seeking to understand and develop the ESE research/policy interface as this relation emerges under more complex conditions. In particular, we respond to the finding in the systematic review of ESE policy research undertaken by Aikens, McKenzie and Vaughter (2016) which reports a geographic under-representation of Africa (amongst other places) in ESE policy studies, and González-Gaudiano (2016, 118)'s insight that ESE policy research in current neo-liberally dominated political conditions and as political process, is essentially an "open, unsteady, incomplete, and relational process". The Aikens et al. (2016) finding informed our decision to offer a substantive 'meta review' of 30+ years of ESE policy research in South Africa including approximately 150 studies, thus making this body of research more visible and available for scrutiny in the international ESE policy sphere, while also offering us an opportunity for the reflexive introspection that is advised for ESE policy studies by Van Poeck and Lysgaard (2016). The paper develops around a concept of *ESE research as policy engagement* oriented towards a *'politics of potentia'* (Dussel, 2008), framing the ESE policy-research meta-review within a theory of politics.

Introduction: Situating this research paper

Like other countries in the world, South Africa has been engaged in a process of integrating environment and sustainability concerns into their policy system over a period of 30+ years (UNESCO, 2014; RSA, 1995; DEA, 2010). In an earlier policy analysis of this emergent process applied to education policy making, Feinstein, Jacobi and Lotz-Sisitka (2013), comparing ESD policy implementation in three countries (USA, Brazil and South Africa), noted that,

International policy analysis tends to simplify the nation state, portraying countries as coherent units that can be described by one statistic or placed into one category. As scholars from Brazil, South Africa, and the USA, we find the nation-centric research perspective particularly challenging. In each of our home countries, the effective influence of the national government on education is quite limited, particularly in fringe and emerging areas of education such as Education for Sustainable Development (ESD) and Climate Change Education (CCE) ... We consider several layers of decentralized governance, but ultimately come to the conclusion that ESD governance in our respective countries is polycentric (pg. 218).

In this paper, we consider this finding further, with emphasis on the relationship between ESE research and policy within a nation state boundary frame, in which we frame *ESE research as a process of ongoing policy engagement* within a multi-levelled, polycentric policy system over a 30 year period. By this we mean that ESE research involves ongoing iterative engagement with policy processes that include inter-alia policy making, policy sense-making, policy implementation, policy evaluation and learning via policy frustrations. These processes are not linear. In the South African context, policy processes are in a state of flux. We, like Aikens, McKenzie and Vaughter (2016) in their systematic review of ESE policy, recognize that there are inadequate reflections on the complexity of policy engagement and enactment in ESE policy research, hence we address this in our paper.

Policy engagement under complex conditions of policy flux

South Africa offers a particularly richly textured context for policy studies, and for the emergence of relations between ESE research and ESE policy, as both have been emerging 'in tandem' in the post 1990 period as discussed later. 1990 is the year that the African National Congress (ANC) was unbanned in South Africa, and is also the year that Nelson Mandela was released from prison. In the 30+ years since 1990, South Africa has been undergoing a complex and oftentimes paradoxical transformation process – broadly framed as a massive shift from apartheid state that excluded the majority of the country's people from education, land and more; to a more inclusive society that has sought to bring human rights, social justice, sustainable development and transformation of society into being.

A critical part of this transformation process has been policy engagement – first via a period of policy formulation driven by strong ideological imperatives necessary at the time for replacing apartheid state policies; then a period of policy implementation ushering in a myriad of new structures, often without the agency, knowledge and other resources to carry through ambitious policy intentions; leading to various policy revision(s) and policy fatigue. Civil society started to experience disenchantment with policy engagement as policy failures emerged, with some analysts critically and reflexively remarking that much of the post-apartheid policy was shaped by inadequate political economy analyses of emerging democracies and economies (e.g. Fakir, 2017), while others commented on the impact of the shift from originally-intended developmental state trajectories under the first post-apartheid Reconstruction and Development Programme (RDP) (ANC, 1994) to neo-liberal policy trajectories (e.g. Carmody, 2002; Peet, 2002). Most recently, strategies of rent seeking, political entrepreneurship, political piracy, and even the emergence of a so-called 'shadow state' structure, are being reported (Fakir, 2017; Bhorat et al. 2017), which in short refer to a variety of practices associated with the emergence of corruption in the policy system (ironically not unlike strategies used under the apartheid regime). These are currently the subject of much public debate and national reflexivity, as shown via the institution of a commission of inquiry into the workings of state capture.

Broadly, this shifting policy trajectory can be summarized into four (roughly delineated) critical incident periods (see Figure 1 below) in which our ESE research as policy engagement manifested over a period of 30+ years. We identify these as:

1990-1994 POLICY PREPARATION

Unbanning of the African National Congress.

Preparatory policy making for a new democracy featuring environmental justice, environmental education, sustainable development discourses.

Early education policy social movements engage with environment, land and water issues.

These are noted as significant matters for societal transformation, thus placing them on the educational transformation agenda.

1994-2000 POLICY PROLIFERATION

New policy formulation across sectors including education and environment.

Shift in focus from reconstruction and development (more socialist) policies (ANC, 1994) to neo-liberal policy framing (Carmody, 2002; Peet 2002; Allais, 2003).

The first national curriculum policy is delineated with environment as a cross cutting concern.

This is framed within a human rights and social justice perspective.

This carries through two subsequent curriculum reviews (in 2002 and again in 2010).

New standards and qualifications are defined for the post-schooling system.

Environment and sustainability is recognised as a new skill and competence area on the national landscape.

2000-2010 INITIAL POLICY FAILURE

Start of serious post-apartheid policy failure in the new democracy.

From mid-2000's, concerted policy reviews and strategy development attempting to address gaps and streamline over-ambitions policies.

Following shifts towards neo-liberal models, government tends to focus on sector-based performance monitoring and performativity.

This reduces earlier forms of state-civil society cooperation.

It hampers the ability of data collection / research processes to contribute to learning and system development.

This affects environment and environmental education and sustainability sector.

In 2010 a study shows a largely re-active skills planning system for ESE needs.

2010-2019 POLICY INCONSISTENCY

Efficacy of policy system in question with efforts to resolve this via National Development Planning.

Lack of integrated and aligned policy engagement increasingly evident.

Following the 2011 Conference of the Parties (COP17) in South Africa, and the Sustainable Development Summit in Rio de Janeiro in 2012, the concept of an inclusive green economy is introduced.

It is in contradiction with the neo-liberal direction of earlier policies.

Efforts are made to introduce a developmental state structure, but this is hampered by corruption (Jain, 2010; Fakir, 2017; Statistics South Africa, 2017).

This affects skills and ESE implementation which lacks coherence and co-ordination.

Figure 1. Four critical incident periods showing the context of broader education policy flux and the effects on ESE policy.

- 1990-1994: Policy Preparation (referring to a period in which the South African liberation movement were preparing policy for the immanent post-apartheid state following the 1994 democratic elections)
- 1994-2000: Policy Proliferation (referring to a period in which virtually all policies in South Africa were transformed, or developed anew)
- 2000-2010: Initial Policy Failure (referring to a period in which significant policy failures became evident due mainly to over-ambitious policies, as well as lack of internal coherence in policy framing, and lack of adequate skills at a national level)
- 2010-2019: Policy Inconsistency (referring to a period in which state corruption, and deep seated contradictions in the policy framework produce policy implementation difficulties)

We note too that, as we write and finalise this paper in early 2020, that the policy trajectory is shifting again in response to the processes of national reflexivity emerging via inquiries into corruption and state capture impacts by the most recent leadership in the ANC government.

Figure 1 shows the context of broader education and national development policy, and how shifts here influenced ESE policy processes. Later we show how research processes overlay with the broad periodic framework we use for our meta-analysis.

As indicated above, the four critical incident periods reflect the state of broader national and educational policy flux and show good intent and high levels of participation in policy processes initially after 1990/94, which deteriorate into inconsistencies and oftentimes paradoxical decision-making by the mid 2000s, uncertainty, rapid change and widespread social protest as policy failures become evident post 2010. Overall, there is rapid policy emergence, policy transformation, policy direction switches, policy failures, policy reviews, policy implementation blockages, and ongoing reflexive, but also sometimes disruptive event-based searches for policy synergy, policy efficacy and policy impact in social, economic, educational and environment and sustainable development policy spheres, all of which have shaped the ESE research we have undertaken.

We, as authors of this paper, are all educational researchers in universities that have been deeply embedded in, and engaged in the policy processes outlined above, from 1990 onwards as we first worked with liberation movements to conceptualise ESE policy in the early 1990s, used research to help shape new policy developments, and then later to deepen understanding of the emerging complexities and contradictions in the policy system as these emerged. We have constantly sought ways of engaging critically, generatively and reflexively with the policy system through our research, a stance that we found necessary given the high demands for transforming a society following the watershed political change in 1994. The relatively time frames involved, as well as the need for ongoing capacity building amongst researchers for policy engaged research in situation of policy flux further created the need for such an orientation to the research-policy relationship. Most recently, we have continued to critically engage with the policy system with depth analysis illuminating the deep seated contradictions and problems surrounding policy inconsistency (see below) and agree with Fakir (2017), who argues that in such a context, there is need to give renewed attention to policy and praxis realism[1]. It is in these wider policy flux conditions that we have continued to develop ESE policy research *as a process of policy engagement* over a 30+ year period, as we outline further below.

ESE policy studies under complex conditions

Given the above context, we position this paper within an emerging body of ESE policy studies internationally that seek to consider the emergence of ESE policy under more complex conditions (Laessøe, Feinstein and Blum, 2013; Aikens, McKenzie and Vaughter, 2016; VanPoeck & Lysgaard (Editors of a VSI edition on ESE policy studies), 2016; González-Gaudiano, 2016; Bengtsson, 2016). González-Gaudiano (2016, 118)'s insight that ESE policy research in current neo-liberally dominated political conditions and as political process, is essentially an "open, unsteady, incomplete, and relational process" is intriguingly familiar, given the state of policy flux we have experienced, outlined above. Aikens et al. (2016) recommend giving attention to intersectionality in ESE policy studies while Van Poeck and Lysgaard, (2016) comment on changing roles for ESE researchers as new relations between researchers and policy actors become important for responding to the political complexity of the field (i.e.ESE research is not a-political). Here researchers seldom have the luxury of being mere documenters of policy (Van Poeck et. al, 2014), and thus need to re-think the research-policy relation as ongoing critically reflexive engagement, as modelled in the paper by McKenzie, Bieler and McNiell (2015) who critique the mobility of ESE policy under education policy neoliberalisation, noting that under such conditions, ESE policy may ironically lead to undermining aspirations of, and action on environmental sustainability. Van Poeck and Lysgaard (2016) comment on the role of ESE research in filling a complex space of critique and engagement. Linking to this, Laessøe et al. (2013, 231) in their review of ESE policy research, recommend giving attention to an "interactive policy-engaged approach to research" a position which we frame more politically as giving attention to (re)-invigorating a *'politics of potentia'* (after Dussel, 2008 – see below).

Methodology and theory guiding our review: Policy realism and (re) invigoration of *'politics as potentia'*

The 30+ year ESE research-policy story that we offer below is essentially a truncated meta-review i.e.it is not possible to offer all of the detail related to the actual policy processes and research that span the 30+ year period of Environmental Education and ESE[2] research in South Africa. A meta review or meta synthesis is designed to bring new interpretations to primary research in order to obtain broader understandings of a body of work (Whittemore and Knafl, 2005; Cooper, Hedges and Valentine, 1994). In this meta-review we focus mainly on major national studies, evaluations of national level ESE policy interventions, and a corpus of policy oriented studies (mainly post-graduate studies) *that have enabled policy engagement throughout this period, and which have helped to deepen understanding of how we might (re)-invigorate a 'politics of potentia' in the current time of flux*. Most of the research we review (See Appendix A) emerges out of the research programme that we have been involved in[3]. While we recognize that there may be inherent bias in the way we represent our research, we have also sought to be widely reflexive of the research programme. While other studies into ESE policy have been conducted in South Africa, and we include them where relevant, the research that has emerged via our postgraduate programmes and multi-institutional partnerships (most often involving other major national ESE researchers and research programmes) remains the largest body of ESE policy related research in the country. Additionally, almost all of the ESE policy research under this programme has been combined with policy engagement in South Africa over the past 30+ years; involving over 100 policy partners and major national policy engagement institutions including state, parastatal, university partners, unions, civil society organisations and social movements. Our research Centre is home to the country's first Chair in Environmental Education which was established in 1990. It currently hosts the most extensive ESE research programme in the country. It was established in the same year that the ANC was unbanned (1990) and has been an integral part of most national environmental and education (and hence also ESE) policy processes since 1990.

In reflecting on this work, we propose that during policy flux, and particularly when policy failure emerges to the extent is currently the case in South Africa, there is need for a theory of politics to guide policy engaged research that can anchor policy realism - not in neo-positivist ways - but in ways that critically and generatively take account of the underlying and contemporary realities of the day. An example of policy engaged research that can anchor policy realism can be found in the green skills research programme we refer to below, in which we undertook critically constituted economic system, demand, supply and transitioning studies for new green economy learning pathways. We critically and reflexively embedded these in multi-level system analysis in order to inform a more comprehensive transformative praxis approach to developing the national organizing framework for occupations which is the key instrument used by government to release funding for ESE training in the country. This required extensive, and ongoing critically reflexive engagements with skills development system policy actors in terms of conceptualization, critique and uptake of the policy research, it also required research to re-frame mainstream economic thinking guiding (neo-liberal) government policy praxis for skills planning (cf. Rosenberg, Ramsarup and Lotz-Sisitka, 2020). In framing the meta-review, we agree with Van Poeck and Lysgaard (2016) that ESE research ought not to be or become "a machine that produces evidence-based solutions to complex issues", hence we see ESE research *as policy engagement* (i.e.a more complex, contested process; not narrowly constituted instrumental policy development, implementation or assessment processes only).

Policy realism in such a context requires a theory of politics that can guide ESE research as a process of policy engagement beyond the above noted instrumentalist framings, and associated neoliberal globalisation ideology which is shaping the post-apartheid state and the current policy condition as outlined above in Figure 1. According to Dussel (2008), instrumentalism and associated practices that emerge from neo-liberal globalization ideology, abolishes a politics of *potentia* as it subordinates the political to the economic and the economic to the technological (including methodologically). This subordination results in "the negation of human life, not just as naked existence, but as collective, dialogical, communicative freedom" (Mendieta, 2008, vii), reflecting a form of 'necropolitics' (Mbembe, 2003) that turns human possibilities for engaging politically into an anti-human lust for profit and destruction of life systems. Dussel (2008) explains *'Politics as Potentia'* as combining the strength of the 'will-to-live' of members of a community, or of the *people*. He suggests that this is a fundamental material determination of the definition of political power. He explains the term *potentia* as "the power that is a faculty or capacity inherent in the *people* as the final instance of sovereignty, authority, governability, and the political" (pg 17)[4]. Significantly for a polycentric, multi-layered and multi-dimensional approach to ESD research as policy engagement, "[t]his power as *potentia* – which spreads like a network over the entire political field, and within which every political actor is a node ... - develops on *various levels and in various spheres* (Dussel, 2008, 17, emphasis original). This allows us a way of thinking about the ESE research-policy relation as an open ended, relational (González-Gaudiano, 2016) *horizon of the possible* infused by "a politics of life and for life" (see also Lotz-Sisitka, 2016). This occurs in the always-in-tension dialectical space of building solidarity and freedom (Bhaskar, 1993). Here Dussel (2008) argues for *potentia***, in relation to** *potestas*. He describes this relation - as currently constituted - as an ontological 'split' between within the primary power of the political community (*potentia*/of the people), and the delegation of the exercise of power through institutions, policies and representatives (*potestas*/'those who command'). Figure 1 shows the emergence of such an ontological split, hence our interest in ongoing (re)-invigoration of a politics of potentia via ESE research as policy engagement. As indicated in the example above, the idea of 'potentia' is not in conflict with policy realism, as 'potentia' emerges in and through the policy research and engagement process in open systems.

The Meta-review: 30+ years of ESE research *as* policy engagement with four trajectories emerging

The Table included in Appendix A provides a summative meta-review of the body of ESE research undertaken by ourselves, our post-graduate students, colleagues, organizational partners (including researchers from other universities and research centres) over the 30+ years since the advent of democracy in South Africa. It provides the foundation for the review and conclusions that follow. While the table greatly condenses the body of roughly 150 studies and reports, it goes some way towards reflecting the complex nature of South African ESE related research-policy processes over time, offering a study that explores the ESE research-practice relationship over a long period of time (i.e.30+ years). Through references to the theoretical and methodological influences, as well as research methodologies used by the researchers, it demonstrates the multi-modal nature of productive ESE policy research and how the ESE policy-practice relationship changed over the 30+ year period. Different to cases of ESE policy-practice research (e.g. Ramsarup, 2017a), systematic reviews of ESE policy-practice research (e.g. Mc Aikens et al. 2016), or comparative ESE policy studies (e.g.Feinstein, Jacobi and Lotz-Sisitka, 2013), this meta-review offers a vantage point that has the benefit of reflexive review of a substantive body of policy-practice research over a longer period of time. We structured the table around the critical incident points referred to in Figure 1 above. Note, however, that these critical incident points or periods are somewhat artificial demarcations for the purpose of mapping broad trends in the policy research and engagement process. In particular, we are interested in marking out the policy-research relationship that has unfolded over time within this meta-level review, rather than synthesizing the findings of the policy research. Whilst we foreground broad trends, we are conscious that parallel and sometimes contested processes were also occurring. We therefore focus on those incidents and research trends that emerged as being most significant in terms of

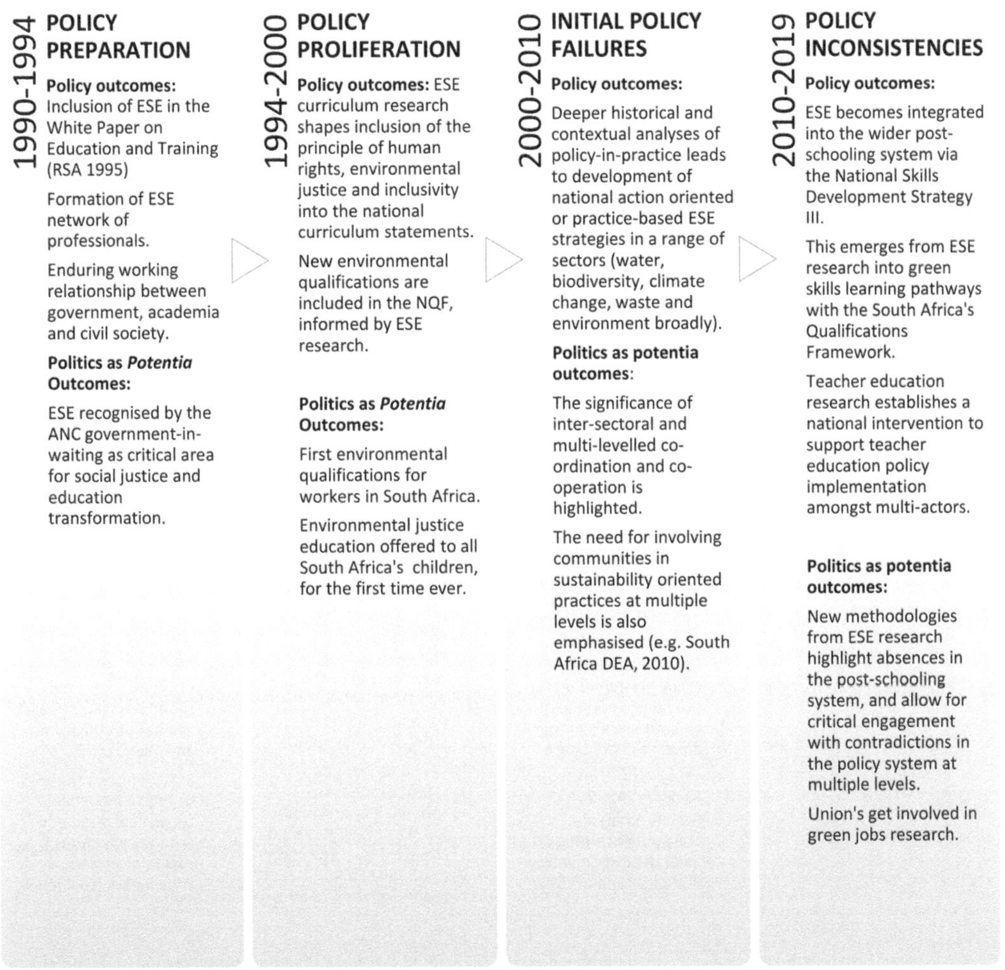

1990-1994 POLICY PREPARATION

Policy outcomes:
Inclusion of ESE in the White Paper on Education and Training (RSA 1995)

Formation of ESE network of professionals.

Enduring working relationship between government, academia and civil society.

Politics as *Potentia* Outcomes:

ESE recognised by the ANC government-in-waiting as critical area for social justice and education transformation.

1994-2000 POLICY PROLIFERATION

Policy outcomes: ESE curriculum research shapes inclusion of the principle of human rights, environmental justice and inclusivity into the national curriculum statements.

New environmental qualifications are included in the NQF, informed by ESE research.

Politics as *Potentia* Outcomes:

First environmental qualifications for workers in South Africa.

Environmental justice education offered to all South Africa's children, for the first time ever.

2000-2010 INITIAL POLICY FAILURES

Policy outcomes:
Deeper historical and contextual analyses of policy-in-practice leads to development of national action oriented or practice-based ESE strategies in a range of sectors (water, biodiversity, climate change, waste and environment broadly).

Politics as potentia outcomes:

The significance of inter-sectoral and multi-levelled co-ordination and co-operation is highlighted.

The need for involving communities in sustainability oriented practices at multiple levels is also emphasised (e.g. South Africa DEA, 2010).

2010-2019 POLICY INCONSISTENCIES

Policy outcomes:
ESE becomes integrated into the wider post-schooling system via the National Skills Development Strategy III.

This emerges from ESE research into green skills learning pathways with the South Africa's Qualifications Framework.

Teacher education research establishes a national intervention to support teacher education policy implementation amongst multi-actors.

Politics as potentia outcomes:

New methodologies from ESE research highlight absences in the post-schooling system, and allow for critical engagement with contradictions in the policy system at multiple levels.

Union's get involved in green jobs research.

Figure 2. ESE research engagement policy and politics as potentia outcomes flowing from ongoing ESE research as policy engagement processes (with further elaboration in Appendix A).

enabling or generating ESE related policy outcomes and that have advanced a *'politics of potentia'*. We also flag, where relevant, what turned out to be less productive or dead end methodological tools and approaches. We summarise the main tenets of this review in Figures 2–4 under the four trajectories observed in the meta-review, discussed next.

Via the meta review outlined in Appendix A, and the body of ESE policy research and engagements on which it is based, a number of trajectories crystalized. Trajectories here refer to developments over time that have influenced and shaped the ESE policy-research relationship in a context of policy flux. The first trajectory relates to Figure 1, which outlines the broader relationship between broader macro-level policy developments and ESE policy outcomes (cf. Figure 2). The latter three trajectories outlined reflect more on the way in which research has changed in this context (cf. Figures 3 and 4) from a theoretical influence and methodological perspective. The latter trajectories are our reflections as researchers on the forms of research that have emerged in the ESE policy-research relation over time. The Figures 2–4 can be read as 'overlays' or deepening of the policy-research relation over time, offering a multi-facetted view of the policy-research relation over time.

Next we outline four of the trajectories we identified below, with some reflection on the process that takes us more deeply into the nature of *ESE research as policy engagement*. We

POLICY PREPARATION 1990-1994	POLICY PROLIFERATION 1994-2000	INITIAL POLICY FAILURES 2000-2010	POLICY INCONSISTENCIES 2010-2019
ESE research theoretical tools and influences:	ESE research theoretical tools and influences:	ESE research theoretical tools and influences:	ESE research theoretical tools and influences:
Critical and reflexive forms of paticipatory action research to mobilise a policy engagement constituency across resistance movement, newly emerging state actors, civil society and research entities.	Scoping, contextual profiling and analytical research to put forward policy proposals via enabling documents and policy toolkits.	Post-structural research, indigenous knowledge research, studies on epistmological access, and decolonisation emerge along with ongoing action-oriented research.	Studies in schooling, post-schooling, workplace learning and community education are increasingly framed by critical realist constellational relationality and transformative praxis research designs (Bhaskar, 1993).
Critical social theory emerging from the paradigms debate (Fien, 1993; Mzarek, 1993; Robottom and Hart, 1993).	These provide mediating tools for policy actors during engaged policy making processes.	Influences include Fairclough's (1985) critical discourse analysis and Foucault's (2003) geneological work, as well as social realist curriculum theorists (Bernstein, 1990; Muller, 2012; Muller and Young, 2007; Morrow, 2007).	Boundary crossing becomes a focus of research as does expansive social learning leading to transformative agency (Engestrom and Sannino, 2010).
Rio Earth Summit NGO Forum Principles of Environmental Education based on Freirian pedagogies in the Global South also influential.	Theoretical resources from constructivist, socially critical pedagogy (Vygotsky, 1987, Bruner, 1997; Fien, 1993; Gough and Robottom, 1993), active learning theory (O'Donoghue, 2000) and theories of engaged praxis (Freire, 1996).	Post-colonial theorists offer ways of engaging with indigenous knowledges and neo-coloniality in post-apartheid policy contexts (Mamdani, 1996, Mbembe, 2001).	Decolonisation of policy and praxis (De Sousa Santos, 2014) challenges dominant epistemology.
	Popkewitz's (1990) social epistemology provided a critique of linear research-design-develop-disseminate policy reforms.		Critiques of narrow rationality shape realist evaluations (Pawson and Tilley, 1997).
	Beck's (1992) Risk Society catalyses engagement with risk and reflexivity in policy discourse and praxis.	Lave and Wenger (1991) emphasise situated learning while Bhaskar's (1993) critical realism draws attention to ontology and problems of relativism.	Post-humanist theory begins to influence curriculum discourse around indigenous cosmologies and knowledges (Le Grange, 2012).

Figure 3. ESE research theoretical tools and influences shaping ESE as policy engagement (with further elaboration in Appendix A) developing over the four critical incident periods.

elaborate on a few examples from the body of research to explicate the ESE policy engagement trajectories further, with emphasis on reflexively considering those multi-modal methodologies and processes that we have found to be more productive in (re)-invigorating a politics of potentia. We also note some of those that were less helpful. Here, we seek to show that our research has not been constituted as an instrumental handmaiden to policy, or a simple 'documenting' of policy processes and engagement, but rather that it has been constituted as an ongoing open process of reflexive policy engagement over time where social justice and praxis-based concerns interface with policy processes and institutions. This provides empirical material for understanding the recommendation of González-Gaudiano (2016) that ESE research as policy engagement should be seen as being an "open, unsteady, incomplete, and relational process" that is also political.

● **Trajectory 1: wider policy shifts influence ESE related policy and politics as potentia outcomes**

The critical incident periods in Figure 1 reflect a socio-political trajectory in which initial policy promise gradually came to fail the early ambitions of the social-ecological justice project of the

1990-1994 **POLICY PREPARATION:**	1994-2000 **POLICY PROLIFERATION**	2000-2010 **INITIAL POLICY FAILURES**	2010-2019 **POLICY INCONSISTENCIES**
Intrinsic Studies: Case studies, often with participatory action research methodology formed the foundations of early ESE policy engaged research. Early examples are O'Donoghue (1990), Naidoo (1993), expanding on a small history of attitude and perception studies which marked the early emergence of ESE research in South Africa (O'Donoghue, 1997).	**Intrinsic Studies:** A burgeoning of case studies focussing on the new curriculum policy and implications for ESE and teachers professional development (e.g. Lotz 1995; Du Toit, 1999; Burt, 1999; Lotz-Sisitka and Olivier, 1998; Khumalo, 2000). **Extrinsic, theoretical and meta-review studies:** Janse van Rensburg (1995) offers a meta-theoretical review of ESE research and calls for reflexivity in the choice of research methodology; O'Donoghue (1997) introduces longer term social historical processes to guide ESE reserach. Evaluation studies inform qualifications design (Janse van Rensburg & Le Roux, 1998; Hattingh, 1999), and a broad study on ESE teacher education (Wagiet, 1997) and formative and summative evaluations of ESE curriculum projects (Janse van Rensburg & Lotz, 2000; Lotz-Sisitka & Raven, 2001) shape the establishment of a National Environmental Education Programme situated in the Minstry of Education. This shapes national curriculum policy outcomes.	**Intrinsic Studies:** Case studies continue, showing weaknesses of the outcomes-based curriculum (e.g. Lotz-Sisitka, 2002; Mbanjwa, 2003; Nduna, 2004); exclsions of indigenous knowledge (e.g. Van Damme & Neluvhalani, 2004; Shava 1999; 2008). These deepen understanding of curriculum (re)contextualisation, epistemic access and educational quality. **Extrinsic, theoretical and meta-review studies:** A large scale multi-institutional evaluation of the National Environmental Education Programme confirms weaknesses of the outcomes-based curriculum and feeds into curriculum policy review. Skills system weaknesses lead to a multi-year national research programme to develop the first ever Environmental Sector Skills Plan for South Africa (DEA, 2010) Price (2007) offers a meta-review and transdisciplinary explanatory critique of ESE research as shaped by positivism and post-structuralism and argues for critical realist research. Lotz-Sisitka (2004) shows up the political economy of sustainable development as driver of ESE into the UN Decade of ESD.	**Intrinsic Studies:** Case studies focussing on specific policy implementation concerns continue. They inform multi-actor national policy-praxis learning networks e.g. the Fundisa for Change learning network Shudel 2012, 2014; Songqwaru 2012, 2020); the Green Skills Learning Network (Cobban et al. 2017; Ramsarup et al. 2018; Rosenberg et al. 2016). **Extrinsic, theoretical and meta-review studies:** Studies make use of multi-layered analytical frameworks to probe depth ontologies and absence in policy systems (e.g. Ramsarup, 2017a), and contradictions and absences in policy and practice epistemic frameworks (e.g. Vallabh, 2017). Evaluations continue to be important forms of extrinsic research and use realist approaches (e.g. Songqwaru, 2020), leading to new models of evaluating ESE and offering stronger analytical tools for transformative change at multiple levels. A synthesis of green skills studies provides a critical realist framework for sustainable development and educational policy (Lotz-Sisitka & Ramsarup, 2020) .

Figure 4. ESE research as policy engagement in 'multi-modal' forms (with further elaboration in Appendix A) over the four critical incident periods.

new South Africa. As discussed above, we see a shift from an initial focus in the early 1990s on redistributive, reconstitutive and reconciliatory justice in the first ANC government's Reconstruction and Development Plan (i.e.a more socialist policy intention), to neo-liberal macro-level development policy; and we see a continuation of exploitative and extractivist economic activity, associated with examples of necropolitics, vested interests and corruption interfering with policy realization in the latter years (2010-2018/9). Nonetheless ESE policy research continued throughout (see Appendix A and Figures 2–4). The outcomes column of Appendix A, summarized in Figure 2, shows that this has been a complex, difficult, yet productive process with ESE policy outcomes as well as ESE related *politics as potentia* outcomes showing the continued dialectical engagement between politics as *potentia* (people's empowerment) and politics as *potestas* (state control). We differentiate policy outcomes as concrete policy developments. Politics as potentia outcomes are outcomes that reflect social and environmental justice movement in the policy landscape related to the policy outcomes and related processes.

From the above (see also Appendix A), there were significant uptakes of ESE policy in the national system at the start of the 30+ year period, and actors in the national system continue to respond to ESE research, and policy gains continue to be made, even though they are often smaller than hoped for, and the context/realpolitik always surprisingly complex and difficult to navigate. This, as we see in Figure 3, has required ESE researchers to constantly develop their research orientations theoretically and methodologically, and socially via various forums and network structures (see also Appendix A).

From an ESE policy outcomes perspective, Figure 2 (see Appendix A for further elaboration) shows that there have also been shifts in the types of policy outcomes. These have been from early framing policy, such as the Constitutional framing of environment, human rights and social justice (RSA, 1996), reflected in the principle statement in the White Paper on Education and Training (RSA, 1995), the national curriculum statements (South Africa: DoE, 1997, 2012), and the national qualifications framing policy, towards a stronger focus on sector-based policy implications of these framing policies. This later phase includes strategies to make policy more workable in field, for example the production of human capacity development strategies for environment and sustainability and the development of a national Environmental Sector Skills Plan in 2010 (DEA, 2010) to guide state-civil society engagement with ESE policy actions.

From a politics of *potentia* perspective, the shift is from initial policy that was inclusive at a broad, idealistic level, to policy processes that were more critical of idealism and ongoing marginalization and exclusion, to a more recent focus on contradictions and absences in the policy system and their implications, but also approaches that address these. Examples of such approaches include giving attention to 'strategy-as-practice' (Jarzabkowski and Spee, 2009) in ESE policy work where multi-voiced actors engage practically to work out how to respond to policy intentions or absences at different levels of the system, and in diverse sites. Some examples include a learning network focusing on the absence of rainwater harvesting knowledge and climate smart agriculture in agricultural education policy and curricula (Lotz-Sisitka et al. 2016); or development of a Unit-based Sustainability Assessment tool for universities to reflexively review institutional policies and sustainability responses (Togo and Lotz-Sisitka, 2013). Other examples of policy-in-practice initiatives that have sought to broaden participation in policy processes include development of auditing tools for schools to develop local Eco-Schools policy and practice (http://wessa.org.za) and development of sourcebooks for sector education and training authorities to undertake sector skills planning in ways that give attention to the unlocking of 'latent' green jobs in sector-based value chains, thus addressing the high demand for decent work and employment (Ramsarup and Ward, 2017). These research-led co-engaged approaches developed throughout the 30+ year period, and have been a key mechanism for maintaining focus on people's participation in policy processes in a context of policy flux.

- *Trajectory 2: relational and embedded nature of ESE research and evaluation*

Much of the research mapped in the Table in Appendix A aimed to contribute, in one way or another, to building the capacity of the national system of government and its social partners to develop, review and implement ESE and related policies, indicating the importance of co-engaged relations between state system policy actors, academics and social partners. Important for constituting the relational approach is that the ESE policy outcomes captured in Figure 2 (elaborated in Appendix A) have not been achieved only through research. Appendix A also documents some of the related processes that have enabled or supported ESE policy outcomes. These include the establishment of formal and informal policy-engagement networks, forums and other system engagement structures, as well as courses and capacity building programmes that allow for state policy actors to engage with other actors from NGOs, universities and civil society movements in learning-centred spaces. Among the former, the Environmental Education Policy Initiative (EEPI), Environmental Education Curriculum Initiative (EECI) and Standards Generating Bodies (SGBs) were particularly important during the initial policy development period, and the National Environmental Skills Planning Forum (NESPF) become increasingly important in the later period.

Courses and capacity building programmes and the professional learning networks that sprung from them, were significant throughout. We noted during the review that these courses and networks were in multiple and productive ways linked to ESE research and policy processes, most often involving state policy actors as well as civil society and private sector actors in multi-voiced formations, actively engaged at different levels of the polycentric system, allowing for boundary crossing learning and policy engagement. For example, ESE research led to the development of ESE courses that enrolled a multiplicity of government officials and other policy actors who were motivated to attend because they were part of shared ESE policy networks; courses and networks generated deepening engagement with ESE concerns, motivating policy actors to undertake situated, embedded ESE research from within the policy system itself (e.g. Sauls, 2018; Giqwa, 2018). Given the multi-actor nature of the networks, alignment across sectors and fields has been encouraged and today the ESE sector in South Africa supports a range of 'changing practice' courses for multi-actors to activate policy-praxis research-and-learning networks. For example: the Amanzi [Water] for Food learning network in the Eastern Cape supporting water policy engagement for small scale farmers, (Pesanayi, 2016, 2019; see www.amanziforfood.co.za), the Fundisa [teaching] for Change teacher education network supporting curriculum policy engagement (Songqwaru, 2020; see www.fundisaforchange.co.za), and the Limpopo Basin Curriculum Innovation Network in the Limpopo Province (supporting climate change policy engagement in Higher Education, see www.lbcin.org).

- *Trajectory 3: expanding and deepening theoretical work over time*

Over time (as framed by the four critical incident periods outlined above) the ESE research in totality shows a growing engagement with, deepening of and use of a broader body of educational, social and economic theory as shown in Figure (see also Appendix A for more detail). In keeping with the transformation project many studies have a strong critical element, in intent and in the theory utilized, and this overall commitment to critical research is maintained throughout the 30+ year period. Earlier research (first two time periods) show a commitment to critical and constructivist theories emerging from the early paradigm deliberations in environmental education research globally (e.g. Mrazek, 1993; Fien, 1993, Robottom and Hart, 1993). However, the newer theory drawn on in the latter two periods shows a broader engagement with a wider range of critical and social theories including critical realism and decolonial theoretical influences which were less present early on. We found that the latter bodies of theory have enabled a greater engagement with the multi-layered complexity of our context of policy flux. Power, for example, is understood not to be static or a simple dialectic of powerful and oppressed, but is more aligned with agency formation in multi-actor groups for the common good; with the dynamically shifting and ambivalent nature of power including understanding of researchers' own complicity and complex roles in ESE policy processes becoming better understood. Hence with the latter theoretical tools, our ESE policy research becomes better equipped to grasp and engage more fully with the complexity of ESE policy and policy enactment.

A growing use of stronger conceptual and social engagement tools (like cultural historical activity theory, social and expansive learning, and community of practice constructs) and a stronger theorization of the role of ethics and ontology, have proven to be generative by allowing researchers to overcome the relativism that trapped some earlier participatory and constructivist studies. A second line of emergence lies in an ongoing deepening of critiques of naïve or pessimistic critical theory, started by Lotz (1996; Lotz-Sisitka 2016b) supported by meta-theoretical perspectives for enhancing inclusive learning and transformation such as those provided by O'Donoghue (2016a), and the deepening of reflexivity, started by Janse van Rensburg (1995) and carried through into the reflexivity that is now central to critically constituted generative ESE policy-in-praxis research in southern Africa (Price and Lotz-Sisitka, 2016).

The Table in Appendix A, (see also Figure 3) shows a trajectory in which social theory and notably the work of Bhaskar (1978, 1979, 1993, 2016) proved valuable and started to inform ESE research programmes. Bhaskar's work found resonance in the South African context because it provides non-anthropocentric ontological, methodological and axiological tools for emancipatory research in transforming societies (i.e.giving meaning to the *'politics of potentia'*) through learning and agency formation. Bhaskar's (1993) notion of criticality in critical realism, is based on a critical realist dialectic that engages absence and emergence in an onto-axiological chain of being and becoming, and provides philosophical and methodological tools for enabling De Sousa Santos' (2014) recommendation for giving attention to both sociologies of absence and emergence, which are interrelated projects in decolonizing and transforming societies. Deleuzian critical theory also emphasizes processes of being and becoming (Le Grange, 2012) but in a different way to Bhaskar's dialectical approach. Both Bhaskarian and Deleuzian critical theories allow for criticality that is generatively constituted from ontological experience i.e.that is not ideologically impositional with important implications for a policy context where policy has a long social history of imposition and oppression (Lotz-Sisitka and Schudel, 2007). As an underlabourer in policy research, critical realism encouraged searches for absent perspectives in the ESE policy landscape, for example commons theory (Ostrom, 2010; Amin and Howell, 2016); transitioning systems theory (found in Geels, developed for emerging economies by Fakir, 2017 and Swilling et al. 2016) and anti-capitalist regenerative economics theory (e.g. Moore, 2015; Streek, 2014 - summarized and developed into a useful educational and praxis framework by Raworth, 2017), as well as wider theories of post-human environment relations (Braidotti, 2013) reflecting the ongoing 'outside-in' dynamic of ESE policy research as being important to our ongoing 'inside-out' work (Van Poeck and Lysgaard, 2016).

The stronger theoretical tools for deeper insights, and the expanding range of theory and method, has given rise to a multi-modal spectrum of research approaches (see below) that in totality seem appropriate for engaging with the diverse dimensions of and actors in ESE policy, and for helping to deal reflexively (but not without difficulty) with the 'ontological split' between *'potentia'* and *'potestas'* in politics and policy relations referred to by Dussel (2008).

- ***Trajectory 4: emergence of Multi-Modal nature of ESE research and evaluation***

From an early engagement with the paradigms debate about which forms of research were most suitable for ESE research (see Figure 3), we have come to see a landscape of multi-modal research, adopting a term used by Coole and Frost (2010) to refer to broad forms of research and evaluation. Informed by the theoretical developments noted above, and the ongoing need for engagement in the research-policy engagement context, we found a need for ongoing deepening of research-policy relations using case studies, but also extensive nationally and more broadly framed theoretical and synthesizing studies reflected in Figure 4. To further concretise the theoretical developments and diversity of types of studies we have worked on within a wider research-policy relation, and based on the scope of research modalities reviewed and reflected in the Table in Appendix A, we use Sayer's (2010) conceptualisation of concrete/intensive research, extensive (generalizing) research; abstract or theoretical research; and synthesis or meta-research, as four complementary forms or modalities of research (see Figure 4) that have emerged drawing on the methodological perspectives above. All of these were found to be important in the 30+ year ESE research as policy engagement process reflected in Appendix A and in Figure 4 . They also contributed to the dialectical relationship embedded in the politics of potential concept, allowing ESE researchers and state policy actors to co-engage with other interest groups in society to develop the ESE policy-relation and trajectory over the four critical incident periods.

In reflecting on the body of work and related outcomes as captured in brief in Figure 4, it seems evident that a multi-modal approach involving a mix of intrinsic, extrinsic, synthesis and abstract research is valuable for ESE policy engagement and outcomes. This does not mean that all approaches and tools seemed equally useful. Within this mix, among the dead ends were approaches that simply described the situation, the differences between groups, or people's views, without scope to be generative of new possibilities, and approaches that had inadequate tools for agency formation and analysis. More generative approaches allowed for productive engagement with contradictions, or new opportunities to bring together policy actors and ideas in co-productive, but open-ended ways. Evaluations using generic sets of indicators, or simply seeking all stakeholders' opinions, failed to support organizational learning and inform further policy development. In the schools' context, an evaluation of the Eco-Schools programme (Rosenberg, 2008, 2009a) shared teachers' voices, but did not test their hypotheses (that participating in Eco-Schools improved learner outcomes within an otherwise failing system) and fell short of probing generative mechanisms shaping teachers experiences or collecting (extensive) national data that could be correlated with learner outcomes to further test teachers' hypotheses. Thus it did not provide a powerful enough statement to guide policy. Hence we have since then developed an interest in realist evaluation methodologies for guiding ESE policy engaged research (Songqwaru, 2020; see also Rickinson, Hall and Reid, 2016).

Many practitioner-led, small scale case studies detailed the ways in which policy was being enacted in a variety of contexts. These studies were often evaluative in nature, *concrete* and *intensive* (Sayer, 2010) and valuable for understanding contexts of implementation (and the importance of context) and how policy does or does not play out at a micro-level. What was often lacking however was a system wide perspective, a way of linking broader and deeper underlying factors to the individual contexts being studied, hence we found the need to complement these with wider national level studies, such as the extensive study undertaken to inform the development of a National Environmental Sector Skills Plan (South Africa: DEA, 2010). Similarly, workplace case studies focused only on individual courses or organisations, lacked the macro-level and system-wide insight that later proved to be essential for engaging the complex world of work and sustainability, hence we found the need for developing research frameworks and tools that work with a multi-levelled systems perspective which crosses the macro-micro divide (Lotz-Sisitka and Ramsarup, 2017a, 2017b; Ramsarup & Lotz-Sisitka, 2017; Ramsarup, 2017a, 2017b).

Appendix A and Figures 3 and 4 reflect that in the last decade, several researchers started under-labouring[5] research with critical realism, and introduced critical realist tools such as retroduction, immanent critique and dialectical transformative praxis (Bhaskar, 1993, 2016). More recently studies are also focussing on decolonisation logics via theoretical and meta-reviews of existing orientations and approaches to ESE research in and as policy engagement (e.g. Le Grange, 2012; Kulundu, 2017; Vallabh, 2017). The studies informed by these approaches are helping us understand why policy might not be 'working'. They provide a greater grasp of the real-politik, complexity, multiple 'layers' of reality (relationally material and social-historical-cultural in construction) and how they interact to give rise to policy enactment, or remain in 'lock-ins'. Research in the latter period has started not only to identify contradictions and obstacles, but to look more systemically, and more deeply to identify underlying structural tendencies and generative mechanisms or 'generative complexes' that shape the more readily observed events, trends and outcomes patterns (Sayer, 2010; Bhaskar, 1993). Evaluations using realist approaches hold the promise of surfacing the deeper programme and generative mechanisms that make some ESE programme aspects work for some participants, and not for others, hence allowing generalisability at the level of generative mechanism (e.g. values or coloniality) across individual contexts (Pawson and Tilley, 1997; Songqwaru, 2020) and the surfacing of a *'politics of potentia'* that allows otherwise marginalised voices to be heard in context.

In summary, various modes of research can provide insight into the various (ontologically) related layers of a complex multi-tiered policy reality. However, they need to be (re)viewed and to some extent designed and considered in relation to each other, for the important interactions between the different layers of the phenomenon of ESE policy to become evident. This reveals that a multi-modal approach is not the same as a mix of quantitative and qualitative methods; but an approach to using different forms of research in combination for understanding complexities over time. A collection of studies/body of work, or a single study can take a multi-modal approach. This multi-modal methodological frame for ESE research is reflected in the Table in Appendix A, and in Figure 4 , and illuminates an overarching perspective for interpreting *ESE research as policy engagement* via ongoing processes over time.

Conclusion

In this paper, we have given attention to a theory of policy realism in the form of (re)-invigoration of a *'politics of potentia'* as described by Dussel's (2008) work. As noted above, Dussel raises the issue of the ontological 'split' within the primary power of the political community (*potentia*/ 'of the people'), and the delegation of the exercise of power through institutions, policies and representatives (*potestas*/'those who command'). With this as background, and with the rapidly transforming and increasingly paradoxical policy environment in which we have been ESE researchers and policy engagement activists, we have worked with a concept of multi-modal *ESE research as policy engagement* over time. This meta review has revealed that we have, via our research and research leadership roles in the field, been reflexively engaging with and producing multi-modal research approaches via a mix of intensive, extensive, theoretical and meta-analytical modalities, that have allowed for exploration of an iterative and complex engagement with policy processes in a time of significant policy flux. Relationality between research, policy processes, learning and networking have been a hallmark of the concept of ESE research *as policy engagement*, and this relationality, coupled with ongoing reflexivity and evaluation, has helped us to straddle the ontological divide between 'potentia' and 'potestas', developing not a bifurcated power relation between people andstate in ESE research and policy, but rather a power that can (albeit at times with immense difficulty) combine 'potentia' and 'potestas' productively in the interests of the marginalized and excluded, including the ecological systems and foundations of life which are increasingly more marginalized and excluded from policy and praxis in a neo-liberal dominated world order.

Our argument is that it is necessary to reflexively deepen and expand multi-model ESE research *as policy engagement* in a context of policy flux, where more complex conceptualisations of ESE policy research are required, as also argued by González-Gaudiano (2016) and McKenzie et al. (2015), and as alluded to in the various recommendations for ESE policy research trajectories outlined in the introduction above. This allows for an ongoing re-thinking of the ESE research-policy interface as co-engaged processes of research-and-policy engagement with potential to reduce the negative consequences of the ontological split that Dussel (2008) refers to. Overall, we have argued for ways of considering ESE research *as policy engagement* in ways that are not instrumentalist, and that do not fall into the naïve trap of thinking that linear policy progressive approaches to ESE research-policy engagement are possible in contexts of policy flux. Instead, we suggest that a multimodal approach to ESE research, *if broadly, explicitly and constantly oriented towards a (re)-invigoration of a politics of potentia*, despite the difficulties of this, has potential to enable a generative process of 'staying with the trouble' (Haraway, 2016), while also reflexively reducing the ontological split in the *potentia-potestas* relation.

As shown above, our meta-review has been limited to an extensive body of research (over 150 studies) in one context, South Africa. We have found it quite complex to make sense of this body of research in our meta-review. We found it important to review all the studies and analytically approach them in the time periods from different vantage points (the four trajectories outlined above), but also in relation to the wider macro-policy environment. We have found it useful to do so, to point out that ESE policy research and its actual relationship to policy outcomes and processes are not simplistic, and that they develop differently over time via multi-modal approaches, theoretical deepening, and an ongoing commitment to the possibilities embedded in a *politics of potentia*. As many countries now have the hindsight of 30+ years of ESE policy making and policy-research relations, it may be interesting to conduct similar studies to trace how diverse contexts of policy flux influence the emergence of policy-research relationships and approaches over time.

Notes

1. Fakir (2017) writes in the context of sustainability-oriented transitioning theory, and proposes 'transitioning realism' for emerging economies, noting that transitioning theory overall has fallen foul to socio-technical idealism and instrumentalism, lacking adequate political economy theory, and situated analysis as guide.
2. We use the terms EE and ESE interchangeably, because in South Africa since 1992, sustainability and social-ecological justice concerns have been central to environmental education, the term which was initially favoured as in many global South countries (e.g. Leff, 2009). Over the years, the term and its use has morphed into ESE. Here we agree with Kopnina (2012, 198) who argues that "… the field should put less emphasis on internal discussions about names (EE/ESD) and subnames (sustainable development education, learning for sustainability, education for sustainability, etc.), and instead insist on a radical turn away from neo-liberally and anthropocentrically-biased education" (Van Poeck and Lysgaard, 2016).
3. This is the research programme based at Rhodes University's Environmental Learning Research Centre, but which has worked widely with researchers across the country and with state and civil society actors and other universities engaged in ESE Research in various national coalitions and collaborative ESE policy research and praxis programmes over the past 30+ years.
4. This is not unlike what Bhaskar (1993) refers to as Power 1.
5. Under-labouring here refers to 'philosophical underlabouring' as described by Bhaskar (2016, 1), which means that the research is philosophically informed by critical realist critiques of positivism and hermeneutics.

Disclosure statement

No potential conflict of interest was reported by the author(s).

ORCID

Heila Lotz-Sisitka http://orcid.org/0000-0002-5193-9881
Eureta Rosenberg http://orcid.org/0000-0001-7421-7120

References

Adler, P. 2015. "Book Review Essay: The Environmental Crisis and ItsCapitalist Roots. Reading Naomi Klein with Karl Polanyi." *Administrative Science Quarterly* 60 (2): NP13–25. https://. doi:10.1177/0001839215579183.
Aikens, K., M. McKenzie, and P. Vaughter. 2016. "Environmental and Sustainability Education Policy Research: A Systematic Review of Methodological and Thematic Trends." *Environmental Education Research* 22 (3): 333–359. doi:10.1080/13504622.2015.1135418.
Allais, S. 2003. "The National Qualifications Framework in South Africa: A Democratic Project Trapped in a Neo-Liberal Paradigm?" *Journal of Education and Work* 16 (3): 305–324. doi:10.1080/1363908032000099467.
Amin, A., and P. Howell. 2016. *Releasing the Commons. Rethinking the Future of the Commons*. London: Routledge.
African National Congress (ANC). 1994. *The Reconstruction and Development Programme*. Johannesburg: Umanyano Publishers.
Archer, M. S. 2007. *Making Our Way through the World: Human Reflexivity and Social Mobility*. Cambridge: Cambridge University Press.
Bateson, G. 1972. *Steps to an Ecology of Mind: Collected Essays in Anthropology, Psychiatry, Evolution, and Epistemology*. Chicago: University of Chicago Press.
Bengtsson, S. 2016. "Hegemony and the Politics of Policy Making for Education for Sustainable Development: A Case Study of Vietnam." *The Journal of Environmental Education* 47 (2): 77–90. doi:10.1080/00958964.2015.1021291.
Bhaskar, R. 1978. *A Realist Theory of Science*. Brighton: Harvester Press.
Bhaskar, R. 1979. *Philosophy and the Human Sciences: The Possibility of Naturalism: A Philosophical Critique of the Contemporary Human Sciences*. Brighton: Harvester Press.
Bhaskar, R. 1993. *Dialectic: The Pulse of Freedom*. London: Verso.
Bhaskar, R. 2016. *Enlightened Common Sense: The Philosophy of Critical Realism*. London: Routledge.
Bhorat, H., M. Buthelezi, I. Chipkin, S. Duma, L. Mondi, C. Peter, M. Qobo, M. Swilling, and H. Friedenstein. 2017. Betrayal of the promise. How the nation is being stolen. Interdisciplinary and Interuniversity research partnership: State capacity research project. Accessed May 2017. http://pari.org.za/wp-content/uploads/2017/05/Betrayal-of-the-Promise-25052017.pdf
Beck, U. 1992. *Risk Society: Toward a New Modernity*. London: Sage.
Bernstein, B. 1990. *The Structuring of Pedagogic Discourse: Vol IV Class, Codes and Control*. London: Routledge.
Braidotti, R. 2013. *The Posthuman*. Cambridge: Polity.
Bruner, J. 1997. *The Culture of Education*. Cambridge: Harvard University Press.
Burt, J. C. 1999. "Dramatic Learning. A Case Study of Theatre for Development and Environmental Education." M.Ed. diss., Rhodes University.
Burt, J. C., and T. Lusithi. 2017. "Being the Earth's Comrade." In *Forging Solidarity: Popular Education at Work*, edited by A. von Kotze and S. Walters, 105–116. Rotterdam: Sense Publishers.
Carmody, P. 2002. "Between Globalisation and (Post) Apartheid: The Political Economy of Restructuring in South Africa." *Journal of Southern African Studies* 28 (2): 255–275. doi:10.1080/03057070220140694.
Carr, W., and S. Kemmis. 1986. *Becoming Critical*. Lewes: Falmer.
Cobban, L. and Z. Visser. 2017. *Green Skills for Climate-Smart Agriculture. A case study of poultry, winter grains and deciduous fruit value chains in the Western Cape*. Green Skills Technical Report. Cape Town: University of Cape Town Africa Climate and Development Initiative (ACDI).
Coole, D., and S. Frost. 2010. *New Materialisms: Ontology, Agency and Politics*. Durham: Duke University Press.
Cooper, H., L. Hedges, and J. Valentine, eds. 1994. *The Handbook of Research Synthesis and Meta-Analytical Review*. 2nd ed. New York: Russel Sage Foundation.
Cornbleth, C. 1990. *Curriculum in Context*. London: Falmer Press.
Daniels, H. 2008. *Vygotsky and Research*. New York: Routledge.
De Sousa Santos, B. 2014. *Epistemologies of the South: Justice against Wpistemicide*. New York: Routledge.
Dussel, E. 2008. *Twenty Theses on Politics*. Durham and London: Duke University Press.
Du Toit, D. 1999. "Through Our Eyes: Teachers Using Cameras to Engage in Education Curriculum Development Processes." MEd diss., Rhodes University.
Engeström, Y. 1987. *Learning by Expanding: An Activity-Theoretical Approach to Developmental Research*. Helsinki: Orienta-Konsultit.
Engeström, Y., and A. Sannino. 2010. "Studies of Expansive Learning: Foundations, Findings and Future Challenges." *Educational Research Review* 5 (1): 1–24. doi:10.1016/j.edurev.2009.12.002.

Fakir, S. 2017. *Transition Realism: The Implications of Rent-Seeking to Achieve South Africa's Low-Carbon Technology Ambition*. South Africa: WWF.

Fairclough, N. 1985. "Critical and Descriptive Goals in Discourse Analysis." *Journal of Pragmatics* 9 (6): 739–763. doi: 10.1016/0378-2166(85)90002-5.

Feinstein, N. W., P. R. Jacobi, and H. Lotz-Sisitka. 2013. "When Does a Nation-Level Analysis Make Sense? ESD and Educational Governance in Brazil, South Africa, and the USA." *Environmental Education Research* 19 (2): 218–230. doi:10.1080/13504622.2013.767321.

Fien, J. 1993. *Education for the Environment: Critical Curriculum Theorising and Environmental Education*. Victoria: Deakin University Press.

Freire, P. 1996. *Pedagogy of the Oppressed (Revised)*. New York: Continuum.

Foucault, M. 2003. *The Essential Foucault: Selections from Essential Works of Foucault, 1954-1984*. New York, NY: The New Press

Geels, F. W. 2002. "Technological Transitions as Evolutionary Reconfiguration Processes: A Multi-Level Perspective and a Case-Study." *Research Policy* 31 (8-9): 1257–1274. https://doi.org/10.1016/S0048-7333. (02)00062-8 doi:10.1016/S0048-7333(02)00062-8.

González-Gaudiano, E. 2016. "ESD: Power, Politics, and Policy: "Tragic Optimism" from Latin America." *The Journal of Environmental Education* 47 (2): 118–127. doi:10.1080/00958964.2015.1072704.

Gough, Annette Greenall, and Ian Robottom. 1993. "Towards a Socially Critical Environmental Education: Water Quality Studies in a Coastal School." *Journal of Curriculum Studies* 25 (4): 301–316. doi:10.1080/0022027930250401.

Giqwa, N. 2018. "Waste Management Knowledge, its Production, Recontextualisation and Circulation in Expanded Public Works Programme (EPWP) Training Programmes." PhD Diss., Rhodes University.

Habermas, J. 1972. *Knowledge and Human Interests*. London: Heinemann.

Haraway, D. 2016. *Staying with the Trouble: Making Kin in the Chthulucene*. Durham and London: Duke University Press.

Hattingh, J. 1999. "Finding Creativity in the Diversity of Environmental Ethics." *Southern African Journal of Environmental Education* 19: 68–84.

Jain, H. 2010. "Community Protests in South Africa: Trends, Analysis and Explanations. University of Western Cape." *Community Law Centre (Local Government Working Paper Series No. 1)*.

Janse van Rensburg, E. 1995. "Environmental Education and Research in Southern Africa: A Landscape of Shifting Priorities." PhD diss., Rhodes University.

Janse van Rensburg, E., and H. Lotz-Sisitka. 2000. *Learning for Sustainability: An Environmental Education Professional Development Case Study Informing Education Policy and Practice*. Johannesburg: Learning for Sustainability Project.

Janse van Rensburg, E., and K. Le Roux. 1998. *Gold Fields Participatory Course in Environmental Education: An Evaluation in Process*. Howick: Sharenet.

Jarzabkowski, P., and A. P. Spee. 2009. "Strategy as Practice: A Review and Future Directions for the Field." *International Journal of Management Reviews* 11 (1): 69–95. doi:10.1111/j.1468-2370.2008.00250.x.

Jenkin, N., P. Molebatsi, E. Rosenberg, and P. Ramsarup. 2016. Green Skills in the South African Surface Coatings Sector: A Focus on Paint. Green Skills Technical Report: Chemicals Industry Education and Training Authority (CHIETA). www.greenskills.co.za.

Khumalo, F. E. 2000. "Environment as Integrating Organiser: A Case Study of Curriculum 2005 in KwaMhlanga, South Africa." MEd diss., Rhodes University.

Kopnina, H. 2012. "Education for Sustainable Development (ESD): The Turn Away from 'Environment' in Environmental Education?" *Environmental Education Research* 18 (5): 699–717. doi:10.1080/13504622.2012.658028.

Kurtz, C. F., and D. J. Snowden. 2003. "The New Dynamics of Strategy: Sense-Making in a Complex and Complicated World." *IBM Systems Journal* 42 (3): 462–483. DOI: 10.1147/sj.423.0462

Kulundu, I. 2017. "Change Drivers at the Front Lines of the Future: Rising Cultures for Sustainability Education in Contemporary South Africa." In *Envisioning Futures for Environment and Sustainability Education*, edited by P. Corcoran, J. Weakland & A.E.J. Wals,419–426. Wageningen: Wageningen Academic Publishers. 10.3920/978-90-8686-846-9_33.

Laessøe, J., N. W. Feinstein, and N. Blum. 2013. "Environmental Education Policy Research – Challenges and Ways Research Might Cope with Them." *Environmental Education Research* 19 (2): 231–242. doi:10.1080/13504622.2013.778230.

Lather, P. 1991. *Getting Smart: Feminist Research and Pedagogy with/in the Postmodern*. New York: Routledge.

Latour, B. 1987. *Science in Action*. Cambridge: Harvard University Press.

Lave, J., and E. Wenger. 1991. *Situated Learning: Legitimate Peripheral Participation*. Cambridge: University of Cambridge Press.

Leff, E. 2009. "Latin American Environmental Thought." Paper Presented at the 6th Latin American Congress of Environmental Education, San Clemente de Tuyu, Argentina, September 19, 2009.

Le Grange, L. 2012. "Ubuntu, Ukama and the Healing of Nature, Self and Society." *Educational Philosophy and Theory* 44 (Supp 2): 56–67. doi:10.1111/j.1469-5812.2011.00795.x.

Le Grange, L., and C. Reddy. 1997. "Environmental Education and Outcomes-Based Education in South Africa: A Marriage Made in Heaven?" *Southern African Journal of Environmental Education. 17: 12-18.*

Le Grange, L., and C. Reddy. 2000. "Introducing Teachers to Outcomes-Based Education and Environmental Education: A Western Cape Case Study." *South African Journal of Education* 20 (1): 21–25.

Long, S. S. 1994. "Towards the Development of an Environmental Curriculum for Members of the Planning Professions." MEd diss., Rhodes University.

Lindley, D. 2014. "Can Expansive (Social) Learning Processes Strengthen Organisational Learning for Improved Wetland Management in a Plantation Forestry Company, and if so how? A Case Study of Mondi." PhD Diss., Rhodes University.

Lotz, H. 1996. "The Development Of Environmental Education Resource Materials for Junior Primary Education through Teacher Participation: The Case of the We Care Primary Project." PhD diss., Stellenbosch University.

Lotz-Sisitka, H. 2000. "The Learning for Sustainability Project: Insights into Policy Implementation in South Africa." In *Monograph: Learning for Sustainability: An Environmental Education Professional Development Case Study Informing Education Policy and Practice*, edited by E. Janse van Rensburg & H. Lotz-Sisitka, 103–113. Johannesburg: Learning for Sustainability Project.

Lotz-Sisitka, H. 2002. "Curriculum Patterning in Environmental Education: A Review of Developments in Formal Education in South Africa." In *EEASA Monograph: Environmental Education, Ethics and Action in Southern Africa*, edited by E. Janse van Rensburg, J. Hattingh, H. Lotz-Sisitka & R. O'Donoghue, 97–120. Cape Town: HSRC Press.

Lotz-Sisitka, H. 2004. *Positioning Southern African Environmental Education in a Changing Context.* Howick: Share-Net/SADC REEP.

Lotz-Sisitka, H. 2008a. Change oriented workplace learning and sustainability practices. Research proposal for the SAQA Work and Learning Research Partnership Programme, Rhodes University, South Africa.

Lotz-Sisitka, H. 2008b. "Environmental Education and Educational Quality and Relevance: Opening the Debate." *Southern African Journal of Environmental Education* 25: 5–12.

Lotz-Sisitka, H. 2009. "Epistemological Access as an Open Question in Education." *Journal of Education* 46: 57–79.

Lotz-Sisitka, H. 2011. "Teacher Professional Development with an Education for Sustainable Development Focus in South Africa: Development of a Network, Curriculum Framework and Resources for Teacher Education." *Southern African Journal of Environmental Education* 28: 30–71.

Lotz-Sisitka, H. 2014. "We Must Start with Our Own Children: Reflectively Researching Intergenerational Leadership for Social Justice, Education, and Sustainability." In *Intergenerational Learning and Transformative Leadership for Sustainable Futures*, edited by P.B. Corcoran & B. Hollingshead, 43–64. Wageningen: Wageningen Academic Press.

Lotz-Sisitka, H. 2016a. "Reviewing Strategies in/for ESD Policy Engagement: Agency Reclaimed?" *The Journal of Environmental Education* 47 (2): 91–103. doi:10.1080/00958964.2015.1113915.

Lotz-Sisitka, H. 2016b. "A Review of Three Generations of Critical Theory: Towards Reconceptualsing Critical HESD Research." In *Routledge Handbook of Higher Education Research for Sustainable Development*, edited by M. Baarth, G. Michelsen, M. Rieckmann & I. Thomas, 207–222. London: Routledge.

Lotz-Sisitka, H. 2017a. "Decolonising as Future Frame for Environment and Sustainability Education." In *Envisioning Futures for Environment and Sustainability Educationm*, edited by P. Corcoran, J. Weakland & A.E.J. Wals, 45–62. Wageningen: Wageningen Academic Publishers. 10.3920/978-90-8686-846-9_2.

Lotz-Sisitka, H. 2017b. "Education and the Common Good." In *Post-Sustainability: Remaking Education*, edited by B. Jickling & S. Sterling, 63–78. London: Palgrave MacMillan.

Lotz-Sisitka, H., and J. Burt. 2006. A critical review of participatory practice in integrated water resource management. WRC report No. 1434/1/06. Pretoria: Water Research Commission.

Lotz-Sisitka, H., and J. Lupele. 2017. "ESD, Learning and Quality Education in Africa: Learning Today, for Tomorrow." In *Schooling and Sustainable Development in Africa. Schooling for Sustainable Development*, edited by H. Lotz-Sisitka, O. Shumba, J. Lupele & D. Wilmot, 3–24. Cham: Springer. 10.1007/978-3-319-45989-9_1.

Lotz-Sisitka, H., and C. Olivier. 1998. "Clarifying Orientations to Learning Programme Development within the OBE Curriculum Framework and the Learning for Sustainability Curriculum 2005 Pilot Project in Gauteng and Mpumalanga. Unpublished paper presented at the Outcomes Based Education International Symposium, Vista University, 17-18 November, 1998.

Lotz-Sisitka, H., T. Pesanayi, K. Weaver, C. Lupele, L. Sisitka, R. O'Donoghue, J. Denison, and K. Phillips. 2016. *Water use and food security: Knowledge dissemination and use in agricultural colleges and local learning networks for home food gardening and smallholder agriculture. Volume 1: Research and development report*. WRC Research Report No. 2277/1/16, 198.

Lotz-Sisitka, H., and P. Ramsarup. 2017a. "Learning Pathways and Articulation: Early Conceptual Explorations and Implications for Research Design(s)." *SAQA Bulletin: Learning Pathways, the National Qualifications Framework (NQF), and Lifelong Learning in South Africa* 17 (1): 27–50.

Lotz-Sisitka, H., and P. Ramsarup. 2017b. "Using Dialectical Critical Realism in the Analysis of Career Stories in Learning Pathways Research." *SAQA Bulletin: Learning Pathways, the National Qualifications Framework (NQF), and Lifelong Learning in South Africa* 17 (1): 109–136.

Lotz-Sisitka, H. B., and P. Ramsarup. 2020. "Green Skills Research: Implications for Systems, Policy, Work and Learning." In *Green Skills Research in South Africa. Models, Cases and Methods*, edited by E. Rosenberg, P. Ramsarup & H. Lotz-Sisitka, 208–223. London: Routledge.

Lotz-Sisitka, H., and G. Raven. 2001. *Active Learning in OBE: Research Report of the National Environmental Education Programme – GET Pilot Research Project*. Pretoria: Department of Education.

Lupele, J. 2008. "Networking: Enabling Professional Development and Institutionalization of environmental education courses in southern Africa." PhD diss., Rhodes University.

Mamdani, M. 1996. *Citizen and Subject: Contemporary Africa and the Legacy of Late Colonialism*. Kampala: Fountain Publishers; London: James Currey; Princeton: Princeton University Press.

Mbanjwa, S. 2003. "The use of environmental education learning support materials in OBE: The case of the creative solutions to waste project." MEd diss., Rhodes University.

Mbembe, A. 2001. *On the Postcolony*. 41 Vols. California: University of California Press.

Mbembe, A. 2003. "Necropolitcs." *Public Culture* 15 (1): 11–40. doi:10.1215/08992363-15-1-11.

Mbengashe, P. M. 1994. "Environmental Perceptions And Knowledge Among Political Leaders in the Eastern Cape Province and Some Implications for Environmental Policy." MEd diss., Rhodes University.

McGarry, D. 2013. "Empathy in the Time of Ecological Apartheid. A Social Sculpture-Practice Led Inquiry into Developing Pedagogies for Ecological Citizenship." PhD diss., Rhodes University.

McKenzie, Marcia, Andrew Bieler, and Rebecca McNeil. 2015. "Education Policy Mobility: Reimagining Sustainability in Neoliberal Times." *Environmental Education Research* 21 (3): 319–337. doi:10.1080/13504622.2014.993934.

Meadows, D. H. 2008. *Thinking in Systems*. Vermont: Chelsea Green Publishing.

Mendieta, E. 2008. "Foreword: The Liberation of Politics: Alterity, Solidarity, Liberation." In *Twenty Theses on Politics*. Translated and edited by George Ciccariello-Maher & E. Dussel, vii–xiii. Durham, NC and London: Duke University Press.

Mignolo, W. D. 2002. "The Geopolitics of Knowledge and the Colonial Difference." *South Atlantic Quarterly* 101 (1): 57–97. doi:10.1215/00382876-101-1-57.

Molose, V. I. 2000. "Materials in Flexible Learning Teacher Education Courses in Environmental Education: An Evaluative Case Study." MEd diss., Rhodes University.

Mohanoe, N. 2014. "Learning Pathways of Key Occupations Relevant to Sustainable Development in Makana Municipality." MEd diss., Rhodes University.

Morrow, W. 2007. *Learning to Teach in South Africa*. Pretoria: HSRC Press.

Moore, J. W. 2015. *Capitalism in the Web of Life: Ecology and the Accumulation of Capital*. New York: Verso Books.

Mrazek, R. 1993. (Ed.). *Alternative Paradigms in Environmental Education Research. Monographs in Environmental Education and Environmental Education Studies*. Troy: North American Association of Environmental Education.

Mukute, M. 2010. "Expanding and Exploring Learning in Sustainable Agriculture Activity Systems." PhD diss., Rhodes University.

Mukute, M., and H. Lotz-Sisitka. 2012. "Working with Cultural Historical Activity Theory and Critical Realism to Investigate and Expand Farmer Learning in Southern Africa." *Mind, Culture and Activity Journal* 19 (4): 342–367. doi:10.1080/10749039.2012.656173.

Muller, J. 2012. *Reclaiming Knowledge: Social Theory, Curriculum and Education Policy*. London: Routledge.

Naidoo, P. 1993. "Collaborative Teacher Participation in Curriculum Development: A Case Study in Junior Secondary General Science." MEd diss., Rhodes University.

Nduna, N. R. 2004. "The Use of Environmental Learning Support Materials to Mediate Learning in Outcomes-Based Education: A Case Study in an Eastern Cape school." MEd diss., Rhodes University.

NEEP-GET. 2005. *A Critical Dialogues Monograph. Building Capacity for Environmental Learning in South Africa's Education System: Openings for the UN Decade on Education for Sustainable Development*. Howick: National Environmental Education Project for General Education and Training/share-Net.

Nhamo, G. 2005. "Environmental Policy Processes Surrounding South Africa's Plastic Bags Regulations: Tensions, Debates and Responses in Waste Product Regulation." PhD Diss., Rhodes University.

Nsubuga, Y. 2010. "The Integration of Natural Resource Management into the Curriculum of Rural Under-Resourced Schools." PhD Diss., Rhodes University.

O'Donoghue, R. 1990. "Environmental Education, Evaluation and Curriculum Change: The Case of the Action Ecology Project 1985-1989." MEd Diss., University of Natal, Pietermaritzburg

O'Donoghue, R. 1993. *The Environment, Development and Environmental Education: Environmental Education Policy Initiative (EEPI)*. Howick: Share-Net.

O'Donoghue, R. 1997. "Detached Harmonies: A Study in/on Developing Social Processes of Environmental Education in Eastern Southern Africa." PhD Diss., Rhodes University.

O'Donoghue, R. 2000. *Environment and Active Learning in OBE: NEEP Guidelines for Facilitating and Assessing Active Learning in OBE*. Howick: Share-Net.

O'Donoghue, R., and E. Neluvhalani. 2002. "Indigenous Knowledge and the School Curriculum: A Review of Developing Methods and Methodological Perspectives." In *EEASA Monograph: Environmental Education, Ethics and Action in Southern Africa*, edited by E. Janse van Rensburg, J. Hattingh, H. Lotz-Sisitka & R. O'Donoghue, 121–134. Cape Town: EEASA/Human Sciences Research Council.

O'Donoghue, R. B. 2016a. "Evaluation and Education for Sustainable Development (ESD): Navigating a Shifting Landscape in Regional Centres of Expertise (RCEs)." In *Routledge Handbook of Higher Education Research for Sustainable Development*, edited by M. Baarth, G. Michelsen, M. Rieckmann & I. Thomas, 223–238. London: Routledge.

O'Donoghue, R. 2016b. "Working with Critical Realist Perspective and Tools at the Interface of Indigenous and Scientific Knowledge in a Science Curriculum Setting." In *Critical Realism, Environmental Learning and Social-Ecological Change*, edited by L. Price & H. Lotz-Sisitka, 159–177. London: Routledge.

O'Donoghue, R. 2017. "Situated Learning in Relation to Human Conduct and Social-Ecological Change." In *Schooling for Sustainable Development in Africa. Schooling for Sustainable Development*, edited by H. Lotz-Sisitka, O. Shumba, J. Lupele & D. Wilmot, 25–38. Cham: Springer. 10.1007/978-3-319-45989-9_2.

Olvitt, L., V. Malema, and H. Lotz-Sisitka. 2005. *Analysis of the education and training needs implied in selected key environmental legislation. An analytical study conducted for the Department of Environmental Affairs and Tourism.* Technical Research Report, 108. South Africa: Place A& DEAT.

Olvitt, L. 2004. "The Adaptive Development and use of Learning Support Materials in Response to the First Principle of the Revised Curriculum Statement: The Case of Hadeda Island." MEd diss., Rhodes University.

Olvitt, L. 2012. "Deciding and doing what's Right for People and Planet: An Investigation of the Ethics-Orientated Learning of Novice Environmental Educators." PhD diss., Rhodes University.

Ostrom, E. 2010. "Beyond Markets and States: Polycentric Governance of Complex Economic Systems." *American Economic Review (American Economic Association)* 100 (3): 641–672. doi:10.1257/aer.100.3.641.

Pahl-Wostl, Claudia, David Tàbara, Rene Bouwen, Marc Craps, Art Dewulf, Erik Mostert, Dagmar Ridder, and Tharsi Taillieu. 2007. "Social Learning and Water Resources Management." *Ecological Economics* 64 (3): 484–495. doi:10.1016/j.ecolecon.2007.08.007.

Pawson, R., and N. Tilley. 1997. *Realist Evaluation*. London: Sage.

Peet, R. 2002. "Ideology, Discourse, and the Geography of Hegemony: From Socialist to Neoliberal Development in Postapartheid South Africa." *Antipode* 34 (1): 54–84. doi:10.1111/1467-8330.00226.

Pesanayi, T. 2016. "Exploring Contradictions and Absences in Mobilizing 'Learning as Process' for Sustainable Agricultural Practices." In *Critical Realism, Environmental Learning and Social-Ecological Change*, edited by L. Price & H. Lotz-Sisitka, 230–253. London: Taylor and Francis.

Pesanayi, T. 2019. "Boundary Crossing Expansive Learning Across Agricultural Learning Systems and Networks in Southern Africa." PhD diss., Rhodes University.

Popkewitz, T. 1991. *A Political Sociology of Educational Reform: Power/Knowledge in Teaching, Teacher Education and Research*. New York: Teachers College Press.

Price, L. 2007. "A Transdisciplinary Explanatory Critique of Environmental Education." PhD PhD diss., Rhodes University.

Price, L., & Lotz-Sisitka, H. eds. 2016. *Critical Realism, Environmental Learning and Social-Ecological Change*. London: Routledge.

Patton, M. Q. 2011. *Developmental Evaluation. Applying Complexity Concepts to Enhance Innovation and Use*. New York: Guilford.

Ramsarup, P. 2006. "Cases of Recontextualising the Environmental Discourse in the National Curriculum Statement (R-9)." MEd diss., Rhodes University.

Ramsarup, P. 2016. "Absenting the Absence of Parallel Learning Pathways for Intermediate Skills: The 'Missing Middle' in the Environmental Sector in South Africa." In *Critical Realism, Environmental Learning and Social-Ecological Change*, edited by L. Price & H. Lotz-Sisitka, 116–136. London: Routledge.

Ramsarup, P. 2017a. "A Critical Realist Dialectical Understanding of Learning Pathways Associated with Two Scarce Skill Environmental Occupations within a Transitioning Systems Frame." PhD Diss., Rhodes University.

Ramsarup, P. 2017b. "Systems Elements Influencing the Emergence of Learning Pathways from a Green Skills Perspective." *SAQA Bulletin: Learning Pathways, the National Qualifications Framework (NQF), and Lifelong Learning in South Africa* 17 (1): 217–254.

Ramsarup, P., and H. Lotz-Sisitka. 2017. "An Expanded Methodological View on Learning Pathways as Educational and Occupational Progression: A Laminated Systems Perspective." *SAQA Bulletin: Learning Pathways, the National Qualifications Framework (NQF), and Lifelong Learning in South Africa* 17 (1): 255–280.

Raven, G. 2005. "Enabling Reflexivity and the Development of Reflexive Competence within Course Processes: a Case Study of an Environmental Education Professional Development Course." PhD diss., Rhodes University.

Ramsarup, P., and M. Ward. 2017. Enabling Green Skills pathways to sustainable development. A source book to support skills planning for green economies. Environmental Learning Research Centre/Wits REAL. www.greenskills.co.za

Ramsarup, P., E. Rosenberg, H. Lotz-Sisitka, and N. Jenkin. 2018. "Green Skills: Transformative Niches for Greening Work." In *Sustainability Transitions in South Africa*, edited by N. Mohammed. London: Routledge.

Raworth, K. 2017. *Doughnut Economics: Seven Ways to Think like a 21st-Century Economist*. London: Random House.

Reddy, C. 2004. "Democracy and in-Service Processes for Teachers: A Debate about Professional Teacher Development Programmes." In *Imaginaries on Democratic Education and Change*, edited by Y. Waghid & L. Le Grange. Pretoria: Southern African Association for Research and Development in Higher Education.

Reddy, C. 2017. "Inaugural Address: Environmental Education and Teacher Development." *Southern African Journal of Environmental Education* 33 (1): 117–129. doi:10.4314/sajee.v.33i1.9.
Republic of South Africa (RSA). 1995. *White Paper on Education and Training*. Pretoria: Department of Education.
Republic of South Africa (RSA). 1996. *Constitution of the Republic of South Africa*. Pretoria: Government Printers.
Republic of South Africa (RSA). 1998. *National Water Act 36*. Pretoria: Government Printer.
Rickinson, M., M. Hall, and A. Reid. 2016. "Sustainable Schools Programmes: What Influence on Schools and How Do we Know?" *Environmental Education Research* 22 (3): 360–389. doi:10.1080/13504622.2015.1077505.
Rivers, N. 2014. "The Mediating Processes within Social Learning: Women's Food and Water Security Practices in the Rural Eastern Cape." PhD Diss., Rhodes University.
Robottom, I. 1991. "Technocratic Environmental Education: A Critique and Some Alternatives." *Journal of Experiential Education* 14 (1): 20–25. doi:10.1177/105382599101400103.
Robottom, I., and P. Hart. 1993. *Research in Environmental Education – Engaging the Debate*. Australia: Deakin University.
Rosenberg, E., and J. Taylor. 2005. *Mondi Wetlands Project Evaluation: Final Report*. MWP, Pretoria: South Africa.
Rosenberg, E. 2008. "Eco Schools and the Quality of Education in South Africa. Realising the Potential." *Southern African Journal of Environmental Education* 20: 25–43.
Rosenberg, E. 2009. *Evaluation of the Eco-Schools South Africa Programme: 2007-2008*. Howick: WESSA.
Rosenberg, E., H. Lotz-Sisitka, P. Ramsarup, M. Togo, and A. Mphinyane. 2015. *Green Skills for the Mining Sector*. Green Skills Technical Report on Research for the Mining Qualifications Authority. Rhodes University and MQA. www.greenskills.co.za
Rosenberg, E., G. Rosenberg, P. Ramsarup, and H. Lotz-Sisitka. 2016a. *Green Economy Learning Assessment South Africa: Critical Competencies for Driving a Green Transition*. Pretoria: DEA, DHET, UNITAR.
Rosenberg, E., P. Ramsarup, S. Gumede, and H. Lotz-Sisitka. 2016b. "Building Capacity for Green, Just and Sustainable Futures: A New Knowledge Field Requiring Transformative Research Methodology." *South African Journal of Education* 65: 95–122.
Rosenberg, E., P. Ramsarup, and H. B. Lotz-Sisitka. 2020. *Green Skills Research in South Africa: Models, Cases and Methods*. London: Routledge.
South African National Biodiversity Institute (SANBI) / Lewis Foundation. 2010. *National Biodiversity Human Capital Development Strategy*. SANBI and Lewis Foundation, Pretoria.
Sayer, A. 2010. *Method in Social Science: revised 2nd Edition*. London: Routledge.
Sayer, A. 2000. *Realism and Social Science*. London: Sage
Sauls, G. 2018. "The National Skills Fund and Green Skills: Towards a Generative Mechanism Approach." PhD diss., Rhodes University.
Shava, S. 1999. "The Use of Indigenous Plants as Food by a Rural Community in the Eastern Cape: Tuku 'A' Village, Peddie." *Southern African Journal of Environmental Education* 19: 85–97.
Shava, S. 2008. "Indigenous Knowledges: A Genealogy of Representations and Applications in Developing Contexts of Environmental Education and Development in Southern Africa." PhD diss., Rhodes University.
Schön, D. A. 1987. *Educating the Reflective Practitioner: Toward a New Design for Teaching and Learning in the Professions*. Hoboken, NJ: Jossey-Bass.
Schudel, I. 2012. "Examining Emergent Active Learning Processes as Transformative Praxis: The Case of the Schools and Sustainability Professional Development Programme." PhD diss., Rhodes University.
Schudel, I. 2014. "Exploring a Knowledge-Focused Trajectory for Researching Environmental Learning in the South African Curriculum." *Southern African Journal of Environmental Education* 30: 96–117.
Schudel, I. 2017. "Deliberations on a Changing Curriculum Landscape and Emergent Environmental and Sustainability Education Practices in South Africa." In *Schooling for Sustainable Development in Africa. Schooling for Sustainable Development*, edited by H. Lotz-Sisitka, O. Shumba, J. Lupele, D. Wilmot, 39–54. Cham: Springer. 10.1007/978-3-319-45989-9_3.
South Africa: Department of Education. 1997. *Curriculum 2005 Learning Area Statements*. Pretoria: Government Printer.
South Africa: Department of Education. 2012. *Curriculum and Assessment Policy Statement*. Pretoria: Government Printers.
South Africa: Department of Higher Education and Training (DHET). 2009. *National Skills Development Strategy III*. Pretoria: DHET.
South Africa: Department of Higher Education and Training (DHET). 2013. *White Paper for Post-School Education and Training: building an Expanded, Effective and Integrated Post-School System*. Pretoria: DHET.
South Africa: Department of Environmental Affairs (DEA). 2010. *Environmental Sector Skills Plan. Towards a Systemic Approach to Human Capacity Development*. Pretoria: DEA
South Africa. Department of Science and Technology (DST). 2010. *Human Capital Development Strategy for the Global Change Grand Challenge*. Pretoria: DST.
South Africa. Economic Development Department. 2011. *New Growth Path Accord 4: Green Economy Accord*. Pretoria: Government Printers.

South Africa. National Planning Commission (NPC). 2011. *National Development Plan 2030: Our Future - Make It Work*. Boksburg: Sherino Printers.

Songqwaru, N. Z. 2012. "Supporting Environment and Sustainability Knowledge in the Grade 10 Life Sciences Curriculum and Assessment Policy Context: A Case Study of the Fundisa for Change Teacher Education and Development Programme Pilot Project. South Africa." MEd diss., Rhodes University.

Songqwaru, N. Z. 2020. "A Theory-Based Approach to Evaluating a Continuing Professional Development Programme Aimed at Strengthening Environment and Sustainability Education." PhD Diss., Rhodes University.

Streeck, W. 2014. *Buying Time: The Delayed Crisis of Democratic Capitalism*. New York: Verso Books.

Swilling, Mark, Josephine Musango, and Jeremy Wakeford. 2016. "Developmental States and Sustainability Transitions: Prospects of a Just Transition in South Africa." *Journal of Environmental Policy & Planning* 18 (5): 650–672. doi:10.1080/1523908X.2015.1107716.

Togo, M. 2009. "A Systems Approach to Mainstreaming Environment and Sustainability in Universities: The Case of Rhodes University. South africa." PhD diss., Rhodes University.

Togo, M., and H. Lotz-Sisitka. 2009. *Unit-Based Sustainability Assessment Tool. A Resource Book to Complement the UNEP Mainstreaming Environment and Sustainability in African Universities Partnership*. Howick: UNEP/Share-net.

Togo, M., and H. Lotz-Sisitka. 2013. "Exploring a Systems Approach to Mainstreaming Sustainability in Universities: A Case Study of Place Ain South Africa." *Environmental Education Research Journal* 19 (5): 673–693. doi:10.1080/13504622.2012.749974.

Tshiningayamwe, S., and N. Z. Songqwaru. 2017. "Towards Professional Learning Communities: A Review." In *Schooling for Sustainable Development in Africa*, edited by H. Lotz-Sisitka, O. Shumba, J. Lupele, D. Wilmot, 259–257. Cham: Springer. 10.1007/978-3-319-45989-9_19.

Vallabh, P. 2017. "Transforming Epistemic Cultures in ESE with Citizen and Civic Sciences as Means for Reframing Participation in the Commons." In *Envisioning Futures for Environment and Sustainability Education*, edited by P. Corcoran & J. Weakland. Wageningen: Wageningen Academic Publishers.

Van Damme, Lynette Sibongile Masuku, and Edgar Fulufhelo Neluvhalani. 2004. "Indigenous Knowledge in Environmental Education Processes: Perspectives on a Growing Research Arena." *Environmental Education Research* 10 (3): 353–370. doi:10.1080/1350462042000258189.

Vass, J., B. Bantwana, and A. Wildschutt. 2009. *Guidelines towards a Human Capital Development Strategy in the Biodiversity Sector*. Pretoria: HSRC (Human Sciences Research Council).

Van Poeck, Katrien, Joke Vandenabeele, and Hans Bruyninckx. 2014. "Taking Stock of the UN Decade of Education for Sustainable Development: The Policy-Making Process in Flanders." *Environmental Education Research* 20 (5): 695–717. doi:10.1080/13504622.2013.836622.

Van Poeck, Katrien, and Jonas A. Lysgaard. 2016. "Editorial: The Roots and Routes of Environmental and Sustainability Education Policy Research." *Environmental Education Research* (VSI Special Issue), 22 (3): 305–318. doi:10.1080/13504622.2015.1108393.

Vygotsky, L. S. 1978. *Mind in Society: The Development of Higher Psychological Processes*. Cambridge: Harvard University Press.

2007. Wals, A.E.J. (Ed.) *Social Learning towards a Sustainable World*. Wageningen: Wageningen Academic Publishers.

Wagiet, M. F. 1996. "Teaching the Principles of Ecology in the Urban Environment: An Investigation into the Development of Resource Materials." MEd diss., Rhodes University.

Wagiet, R. 1997. Environmental Education: A Strategy for Primary Teacher Education." PhD Diss., Rhodes University.

Ward, M., N. Jenkin, E. Rosenberg, and P. Ramsarup. 2016. "Occupationally directed skills development for green public supply chain management." *PSETA and Rhodes University*, www.greenskills.co.za

Whittemore, Robin, and Kathleen Knafl. 2005. "The Integrative Review: Updated Methodology." *Journal of Advanced Nursing* 52 (5): 546–553. doi:10.1111/j.1365-2648.2005.03621.x.

Young, M. I. C. H. A. E. L., and J. O. H. A. N. Muller. 2010. "Three Educational Scenarios for the Future: Lessons from the Sociology of Knowledge." *European Journal of Education* 45 (1): 11–27. doi:10.1111/j.1465-3435.2009.01413.x.

Appendix A. Meta-review of ESE research over A 30+ year period

Critical Incident Period	Wider methodological processes and theory shaping ESE research in this period:	South/ern Africa ESE research-policy engagement processes and selected studies contributing to the ESE policy engagement trajectory:	Outcomes of the research-policy engagement processes – in terms of policy, but also in terms of engaging the 'ontological split' between a politics of *potentia* and *potestus*; and (re)-invigorating a politics of *potentia*
POLICY PREPARATION Early 1990's (1992 – 1996) Unbanning of the African National Congress and preparatory policy making for a new democracy featuring environmental justice, sustainable development discourses.	Critical and reflexive forms of participatory action research to mobilise a policy engagement constituency and policy engagement capital across resistance movement, newly emerging state, civil society and research entities. Theoretical resources included critical social theory (Carr and Kemmis, 1986; Fien, 1993); critiques of positivist research (Robottom, 1991) and the 'paradigms debate' (Mrazek 1993; Robottom and Hart, 1993); the concepts of democracy and social justice and the notion of sustainable development as integrating poverty and environmental concerns (1992 Earth Summit and UNCED). Principles of Environmental Education released by the NGO Forum at the 1992 Rio Earth Summit are particularly influential in shaping EE research and praxis in southern Africa. Local theorist O'Donoghue (1993) is particularly influential with his work informing the inclusion of environment and sustainability across the national system as an inclusive, transformatory, critically reflexive approach to development, rather than its opposite.	National policy network formations such as the Environmental Education Policy Initiative (EEPI) are formed as state-civil society partnership engagement forums, where research and policy could 'compost'. The post-apartheid Environmental Justice Network was a key participant in shaping early environmental and environmental education policy and praxis in the country and formed part of the civil society and research actors engaging with new state formation policies, the EEPI and later also the EECI. Case studies, often with a participatory action research methodology, including O'Donoghue (1990), Naidoo (1993); Lotz (1996); Wagiet (1996) formed the early foundations of ESE policy engaged research. Mbengashe (1994) and Long (1994) were among those who looked at EE/ESE needs for professional development to inform policy for government and industry contexts.	From a policy outcomes perspective: Inclusion of environmental education in the *White Paper on Education and Training* (RSA, 1995); the formation of a network of emerging ESE professionals and the establishment of an enduring working relationship between academia, civil society and government departments around environment and education, that is still used today for policy comment, input and implementation strategies. This is consolidated by the parallel process of inclusion of environment as a human right in the Bill of Rights in the South African Constitution (RSA, 1996), henceforth shaping ESE policy substantively. From a politics as *potentia* perspective: Environmental education was recognised within the ANC as holding 'politics as *potentia*' and as a critical area for social justice and claiming of inclusivity in relation to the country's natural resources, land and participation in environmental justice. The relationship between environment, human rights, social justice and sustainability is enshrined in the Constitution in 1996 and significantly shapes a 'politics as *potentia*' orientation to ESE praxis and ongoing research.
POLICY PROLIFERATION: Mid-end 1990's (1994-2000) New policy formulation across sectors including education and environment (policy proliferation).	Scoping, contextual profiling and analytical research to put forward 'policy proposals' via a series of 'enabling documents' and policy engagement 'toolkits'. These provided resources or mediating tools for policy actors to draw on during engaged policy making	Formation of the Environmental Education Curriculum Initiative (EECI) out of the EEPI; Standards Generating Bodies; professional learning networks and courses; and a burgeoning of studies in, of and for EE/ESE, including case studies by Du Toit (1999); Burt	From a policy outcomes perspective: Inclusion of the relational principle of environmental justice, human rights and inclusivity in the national curriculum statements (South Africa: DoE, 1997); and early efforts of integrating this principle into curriculum praxis in schools

(continued)

Appendix A. Continued.

Critical Incident Period	Wider methodological processes and theory shaping ESE research in this period:	South/ern Africa ESE research-policy engagement processes and selected studies contributing to the ESE policy engagement trajectory:	Outcomes of the research-policy engagement processes – in terms of policy, but also in terms of engaging the 'ontological split' between a politics of *potentia* and *potestus*; and (re)-invigorating a politics of *potentia*
National ESE projects and programmes in partnership with international donor agencies shape local curricula and policy.	and sense-making processes (e.g. O'Donoghue, 1993). Theoretical resources for this research were drawn from constructivist (Vygotsky, 1978; Bruner, 1997); socially critical pedagogy (Fein, 1993; Gough & Robottom, 1993); active learning theory (O'Donoghue, 2000), and the theories and methodologies of critically engaged praxis (Freire, 1996; Schön, 1987; Lather, 1991). Habermas' (1972) technical, practical and emancipatory knowledge interests help to ground and deepen engagement with these orientations, and Cornbleth's (1990) critical curriculum theorizing frames curriculum policy research as both 'blueprint' and contextualized social process. Popkewitz's social epistemology (1991) provided a critique of linear research-design-develop-adopt policy reforms and Beck's (1992) (Risk Society) introduces the concepts of risk and reflexivity.	(1999); Lotz-Sisitka and Olivier (1998); Molose (2000); Khumalo (2000) providing early insights into the implications of the new outcomes-based national curriculum and associated professional learning of teachers and educators. Janse van Rensburg (1995) called for reflexivity in the choice of research design for transformatory purposes; O'Donoghue's PhD (1997) introduces longer term social historical process to guide ESE research, and introduces a focus on indigenous knowledge into educational policy dialogues. Early research and evaluation of ESE courses informs qualifications design on the NQF (Janse van Rensburg and Le Roux, 1998; Molose, 2000) and engagement with ethics research (Hattingh, 1999) informs the first ESE ethics-based unit standard influencing qualifications design and development. Wagiet draws on her own research (1997), and formative evaluations and summative pilot evaluations of national ESE projects (Janse van Rensburg & Lotz-Sisitka, 2000; Lotz-Sisitka & Raven, 2001) to establish a National Environmental Education Programme for schools in her role as advisor to the Education Minister.	and teacher professional development contexts. Research informs the national curriculum statements, and national approaches to teacher professional development as well as new standards and qualifications design processes under the new National Qualifications Framework. **From a politics as *potentia* perspective:** Development of the first environmental qualifications for workers in South Africa in the context of the new South African national qualifications framework in areas of environmental management and environmental health. The study field of environment (framed within a human rights, social justice and sustainability orientation) becomes available for the majority of South Africa's people, including all of the nation's children, for the first time in the country's history.
INITIAL POLICY FAILURES: Early 2000's (2000 – 2005) Start of serious post-apartheid policy failure in the new democracy	The introduction of post-structural research, indigenous knowledge research, continuation of contextual profiling, critical reviews and action-oriented research. A large scale bi-lateral programme in biodiversity provides opportunities for renewed focus on EE/conservation education at all levels of society, from schools to workplaces; this work is comprehensively	Formation of research and policy forums around interest areas such as indigenous knowledge; biodiversity education; curriculum innovation in Higher Education; and workplace skills for sustainability. Critical ESD policy engagement intensifies (Lotz-Sisitka, 2000, 2004) and growing critiques of outcomes-based education and donor influences on ESE policy emerge (Le Grange	**From a policy outcomes perspective:** A deepening understanding of the societal and changing social-ecological context in which policy engagement was taking place; tracking back to structural dynamics and constraints and continuities in post-colonial power relations, marginalisations and system malfunctions. A sense of policy disillusion and 'drying up' seems to form as significant

(*continued*)

Appendix A. Continued.

Critical Incident Period	Wider methodological processes and theory shaping ESE research in this period:	South/ern Africa ESE research-policy engagement processes and selected studies contributing to the ESE policy engagement trajectory:	Outcomes of the research-policy engagement processes – in terms of policy, but also in terms of engaging the 'ontological split' between a politics of *potentia* and *potestus*; and (re)-invigorating a politics of *potentia*
	evaluated but standardized approaches prove unsuitable for evaluating educational components. Theoretical influences included Fairclough's critical discourse analysis (1985) and Foucault's (2003) genealogical work. Postcolonial theorists begin to offer ways of engaging with indigenous knowledge and the deeply entrenched historical legacies of colonial and apartheid impositions (Mamdani, 1996, Mbembe 2001). The work of Lave and Wenger (1991) and Latour's (1987) Actor Network Theory extends constructivist approaches introducing socio-material analyses and situated workplace learning studies, with these influences informing post-schooling ESE.	and Reddy 1997, 2000). A number of case studies point to weaknesses in the OBE curriculum and its underlying assumptions (Lotz-Sisitka, 2002; Mbanjwa, 2003; Nduna, 2004: Olvitt, 2004), findings which are borne out through a large scale multi-institutional evaluation of the National EE Programme (NEEP-GET, 2005) pointing also towards weaknesses in teacher education policy and planning (Reddy, 2004). Studies demonstrate a widening scope of foci, e.g. indigenous and community knowledge (e.g. Shava, 1999, 2008), professional learning and institutional policy and praxis (Raven, 2005; Reddy, 2004); and research methodologies, especially the limitations of both post-structural and positivist research designs for mobilizing emancipatory education (Price, 2007), and a 'politics of potentia'. In the first explicit socio-material studies, Nhamo (2005) uses actor network theory to analyse environmental policy and implications for ESE.	weaknesses in the post-apartheid policy frameworks and their assumptions become more evident via deeper historical and contextual analysis of policy-in-practice. **From a politics as potentia perspective:** Issues of idealism, relevance and inclusion emerge as critical issues in the wider policy landscape. Studies seek to deepen inclusivity via indigenous knowledge, giving more attention to teachers' knowledge and experience, and broadening focus to include communities, and new policy developments such as the promulgation of the plastic bag regulations. From this, critical orientations emerge as to how policy does or does not benefit people, leading also to major revisions in emancipatory research designs and assumptions.
POLICY FAILURES CONT .. **Late 2000's (2005-2010)** Concerted policy reviews and strategy development attempting to address gaps but also to 'streamline' over-ambitious, ideologically driven policy of the early post-apartheid period. Following shifts towards neo-liberal models, government tends to focus on sector-based performance monitoring and performativity that reduces earlier forms of state-civil society	Introduction of studies seeking to understand policy re-contextualisation processes; knowledge structuring, and epistemological access concerns within an emerging decolonization frame guiding research. Critical analysis expands to incorporate stronger ontological congruence, and identification of absences, which opens the platform for stronger theorizing of the absence and emergence relation (Bhaskar, 1993). With revision of the NQF Act in 2008, the South African Qualifications Authority (SAQA) mandate changes to leading co-ordination and co-operation across the education and	Significant broadening of ESE research beyond a focus on the school curriculum, strengthening of ESE research in higher and further education curriculum and workplace-based learning. The SAQA research partnership provides opportunities for 'composting' of ESE research at the highest level amongst ESE policy actors; informing policy and praxis in the general education and training sector, the further education and training sector, and the higher education and training sector. Consultative strategy development and review / evaluation processes using multi-modal approaches, critical realist analyses and	**From a policy outcomes perspective:** National ESE strategies in a range of sectors (water, biodiversity, global change including climate change, environment broadly) and for a range of government departments (South Africa: DEA 2010; SANBI/Lewis, 2010; South Africa: DST 2010); these were 'action oriented' or practice-based strategies and based on consultative processes that also left some professional development, implementation and coordination networks in place. Key among them is the National Environmental Skills Planning Forum (NESPF) through which policy inputs are still made by a government-

(continued)

Appendix A. Continued.

Critical Incident Period	Wider methodological processes and theory shaping ESE research in this period:	South/ern Africa ESE research-policy engagement processes and selected studies contributing to the ESE policy engagement trajectory:	Outcomes of the research-policy engagement processes – in terms of policy, but also in terms of engaging the 'ontological split' between a politics of *potentia* and *potestus*; and (re)-invigorating a politics of *potentia*
cooperation and hampers the ability of data collection / research processes to contribute to learning and system development.	training system via research. ESE research in South Africa is recognized by the South African Qualifications Authority (SAQA) through a two phase national research partnership (2008-2014) to develop insights into workplace learning and sustainability practices, and green skills learning pathways to inform standard setting and articulation policy (Lotz-Sisitka, 2008a). Along with the influence of indigenous knowledge in curriculum research (O'Donoghue and Neluvhalani, 2002), curriculum and knowledge research is partly influenced by Bernstein's (1990) social realist theory of the pedagogical device and his views on horizontal and vertical knowledge structures (Muller, 2012; Young and Muller, 2010). Morrow's (2007) concept of epistemological access allows for more in-depth, critical and transformative theorizing of curriculum and pedagogical praxis. Critical analysis expands to incorporate stronger ontological congruence, and identification of absences (Bhaskar, 1993). ESE research moves beyond the 'paradigms debate' of the 1990's with critical and social realist (including some socio-material) framings (Bhaskar, 1993; Sayer, 2000; 2010; Latour, 1987). An interest in 'absenting absences' (Bhaskar, 1993), generativity and transformative praxis and transformative learning in ESE research is amplified and given depth and rigour through the introduction of expansive learning and cultural historical activity theory (CHAT), a form of post-Vygotskian cultural psychology (Engeström, 1987; Daniels, 2008).	critical policy implementation reviews in various areas of ESE, in schools, universities, communities and workplaces. Several multi-modal research-based national strategies and skills plans are developed in collaborative government-social partner processes, despite the dominant model of consultancy-based / outsourced research. A deepening understanding of ESE curriculum (re) contextualization, epistemological access, and knowledge is developed (e.g. Ramsarup, 2006; Lotz-Sisitka, 2009; Nsubuga, 2010; Shava, 2008), shaping a wider regional research programme on Educational Quality and Relevance (Lotz-Sisitka, 2008b; Lotz-Sisitka et al. 2017) to address major policy and epistemological framing weaknesses in curriculum and teacher education (Reddy, 2017), which by now were visible and in need of urgent resolution. Le Grange (2012) works with Ubuntu and Ukama to theorise post-human relations in indigenous cultures. A deepening engagement with qualifications and standard setting system issues emerge with ESE being articulated as a largely neglected cross-sectoral policy concern. Studies for these include Olvitt, Lotz-Sisitka and Malema (2005); and multi-year ESE policy research combined with ongoing country-wide consultations by Lotz-Sisitka, Ramsarup and Mosidi to inform and develop South Africa's first ever Environmental Sector Skills Plan (South Africa: DEA, 2010). At the same time, supported by research conducted by the Human Sciences Research Council (Vass et al. 2009), Rosenberg leads the	civil society collective. **From a politics as *potentia* perspective:** Further critical issues associated with post-apartheid policy making and implementation are researched and illuminated, especially the implications and consequences of a lack of inter-sectoral co-ordination, and a lack of adequate attention to the relationship between knowledge, skills, empowerment and transformation in the environmental sector, which was hampered by over-emphasis on industrial sectors over public good sectors (South Africa: DEA, 2010), pointing to a weakening of capability for environmental management, change and transformation in various sectors including water, climate change, biodiversity and within the state sector itself who carried the mandate for managing environmental concerns as a public good.

(continued)

Appendix A. Continued.

Critical Incident Period	Wider methodological processes and theory shaping ESE research in this period:	South/ern Africa ESE research-policy engagement processes and selected studies contributing to the ESE policy engagement trajectory:	Outcomes of the research-policy engagement processes – in terms of policy, but also in terms of engaging the 'ontological split' between a politics of *potentia* and *potestus*; and (re)-invigorating a politics of *potentia*
	In the wider social-ecological sciences, systems theory analytical frameworks become more sophisticated, drawing inter alia on Meadows (2008) and the notion of complex systems (Kurtz and Snowden, 2003) launching complexity science-based transdisciplinary studies in which 'learning' is seen to be central (Pahl-Wostl et al. 2007). In this context learning is theorized as single, double and triple loop learning (ibid), building on earlier work of Bateson (1972) and social learning gains popularity in natural resources management (Wals, 2007). 'Learning to Change our World' is defined the theme of the World EE Congress hosted in South Africa in 2007.	development of a national Biodiversity Human Capital Development Strategy (SANBI, 2010). In Higher Education Studies, Lupele (2008) combines actor network theory and communities of practice with post-colonial theory to analyse higher education curriculum innovations and institutional development in southern African countries, a process which catalyses ongoing ESE in higher education studies with significant on-campus policy influence across Africa. Togo (2009) uses critical realism and systems theory to develop a Unit-Based Sustainability Assessment tool for policy and praxis review in African universities (Togo and Lotz-Sisitka, 2009, 2013). Evaluations by Rosenberg (2006, 2008), Lotz-Sisitka and Burt (2006), Rosenberg and Taylor (2005) start to explore multi-modal approaches to evaluation and Price (2007) introduces critical realist transdisciplinary explanatory critique of industry-based environmental education using critical realism.	
POLICY INCONSISTENCIES **Early 2010's – 2017** Efficacy of policy system in question; lack of integrated and aligned policy engagement increasingly evident; following the 2011 Conference of the Parties (COP17) in South Africa, and the Sustainable Development summit in Rio de Janeiro in 2012, we saw the introduction of the notion of	Studies in schooling, post-schooling and workplace contexts are increasingly framed by critical realist constellational relationality and transformative praxis orientations. These guide laminated system research designs for identification of learning pathways in the national system of education and training, where boundary crossing also becomes a focus of research. The emphasis on generative research approaches strengthens commitment to De	Research processes *with* rather than *for* government (despite a now established culture of contracting consultants to do research). The introduction of new generative courses and skills development processes that are focused on Changing Practice as strategy to engage policy. These research-and-co-learning courses feed into and are supported by a range of associated ESE policy-practice learning networks, especially the National Environmental Skills Planning Forum, but also	*Policy related outcomes:* Improved tools and approaches for ESE policy engagement including learning networks, capable and motivated policy actors including government officials, and complexity-aligned review processes for adaptive programme implementation processes. Inclusion of 'green economy' as a sustainable, low-carbon growth path in the National Development Plan (South Africa: NPC, 2011) and a Green Economy Accord (South Africa:

(*continued*)

Appendix A. Continued.

Critical Incident Period	Wider methodological processes and theory shaping ESE research in this period:	South/ern Africa ESE research-policy engagement processes and selected studies contributing to the ESE policy engagement trajectory:	Outcomes of the research-policy engagement processes – in terms of policy, but also in terms of engaging the 'ontological split' between a politics of *potentia* and *potestus*; and (re)-invigorating a politics of *potentia*
an inclusive green economy to complement the concept of sustainable development.	Sousa Santos' argument that there is need for both: a *sociology of absence and a related sociology of emergence* in post-colonial / decolonizing societies such as South Africa (Lotz-Sisitka, 2017a). A history of critique proves to be inadequate (Lotz-Sisitka, 2016b) and research designs seek to strengthen generativity and emergence in dialectical engagement with more carefully articulated and ontologically situated notions of absence (Price and Lotz-Sisitka, 2016). Examples of these forms of research include the surfacing of latent demand for green work in green skills learning studies in place-based and policy engaged learning networks; and evaluation research that takes reflexive learning as key focus, informed by deepening multi-modal methodologies. Conceptual and methodological tools are drawn from Bhaskar (1993), Archer (2007), Engeström and Sannino (2010), Daniels (2008), De Sousa Santos (2014), and post-colonial / decolonization theorists Mamdani (1996), Leff (2009), Dussel (2008), Mignolo (2002), Mbembe (2001) and Freire (1996) amongst others. Socio-technical transitioning systems theory offers some, if limited, resources (Geels, 2002) and new economists offering deeper critiques of, and alternatives to capitalism such as Moore (2015), Streeck (2014), Adler (2015), and Raworth (2017) are drawn on to guide engagement with absence and emergence in ESE research programmes. Evaluation design with a critical realist underpinning draws on Pawson and Tilley	the Green Skills Research-Policy Forum, Fundisa [Teaching] for Change programme and the Amanzi [Water] for Food Learning Network, all of which are constituted as state-civil society partner networks where ESE research 'composting' is possible. Associated research emerging within, and shaping these networks include Lotz-Sisitka (2011), Schudel (2012, 2014), Songqwaru (2012), Mohanoe (2014), Rosenberg et al. (2015), Jenkin et al. (2016), Ward et al. (2016), Ramsarup (2017a), Cobban et al. (2017); Rosenberg et al. (2016a); Rosenberg et al. (2016b); Ramsarup et al. (2019), Lindley (2014); Rivers (2014), Pesanayi (2016; 2019), Tshiningayamwe and Songqwaru (2017), Schudel (2017), and O'Donoghue (2017) amongst others. Mukute (2010) and Mukute and Lotz-Sisitka (2012) introduce an expansive learning perspective and Olvitt (2012) and McGarry (2013) deepen approaches to ethics in ESE research. Many of these studies have a socio-material / critical realist underlabouring and individual studies make use of multi-layered methodologies, considering concrete experiences at the micro-level in relation to meso- and macro-factors in wider transitioning and transforming systems and society. The dialectical focus on *absence and emergence* in decolonizing society is more widely visible across the study field, as is a stronger commitment to ESE policy making and praxis framed as a contemporary re-invigoration of 'politics as potentia' with commitments to the public good and the	EDD, 2011), and reference to 'green' skills and sustainability related occupations in the National Skills Development Strategy (NSDS III of 2009) (South Africa: DHET, 2009), national Scarce Skills List and national list of Occupations in High Demand – all of which are now framed within a new post-schooling White Paper (South Africa: DHET, 2013) that seeks to develop an integrative approach. The Curriculum and Assessment Policy Statement continues to include an environmental and sustainability education focus (South Africa: DoE, 2012). *From a politics of potentia perspective:* New methodologies allow for identification of absences, and processes of 'absenting absence' via expansive learning in and across activity systems and via giving attention to re-dressing flaws in system development. This allows for engagement with deep seated contradictions in the policy systems, and for multi-actor engagement, giving more voice to those who continue to be excluded from policy benefits (e.g. water activists in the South African Water Caucus; farmers and college lecturers; black women and youth), and opening up engagement with critical absences (e.g. the missing middle / lack of attention given to technical environmental qualifications as 'alternative learning pathways' into the sector (Ramsarup, 2016, 2017a). Sector Education and Training Authorities across all sectors start to commission research into skills for sustainability and green economic

(continued)

Appendix A. Continued.

Critical Incident Period	Wider methodological processes and theory shaping ESE research in this period:	South/ern Africa ESE research-policy engagement processes and selected studies contributing to the ESE policy engagement trajectory:	Outcomes of the research-policy engagement processes – in terms of policy, but also in terms of engaging the 'ontological split' between a politics of *potentia* and *potestus*; and (re)-invigorating a politics of *potentia* development.
	(1997) and Patton's (2011) work on developmental evaluation in complex systems, while Appreciative Enquiry and Most Significant Change Stories are also used in developmental contexts (e.g. O'Donoghue's 2016a RCE evaluation), offering a range of methodologies to strengthen the absence – emergence relation.	commons (Lotz-Sisitka, 2014, 2016a, 2016b, 2017a, 2017b; Kulundu, 2017; O'Donoghue, 2016b; Vallabh, 2017; Burt and Lusithi, 2017). Evaluations also start to use realist and multi-modal approaches, the following multi-year evaluations all being currently underway: Songqwaru (2020); Giqwa (2018), Rosenberg et al. (in press); and a Rhodes University-Department of Environment Affairs partnership to develop a new model for evaluating national natural resource management public works programmes combining intensive, extensive, participatory and synthesis research methodologies, is being explored.	Evaluation methodologies seek out deep seated mechanisms shaping 'what counts for whom under what conditions', revealing flaws in ontologically weakly developed theories of change, and foregrounding the reflexive learning potential of evaluation research.

Unions get involved in 'green jobs' and see the potential for skills development for climate resilient development in the country, and researchers seek to illuminate 'latent' jobs in value chains that address a broader framing of economy in household, state, market and the commons spheres (Rosenberg et al. 2020).

A synthesis of green skills studies provides a critical realist framework for sustainable development and educational policy (Lotz-Sisitka & Ramsarup, 2002). |

Reflections on the science–policy interface within education for sustainable development in Germany

Mandy Singer-Brodowski ⓘ, Antje Brock, Julius Grund and Gerhard de Haan

ABSTRACT
While science–policy interfaces (SPIs) are argued to be crucial in developing and implementing effective public policy programmes, what happens in a particular SPI policy-research relationship remains under-researched, particularly in relation to 'success criteria' for policy makers and researchers. In this article, we address this gap by examining the SPI created for monitoring the national implementation of UNESCO's Global Action Programme for Education for Sustainable Development (ESD) policies in Germany. Our study used analytical autoethnography and intersubjective group discussions with the ESD-SPI researchers. Findings illustrate key considerations for fostering productive working relationships. These include: (i) dealing with different expectations and perspectives on measuring policy implementation; (ii) reflecting on the diverse ways an evidence base is used; and (iii) becoming more aware of and factoring in power dynamics, at the SPI. We conclude with a series of questions for further examining 'critical detachment' by researchers and 'constructive involvement' with policymakers in SPIs.

Introduction

This article explores the relationships between research and policy within scientific advisory and monitoring work related to Education for Sustainable Development (ESD) implementation in Germany. We deploy the concept of a science–policy interface (SPI) and analyse our experiences of working as researchers within this context through an analytic autoethnographic approach. SPIs in general can be defined as 'social processes which encompass relations between scientists and other actors in the policy process, and which allow for exchanges, coevolution, and joint construction of knowledge with the aim of enriching decision-making' (van den Hove 2007, 815). This understanding of SPIs goes beyond simple assumptions about linear knowledge transfer from science to policy. It also acknowledges the complex processes of knowledge construction and translation that are involved, and recognises the iterative and multidirectional dialogue and learning that can happen between the stakeholders (Sarkki et al. 2015).

The strategies used by researchers at the interface between research and policy represent a relatively new field of analysis in Environmental and Sustainability Education (ESE) (Aikens, McKenzie, and Vaughter 2016; van Poeck and Lysgaard 2015). It has been argued that ESE policy research could benefit from critical policy research perspectives that understand 'policy processes as complex, with multiple actors intervening in ways that influence what issues are identified as policy problems, what solutions are available, and how these policy solutions are championed, borne out, resisted, or subverted in practice' (Aikens, McKenzie, and Vaughter 2016, 350). This critical policy perspective in the context of ESE leads to several questions concerning the SPI, such as: How should researchers position themselves regarding ESD policy (Læssøe, Feinstein, and Blum 2013, 234)? To what extent should researchers maintain their independence and only analyse policy processes and their effects from a distant point of view? How close ought they work together with policymakers, government officials and other stakeholders?

Responding to such issues is far from easy. On the one hand, being unreflective and too close to the interaction between science and policy might prevent scientists from independently evaluating policy strategies. That is, research projects that are conducted in close cooperation with governments can become optimistic self-descriptions that lack aspects of critical empirical research (Nazir et al. 2009). On the other hand, significant sustainability challenges give rise to an urgent need to collaborate to integrate scientific evidence into policymaking and thus accelerate sustainability transitions, including ESE. This has led to calls for researchers to alternate 'between critical detachment and constructive involvement' (Læssøe, Feinstein, and Blum 2013, 233 with reference to Mathiesen 1982). However, it is not sufficiently clear what this process of alternation should look like and what challenges it can involve.

To better understand the dynamics emerging at the SPI, we analyse the experiences of working at the ESD-SPI in Germany. We start by describing the structure and development of the ESD-SPI in Germany. We then explain the process by which we have reflected on our experiences of working within this context in terms of the conceptual model used (typology of SPIs) and the analytical approach followed (intersubjective group discussions based on autoethnography). The resulting insights into the SPI are then discussed in relation to three questions:

- How to deal with different expectations of 'measuring' ESD?
- How to deal with and support different ways of using the evidence base at the SPI?
- How to deal with different kinds of power at the SPI?

We conclude by sharing reflections and posing questions that may be helpful for the work of other researchers who are operating at the ESD-SPI.

ESD implementation and monitoring in Germany

The main object of investigation, the ESD-SPI in Germany, is embedded within a broader structure of ESD implementation in Germany. This section therefore provides an overview of this broader context, as well as the scientific advisory and monitoring work of the team of authors.

Structure of the Global Action Programme on ESD in Germany

As follow-up to the activities during the UN Decade of ESD (2005–2014), UNESCO proclaimed the ESD Global Action Programme (GAP) (2015–2019) in order to further catalyse and mainstream ESD internationally. When considering the national process of implementing the GAP on ESD in Germany, it is important to emphasise the federal structure of the German education system. The constitution grants the German government very few opportunities to influence the education system; responsibility rather lies with the federal states in terms of the legislation, administration and financing of education, science and culture (Hepp 2011). For this reason, the 16 federal states contribute a large proportion of funding to the education system, followed by local authorities (local authorities are the smallest administrative unit in Germany after the federal states and the federation) (ibid.). Besides single areas of authority that remain on a national level (e.g. extra-curricular vocational training), there are voluntary, non-binding structures of cooperation between federal states, such as the Standing Conference of the Ministers of Education and Cultural Affairs of the Länder in the Federal Republic of Germany (Kultusministerkonferenz, KMK), which aim to align the different education systems (ibid.).

The strategy to implement the GAP for ESD in Germany consisted of a complex multi-stakeholder process led by the Federal Ministry of Education and Research. In order to ensure effective implementation of ESD, in 2015 a governance structure was established, with three main bodies including top-down and bottom-up processes. These bodies include: (i) the National Platform ESD; (ii) Expert Forums, including a Youth Panel and (iii) Partner Networks. Each of these bodies includes participation by stakeholders from the fields of politics and administration, educational practice, civil society and academia (Figure 1).

The National Platform is the central decision-making body concerning strategic questions of ESD implementation in Germany and brings together key actors from different sectors of society and from different fields of action. It is complemented by one international advisor as well as one scientific advisor (Prof. Gerhard de Haan). The six Expert Forums are structured according to the educational areas of early childhood education, school, vocational education and training, higher education, non-formal/informal learning/youth and local authorities. They include key stakeholders working on strategies to strengthen ESD within the different educational areas. The Partner Networks represent open and low-threshold networks of ESD practitioners offering opportunities for exchange and activities. They are differentiated according to various educational areas and topics (such as the media, the economy, cultural education) and are closely engaged with the Expert Forums, with some committee members being involved with both bodies. The actors within this landscape met in 2016 and 2017 for the Agenda Congress. Besides providing an opportunity for professional exchange regarding ESD, this national congress hosted award ceremonies, honoring exemplary educational efforts from learning locations, networks and local authorities within ESD. One of the most important milestones and achievements in the implementation of the GAP was the preparation and adoption of a National Action Plan on ESD in June 2017 containing 130 objectives and 349 concrete recommendations for action (National Platform on Education for Sustainable Development 2017). The ESD Tour introduced and

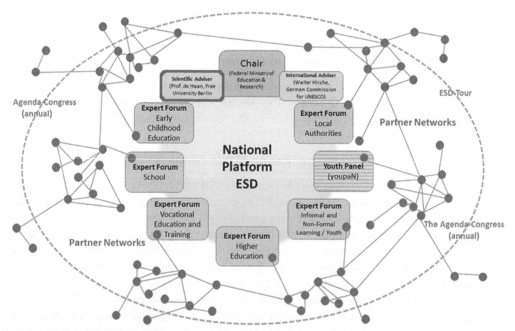

Figure 1. Structure of the national process of the GAP on ESD in Germany, Source: BNE-Portal 2019[2]. (Note: The location of the scientific advisory team, whose work is the focus of this paper, is highlighted in red).

discussed the National Action Plan by means of 25 nationwide events from February to December 2018. Besides the National Action Plan, different federal states have developed their own ESD strategies (United Nations Economic Commission for Europe 2018, 12).

This article is written from the perspective of the department of the aforementioned scientific advisor for GAP implementation in Germany at the Freie Universität Berlin. The scientific advisor has long-standing experience of advising the Federal Ministry of Education and Research and other stakeholders on EE and ESD. The two main functions of the department of the scientific advisor are to conduct nationwide monitoring of ESD (see the next section) and to scientifically advise actors of the GAP on ESD in Germany. The team provides an academic perspective on points of discussion during meetings of the GAP's central bodies on ESD, presents regular research results from the monitoring project at these meetings and is involved in general strategic decisions throughout the ESD implementation process. For example, the team has been involved in long-term strategic questions and future strategies of the successor programmes of the GAP. Thus, the department of the scientific advisor is situated at the very core of the ESD-SPI in Germany and so represents an interesting context and perspective for reflection on the nature and dynamics of the science–policy interface.

Nationwide monitoring of ESD in Germany

The department's scientific advice on the SPI derives from other national and international research results, and, to a large extent, from transdisciplinary mixed-methods ESD monitoring. Educational monitoring can be described as indicator-based observation of an education system (Ioannidou 2010; Döbert and Weishaupt 2012) in order to inform experts and policymakers and build a foundation for evidence-informed policymaking. The nationwide research project on monitoring ESD has been conducted by this department for over 5 years now. Overall, it is based on a transdisciplinary approach which aims to integrate perspectives of actors from beyond the university into the research project design, knowledge generation and communication of results (Lang et al. 2012). It thereby follows a comprehensive mixed-method design to inform different target groups: the Federal Ministry of Education and Research; members of the official ESD implementation structure (Figure 1); ESD practitioners; the scientific community and the interested public. To capture the multi-faceted reality of ESD, the mixed-method monitoring analyses different levels of ESD implementation in Germany (Figure 2).

By means of document analyses performed in 2016, 2017 and 2019 (Desk Research I-III), analysis was conducted on the extent and types of references to ESD and similar educational concepts in more than 4500 documents (including curricula, examination-related documents and policy documents from the different educational areas and federal states). This research phase was structured according to a set of indicators. The selection of indicators was structured along different educational phases (e.g. early childhood, school, vocational education and training, higher education) and drew on relevant international ESD implementation indicators, such as the role of ESD in curricula or in documents relevant for the qualification of educators (e.g. UNECE Steering Committee on ESD 2007). This process also took account of the potential drawbacks of indicators – in particular, that they can often fail to adequately represent complex issues to the degree of precision and insight that is needed or expected. The selection of individual measurable facets of a complex issue such as ESD implementation, for example, is necessarily reductive and will determine the content of the evidence base that will be produced to inform processes at the SPI. Contextual appropriateness is also important and the indicator-based selection of relevant document groups was adapted where necessary in order to ensure relevance to the German educational context and to fit the different educational areas (Brock 2018).

Additionally, following the transdisciplinary research design, the selection of document groups was informed by the feedback of experts in the practical and political field of ESD. For all selected documents, a lexical analysis based on the software MAXQDA was conducted to identify

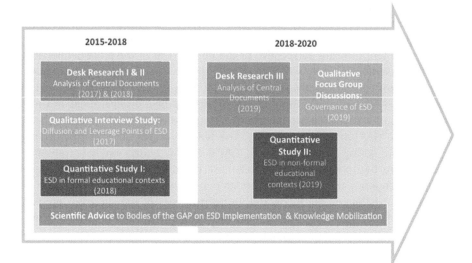

Figure 2. Mixed-method design of nationwide ESD monitoring in Germany.

each sequence of text containing one or more keywords from a comprehensive list related to ESD (such as EE, global learning and nature pedagogy). Each of the software-based findings in the text was then individually coded for context and connotation. The analysis was designed as a longitudinal study, and was repeated after two years for document types with short update intervals (for methodological details see Singer-Brodowski et al. 2019; Holst et al. 2020).

Qualitative research was conducted via 66 expert interviews. Experts from ministries, academia, educational practice and civil society organisations (CSOs) were asked to identify ESD implementation processes and leverage points for mainstreaming ESD. The objective was to capture the diffusion processes of ESD in the four formal educational areas outlined above as well as in non-formal education, local authorities and within youth participation. Given the aim of informing, strengthening and supporting educational work across the country, transformation paths of ESD in the different educational areas were identified (i.e. an educator-oriented capacity-building transformation path in early childhood education and an organisation-oriented transformation path in higher education) (Singer-Brodowski, Etzkorn, and von Seggern 2019). Additionally, in 2019, focus group discussions with experts from the ministries, academia, educational practise and CSOs regarding the governance of ESD in Germany were conducted and analysed (Singer-Brodowski et al. 2020).

The monitoring project's quantitative studies include a nationwide online survey of young people aged 14–24 ($n = 2564$) and teachers ($n = 525$) in formal educational settings (Grund and Brock 2019a, 2019b). These surveys enabled analysis of several dimensions such as actual and wished-for ESD implementation (Grund and Brock 2020), as well as emotions, attitudes and knowledge concerning SD. Further in-depth analyses of the data focused on the interplay between expected and wished-for future scenarios and the role of constructive hope, including concrete implications for ESD practice (Grund and Brock 2019c). In 2019/2020, several additional online surveys were carried out in the area of non-formal and informal education. These surveys involved transdisciplinary cooperation with various ESD educational organisations in civil society that worked with the research team on processes such as co-designing the questionnaires.

Specifying SPIs and analysing interactions within them

The findings of this mixed-methods ESD monitoring feed into the process of advising actors at the SPI. The aim of this article is to arrive at a better understanding of the complex interplay and non-linear processes of knowledge production and knowledge integration at the SPI. First, this must be based on a differentiated view of the kind of SPI under discussion. Second, our own interactions with others at the SPI form a considerable part of the research object. So how can one systematically gain a more nuanced and reflective understanding of these interactions – as the researcher and as the research object at the same time? The following two sections outline these theoretical and methodological elements.

Different models of SPIs

SPIs can be manifested in various forms. According to a typology by Kaaronen (2016), seven models of SPIs can be distinguished in the context of sustainability: the independent, integrated, assignment, nested, advisor, platform and the mixed model (see Table 1).

Given the typology above, the department of the scientific advisor can be seen to contain features especially of both the independent and the advisor models. It aligns with the independent model in so far as it covers aspects of reporting on relevant scientific insights, providing critical feedback and monitoring (watchdog), producing knowledge in a 'think tank' way as well as contributing to strategic issues and facilitating deliberation between stakeholder groups (Kaaronen 2016). The freedom from constraints and the resulting possibilities of creativity and the ability to articulate critical standpoints are essential advantages of this model (ibid.). Nevertheless, its challenges are seen in the potentially low impact of the findings and suggestions for policymakers (ibid.). At the same time, the work of the scientific advisory team is linked to the category of the advisor model, for obvious reasons. While the advantages of an advisor model lie in the potential for individuals to function as impactful spokespersons representing good science and advancing sustainability (ibid.), the disadvantages can be seen in a lack of socially robust knowledge and the potential for the impactful proximity to decision-makers to compromise the research (ibid.). The work at our department therefore represents a mixed model in which goals and features potentially complement one another, such as being independent and at the same time impactful and sufficiently involved.

Methodological background to analysing our own work at the SPI

Our location at the ESD-SPI presents us with challenges and opportunities. One of the challenges is that our advisory work and dissemination of research results has to address multiple actor groups with different needs. This need for the research to be target group-specific is, at the same time, an opportunity for our work to have increased impact and provide a profound understanding of the aims and expectations of the different actors involved. It was in responding to these kinds of challenges and opportunities that we began to broaden our knowledge about wider scholarship on SPIs, within and beyond the field of sustainability. This was in order to better understand our own roles, strategies and practices in relation to the dynamics of an ESD-SPI.

We therefore initiated analyses of our work at the ESD-SPI and developed and exchanged experiences in the context of advisory work within our team against the background of analytic autoethnography. Analytic autoethnography concerns the analysis of the relations between individual persons and the social structure (Anderson 2006, 390), in our case the ESD-SPI. According to this methodology, five different features are crucial for this analytical perspective (see for the following ibid., 378 ff.).

The first feature is that the researchers are part of the context they analyse, which constitutes their dual role as observers and participants simultaneously, as is typical of ethnography. This is given, as stated above, because our department is situated directly at the SPI. The analytical, more reflective participation within the group under study does not, however, imply a 'panoptical or non-problematic positionality' (ibid., 380). Hence it is crucial to consider the limitations of one's perspective and recognise the plurality of aims, values etc. within the group (ibid., 380 f).

Table 1. Typology of SPIs as differentiated by Kaaronen (2016, 20 ff).

Typology of science–policy interfaces

	Independent Model	Integrated Model	Assignment Model	Nested Model	Advisor Model	Platform Model	Mixed Model
Core features	Assessment, advice and monitoring of independent scientific/expert groups.	Similar to independent model, difference see below	Demand-driven funding of external (university, think tank) advice by policy sector	Nested and hierarchically structured design of advisory bodies (task forces, expert groups etc.)	Single Chief Scientific Advisor responsible for policy advice, knowledge diffusion or monitoring	Third party organises platform for deliberative and impartial exchange of different stakeholder groups	Hybrids of the different types with mixed core features
Relation between science and policy	Independent experts/scientists bring or 'push' knowledge into policy sphere, but often commissioned or funded by governmental bodies	Closeness to governments through membership of scientists, parliamentarians, ministers etc. in councils	Governments look for external advice. Demand/'pull' model of science–policy interaction	Similar to independent model, but hierarchy of scientific bodies producing knowledge towards policy sphere	(Appointed) chief advisor as representative of science, informs high political authorities	Platform includes scientists, policy and other stakeholders for co-production of knowledge and solutions	Different features and degrees of independence/cooperation, demand- or supply-driven production of knowledge

The second feature of analytic autoethnography concerns analytic reflexivity, whereby the awareness of the mutual influences between the researchers and their research object is important (ibid., 382). This reflexivity is of particular relevance for considering and counterbalancing the potential challenges connected to the different SPI models by Kaaronen. For example, reflecting on the lack of impact of the independent model or, conversely, the potential lack of social robustness of the advisor model.

Besides the necessary self-reflexivity, it is also crucial to ensure the visibility of researchers in the outputs of their analysis, which is the third feature of analytic autoethnography (ibid., 384). Hence, we sought not just to make ourselves visible in this text, but also to provide contextual knowledge on our work and our positioning within the ESD-governance structure and the SPI.

The fourth feature of analytic autoethnography is exchange with other sources of information on the context of analysis, be it empirical findings or other persons beyond one's own group of researchers (ibid., 385 f). It is important to us to remain aware of the limitations of our own experiences and although we did not include other persons in our own analytical reflection processes, our work involves regularly exchange with other groups (scientists beyond the educational field and the field of sustainability, practitioners and policymakers). Additionally, we reviewed the literature on other SPIs in the field of climate change, biodiversity and health issues with the aim for systematically analysing our experiences against the background of the wider knowledge base.

This last point connects with the fifth and final feature of analytic autoethnography (ibid., 386), which is commitment to an analytical agenda beyond providing an 'insider's perspective' (ibid.), striving for theoretical development and refinement. Here, the aim of our analysis was to better understand ESD-SPIs by reflecting on our experiences using ideas from the literature, particularly in relation to how SPIs, and sustainability-related SPIs specifically, work. This process was in order to be able to synthesise this knowledge into formulating recommendations for working and acting as a researcher at an SPI.

Based on this approach of analytic autoethnography, we organised a process of exchanging what might be individual or shared reflections on our observations at the ESD-SPI in Germany. Therefore, we organised intersubjective group discussions among the five researchers and the scientific advisor. These discussions were held against the background of literature regarding the SPIs and in turn led to a more specific search for literature. We used intersubjective validation (Steinke 2007) to capture individual observations and reflections and discussed them critically until a sufficiently reflective intersubjective interpretation was reached. The aim was to gain 'a discursive form of generating intersubjectivity and transparency through explicit handling of the data and their interpretation' (Steinke 1999, 214, own translation).

In the vein of self-reflexivity, and understanding the limitation of one's own viewpoint, the discussion did not focus on areas of commonality, but rather on instances of diverging perspectives. In this way, diverging and converging perspectives could be discussed with regard to their complementary aspects. Where there were tensions and synthesis could not be reached, it was often possible to at least acknowledge their consistency and functionality within the respective rationalities. Throughout these intersubjective discussions, we were able to develop more reflective and robust interpretations of our experiences at the SPI, which gradually led to a more detailed understanding of our SPI. Besides that, the discussions brought up new and unanswered questions that increased complexity.

Insights into the science–policy interface within ESD in Germany

The insights that emerged from our analysis of working within the German ESD-SPI can be considered in terms of three key issues:

- How to deal with different expectations of 'measuring' ESD?
- How to deal with and support different ways of using the evidence base at the SPI?
- How to deal with different kinds of power at the SPI?

How to deal with different expectations of 'measuring' ESD?

As we will argue, wider international developments regarding evidence-informed education and standardisation are influencing both our own and external expectations concerning monitoring and evaluation. The response to both sets of expectations includes dealing with ambivalent or contradictory aims.

Conceptual and methodological decisions within the monitoring project, as well as the understandings and expectations of other stakeholders at the SPI, are being shaped against the background of wider, international trends and discourses. These trends include the growing evidence-orientation in education policy, coinciding with increasing standardisation and measurability in education (Biesta 2016). These trends have implications that are in tension with each other. They make certain educational outcomes quantifiable and easily communicable, thereby drawing attention to the topic of educational outcomes and creating a pull effect to increase educational quality. At the same time, the growing prevalence of evidence-based (Nutley, Walter, and Davies 2007) or evidence-informed (educational) policies (on the difference between evidence-based and evidence-informed see, for example, Nevo and Slonim-Nevo (2011)) entails the risk that educational processes and results are reduced to cognitive, measurable and thus comparable competencies. This is because the complex multi-faceted learning processes of individuals, and the cultural context in different educational systems, are considerably more challenging to grasp and compare by means of standardised measures.

The mode of educational governance that is connected with these trends of standardisation is described as governance of comparison (Martens and Niemann 2010). Here, the evidence base is produced and communicated in such a way that, in the example of PISA (the Programme for International Student Assessment), international organisations significantly influence national educational policies, exerting a powerful steering function via governance by comparison (OECD 2007). One implication of standardisation and the necessary reduction of complexity is narrowing education down to what is of economic value. Educational achievements are increasingly interpreted and measured in terms of their function as a driver of economic development (Lawn and Lingard 2002, 291).These problematic aspects of evidence-based approaches can be subsumed as misplaced reduction of complexity as well as misplaced concreteness (governance by comparison, suggesting comparability at the cost of contextual factors and important, incomparable aspects).

In relation to ESD in Germany, the increased emphasis on monitoring can be viewed as part of wider trends in education policy (Exley, Braun, and Ball 2011). Indeed, interest in the evidence base within the national ESD implementation strategy was a driver for ESD monitoring, of which our work is a part. In this way, the trends related to evidence-informed approaches, comparability and internationalisation in education more widely serve to justify and support our work. Yet creating this evidence base at the SPI invites expectations around measuring ESD in line with wider trends in educational policy internationally. During our intersubjective group discussions we debated the benefits and limitations that stem from expectations regarding 'measuring' ESD. Relativising the problematic facets of standardisation was of special importance given the federal structure of the educational system and the potential relevance of governance by comparison in a country with a high level of federal autonomy.

For example, the design of the desk research as large-scale assessments of ESD-relevant documents was federal state-specific with respect to most document types (e.g. curricula, educational plans). The comparative and quantification-based modes of analysis were applied and contributed to public and scientific visibility and thereby generated a leverage effect for political actions. Such large-scale endeavors, however, also run the risk of overstraining the comparability of different types of documents (in terms of length, structure and content) given the breadth and heterogeneity of the database. In order to counterbalance reductionist and decontextualised conclusions on the analysis of these large bodies of documents, the results have been framed and partly interpreted in more depth (Singer-Brodowski, Brock, and Etzkorn 2019). For example, not only have the educational plans for early childhood education of the different federal states been compared with respect to the quantitative results (mentions of ESD and related educational concepts), but qualitative aspects of ESD have also been analysed (context and significance of use of ESD-related text passages). Here, we sought to acknowledge and engage with the complexity of ESD implementation through the use of triangulation and mixed-methods designs.

Another challenge concerning standardisation and comparability came with monitoring ESD in the field of non-formal and informal learning with its diverse actors, organisations and content. It was an important area to include within our quantitative work, though, because of its capacity for deep-rooted and self-motivated educational processes. Also, the most important ways of coming into contact with sustainability issues seem to be located in this field (Grund and Brock 2019a). Nevertheless, the organisations where non-formal learning takes place (mostly in civil society) are under-researched, especially quantitatively. The quantitative study was conceptualised to capture the complexity and heterogeneity of this educational field and to include questions of genuine interest to the practitioners by means of a transdisciplinary research design. The study, conducted in 2019/2020, was thus co-designed and co-conducted with several nationwide associations in the field of non-formal ESD, EE and Global Citizenship Education. The questionnaires were partly standardised and partly individualised for each of the organisations. Again, this was an example of seeking to move at the boundaries of the methodologies chosen, to utilise their advantages and limit their potential drawbacks (such as generalisable insights from a large sample versus context-sensitivity and collecting organisation-specific information). With this approach, we compromised on maximising sample size, comparability of results and representativeness and hence probably also on an easily communicable story and on meeting lay expectations at the SPI concerning quantitative nationwide monitoring approaches.

In summary, in our intersubjective group discussions we intensively discussed how to deal with different stakeholder expectations and thereby leverage the advantages, and at the same time counterbalance problems of standardisation and measurability in the monitoring approach. The quantification focus inherent in monitoring has been discussed in terms of tensions between increasing visibility and being potentially reductionist. This issue played out on the level of conceptualising the research and communicating its results. We therefore consider it essential for ESD researchers to be mindful of the broader picture of tensions or contradictions associated with global trends such as evidence-informed educational policies and standardisation. In this way, researchers will be better able to deal in a more nuanced way with expectations of measuring ESD and/or distance themselves from such expectations by following the independent model of scientific advice for example.

How to deal with and support different ways of using the evidence base at the SPI?

A second area of insight relates to the ways in which evidence is used by different stakeholders involved in the SPI, and how researchers can support these uses. Important themes here were recognising and responding to the distinctive needs and interests of different actors, understanding how the role of evidence will vary at different stages in the processes of policy making, and the potential of designing and conducting research and evaluation in a transdisciplinary way.

Science and policy are often described as two fundamentally different systems, communities or orbits (Orland 2012) which need to be bridged or at least translated into each other. Current evidence-informed policymaking at the SPI 'takes place within an ecosystem' (Gluckman 2016, 969) which is characterised by complex communication, interpretation and negotiation processes. The uptake and negotiation of the evidentiary basis in these processes can, therefore, be somewhat nebulous and include tensions (Singer-Brodowski, Brock, and Etzkorn 2019). Furthermore, to enhance the use of evidence, it is crucial to identify which roles different actors play in the ecosystem of actors. In this section, we focus first on policy actors and second on the broader policy ecosystem, such as civil society actors.

At the beginning of the overall monitoring research programme, it was essential for us to gain a better understanding of the roles played by the diverse policy actors involved in the German GAP implementation (including their heterogeneous aims and expectations concerning ESD implementation). Most of the policy actors are from the education administration of the federal states or the German Ministry of Education and Research – i.e. they are not policymakers in the sense of parliamentary representatives, but government officials who have broad operational responsibilities. While the scientific advisory team interacts regularly with policymakers with small- to medium-scale decision-making authority concerning ESD implementation, far fewer interactions take place with policymakers with large-scale decision-making authority. Within those interactions, constructive personal relationships are essential in communicating research results (Oliver, Lorenc, and Innvaer 2014), and can support the uptake of evidence in policy making. Overall, we put considerable effort into developing trustful and synergetic cooperation with the individual policy actors. Within our intersubjective group discussions, we identified the kind and scope of influence of the different levels of state actors. We also adapted the evidence base to the specific context and sphere of influence.

In relation to the processes of policymaking, Geden states that there is a relevant inconsistency at the centre of policymaking: the inconsistency between talking, deciding and acting, with talking and deciding being more progressive than the resulting action (Geden 2016, 791). The reason for this is identified in addressing different stakeholders: some 'through talk, some through decisions, and some through actions' (ibid., 794). Following Geden (2016), actors at the SPI need to be aware of the general tendency for the level of acting in policy to lag behind the levels of talking and decision-making. Or, put another way, words and even decisions do not necessarily (immediately) trickle down to the level of actions. One example of this is a broad participative process of suggesting indicators to measure the status quo and progress in terms of ESD to update Germany's National Sustainable Development Strategy.[1] As mentioned earlier, indicators focus on specific facets that are representative of broader issues. Their selection depends on various issues that, due to their steering relevance, are not limited simply due to feasibility issues such as the availability of relevant data. They might also include political tendencies for complexity to be reduced in such ways that 'demotivating' stories are avoided or overlooked in favour of accounts of partial successes. In terms of the indicators for the National Sustainable Development Strategy, the participative process informed by science and an interested public does not necessarily lead to the implementation of progressive indicators in a linear way. Their final selection was guided by a less transparent or non-participative political process involving only selected players and tactical decisions at a higher political level.

Besides such inconsistencies, another lack of linearity and predictability concerns the uptake of the evidence base within the broader policy ecosystem, including civil society organisations. This complexity and unpredictability of knowledge uptake was one of the considerations behind our use of a transdisciplinary research approach (Lang et al. 2012) as a central approach of the ESD-monitoring project's research design. Using a transdisciplinary approach enabled us to achieve greater legitimation within the broader policy environment of (E)SD and supported the uptake of the results by the different actors. For example, the data for the quantitative studies were gathered in the context of non-formal and informal learning in 2019 in close cooperation with CSOs. Relevant parts of the collected data are thus shaped by and shared with the institutions and provide valuable insights into their organisational structures and the perspectives of their practitioners (e.g. on enablers and barriers of ESD implementation) which can be used for organisational development.

The transdisciplinary research approach also led to weighting or even prioritising different and often conflicting requirements, and an ongoing search for an appropriate balance between scientific and societal impact within our intersubjective group discussions. With the aim of broadening both these kinds of impacts, we published our findings in various formats, consisting of articles in professional journals for practitioners and monographs containing detailed descriptions of the research process and findings for the scientific community. Additionally, executive summaries have been published in less academic language. Although the uptake of scientific research results in policy processes is more likely when scientists provide simple stories (Cairney and Oliver 2017, 7), in our case it was important to maintain complexity and avoid simple stories in the executive summaries. Furthermore, especially for educational practitioners with limited time or even access to the original publication, the scientific papers were summarised, enriched with practical advice and published in German (i.e. Grund and Brock 2019a).

Further, one of the central insights arising from numerous years of consulting within the ESD policy environment in this context is that adaptation of scientific results is more likely when it can be well aligned with the overall policy agendas. This represents a challenge if SPI scientific advisory work is to go beyond confirming and legitimising the current policy agendas (which are often less ambitious than civil society and the recommendations of academia) but also maintain the trust of policymakers. Here, the detachment–involvement balance again has significance.

To sum up this discussion of how to support different ways of using the evidence base at the SPI, several factors appear to be decisive. Starting from an understanding of bridging the different 'orbits' or 'ecosystems' of science and policy, a more nuanced understanding of different stakeholders, their mandates and aims becomes a vital precondition of powerfully striving for a common aim at the SPI. Here, the inconsistencies generic to the field of policymaking also have to be considered. Another way of increasing the impact, commitment and effectiveness of research use at the SPI is to design and conduct research in a transdisciplinary way. While research results that cannot be aligned with a broader policy agenda have a low chance of uptake and practical implementation, trustful and synergetic cooperation at the SPI does increase the relevance and impact of researchers' involvement at the SPI.

How to deal with different kinds of power at the SPI?

The third area which became prevalent in reflecting on our experiences at the SPI was the role of power dynamics within SPIs. Morrison et al. (2019, 2, original emphasis) made clear that '[S]cientists and policymakers can improve their ability to explain and enhance the environmental outcomes of polycentric systems by *re-conceiving polycentric governance* [...] as [...] *influenced by power-laden social relationships*'. While it is hard to put into practice systematically, it is all the more crucial to include power dynamics in the description of SPIs, since this very interface, as well as governance processes more generally, are noticeably influenced by power (Krott et al. 2014, 4). Power is still a blind spot in analysing issues of sustainability transitions. While it often has a negative connotation, power can be constraining, but also enabling. It can be understood as 'the uneven capacity of different actors to influence the goals, process, and outcomes of polycentric governance' (Morrison et al. 2019, 2). Power matters in all governance processes, since it is relevant for determining and explaining the effectiveness of these processes (ibid., 3).

While addressing power dynamics in the context of governance, in general, is certainly not a new topic, it is only recently being analysed in the context of polycentric governance (which is the case for ESD governance). Hitherto, power in this context has often been seen as a 'black box of politics' (ibid.). Especially at the SPI, the involved actors including scientists 'can also find power dynamics sensitive and uncomfortable, and therefore may often deliberately or inadvertently overlook them' (ibid.). Probably some of the most central ESD-relevant power dynamics in Germany, at least in the sector of formal education, might be those between the Federal Ministry of Education and Research (which has some regulatory and significant symbolic power), and the ministries responsible for education in the 16 federal states (which have extensive regulatory power). Due to federalism, the remunerative power at the national level is limited to providing and financing the GAP implementation structures as described above and does not extend to being able to directly financially support implementation at the federal level. The federal level, in contrast, is equipped with remunerative power (Etzioni 1975, 32), while the level of practitioners is equipped with pragmatic power. They realise what Morrison et al. (2019) call the 'day-to-day practice and implementation of formal and informal rules and norms' (ibid., 3), and therefore they are the ones who decide what type and extent of ESD is eventually put into practice. Another form of indirect steering power can be seen in the governance by comparison strategies of the OECD described above, since they create a pull factor for what is being compared. This is especially so for the jurisdictions or organisations that appear as 'laggards' in this respect, but at the same time it constitutes an opportunity for effectively promoting important topics.

Against this background of how crucial different kinds of power shape the SPI as a whole, the monitoring itself and the methods described above can also be viewed in this light. Here, the scientific advisory team can be seen to be provided or lent symbolic and pragmatic power to conduct research and inform the SPI on the status and progress of ESD. At the same time, the role and distribution of different kinds of power within ESD governance can potentially be disrupted by approaches such as transdisciplinary monitoring, because this design includes the perspectives and interests of different groups. It might alter power dynamics through giving voice to, and increasing the visibility of, groups with less specific types of power (e.g. the non-formal learning organisations).

During our intersubjective group discussions, however, we became more aware of an important methodological limitation of transdisciplinary approaches in regard of power issues. On the one hand, including different actors and their different levels of influence in our research design as well as reflecting on our own involvement in the research setting might increase our awareness of potentials and drawbacks of kinds and extents of power. On the other hand, these methods are not meant to and, in most cases, will not, considerably contribute to significant changes in facets of power at the SPI regarding ESD implementation (for instance by strengthening positive aspects or limiting their problematic elements). For example, the high autonomy and pragmatic power of the individual federal states that can be seen as a barrier to effective and swift mainstreaming of ESD will largely remain unchanged regardless of whether or not this obstacle is diagnosed.

In relation to using the SPI for strengthening ESD, it is important to recognise that 'the values and perceptions of the actors involved are often more critical than the design properties of the governance mechanism itself' (Morrison et al. 2019, 4). Building on this, a future research contribution to SPIs would be to analyse the weighting between the levels of autonomy, ownership and meaningful co-creation of ESD governance, practice and research. Laying out differences in this issue of weighting appears supportive and occasionally even has a mediating influence at the SPI. For future analyses, stronger consideration of the role of power in these weighting decisions appears to be a vital and presumably empowering contribution to ESD research, governance and practice at the SPI.

Conclusion and outlook

The objective of this article was to reflect on experiences from the ESD monitoring project in Germany as an example of a formalised ESD-SPI in action and link them to more general characteristics and trends at (SD-related) SPIs. To this end, we used an analytic autoethnographic approach and organised regular intersubjective group discussions in which the individual analytical perspectives on dynamics at the ESD-SPI and our own roles were systematically examined. We also used the literature on evidence-informed trends in educational policies, the uptake of scientific results in policy making and questions of different kinds of power, to generate insights into working at the SPI.

One recurring theme concerned the need for researchers to alternate between critical detachment and constructive involvement with policymakers, as also argued by Læssøe, Feinstein, and Blum (2013, 233). Based on our reflections, this alternation needs to involve subtle shifting between both approaches, which often turned out to be a question of the right dose and timing. It has been argued that more explicit reflection on the dynamics emerging at the SPI makes scientific work more policy-relevant and thereby contributes to an accelerated and solution-oriented research agenda (Miller et al. 2014) of ESD. In this regard, the use of a transdisciplinary mixed-methods research design was helpful for us in addressing the needs of different stakeholders as well as maintaining sensitivity to the complexity inherent in ESD.

We would encourage other ESD researchers working in similar kinds of situations to build in systematic observation of, and reflection on, their work and interactions with others at the SPI. Informed by the approach of analytic autoethnography, we were able to systematically observe and analyse our own role and practices at the SPI. Our process, though, was not without limitations. Although we discussed various reflections in our intersubjective discussion, we did not directly involve the perspective of other groups of actors within the SPI. Therefore, our process lacked the views of different actors on issues such as effective ways of governing ESD. This issue also affected our understanding of which aspects of the evidence produced by us were received and used by different stakeholder groups. Furthermore, a recurring challenge in our intersubjective group discussions was differences in weighting the roles of involved insiders and critical outsiders against the background of our involvement at the SPI and maintaining trustful relationships with other actors.

Nevertheless, we recognise the potential of such a systematic approach that can also be used by other researchers to analyse their own involvement and strategies at the SPI. One simple starting point would be to use research journals to help document, discuss and study one's individual and collective reflections over a period of time. Connected with this, there were a number of questions that featured in our work in an ongoing way from the outset. These may be helpful for the work of other researchers who are operating at the ESD-SPI. These questions concerned:

- Which type(s) of SPI (see Kaaronen's differentiation above) are we part of?
- Who is involved in the SPI and in what way?
- What kinds of power relations are shaping the SPI and what are the roles of the actors involved?
- How are we involved in the SPI and which power relations are shaping our work as researchers?
- How can we find an appropriate balance between detachment and involvement with policy actors?
- What kinds of expertise, functions and expectations do actors bring to the SPI, especially with regard to measuring ESD?
- Which sector-specific timelines should be considered in advance?
- Which formats for dissemination of information should be used to address the different target groups of an SPI constructively?

In our experience, frequently updating one's answers to these questions – for example by means of intersubjective group discussions – can help to advance the understanding of SPIs and holds the potential to increase the policy relevance of a solution-oriented ESD research. In the upcoming work of German ESD monitoring, a central aim will be to increase reflexivity through analytic autoethnography and other possible approaches such as the Reflexive Monitoring Approach in Action (van Mierlo et al. 2010). We will expand the spaces for enhancing reflexivity and include groups of other stakeholders from the SPI and beyond. Workshops with members of the ESD-bodies will be organised with the aims of identifying un(der)used potential and negotiating conflicting interests or diverging system logics. In conclusion, we feel strongly that realising the potential of science–policy interfaces in ESE depends not only on how carefully they are navigated but, connected to that, how deeply they are reflected upon. Such reflections are vital for co-creating good ESD-policy and for effectively accelerating its implementation.

Notes

1. https://www.bundesregierung.de/resource/blob/975292/1559082/a9795692a667605f652981aa9b6cab51/deutsche-nachhaltigkeitsstrategie-aktualisierung-2018-download-bpa-data.pdf?download=1
2. https://www.bne-portal.de/en/education-sustainable-development-germany/gap-implementation-structures-germany

Disclosure statement

No potential conflict of interest was reported by the authors.

ORCID

Mandy Singer-Brodowski http://orcid.org/0000-0002-9176-318X

References

Aikens, Kathleen, Marcia McKenzie, and Philip Vaughter. 2016. "Environmental and Sustainability Education Policy Research: A Systematic Review of Methodological and Thematic Trends." *Environmental Education Research* 22 (3): 333–359. doi:10.1080/13504622.2015.1135418.

Anderson, Leon. 2006. "Analytic Autoethnography." *Journal of Contemporary Ethnography* 35 (4): 373–395. doi:10.1177/0891241605280449.

Biesta, Gert J. J. 2016. *Good Education in an Age of Measurement: Ethics, Politics, Democracy*. Interventions. London: Routledge Taylor & Francis Group.

Brock, Antje. 2018. "Indikatorenset Zur Verankerung Von BNE in Den Verschiedenen Bildungsbereichen." In *Wegmarken Zur Transformation. Nationales Monitoring Von Bildung Für Nachhaltige Entwicklung in Deutschland*, edited by Antje Brock, Gerhard de Haan, Nadine Etzkorn and Mandy Singer-Brodowski, 25–34. Opladen, Berlin, Toronto: Barbara Budrich.

Cairney, Paul, and Kathryn Oliver. 2017. "Evidence-Based Policymaking is Not like Evidence-Based Medicine, so How Far Should You Go to Bridge the Divide between Evidence and Policy?" *Health Research Policy and Systems* 15 (1): 1–11. doi:10.1186/s12961-017-0192-x.

Döbert, Hans, and Horst Weishaupt. 2012. "Bildungsmonitoring." In *Schul- Und Unterrichtsreform Durch Ergebnisorientierte Steuerung: Empirische Befunde Und Forschungsmethodische Implikationen*, edited by Albrecht Wacker, Uwe Maier, and Jochen Wissinger, 155–173. Wiesbaden: VS Verlag.

Etzioni, Amitai. 1975. *A Comparative Analysis of Complex Organizations: On Power, Involvement, and Their Correlates*. Rev. and enlarged ed. New York: Free Press.

Exley, Sonia, Annette Braun, and Stephen Ball. 2011. "Global Education Policy: Networks and Flows." *Critical Studies in Education* 52 (3): 213–218. doi:10.1080/17508487.2011.604079.

Geden, Oliver. 2016. "The Paris Agreement and the Inherent Inconsistency of Climate Policymaking." *Wiley Interdisciplinary Reviews: Climate Change* 7 (6): 790–797. doi:10.1002/wcc.427.

Gluckman, Peter. 2016. "The Science-Policy Interface." *Science* 353 (6303): 969–969. doi:10.1126/science.aai8837.

Grund, Julius, and Antje Brock. 2019a. "Education for Sustainable Development in Teaching and Learning Settings: Quantitative Study in the National Monitoring – Survey of Young People." https://www.ewi-psy.fu-berlin.de/einrichtungen/weitere/institut-futur/publikatione-n/WAP_BNE/index.html.

Grund, Julius, and Antje Brock. 2019b. "Education for Sustainable Development in Teaching and Learning Settings: Quantitative Study in the National Monitoring – Teaching Stuff." https://www.ewi-psy.fu-berlin.de/einrichtungen/weitere/institut-futur/publikationen/WAP_BNE/index.html.

Grund, Julius, and Antje Brock. 2019c. "Why We Should Empty Pandora's Box to Create a Sustainable Future: Hope, Sustainability and Its Implications for Education." *Sustainability* 11 (3): 893–913. doi:10.3390/su11030893.

Grund, Julius, and Antje Brock. 2020. "Education for Sustainable Development in Germany: Not Just Desired but Also Effective for Transformative Action." *Sustainability* 12 (7): 2838. doi:10.3390/su12072838.

Hepp, Gerd, ed. 2011. *Bildungspolitik in Deutschland. Eine Einführung*. Wiesbaden: VS Verl. für Sozialwissenschaften.

Holst, Jorrit, Antje Brock, Mandy Singer-Brodowski, and Gerhard de Haan. 2020. "Monitoring Progress of Change: Implementation of Education for Sustainable Development (ESD) within Documents of the German Education System." *Sustainability* 12 (10): 4306. doi:10.3390/su12104306.

Ioannidou, Alexandra. 2010. "Educational Monitoring and Reporting as Governance Instruments for Evidence-Based Education Policy." In *International Educational Governance*, edited by Karin Amos, 155–172. Vol. 12. Emerald Group Publishing Limited, Bingley.

Kaaronen, Roope. 2016. *Scientific Support for Sustainable Development Policies: A Typology of Science–Policy Interfaces with Case Studies*. Helsinki. https://media.sitra.fi/2017/02/28-142637/Selvityksia118.pdf.

Krott, Max, Axel Bader, Carsten Schusser, Rosan Devkota, Ahmad Maryudi, Lukas Giessen, and Helene Aurenhammer. 2014. "Actor-Centred Power: The Driving Force in Decentralised Community Based Forest Governance." *Forest Policy and Economics* 49: 34–42. doi:10.1016/j.forpol.2013.04.012.

Læssøe, Jeppe, Noah W. Feinstein, and Nicole Blum. 2013. "Environmental Education Policy Research – Challenges and Ways Research Might Cope with Them." *Environmental Education Research* 19 (2): 231–242. doi:10.1080/13504622.2013.778230.

Lang, Daniel J., Arnim Wiek, Matthias Bergmann, Michael Stauffacher, Pim Martens, Peter Moll, Mark Swilling, and Christopher J. Thomas. 2012. "Transdisciplinary Research in Sustainability Science: Practice, Principles, and Challenges." *Sustainability Science* 7 (Suppl 1): 25–43. doi:10.1007/s11625-011-0149-x.

Lawn, Martin, and Bob Lingard. 2002. "Constructing a European Policy Space in Educational Governance: The Role of Transnational Policy Actors." *European Educational Research Journal* 1 (2): 290–307. doi:10.2304/eerj.2002.1.2.6.

Martens, Kerstin, and Dennis Niemann. 2010. "Governance by Comparison: How Ratings & Rankings Impact National Policy-Making in Education." TranState Working PapersUR, https://www.econstor.eu/handle/10419/41595139. https://www.econstor.eu/bitstream-/10419/41595/1/639011268.pdf.

Mathiesen, Thomas. 1982. *Makt og Motmakt*. Oslo: Pax.

Miller, Thaddeus R., Arnim Wiek, Daniel Sarewitz, John Robinson, Lennart Olsson, David Kriebel, and Derk Loorbach. 2014. "The Future of Sustainability Science: A Solutions-Oriented Research Agenda." *Sustainability Science* 9 (2): 239–246. doi:10.1007/s11625-013-0224-6.

Morrison, Tiffany, Neil Adger, Katrina Brown, Maria C. Lemos, Dave Huitema, Jacob Phelps, Lousia Evans, et al. 2019. "The Black Box of Power in Polycentric Environmental Governance." *Global Environmental Change* 57: 101934. doi:10.1016/j.gloenvcha.2019.101934.

National Platform on Education for Sustainable Development. 2017. "National Action Plan on Education for Sustainable Development: The German contribution to the UNESCO Global Action Programme." https://www.bne-portal.de/sites/default/files/downloads/publikationen/BMBF_NAP_BNE_EN_Screen_2.pdf.

Nazir, Joanne, Erminia Pedretti, John Wallace, David Montemurro, and Hilary Inwood. 2009. "Climate Change and Sustainable Development: The Response from Education: The Canadian Perspective." Centre for Science, Mathematics and Technology EducationOntario Institute for Studies in Education, University of Toronto, Toronto

Nevo, Isaac, and Vered Slonim-Nevo. 2011. "The Myth of Evidence-Based Practice: Towards Evidence-Informed Practice." *British Journal of Social Work* 41 (6): 1176–1197. doi:10.1093/bjsw/bcq149.

Nutley, Sandra M., Isabel Walter, and Huw T. O. Davies. 2007. *Using Evidence How Research Can Inform Public Services*. Bristol: Policy Press.

OECD. 2007. *Evidence in Education: Linking Research and Policy*. Paris: OECD Publishing.

Oliver, Kathryn, Theo Lorenc, and Simon Innvær. 2014. "New Directions in Evidence-Based Policy Research: A Critical Analysis of the Literature." *Health Research Policy and Systems* 12 (1): 34. doi:10.1186/1478-4505-12-34.

Orland, Martin. 2012. "Separate Orbits: The Distinctive Worlds of Educational Research and Policymaking." In edited by G. Sykes , B. Schneider, D. N. Plank, and T. G. Ford (Eds), *Handbook of Education Policy Research*, 129–144. London: Routledge. https://content.taylorfrancis.com/books/download?dac=C2009-0-09106-5&isbn=978020-3880968&doi=10.4324/9780203880968-18&format=pdf.

Sarkki, Simo, Rob Tinch, Jari Niemelä, Ulrich Heink, Kerry Waylen, Johannes Timaeus, Juliette Young, Allan Watt, Carsten Neßhöver, and Sybille van den Hove. 2015. "Adding 'Iterativity' to the Credibility, Relevance, Legitimacy: A Novel Scheme to Highlight Dynamic Aspects of Science–Policy Interfaces." *Environmental Science & Policy* 54: 505–512. doi:10.1016/j.envsci.2015.02.016.

Singer-Brodowski, Mandy, Antje Brock, and Nadine Etzkorn. 2019. "Meeting the Expectations of Different Actors at the Science-Policy Interface – Monitoring of Education for Sustainable Development in Germany." In *Doing Educational Research: Overcoming Challenges in Practice*, edited by Marit H. Hoveid, Lucian Ciolan, Angelika Paseka, and Sofia M. d. Silva, 291–314. London [u. a.]: EERA, European Educational Research Association; SAGE.

Singer-Brodowski, Mandy, Antje Brock, Nadine Etzkorn, and Insa Otte. 2019. "Monitoring of Education for Sustainable Development in Germany – Insights from Early Childhood Education, School and Higher Education." *Environmental Education Research* 25 (4): 492–507. doi:10.1080/13504622.2018.1440380.

Singer-Brodowski, Mandy, Nadine Etzkorn, and Janne von Seggern. 2019. "One Transformation Path Does Not Fit All – Insights into the Diffusion Processes of Education for Sustainable Development in Different Educational Areas in Germany." *Sustainability* 11 (1): 269. (doi:10.3390/su11010269.

Singer-Brodowski, Mandy, Janne von Seggern, Anika Duveneck, and Nadine Etzkorn. 2020. "Moving (Reflexively within) Structures. The Governance of Education for Sustainable Development in Germany." *Sustainability* 12 (7): 2778. doi:10.3390/su12072778.

Steinke, Ines. 1999. *Kriterien Qualitativer Forschung: Ansätze Zur Bewertung Qualitativ-Empirischer Sozialforschung*. Weinheim: Juventa-Verlag.

Steinke, Ines. 2007. "Qualitätssicherung in Der Qualitativen Forschung." In *Qualitative Datenanalyse: computergestützt: Methodische Hintergründe Und Beispiele Aus Der Forschungspraxis*, edited by Udo Kuckartz, Heiko Grunenberg, and Thorsten Dresing, 176–187. 2., überarbeitete und erweiterte Auflage. Wiesbaden: VS Verlag für Sozialwissenschaften.

UNECE Steering Committee on ESD. 2007. "Indicators for Education for Sustainable Development. Progress report on the work of the Expert Group".http://www.unece.org/fileadmin/DAM//env/documents/2006/ece/cep/ac.13/ece.cep.ac.13.2006.5.e.pdf.

United Nations Economic Commission for Europe. 2018. "Format for reporting on the implementation of the UNECE Strategy for Education for Sustainable Development (2017–2019)." https://www.unece.org/fileadmin/DAM/env/esd/Implementation/NIR_2018/Germany_N-IR_2018.pdf.

van den Hove, Sybille. 2007. "A Rationale for Science–Policy Interfaces." *Futures* 39 (7): 807–826. doi:10.1016/j.futures.2006.12.004.

van Mierlo, Barbara, Barbara, Regeer, Mariëtte van Amstel, Marlèn Arkesteijn, Volkert Beekman, Joske Bunders, Tjard de Cock Buning, Boelie Elzen, Anne-Charlotte Hoes, and Cees Leeuwis. 2010. *Reflexive Monitoring in Action: A Guide for Monitoring System Innovation Projects*. The Netherlands: Communication and Innovation Studies, Wageningen University; Athena Institute; VU University Amsterdam; Wageningen UR Livestock Research. https://www.researchgate.net/publication/46383381_Reflexive_Monitoring_in_Action_A_guide_for_monitoring_system_innovation_projects.

van Poeck, Katrien, and Jonas A. Lysgaard. 2015. "The Roots and Routes of Environmental and Sustainability Education Policy Research." *Environmental Education Research* 22 (3): 305–318. doi:10.1080/13504622.2015.1108393.

Colombia's national policy of environmental education: a critical discourse analysis

María Angélica Mejía-Cáceres ⓘ, Alejandra Huérfano ⓘ, Alan Reid ⓘ and Laísa María Freire ⓘ

ABSTRACT
This article explores how an environmental education policy text comes to be constituted by discursive strategies that reproduce or challenge particular ideologies of environmentalism in relation to education. Using a qualitative analysis of discourses in the National Policy of Environmental Education of Colombia (NPEEC), we examine how these can be traced to a range of stakeholders. Unsurprisingly, key findings include that the discourses present in the policy strongly reflect broader policy agendas circulating in the country, such that the NPEEC falls in line with neoliberal policy prescriptions for addressing environmental challenges. The NPEEC also omits and transforms certain discourses from the environmental education researcher community, particularly when these offer critical and alternative viewpoints for tackling environmental issues through education. The article illuminates how these gaps and movements might be a result of global pressure on local governments, and how the contributions of nationally-recognised environmental education research and researchers have been reduced in the text of the NPEEC. We conclude this represents a problematic relation between research and policy, and discuss the features of this 'disidentification'.

Introduction

In this article, we explore an example of why relationships characterised by 'disidentification' might emerge between the worlds of environmental education (EE) policy and research. Our study focuses on discursive markers for aspects of research within the *National Policy of Environmental Education in Colombia* (NPEEC) (Ministerio del Medio Ambiente, and Ministerio de Educación Nacional, 2002). Using critical discourse analysis techniques, we illustrate the ways in which ideologies and power relations play out in developing and finalising particular government-level discourses of EE, aspects of which relate to shifting shapes and patterns of relationship between the 'two worlds', while also remaining open to other possibilities and readings.

Our work proceeds from the recognition that while Colombia has been committed to instilling and promoting EE within its decentralised, public education system (Faguet and Sánchez 2008), its presence and outcomes in relation to the realities and impact of EE have been routinely treated as 'failing' to deliver on its commitments by national and international EE researchers (e.g. Macedo and Salgado 2007; Torres Carrasco, 2010a; Florez-Yepes 2015; Gaudiano and Lorenzetti 2012; Gutiérrez 2015; Mora Ortiz 2016; Henao Hueso and Sánchez Arce 2019). To explain this assessment, we argue scholarship on recent policy and policy development should be able to account for the features of actual relationships between the worlds of academia and policy-making, by considering their unique and entwined histories in Colombia. This includes how particular researchers and research have been, and are, positioned in policy-making processes and policy texts.

The article begins with a brief overview of the situation and various policy trajectories that have emerged in Colombia. We then draw on select literature for understanding: (a) educational policy as an ideological tool, and (b) using critical discourse analysis to identify particular relationships between policy and research about education. We then outline the study's methodology and each stage of the research process, followed by extracts from our analysis. The findings focus on the discursive practices regarding the textual dimension, which includes intertextuality and interdiscursivity, and the cognitive dimension, in terms of the modes of operation of ideology that can be detected in the NPEEC. We conclude by outlining a series of challenges and next steps to better understand the relationship between research and policy-making in EE in Colombia, and in similar situations.

Background

To understand the policy configurations and trajectories of the present, we have to consider the effects of the policy conditions and priorities of the past.

The first official stirrings of environmental education (EE) in Colombia can be traced to 1974 (Congreso de la República de Colombia 1974). In the National Code of Natural Resources (Código Nacional de los Recursos Naturales), Congress made a decree (#2811) that articulated a series of policy specifications for the formal education sector. In step with international environmental guidelines from the time, e.g. those discussed at the UN Conference on the Human Environment held in Stockholm (1972), the environmental ideologies associated with these policy specifications were tilted strongly towards a conservationist perspective (O'Brien 1995). However, despite ongoing local, regional and international work by educators and academics to develop localized interpretations aligned with the internationalized conception of EE at Belgrade and Tbilisi by UNESCO and UNEP (UNESCO, 1978, UNESCO 1980)—including in Bogotá, Colombia in the run up to Tbilisi (Teitelbaum 1978)—these initial specifications made little difference to the subsequent work of government ministries responsible for education and the environment in Colombia (Guhl, Wagner, and Zapata 2015).

An immediate barrier to subsequent progress in conceptualisation and practice development in Colombia was the widespread embrace by government of neoliberal ideologies associated with structural adjustment policies (Faguet and Sánchez 2008). These took a strong hold on policy-making in the 1980s, and reinforced a relationship of *subservience* of environmental considerations to economic policy (O'Brien 1995, 16). For Youkhana, Leifkes, and León-Sicard (2018, 22), the initial work of the 1970s only succeeded in "putting ecological education and preservation in the education agenda". It has also been argued EE didn't receive renewed interest in Colombia until the uptake of sustainable development as a concept in the late 1980s (and thus its relation of possible displacement via education for sustainable development (ESD) later on), coupled with the spotlight on renewing national and regional policies at the time of the Rio Earth Summit (Colombia 1992; UNCED, 1992) (see Rodriguez Becerra 1994; Vélez Rojas and Londoño Pineda 2016, 177–179).

Accordingly, it is largely since the 1990s that at state and regional levels, conditions in Colombia have shifted enough to afford any linking or prioritization of the environment, education and EE, in policy. Notwithstanding the ongoing work of NGOs, community organizations, 'popular actions', mass mobilization of environmental and social movements, and other third sector activities in preparing the ground to advance EE (O'Brien 1995, 17–18, and for contemporary illustrations, see the work of Ecogente 83, INDERENA and *Trama*), the major breakthrough at policy level occurred in 1991. The National Constitution of 1991 [*Nueva Constitución*, 1991] (República de Colombia 1991) prepared the ground, shortly followed by the official inclusion of EE in the education system via Law 115 in 1994 (República de Colombia, 1994).

In brief, the new constitution (República de Colombia 1991) enshrined 43 principles and laws on the relationship between the environment and development. These included a declaration that the environment is a common heritage and it is the duty of the State and the individual to protect and conserve that (Article 8), and the individual has the right to a healthy environment (Article 98). The introduction of the concepts of 'sustainable development', 'quality of life' and 'ecological wealth' also helped signal an ideological shift away from the previous 1886 constitution, which had positioned the environment largely in terms of territoriality and natural resources to be exploited (Article 80). As O'Brien (1995, 15) put it at the time:

> "Colombia's environmental movement has gone through four broad stages: that of denunciation, that of environmental education and local environmental work, that of defining alternative strategies of development and finally a formal process of concertation with the state and other groups for a strategy of sustainable development."

Meanwhile, Law 99 of 1993 (República de Colombia, 1993) created the Ministry of the Environment, the first post-UNCED ministry of the environment, and the National Environmental System (*Sistema Nacional Ambiental* - SINA, acronym from Spanish) to oversee environmental protections. The Constitution of 1991 also introduced compulsory schooling for children between 5 and 15 years of age. Article 5 required the creation of plans, educational programs and curricula in the different levels of national education in relation to the environment, to encourage people to 'adopt lifestyles compatible with sustainability gained by proper exploration, exploitation, utilization and management of natural resources' (our translation). Article 67 enshrined education as an important tool to promote environmental awareness and protection ('Education will form the Colombian in the respect of human rights, peace and democracy … for cultural, scientific and technological improvement and for the protection of the environment').

The final addition to this initial national EE policy mix was Law 115 of 1994 (República de Colombia. 1994). It restated the aims and guidelines for Colombian education, focusing on curriculum, educative levels and transversal issues. It is here, and for the first time, that EE was established as an educational policy in Colombia through the School Environmental Project (SEP), creating a norm for all levels of formal education. In addition, the relationships and networks between the Ministry of Education and the Ministry of the Environment were formed. Since this time, EE in Colombia was supposed to respond to intercultural principles, value formation, regionalization, interdisciplinarity, democracy, and participation in all levels of the curriculum. At the same time, the Ministry of Education published Decree 1743 of 1994 (Ministerio de Educación Nacional 1994b) establishing the obligatory creation and application of the SEP.

Together, these legislative provisions determined the legal parameters in which EE would be able to play a role in Colombian policy and civil life, as well as in education programs and institutions (Mejía Cáceres and Zambrano 2018). The provisions also afforded opportunities for synchronization between the work programs of the fledgling Ministry of Environment and the more established Ministry of Education, working together on projects, plans and curricular proposals to strengthen SINA (Ministerio de medio Ambiente & Ministerio de Educación Nacional, 2002).

Complicated histories and currents

Sauvé's (2005) survey of international currents in EE draws attention to the emergence of a bioregional pedagogical model in Colombia. Offered in the work of Talero de Husain and Humaña de Gauthier (1993), the model put the school at the centre of the community's social and environmental development, and places a strong emphasis on a participatory approach to ensure contextual meaning and localized practice development. The model is emblematic of ideal versions of EE policy and practice across Colombia's regions and central and regional universities at the time. It was also popularized via the Interinstitutional Technical Committees of Environmental Education (CIDEA, acronym in Spanish), created by the Ministry of Education and the Ministry of Environment, and as we show below, has particular resonances with ideologies for EE originating in academia.

Returning to 1992, the Ministry of Environment had signed an agreement with CIDEA, from which emerged the requirement of inclusion of an "environmental dimension" in education. There were three work phases: (1) an exploration phase, that resulted in projects, proposals and activities (such as the bioregional model); (2) a theoretical reflection about education and environment (that later allowed the formulation of the General Law of Education); and (3) the creation of a National Policy for EE, based on the 1991 National Environmental Education Plan that introduced EE throughout the primary level (Colombia 1992).

In addition to directing its own EE initiatives, Colombia partnered with its neighbours in Latin America, and with the United Nations, to expand the scope of its environmental protections, including via EE (see Novo 2009, 198). To illustrate the broader constituencies in EE policy making and enactment, we note Colombia secured a 'debt for environment and social swap' from Canada at the Rio Conference in 1992, to fund the administrative costs of *Ecofondo* (1993). This 'aid' ensured Ecofondo's work as an umbrella organisation would continue, bringing together NGO, university and government representatives and a network of regional environmental units. This was despite reservations about continued 'foreign interference' from countries such as Canada in some academic circles and regions in Colombia to develop EE practice (Torres Palacios and Rodriguez Bolanos 2013; cf. Paz, Avendaño C, and Parada-Trujillo 2014).

As stated by Torres Carrasco (2010b), in broad terms, EE in Colombia at that time was intended to be rooted in local guidance for each region, built though participatory means: "collectively and systematically in every social construct, starting with the family, the school, work, the neighbourhood, the town, and the State" (p. 115, our translation). Since 1994, with NPEEC, the government of Colombia included EE in school curricula and made it obligatory. Additionally, the Ministry of Education and the Ministry of Environment had created a document to provide guidelines for the process of EE at different levels and in various contexts, aligned with NPEEC (Torres Carrasco 1996, 1998). While through *Ecofondo* and other brokering organisations, the Ministry of the Environment also partnered with other agencies and local interests to foster support for sustainability and citizen led educational projects, including with universities (GEEP, 2016).

Regarding this emerging work and the National Constitution of 1991, Law 115 of the General Law of Education, 1994 (República de Colombia, 1994), established the necessity and scope of education about environmental protection, ecology and natural resources preservation as mandatory in formal schools (Paz, Avendaño C, and Parada-Trujillo 2014). The National Program of EE followed the Plan, and had been established from these and later 'normative dispositions', while also affording the coordination of the educational system with SINA and other research institutions. As Sauvé et al. (2005, 278), put it, the 2002 version of EE was "a formal recognition of initiatives already progressively developed since 1994", where the proposed actions aimed at introducing the environmental dimension as an integral and holistic part of education, i.e. going beyond mainly being taught alongside the natural sciences. Thus, within the NPEEC, EE (*educación ambiental*), was explicitly positioned as:

"the process that allows an individual to understand the relationships of interdependence with their environment, through reflexive and critical knowledge of their biophysical, social, political, economic and cultural reality, so that attitudes of appreciation and respect for the environment may be promoted by the individual and their community."

(our translation, adapted from Sauvé et al., 2005, 277, based on Ministerio de Educación Nacional, 1998, p. 17; Ministerio del Medio Ambiente & Ministerio de Educación Nacional, 2002, p. 21)

Decree 1743 in Law 114 of 1994 (Ministerio de Educación Nacional, 1994b) had mandated that every school must implement an environmental project in its curriculum (SEP in English, PRAES, plural acronym from Spanish). These pedagogical projects (Ministerio de Educación Nacional 2016, unpaginated, our translation) had to:

"Provide frameworks of conceptual, strategic and projective nature, which from the systemic vision of the environment and the purposes of comprehensive training of individuals and groups, guide the environmental educational actions that are carried out in the country, in the different scenarios and levels of formal education, education for work and human development, and informal education; promoting the construction of region and territory, in the context of an ethical culture for the sustainable management of the environment."

PRAES were regulated by the Ministry of Education (Torres Carrasco 2009; Torres López 2011). In their survey of the situation in Colombia, Sauvé et al. (2005, 277-278) had suggested that contemporary policy on EE was:

"a very rich example of the national institutionalization of the field. This policy is based on an explicit vision of the construction of an 'environmental culture' (of an essentially ethical nature) and an extended theoretical and strategic framework for EE. The adopted conception of sustainability (as one among a plurality of EE issues) has strong ideological, ethical, sociocultural, political and natural components; the economic component is not put forward to the detriment of other components, and important clarifications are given to distinguish 'growth' (*crecimiento*) from 'development' (*desarrollo*). Education is not seen as a mere instrument for a predetermined goal, but as a participatory process for the development of a new citizenry, for personal and social identity construction, valuing cultural diversity and interculturality. Furthermore, a diversity of ways of perceiving the environment is promoted. The environment is not only a pool of resources to be managed and problems to be resolved. It is also a place to live, a community project in which to get involved and to feel a sense of belonging towards collective responsibility. The themes of culture and peace are also very important, and EE is seen as a contributing factor to the emergence of a culture of peace and to the reconstruction of the Colombian society."

Nonetheless, this law was not generalised for every education sector as it did not include higher education. Universities, including teacher preparation courses, were left to interpret their own priorities (Berdugo Silva and Montaño Renuma 2017). The NPEEC (2002) however, was designed to absorb that independence, through the intention of creating a self-improving system such that every scenario and level of education would eventually be included (Ministerio de Educación Nacional 2005a). Monitoring and evaluation of the policy and PRAES, for example, led to opportunities for the active role of researchers in policy and program revision (Ministerio de Educación Nacional 2010). While in 2012, Law 1549 stated:

- Every person has the right and the responsibility to participate in environmental educative processes.
- The Ministry of Education, the Ministry of Environment and other institutions involved are required to reinforce and strengthen the PRAES at all schools in primary and secondary education.
- The PRAES must offer concrete activities and actions that allow children and teenagers to develop environmental cognition as well as ethical and responsive behaviour (our translation, República de Colombia 2012).

However, there were tensions in both policy, practice and research in Colombia. Vélez Rojas and Londoño Pineda (2016, 175, our translation) noted that even with the application of Law

1549, policy and practice "cannot be said to have gone beyond the normative commitment, because there is evidence of a clear disconnect between the formal, non-formal and informal education sectors; for this reason, there are serious environmental and social problems that reflect the need for training of those who make up these sectors". Earlier, Calderón and Cerón (2005) had critiqued an over-reliance on natural science teachers rather than generating or employing EE professionals to meet legislative obligations in the NPEEC. Equally, Gaudiano and Lorenzetti (2012, 175) in their regional survey, strike to the heart of this study, concluding that:

> the environmental education field has shifted progressively towards education for sustainable development. School environmental projects (*proyectos ambientales escolares*: PRAES) supported by the Colombian Ministry of Education have followed this shift. Very little is done in the environmental education research field. Even though the implementation of the decennial plan for environmental education, legally in effect from 2005 until 2014, has contemplated a proposal for a diagnostic research project on the progress of environmental education since its inception in Colombia, the trend experienced by the PRAES has also taken hold with education for sustainable development being included in the plans. Any other studies start with the premise that environmental education is for sustainable development, with the exception of isolated research projects such as that carried out at the National University of Colombia, particularly the Institute of Environmental Studies, which takes a very critical look at the way environmental education had been handled in Colombia (Ángel Maya, 2000; Noguera 2002).

Towards a research design

Treating the NPEEC as a policy text, we recognize the policy draws on contributions from professors, scholars and researchers in Colombia, and will be interpreted and translated by social actors in educational institutions, such as teachers, policymakers, and academics from a range of positions and perspectives (Ball 2015). Moreover, while the NPEEC was being drafted, many discourses were consulted, interpreted and translated, including for setting out the 'normative commitments' noted above, sourced from local and international scholars. So, following Ball (2006), we were motivated to identify whether research discourses are located or dislocated in this policy for schools and educational institutions, including in relation to their physical and cultural environment. On the one hand, this can be to test whether the NPEEC aligns with local conditions, and in so doing, emphasises or silences some aspects over others. On the other, it allows us to test whether there are particular characteristics held to be significant in the formation and realization of this policy. As with Ball, a policy discourse offers a discursive representation of reality, albeit one that is not always recognised by those living and working with that reality, or in other realities. Equally, assuming discourse is a moment of social practice that is a relatively stabilised form of social activity (Fairclough 2001), a discourse analysis of the NPEEC can be used to identify ideological assumptions about educational and environmental discourses embedded in policy texts, and through critique, surface other possibilities.

Theoretical framework

Education policy as an ideological tool

We base this first aspect of our study on Thompson (2004), who considered ideology an index for the problems related to the interrelationship between meaning and power. If we are to develop a critical conception of ideology in education policy, this assumption allows us to treat ideology as an orientation to meaning and power, so we can then undertake a critical analysis of the associated meanings and expectations, normative and otherwise, of various ideologies.

Appraising ideology in the NPEEC is important because it impacts the educational process as much as shapes environmental priorities and outcomes. Ideologies coursing across the terrains of EE typically include neo-liberalism, neo-conservatism, democratic socialism, and authoritarian populism (see Scott, 2010, 34). These are found in a tense coalition of forces in Colombia that enable dominance as well as seek to crush other positions (see Torres Carrasco, 2010b). The educational process is entangled with, regulated by, and contested through the dominant ideology in Colombia (Zuluaga and Echeverri 2003; Torres Carrasco, 2010b, especially p.118, on education). More broadly though, Apple (2006, 49) argues ideology can overcome its own internal contradictions and that 'ideologues' can succeed in radically transforming educational policy and practice. For EE and ESD globally, Jickling and Wals (2008) have noted the dominating power of neoliberalism and its proposals for 'market solutions' to educational problems, as a negative version of this 'success'. As in Colombia, these proposals suggest universal schemes for educational quality (e.g. with policy regimes and protocols emanating from the World Bank). These homogenise the local educational landscape by materialising various global educational policies and international research agendas (Cachelin, Rose, and Paisley 2015; Vélez Rojas and Londoño Pineda 2016; Henao Hueso and Sánchez Arce 2019), such as in relation to transitioning local EE into a globalised form of Education for Sustainable Development (UNESCO 1997).

Policy enactment in education

With this in mind, considering policy as a representation of power through knowledge, we might also suspect power waxes and wanes not in a linear but a complex process. In education policy, this includes through the possibilities of transformation and displacement as it manifests the relationships in a dynamic social network (Maguire et al. 2011; Ball, Maguire, and Braun 2012). Additionally, policy discourses act on and influence one another intertextually (Maguire et al. 2011). Therefore, education policy may interact with other policies not only from the same field but also from other fields, such as economics or resource management. Each policy discourse has different national and international sources, influences and various enactors. While as with Rizvi and Lingard, we note "policy readership is much wider than the practitioners who may enact it, and therefore, policy may seek to suture different, even oppositional ideological positions" (2010, in Spratt 2017, 17).

In elaborating a theory of policy enactments, Ball, Maguire, and Braun (2012) consider three facets of policy work and process, namely: the *material* (physical aspects of schools and context), *interpretative* (problem of the meaning) and *discursive* facets. "None of the three, alone, is considered sufficient to capture, understand, and represent the process of putting politics into action" (Lopes 2016, 5, our translation). Considering that texts themselves are the products of compromises and power struggles, including between academics and policy-makers, we consider whether policymaking has potentially productive and/or constraining effects according to their conception and mobilization of one specific topic (in our case, EE) in educational policy (e.g. McKenzie, Bieler, and McNeil 2015). In other words, we want to notice whether power is reconfigured by policy, and power reconfigures policy, using NPEEC as a test site for these considerations.

Methodology

Critical discourse analysis (CDA)

Critical discourse analysis (CDA) is an interdisciplinary approach to the study of discourse as a form of social practice[1]. As with the aforementioned facets, key assumptions are that discourse is constitutive and contributes to the building of social identity, subjects, social relationships, and systems of knowledge and beliefs. More specifically, discourse is a practice that gives meaning to the world (Fairclough 2001).

For Foucault, knowledge acts a constitutive element of discourse. As a result, it is necessary to consider the relationship between knowledge and power (Fairclough 2001). Foucault's genealogical methods encourage us to reflect on the intimate disciplinary and confessional practices gradually established among individual identities, society and the modern nation state, made visible through the championing and contestation of a public policy discourse. As Bastalich (2009, 4) describes:

> "Genealogy offers socially relevant descriptions of the interrelations of past practice and knowledge that enable reflection on our current condition. Their value lies in their ability to open the field of practice by throwing current rules into doubt."

Researchers of education such as Ball (and his students) have drawn on Foucault's genealogical method of inquiry to elucidate the ways in which discourse, power and knowledge are articulated. However, our work also draws on CDA to identify the connections among the linguistic selections of particular social actors or groups and social aspects.

Thus, in this project, we are interested in how the NPEEC was constituted through hybrid configurations among diverse genres and discourses, which according to Fairclough, drawing on Bakhtin (1981), might be identified through signs of intertextuality. Analysing the intertextuality of the policy through CDA is helpful because, as Ball, Maguire, and Braun (2012, p.15) argue, "policy texts are normally written to be authoritative and persuasive and are accretative and intertextual." Accordingly, we must recognise that discourse can create and mobilise power, as well as subvert existing powers. At the same time, power can be expressed and reproduced through discourse (Van Dijk 2016). Intertextuality may thus show the mobilisation of power in discourse, so that in a Bakhtinian sense, texts and statements are shaped by the 'powers' of previous texts to which they are responding, and by the subsequent texts that they precede (Fairclough 1992, 134).

To understand intertextuality in the NPEEC context then, it is necessary to consider each policy statement as embedded within a chain of communication, albeit some are treated as more authoritative than others. We understand the history of a social practice and its texts within their layers of context (hence our background section), as all text is built by including and responding to other texts from the past. Furthermore, these past texts can be transformed, accentuated, and reworked in successive texts through the constitutive and reconstitutive effects of discourse-related social practices. Intertextuality can thus be seen as incorporating potentially complex relationships given the discursive conventions and options available (genres, discourses, styles, activity types). Similarly, policy texts are often replete with parts of other texts—which may be explicitly demarcated or thoroughly merged—through assimilation, contradiction, ironic echoes, and so forth (Fairclough 1992). Finally, there is also the possibility of interdiscursivity (or constitutive intertextuality), which refers to mixing the configuration of the discourse conventions, such as genres, activity types, and styles associated with different types of discourse (Fairclough 1992).

Research methods

To identify which researchers' discourses are expressed in the NPEEC, we started with questions to organize our analysis of the text. These were: *which categories allow the identification of researchers' discourse? How can ideologies be identified in the text? Does the policy explicitly reference other texts (intertextuality)? Does the policy mix genres, activity types, and styles and form a hybridization of discourses (interdiscursivity)?*

Our methods started with an initial 'preliminary review' driven by these questions, followed by three other stages.

The *preliminary review* aimed to identify those Colombian researchers who had contributed to EE before NPEEC. We reviewed journals and books (journals on the Dialnet platform[2] and books in the Online Public Access Catalogue (OPAC) of the University of Valle, Colombia). Our analysis revealed that only 38 documents (2 papers and 36 books) met our criteria. These two platforms (Dialnet and OPAC) were reviewed by using the keyword 'environmental education' (*educación ambiental*, in Spanish) and were restricted to papers and books published before 2002. Next, we reviewed and selected the papers and books that had an explicit environmental dimension or discussed EE as an approach. Then, we reviewed their bibliography references, and selected the citations of Colombian researchers. Finally, we compared the cited authors between the journals and books. The findings showed an international diversity of authors, but our focus was on the visibility of Colombian authors. We found that only five Colombian researchers were referenced in these journals and books before the NPEEC, namely: *Augusto Ángel Maya, Maritza Torres (Carrasco), Ana Patricia Noguera, Gustavo Wilches Chaux,* and *Julio Carrizosa*.

In brief, among other roles:

- *Carlos Augusto Ángel Maya,* was a Full Professor of the National University of Colombia, and founder of the Institute of Environmental Studies (IDEA) of the same University in 1991
- *Maritza Torres* was the National Coordinator of the Environmental Education Program of the Ministry of National Education of Colombia and Teacher-Researcher of the Faculty of Environment and Natural Resources of the Santafe District University of Bogotá
- *Ana Patricia Noguera* was a Full Professor of the National University of Colombia, holding a chair in Environmental Thought and Philosophy
- *Gustavo Wilches Chaux* was the first Director of the *Ecofondo* and was one of the founding members of LA RED (Social Studies Network on Disasters in Latin America), working as a writer and professor at Externado University of Colombia too
- *Julio Carrizosa* was Director and a Full Professor at IDEA, National University of Colombia.

The second stage involved identifying the textual structure of the NPEEC by identifying the pre-genres and genres of the policy. According to Bonini (2010, 489), drawing on Fairclough's CDA, genre analysis involves identifying "a set of typical actions of textualization, text production and comprehension, which performs at least one social practice within various possible relational chains, carrying out then the discourse and the social structure." Genre frames action, meaning, representation and identification, and how these areas are realized in the various features of texts. When genre presents a high level of abstraction, it is called pre-genre, e.g. narrative, argument, description and conversation (Fairclough 2003).

The third stage involved identifying the codification of each of the aforementioned researchers' discourses. In this stage, we focused on two different moments to identify inductive codes, both of which were established after reading the text. In the first, our goal was to understand the research discourses of each of the scholars whose ideas appeared in the policy. We used emergent coding schemes to code the selections of the authors' ideas and thoughts using the following broad ideas: (1) ideological words to describe the environment; (2) ideological words to describe EE; (3) arguments used in favour of EE; and (4) their proposal for or contribution to the field of EE. Categories were derived directly from the data (Mayring 2000). [The scholars' perspectives and associated ideologies for each inductive code are illustrated in Table 2.]

Our second inductive coding was based on a preliminary scan of the text, from which we identified a theme by understanding it as "a pattern in the information that at a minimum describes and organizes the possible observations and at maximum interprets aspects of the phenomenon" (Boyatzis 1998, 161). Accordingly, we identified a pattern aligned with the researchers' theoretical framework. Terms appearing less than 10 times were not considered in the final analysis.

In the fourth stage, we analysed the discursive practices through categories that referred to the textual dimension through: a) the frequency of discourses, b) intertextuality, and c) interdiscursivity. This involved the following steps:

1. we ran the entire document through AdTAT (concordancing software from the University of Adelaide), which allowed us to identify the position and uses of the discourses' codes, such as the culture, environmental system, and environment;

Table 1. Ideological strategies, modes of operation and features (adapted from Thompson 2004).

Ideological strategies	Associated foci and modes of operation		Typical features of symbolic construction
Legitimization	Representing relations of domination in ways that court acceptance and dissuade dissent	Rationalization	Rational arguments
		Universalization	Dissemination of representations
		Narration	Reproducing stories
Dissimulation	Denying or obscuring relations of domination	Displacement	Adding positive or negative connotations to discussion of fields
		Euphemisms	Positively presented actions
		Trope	Synecdoche, metonym, metaphor
Unification	Deploying symbolic constructions of units in ways that foster collective identity	Standardization	Shared pattern
		Symbolization	Construction of symbols and collectivity
Fragmentation	Accentuating division among individuals or groups	Differentiation	Emphasis on features that divide the community
		Construction of an "enemy"	Capitalizing on polarization and division
Reification	Presenting transient, social, and historical situations as permanent and natural	Naturalization	Social creations treated as natural events
		Externalization	Facts assumed as permanent
		Nominalization and passivity	Obscuring or omitting social actors

2. intertextuality was identified through references incorporated into a text that were either explicitly marked—for example, by quotation marks and reporting clauses—or by using the exact words of the researcher;
3. interdiscursivity was interpreted through the analysis of the particular mix of genres, of discourses, and how different genres, discourses are articulatet; for example, UN-style 'the society we want', 'the future we want' and 'the world we want', echoed in the NPEEC, as "the peaceful society that Colombia wants".

Finally, although we read the entire document, following Fairclough, we focused on identifying the key discourses and modes of operation of ideologies to identify the underlying ideologies in discourses of dominance and resistance. Thus, we also tried to identify gaps, fractures, contradictions, and, thus, possibilities for social transformation, as part of our critical reading.

To identify the discourses of *dominance* (which is connected to the neo-liberal political project of removing obstacles to the new economic order, Gee, Hull, and Lankshear 1996), we looked for terms or evidence related to globalization, governance, flexibility, ethics (as a change of behaviour), employability, exclusion, and nature (as an object or resource). To identify the discourses of *resistance*, we considered, for instance, new management discourses that attempted to resurrect or create management systems based on teamwork and relatively non-hierarchical and networked ways of encouraging participation and managing organisations (Fairclough 2017). In addition, we considered the modes of operation of the ideological strategies proposed by Thompson (2004), namely, legitimization, dissimulation, unification, fragmentation, and reification. In Table 1 below, we explain each mode and typical features of symbolic construction in discourse.

Findings and interpretation

In the first section of our findings, we introduce the pre-genres and genres of the policy. In the second, we identify the researchers' discourses and interdiscursivity through inductive codes. In the third, we analyse how the citation was used or if the citation was omitted.

Textual structure of the national policy of environmental education

The policy text is available online (NPEEC - Ministerio de medio Ambiente & Ministerio de Educación Nacional, 2002). It is 69 pages long and is structured into eight chapters, as follows:

The first offers an introduction, the second presents the background and justification for such a policy, the third defines the aims of the NPEEC, the fourth covers basic conceptual guidelines, the fifth outlines the general principles that guide EE, the sixth refers to the strategies and challenges for EE, the seventh outlines financial resources for implementation, and the final chapter makes recommendations. (These are in terms of financing of the national environmental system, commissions, political actions, and projects of the Office of Research, Participation and Education of the Ministry of the Environment, the EE Program of the Ministry of Education, and the Prevention and Disaster Management Office.)

Unsurprisingly, the NPEEC has a combination of pre-genres, such as exposition and description, because the text provides guidelines about how to enact EE within and across Colombia. When genre transcends specific networks of practices, involves a socio-historical process, and is a less abstract category, it is called *'disembedding'*. It is typical of a national policy, and we note too that the NPEEC has the 'force of law' (Pierce 2015). On the one hand, it performs *directive* and *declarative* speech acts, such as to 'compel, demand, forbid, ban, authorize, approve, and legalize' (Cooren 2004, in Pierce 2015), in the attempt to regulate all citizens' lives concerning EE. On the other, the function of its language is *representative*, because it aspires to inform the receiver, and is *conative* (appellative) because it attempts to influence the behaviour of the receiver. Thus, we can also consider the NPEEC to be a 'doctrinal' text because it offers an interpretation of the law on EE, and it is similar to the liberal humanist genres of the Colombian laws of the time (Appadurai 1996).

Colombian researchers and discourses
In this section, we identify the researchers' discourses in the policy, the inductive codes, interdiscursivity and intertextuality. While reading the researchers' proposals to generate inductive codes, we found that some categories of open coding were key to the discourses, namely: *culture, ecosystem, system, problems, holistic, risk management, ethics, aesthetics, mobilization,* and *territory*. These inductive codes (Table 2) correspond to a principal theme (Table 3) worked into the theoretical framework by each researcher[3], while the degree to which these features are taken up or sidelined in the NPEEC forms the basis of our notion of 'disidentification'.

We chose repetition or frequency as the key criteria to delimit codes in our corpus (Table 2). Repetition and frequency were used because repetition is a rhetorical strategy used to persuade; political texts aim to be persuasive, and their structure is commonly rhetorical (Van Dijk 1997). Based on the results from analysis of frequencies, we noted that the theme with the highest (Table 3) were the word 'culture' used by Augusto Ángel Maya, followed by 'system' and 'problems' by Maritza Torres (Carrasco), then Julio Carrizosa's 'territory', and finally, Ana Patricia Noguera's term 'ethic'. Gustavo Wilches' 'risk management' was found less than ten times, as were the terms 'ecosystem', 'aesthetic', 'experience' and 'mobilization,' as used by other researchers. However, we studied each of the selected themes in detail, considering sentence context and examining whether they corresponded to the authors' perspective, or were used differently.

AdTAT helped count the frequency of the themes and determine the position of the keywords; the tool also enabled us to go back and review the meaning of the inductive code and how it was used, based on its position. In addition, we identified which theme were associated with one another and the key examples of interdiscursivity. We started with culture and identified seven uses, as follows:

Culture.

1. Culture as a *dimension of society or sustainability*: here, culture is considered to articulate the relationship between society and nature. It is a social dimension that represents worldview,

Table 2. Inductive coding for researcher discourses.

Code	Augusto Ángel Maya	Maritza Torres	Gustavo Wilchex Chaux	Ana Patricia Noguera	Julio Carrizosa
Emphases in perspective on the environment	Relationship (between culture and ecosystem; both emerge from nature. In addition, culture is necessary for humans to adapt to the ecosystem)	System	Holistic, A Scenery	Problem, Life network	Denaturalizing, and decoding (the concept of the environment, incorporating the duty to be ethical and aesthetic as well as subjective values towards knowledge and tasks related to environmental management practices)
Snapshot of EE	A process of transformation of the symbols of culture in service of an earth-centred logic; hence ecological education is key	A strategic and integral educative process for addressing environmental challenges	A worldview and a perspective to contextualise all educative processes	A resignification of being, body and life	An instrument for adapting society to the affordances, risks and constraints arising from the physical environment
Key arguments in favour of EE in Colombia	Latin American environmental thinking offers a way of decolonizing and localizing EE	EE is an essential process and feature for education of the social and biological subject	EE is crucial for building sufficiently interdisciplinary social and pedagogic processes	EE is a social imperative that ensures recognition of the world within a new ethics, aesthetics and culture	Society needs an educational form that recognises territory, the deterioration of ecosystem, risk, and limits arising from prevailing forms and the cumulative effects of economic activity
Key features of proposal for EE	Prioritising the environmentalisation of education through the defragmentation of disciplines, combining aesthetics and environmental ethics, and ensuring dialogues about knowledge premised on the assumption that life is fundamentally poetic	All educational levels need to have a progressive series of EE projects, to resolve environmental problems of differing scales and complexities	Reviving the role of sensory and affective experience is essential for the exploration and understanding of reality, particularly as a source of knowledge and maintaining a range of types of education (e.g. non-formal)	A focus on environmental problems is problematic: it leads to the reduction of the human to the knowing subject which also leads to the reduction of the world to an object	Reflection on a concept, a strategy and an environmental policy affords the demarcation of what is properly Latin American in its historical sources. This is a better basis for moving forwards and the construction of an environmental rationality for the sustainable development of the peoples of this region than non-local considerations

Table 3. Inductive categories for key themes of Colombian researchers.

	Augusto Ángel Maya	Maritza Torres	Gustavo Wilchex Chaux	Ana Patricia Noguera	Julio Carrizosa
Key themes	Culture, Ecosystem	System, Problems	Holistic, Risk Management	Ethics, Aesthetics	Mobilization, Territory

ideologies, discourses, and traditions of communities. It is also associated with other themes, such as Torres' 'problems' and Noguera's 'aesthetic' (Noguera 2006).

2. Culture as *system*: similar to the first use, this refers to interactions or adaptations between a natural, social and cultural system. It is necessary to clarify that the NPEEC does not differentiate between a system and a dimension. It is primarily associated with Torres' 'system'.
3. Culture as *condition*: this use is to understand gender, to recognize diversity, to achieve sustainability, and to articulate a reason to educate. Wilches Chaux's 'risk management' is also associated with this use.
4. Culture as *homogenizing strategy*: in contrast with the third use, this use is to improve the relationship among different social dimensions and to establish an appropriate cultural form. This use is partly associated with 'risk management' too.
5. Culture as an *aim to build a sustainable environmental culture*: this refers to the necessity of developing different types of sub-cultures, such as sub-cultures of peace, development, technology, state management, society management, risk management, ecology, interdisciplinarity, sustainable management and participative culture. We found associated uses of culture with those of 'prevention', 'risk', and 'ethics'.
6. Culture as *process*: here, culture reflects an interaction with the beliefs and traditions of ethnic groups or a process to develop society. These was often associated with 'problems', 'ethics' and 'aesthetics'.
7. Culture as *contextualization*: from this perspective, humanity and history develop in specific spaces and times that need to be recognized. This use of culture is associated with the inductive code, 'problems'.

The text below is an excerpt from the fourth general objective of NPEEC (2002, 14§4) regarding culture:

> "Provide instruments that allow openings for critical reflection, regarding the need to move towards development models, that incorporate a concept of sustainability, not only natural but also social and that, of course, locate our cultural diversity as a strength, to achieve one of the great purposes of Environmental Education in the country, such as the qualification of interactions: society-nature-culture and the proper transformation of our environmental realities." (our translation)

The reference to culture in the text articulates how the policy intends to influence social practice. However, policymakers cannot control the meaning of their texts, even if they attempt to control their interpretation (Bowe, Ball, and Gold 1992). Regarding cultural discourse, we found 'development' to be a dominant discourse. This discourse aligns with neoliberal discourses that are written in the coded languages of discourse through words including: model, management, and sustainability. In this case, it is assumed that the integration of economy, equity and ecology are non-problematic (Cachelin, Rose, and Paisley 2015). However, neoliberal discourses of dominance are also synthesized by the NPEEC, in that EE is positioned as an 'answer' to the other policy agendas of the country and the international guidelines by powerful institutions such as the World Bank. These discourses reflect similar findings in the literature review of ESE policies by Aikens, McKenzie, and Vaughter (2016, 342), including a widely found "desire to align with international policy imperatives [operates] as an impetus for the development of sustainability education policy". (See also Lotz-Sisitka, Rosenberg, and Ramsarup 2020, for a deeper analysis in the context of ESE policy in Southern Africa, investigating 'the interests of the marginalized and excluded, including the ecological systems and foundations of life which are increasingly more marginalized and excluded from policy and praxis in a neo-liberal dominated world order', p.14.)

However, these discourses are also contradictory from the perspective of the theme associated with ethics and the researchers who typify resistance discourses. For example, Ángel Maya (1997, 80) had said the following about so-called "development" in a neocolonial and neo-liberal model:

> "The immediate environmental problem of the so-called Third World has more to do with the plundering of resources and with the arbitrary and damaging demands of imposed development." (our translation)

In contrast to the NPEEC then, 'colonization' through a 'development model' to find an environmental culture or a better culture, is indicative of the 'technologization' of discourse. What we detect here is a process of intervention in the sphere of discourse practices with the objective of establishing a new hegemony in the order of discourse (Fairclough 1995, 104). Therefore, the 'hybridization' between policy and researcher's discourses can be used as a strategy for political domination, and disembedding, from Ángel Maya's original intent.

Problem. In the 'problem' category, we found three ways in which this term was used. The first refers to *problem-based learning*. In contrast to the above, given the embedded role of Maritza Torres in government, it was unsurprising to see the NPEEC proposes the generation of projects and an interdisciplinary culture and discourses of resistance as dialogue, as with PRAES. 'Problem-based learning' was also associated with the theme, 'system'.

The second way that 'problem' was used—problem as a *crisis or conflict*—refers to the necessity of interpreting the crisis as a result of economic growth, industrial development, and an inadequate relationship among society, the economy, and nature (see Rodriguez Becerra 1994). In this sense, 'the problem as crisis' was based on the discourses of resistance that could be traced to earlier work by communities and collectives, and emphasised identity, contexts, decisions, and an integral view. In addition, this perspective was associated with themes such as culture, ethics, aesthetics and territory as a way to address the issue and propose a solution, themes familiar to EE from the 1980s, and the work of those associated with IDEA (Ángel Maya, Carrizosa, Noguera).

The last way that 'problem' was used referred to the 'environmental' problem. It presents the problem as a *result of development and a transformation of the environment*. The environmental problem is associated with the two themes of 'system' and 'risk management' (Wilches Chaux). To resolve the environmental problem, the NPEEC notes the necessity of developing education and policy and emphasizes the role of educational institutions. However, since the proposal falls back on a behavioural perspective and not on a constructive perspective, the scope seems to be rather limited. Similarly, the interpretation of the term 'sustainability' can be problematic.

We also identified that colonization continues through the discourse of globalization, but equally, the economic system is criticized by NPEEC. The policy actually recognizes that this is a cyclical process and that its influence on social practice will depend on its translation by social actors (Lima and Marran 2013). Significantly, the policy process does not simply begin when the policy is launched and received as a text by the people in charge of implementation. Therefore, for future analyses of NPEEC-related social practice, it is necessary to understand the histories and ideologies of the people who shape and receive policy texts and what drives them to implement policy in a certain way (Bowe, Ball, and Gold 1992). We recognise that the social actors and groups are in debate and conflict over who has ongoing power and influence through the definition, aims and meaning of the policy and are always in relation to international guidelines, stakeholders, actants, and discourses), e.g. the role of university chairs, research centres, seminars and research in generating and contesting policy (Reid 2020). Indeed, we found that the policy has a strong influence on the implementation of EE in schools because the policy provides some guidelines and topics for consideration for schools in their school environmental projects (SEPs) [PRAES]:

> "In general terms, the proposal can be made from the following topics: a) Work due to an environmental problem, through school projects (PRAES); b) Construction of an open school, with community involvement; c) Ongoing training of teachers and environmental facilitators through research; d) Construction of flexible curricula; e) Training for intersectoral, inter-institutional and intercultural work, f) Training for interdisciplinary work, g) Training for gender recognition." (NPEEC, 2002, 10§3, our translation)

Territory. The theme of 'territory' was used in five ways. The first, *territory*, or any geographical space, was used to denote limited space. The second refers to the *country* of Colombia. The third refers to a *spiritual* or essential place and means a sacred place with a worldview, knowledge, and life through the culture and environment. Therefore, it is strongly associated with the theme of culture too. Among the key discourses, we found resistance to this meaning because it tends to emphasize communities such as indigenous groups, Afro Colombian people, and Raizales, even as it strives to promote participation and autonomy. Next, territory was used to indicate *scenery* where there is a possible dialogue among methods, strategies, content, and conceptualization. Finally, when used as *territorial*, it refers to entities and corresponds to departments, districts, cities and indigenous territory.

For Carrizosa (1992, 49, our translation), the conception of territory depends on the political interests of the moment:

> "Colombia is one of the few countries in the world that has a continuous on-going war for more than fifty years, a continuous sequence of elaboration of national development plans, now converted into a constitutional obligation. Since the World Bank sent the first international mission in the pursuit of development, led by Currie, until the current plan, going through one that aspired to last ten years. Colombians have carried out this ritual every four years, and it is interesting to review the way in which the territory appears and disappears from the dominant vision in each period."

System. System is also used in four ways. The first is to *group or order of elements* that are interrelated and that interact with one other. It is associated with problem, culture, ethics, and managing risk, and it presents the key discourses of dominance, such as quality, strategy, and sustainability. The second refers to system as a *strategy of a mode of appropriation*. The third uses system as *policy* and references the National Environmental System (NES) of Colombia. The last presents different types such as culture, social, value, research, reality, behaviour, production, information, cooperation, disciplinary, educative, formative, institutional, natural, productive and social systems. This shows how the policy uses the ideological strategy of *fragmentation* to indicate the divisions of many systems and possibly creates confusion in the areas of work.

One possible reason why 'system' was used as strategic rhetorical device through repetition was because it corresponds to the thinking of Torres. As noted above, she is the Policies Coordinator and leads the political processes of implementing EE in the country (Ministerio de Educación Nacional, 2013). It also illustrates the dynamic and different roles researchers and their discourses might play in policy and social practice, and the social power between the researchers and institutions, e.g. as the cycle or stick at being, outsider, insider and/or inbetweener (Reid 2020). In other words, it is an example of the social and political roles of language and their speakers in contemporary society, and the embodied positions and relationships between discourse and society, which can lead to unequal relationships of power that can be understood through social semiotics (Wodak and Matouschek 1993; Van Dijk 2007).

Ethics. Finally, we found three ways in which 'ethics' was used. The first use was, *ethics as customs and values*. The policy raises the need to promote an ethic for a good relationship between society and culture. It is usually associated with a critical perspective, which allows us to understand it as resistance. However, it limits ethics to guidelines and behavioural changes. Subsequently, we found *environmental ethics* to refer to the way to achieve environmental sustainability through democracy. *Citizen ethics* is also used as a possibility to establish an ethic through education and to recognize plurality and democracy.

As another example of discourse hybridity, ethics is proposed to *change behaviour*. It is contradictory to Noguera's (2002) perspective. She has criticized ethics as a socially normative instrument. Noguera (1998, 32, our translation) argues that:

> "Ethic is the dynamic factor of decisions and actions. If ethics as a movement of values is centred on an anthropocentric culture, actions will always be directed towards the welfare of man, forgetting his telluric link with nature. If, on the contrary, the actions are directed to the well-being of nature seen as a pure externality, the oblivion of man would lead to an irremediable biologism."

The seeds of disidentification. In this analysis, the ideological aspects of the NPEEC are inevitably structured by linguistic and discursive mixtures of the voices of researchers and policymakers (Table 1). These mixtures can converge or diverge from axiological points of view by establishing relations of contradiction and/or confrontations, resistance or acceptance (Bakhtin 1986). Consequently, our analysis shows that the NPEEC can have discourses that contribute to dissimulating the relations of domination and exploitation conformed by this societal model. This is especially true for the global perspective imposed by the World Bank and other powerful entities that have contributed to environmental and social problems. The analyses also show resistance discourses, for example, the necessity of empowering vulnerable communities. However, the domination discourses prevail over the resistance discourses.

The NPEEC starts with a justification of the policy (i.e. *legitimization*, Table 1). It uses *dissimulation* through the displacement of discourses between international guidelines and the researchers' discourses as the mode of operation of ideology. For example, some issues are presented by the policy as priorities of the political agenda, such as poverty, violence, and the environment (e.g. *unification*). These issues were presented at international UNESCO conferences and seminars (e.g. UNESCO 1997). Then, the policy selectively draws on the discourse of Ángel Maya in the references, "the need to consolidate a new ethos and culture", "EE as a critical discourse of culture", and "cultural change."

However, in the section that pertains to justification and background, the NPEEC uses legal frameworks as citations to justify certain selections of EE, and the research and investigators' discourse is obscured (for example, *reification* of Ángel Maya (2000) perspective) or absent. In contrast, the policy emphasizes the international agenda and globalization as a dominant discourse. It argues for the implementation of the policy at both international and national levels. Accordingly, the NPEEC attempts to establish the relations of the contextual, cultural, political and economic practices of the country. This attempt is seen, for example, when the NPEEC refers to the insertion of EE in ethnic groups (e.g. *fragmentation*).

In this, the national policy mobilizes a deontic logic, in that the logical structure of language through which signs are socially produced, comes to direct how we might live our experiences in relation to the obligations, prohibitions, and permits in a possible legal or moral world (Kress 1993). Based on this logic, SEPs are presented as mandatory because they are one of the social activities that schools must oversee to remain in the national education system (e.g. *unification*). This is instead of teachers and students being speakers located in a discursive and geographical context, and emphasizing the pre-eminence and pre-existence of a social topography (Barbi 1999) for EE in which they already reside (Stevenson 2007). In addition, it obliges schools to employ an 'integrated' perspective in understanding environmental problems (NPEEC, 35, §3ff). In this, we note that most sources are norms or statements for creating strategies and addressing challenges arise from public institutions that express normative propositions. The policy also mobilizes a logic that assumes the creation of a new country characterized by relationships based on peace, which is evidenced in one of the documents that cite "culture for peace, towards a policy of EE" (see also, Ministerio de Educación Nacional 2005a, in contrast to Ministerio de Educación Nacional 2005b, on educating for sustainable development, using PRAES and SINA as the framework).

Intertextuality in the NPEEC – another aspect to research/er disidentification?

Our intertextuality analysis was directed by citation, i.e. when references to another text were incorporated into a text and explicitly marked as such. We searched for the researchers who had been directly cited in the NPEEC and how the citation was used or, in contrast, if the citation was omitted (see Table 1, e.g. strategies of reification). We found that the document cited three researchers—Torres (twice, while appearing six times in the bibliography), Ángel Maya (twice, and four times in the bibliography) and Wilches Chaux (once, and omitted from the bibliography)—and other authors who were not considered in this research. (NB international researchers appear too: Lucie Sauvé is cited on p.32, §3; Andre Giordan appears twice in the bibliography.)

In short, the policy has obscured or omitted the discourses of many nationally-recognised researchers. Equally, the NPEEC uses collective entities as the voices of political discourse to legitimise their selections (Table 1).

First, the policy represents the inclusion of researchers as participants and a function of the construction of the policy, as when it introduces a direct citation of Torres. The excerpt from the policy's introduction clearly illustrates this:

> The Ministry of National Education (accompanied by a group of researchers from the university and some members of non-governmental organizations) has been very important for the development of this proposal ... (Torres, 1998-1999) (NPEEC, 8§1, background and justification)[4].

It is also important to identify the ideological strategies used and their modes of operation in citations. The first citation of Wilches Chaux's work, for example, is used as a strategy of self-legitimization, appearing substantially after the policy text justified the participation of researchers in the policy (p.24). The citation was taken from a document written in collaboration with Eloisa Trellez and Maritza Torres, written in high policy style, and introduced by way of reference to: "with the participation of Maritza Torres from the Ministry of Education". In the NPEEC, it is also used to argue in favour of sustainable development (cf. Carrizosa, 1992 (Carrizosa, 1992), listed in the bibliography, but not cited in offering what is actually a 'counterproposal'). Moreover, the policy uses further modes of dissimulation in attributing the perspective of sustainability to Wilches Chaux, but omits the co-authors in the citation, and replaces their names by 'et al.' In fact, all three names were not included (intentionally or unintentionally) from the corresponding section in the Bibliography (pp. 66-69), nor do they appear in a footnote.

> "Wilches et al. (1998): It includes an ideological and cultural dimension, on which depends the sense or meaning that each community gives to development, the concept of "success" and, in general, the role and responsibility that corresponds to assuming the human being in the universal becoming. Likewise, the concept of sustainability comprises a political dimension of which the concepts of democracy, tolerance, agreement, governance, respect for difference and active valuation of diversity, decentralization and participation are an integral part, without which sustainability is not conceivable." (NPEEC, 2002, 24§3)

In contrast, Ángel Maya's (1997, 2000) ideas were used directly and indirectly. A first example can be found in a discussion about education in universities, and his discourse is employed to explain the necessity of continuing to use technology, but from another perspective to imply changing prevailing perspectives about science. After that, the policy uses a direct citation (p.29) to argue the necessity of a relationship between social and natural sciences, because education has a tendency towards a natural scientific perspective, thereby devaluing the social dimension.

> "the social sciences, says the author, "have been built, however, outside the natural system, as if man [sic] had nothing to do with the rest of nature. This is no more than a landscape for solace or a scene of wars.

The history we have learned has been built without animals and without plants. From the discovery of America we only know the mythicized heroes, but we forget their horses and the plants they carried in their saddlebags. It is easily forgotten that in the encounter of America and Europe, not only the value of soldiers triumphed, but also the Neolithic of wheat and cattle, against the Neolithic of corn and turkey. While the natural sciences want to explain a nature without man, the social sciences prefer a man without nature." (NPEEC, 29§4-30§1).

In this section, then, we have briefly identified how academic discourse is combined with political text in a dual rhetorical strategy of legitimization and delegitimization, through citations to argue in favour of some political interest, such as sustainable development, and by using researchers generally recognised in Colombia, such as Ángel Maya, Torres and Wilches Chaux.

Final considerations and research gaps

This study illustrates how we might come to understand whether and how the voices of EE scholars were deployed, dissimulated, or deleted in the NPEEC (Table 1). Our theoretical framework helped us explore the social processes associated with language in use that can lead to relations of domination; in this instance, crystallising as a form of 'disidentification'. In short, we found that researcher discourses were included in the NPEEC, but the policy gave greater prominence to legislative guidelines and international policy discourses than to previously authoritative, historical and grounded thought and practice. The study also offers an explanatory critique about the dynamics between research and policy in that the NPEEC reduced the contributions of local research by Colombian scholars in its text, i.e. instead of their identification in and with policy, we notice evidence of differing degrees of *disidentification*.

While the results offer insights into the state of the research-policy relationship for the NPEEC, they also illustrate divergence in forms of relationship between EE researchers and policymakers from what is historically expected in Colombia: *to adopt and ensure a collaborative and participatory approach towards research in policy formulation and development* (Youkhana, Leifkes, and León-Sicard 2018). With the NPEEC, we found that policy discourses can use different types of discursive strategies, such as repetition and credibility, through legitimate researcher's discourses to attempt to convince the reader or seek to legitimize a policymaker's discourse. This process provides momentum to the dominance of certain social actors and develops hegemonic positions into policies (e.g. in relation to the work and role of Maritza Torres), which can then have strong legacy effects on subsequent EE. In the text of NPEEC, we also observed genre shifts, such as selective extracts from the argumentative forms of researchers into expositive material. Furthermore, we understand that the issues that policymakers choose from the research responds to global interests, and in this way, the authors and editors of the NPEEC have tried to avoid relaying ideological tensions, while still layering topics to create cohesive collections of policy between international guidelines and national policies.

Elsewhere, other publications about environmental and sustainable education policy research have generated important insights into the dynamics of policy, policy-making, and policy scholarship (i.e. Lysgaard, Reid, and Van Poeck 2016; Stevenson 2013). In this paper, we recognise that our discussion is based only on the NPEEC, and since then, other local EE and ESD researchers and academics have been involved in its enactment (e.g. Alain Boutet, Pablo Ángel Meira Cartea). Equally, we did not analyse the degree of alignment or diversity of social practices in schools, universities, or other institutions where the policy is in effect. We do, however, remain committed to continuing the analysis of social relations and discourses legitimatized in schools recognising it is not a static or prescribed process. Finally, we acknowledge the necessity of conducting an analysis that includes the discourses directly from policymakers, authors/editors, and researchers of EE and related areas, e.g. based on interviews. It will be a challenge to establish networks between policymakers and researchers and to secure financial support. However, it will be a way to voice their perspectives, first, on participation in ESE policy and decision-making;

second, on the relationships between academics and policymakers that need to be rethought or improved; and third, on the methods for establishing connected and productive networks.

In light of this, we believe that the challenge for the EE field of research is to ensure that policymakers are committed to research and researchers and vice versa, notwithstanding the dynamic interplay and shifting of roles framed by the notions of 'insiders', 'outsiders' and 'inbetweeners' (Reid 2020). It is a call that requires a dialogue that repeatedly considers the roles of research and researchers in ESE policy processes, and the engagement of policy and policymakers in the relationship between the development of EE or/and ESD. However, while we consider that public policy needs to be applicable at the national level, it must simultaneously account for the specificities of the work at the local level, in Colombia and elsewhere. In this sense, considering the theoretical framework adopted in this study, a key question to consider is the process of the re-signification of public policies that are expected to work at a local level by policymakers and legislators, and the feedback and feedforward from the social actors who use national policies in ways not necessarily account for at different scales or in other contexts (e.g. in relation to UNESCO 2016, and Ministerio de Ambiente y Desarrollon Sostenible 2016; see again, Lotz-Sisitka, Rosenberg, and Ramsarup 2020).

Accordingly, the findings of this analysis encourage us to continue researching the relationship between the worlds of policymaking and research by reflecting further on questions of power and strategies of imposition, emancipation, and participation within and across scales. Finally, the findings invite us to reflect on the similarities and differences in Latin American contexts, to understand how shared and unique features of context influence the construction of policy therein, and the convergences and divergences in the relationships between policymakers and researchers and the practices of EE, particularly if 'disidentification' is to be avoided and addressed.

Notes

1. Chouliaraki and Fairclough (1999) understand the concept of social practice as a social activity that has oscillation between the perspective of social structure and the perspective of social action and agency (examples could be classroom teaching, television news, family meals, medical consultations).
2. The Dialnet platform is a virtual newspaper and periodical library that contains Hispanic scientific journals and papers.
3. In our analysis, we considered how each theme was used by the authors, which meaning was given to it, and how it was associated with other inductive codes.
4. All the passages referring to the NPEEC were translated by one of the authors of this article.

Disclosure statement

No potential conflict of interest was reported by the authors.

Funding

This study was financed in part by the Coordenação de Aperfeiçoamento de Pessoal de Nível Superior - Brasil (CAPES) - Finance Code 001 (doctoral funding), and process 88881.312004/2018-01 (research funding), and by the Conselho Nacional de Desarrollo Cientifico y Tecnologico CNPq, process number 148873/2016-2 (doctoral funding).

ORCID

María Angélica Mejía-Cáceres http://orcid.org/0000-0003-3486-1952
Alejandra Huérfano http://orcid.org/0000-0003-2922-4879
Alan Reid http://orcid.org/0000-0002-2954-6424
Laísa María Freire http://orcid.org/0000-0002-4573-0969

References

Aikens, K., M. McKenzie, and P. Vaughter. 2016. "Environmental and Sustainability Education Policy Research: A Systematic Review of Methodological and Thematic Trends." *Environmental Education Research* 22 (3): 333–359. doi:10.1080/13504622.2015.1135418.
Ángel Maya, A. 1997. *Desarrollo Sostenible o Cambio Cultural [Sustainable Development or Cultural Change]*. Cali: Corporación Universitaria Autónoma de Occidente, Fondo Mixto para la Promoción de la Cultura y las Artes del Valle del Cauca.
Ángel Maya, A. 2000. *La aventura de los símbolos. Una visión ambiental de la historia del pensamiento [The adventure of symbols. An environmental view of the history of thought]*. Bogotá, Colombia: Ecofondo.
Appadurai, A. 1996. *Modernity at Large: Cultural Dimensions of Globalization*. Minneapo- lis: University of Minnesota Press.
Apple, M. 2006. *Educating the "right" way: Markets standards, God, And Inequality*. New York, NY: Routledge.
Barbi, S. H. 1999. *Discurso e Ensino [Speech and Teaching]*. Belo Horizonte: Autêntica.
Ball, S. 2006. "Sociologia das políticas educacionais e pesquisa crítico-social: uma revisão pessoal das políticas educacionais e da pesquisa em política educacional [Sociology of educational policies and critical-social research: A personal review of educational policies and research in educational policy]." *Curriculo sem Fronteiras* 6 (2): 10–32. http://www.curriculosemfronteiras.org/vol6iss2articles/ball.pdf.
Ball, S. 2015. "What is Policy? 21 Years Later: Reflections on the Possibilities of Policy Research." *Discourse: Studies in the Cultural Politics of Education* 36 (3): 306–313. doi:10.1080/01596306.2015.1015279.
Ball, S. J., M. Maguire, and A. Braun. 2012. *"How Schools Do Policy." Policy Enactments in Secondary Schools*. London: Routledge.
Bakhtin, M. 1981. *The Dialogical Imagination*. Ed. M. Holquist, trans. C. Emerson and M. Holquist. Austin: University of Texas Press.
Bakhtin, M. 1986. *Speech Genres and Other Late Essays*. Ed. C. Emerson and M. Holquist, trans. V.W. McGee. Austin: University of Texas Press.
Bastalich, W. 2009. "Reading Foucault: Genealogy and Social Science Research Methodology and Ethic." *Sociological Research Online* 14 (2): 81–90. doi:10.5153/sro.1905.
Berdugo Silva, N., and W. Montaño Renuma. 2017. "La educación ambiental en las instituciones de educación superior públicas acreditadas en Colombia [Environmental education in accredited public higher education institutions in Colombia." *Revista Científica General José María Córdova* 15 (20): 127–136.]. doi:10.21830/19006586.178.
Bonini, A. 2010. "Critical Genre Analysis and Professional Practice: The Case of Public Contests to Select Professors for Brazilian Public Universities." *Linguagem em (Dis)Curso* 10 (3): 485–510. doi:10.1590/S1518-76322010000300004.
Bowe, R., S. Ball, and A. Gold. 1992. *Reforming Education & Changing Schools*. London: Routledge.
Boyatzis, R. 1998. *Transforming Qualitative Information: Thematic Analysis and Code Development*, Thousand Oaks, CA: Sage.

Cachelin, A., J. Rose, and K. Paisley. 2015. "Disrupting Neoliberal Discourse in Critical Sustainability Education: A Qualitative Analysis of Intentional Language Framing." *Environmental Education Research* 21 (8): 1127–1142. doi:10.1080/13504622.2014.974023.

Calderón, J. J., and P. D. Cerón, 2005. *Educación Ambiental: Una Cuestión de Valores [Environmental Education: A Matter of Values]*. Bogotá: Universidad Nacional de Colombia.

Carrizosa, J. 1992. La viabilidad del desarrollo sustentable en Colombia. Una contrapropuesta En Medio Ambiente y Desarrollo [The Viability of Sustainable Development in Colombia. A Counterproposal in Environment and Development]. Bogotá: Tercer Mundo Editores.

Carrizosa, J. 2001. Reflexiones y Notas sobre Ambiente, Desarrollo y Paz [Reflections and Notes on Environment, Development and Peace]. In: *Que es ambientalismo. La vision ambiental compleda* [What is environmentalism. The complete environmental vision]. PNUMA-IDEA-UN.CEREC. Bogotá. URL: http://www.idea.unal.edu.co/publica/docs/reflexiones.pdf

Colombia. 1992. *Colombia National Report for UNCED*. Bogota.

Cooren, F. 2004. "Textual Agency: How Texts Do Things in Organizational Settings." *Organization* 11 (3): 373–393. doi:10.1177/1350508404041998.

Chouliaraki, L., and N. Fairclough. 1999. *Discourse in Late Modernity*. Edinburgh: Edinburgh University Press.

Congreso de la República de Colombia 1974., *Decreto Ley 2811, Código Nacional de Recursos Naturales y de protección del ambiente [Decree Law 2811, National Code of Natural Resources and protection of the environment]*. Diario Oficial 34.243. Colombia: Bogotá.. https://www.minambiente.gov.co/images/normativa/app/decretos/9d-dec_2811_1974%20. (2).pdf

Ecofondo, 1993. *Corporation Ecofondo Documentos [Ecofondo Corporation Documents]*. Bogotá, Colombia: Ecofondo.

Faguet, J.-P., and F. Sánchez. 2008. "Decentralization's Effects on Educational Outcomes in Bolivia and Colombia." *World Development* 36 (7): 1294–1316. doi:10.1016/j.worlddev.2007.06.021.

Fairclough, N. 1992. *Discourse and Social Change*. Cambridge UK: Polity Press.

Fairclough, N. 1995. *Critical Discourse Analysis: The Critical Study of Language*. London and New York: Longman.

Fairclough, N. 2001. "The Dialectics of Discourse." *Textus* XIV (2): 231–242.

Fairclough, N. 2003. *Analysing Discourse*. Abingdon: Routledge.

Fairclough. 2008. "El análisis crítico del discurso y la mercantilización del discurso público en las universidades [The critical analysis of discourse and the commodification of public discourse in universities]." *Discurso & Sociedad* 2 (1): 170–185.

Fairclough, N. 2017. "CDA as 'Dialectical Reasoning.'" In *The Routledge Handbook of Critical Discourse Studies*, edited by J. Flowerdew and J. E. Richardson, 13–26. Abingdon: Routledge.

Florez-Yepes, G. Y. 2015. "La educación ambiental y el desarrollo sostenible en el contexto colombiano [Environmental Education and Sustainable Development in the Colombian Context]." *Revista Electrónica Educare* 19 (3): 1–12. doi:10.15359/ree.19-3.5.

Gee, J., G. Hull, and C. Lankshear. 1996. *The New Work Order: Behind the Language of the New Capitalism*. Boulder, CO: Westview Press.

Global Environmental Education Partnership (GEEP). 2016. *Colombia - Policy and Practice*. https://thegeep.org/learn/countries/colombia

Gaudiano, E. G., and L. Lorenzetti. 2012. "Trends, Junctures, and Disjunctures in Latin American Environmental Education Research." In *International Handbook of Research on Environmental Education*, edited by R. B. Stevenson, M. Brody, J. Dillon and A. E. J. Wals, 171–177. Abingdon: Routledge.

Guhl, E., M. Wagner, and A. Zapata. 2015. "Evolución del Ministerio de Ambiente de Colombia en sus primeros veinte años: 1994-2014 [Evolution of the Colombian Ministry of the Environment in its first twenty years: 1994-2014]." In *La gestión ambiental en Colombia, 1994-2014: ¿un esfuerzo insostenible? [Environmental management in Colombia, 1994-2014: An unsustainable effort?]*, edited by E. Guhl and P. Leiva, 23–113. Bogotá: Friedrich-Ebert-Stiftung (Fescol).

Gutiérrez, L. 2015. "Problemática de la educación ambiental en las instituciones educativas [Problems of environmental education in educational institutions]." *Revista Científica* 23: 57–76. doi:10.14483/udistrital.jour.RC.2015.23.a5.

Henao Hueso, O., and L. Sánchez Arce. 2019. "La educación ambiental en Colombia, utopía o realidad [Environmental education in Colombia, utopia or reality]." *Revista Conrado* 15 (67): 213–219. https://conrado.ucf.edu.cu/index.php/conrado/article/view/949.

Jickling, B., and A. E. J. Wals. 2008. "Globalization and Environmental Education: Looking beyond Sustainable Development." *Journal of Curriculum Studies* 40 (1): 1–21. doi:10.1080/00220270701684667.

Kress, G. 1993. "Against Arbitrariness: The Social Production of the Sign as a Foundational Issue in Critical Discourse Analysis." *Discourse & Society* 4 (2): 169–192. doi:10.1177/0957926593004002003.

Lima, P., and A. Marran. 2013. "A Avaliação de políticas educacionais por meio da abordagem teórico- analítica do ciclo de políticas [An evaluation of educational policies by means of theoretical-analytical approach to the policy cycle]." *Praxis Educativa* 8 (1): 41–62. doi:10.5212/PraxEduc.v.8i1.0002.

Lopes, A. C. 2016. "A teoria da atuac̦ao de Stephen Ball: E se a noc̦ao de discurso fosse outra? [Stephen Ball's theory of enactment: And what if the notion of discourse was different?]." *Archivos Analíticos de Políticas Educativas* 24 (25), 1-19. doi:10.14507/epaa.24.2111

Lotz-Sisitka, H., E. Rosenberg, and P. Ramsarup. 2020. "Environment and sustainability education research as policy engagement: (re-) invigorating 'politics as *potentia*' in South Africa ." *Environmental Education Research.*, 1-29. doi:10.1080/13504622.2020.1759511.

Lysgaard, J. A., A. Reid, and K. Van Poeck. 2016. "The Roots and Routes of Environmental and Sustainability Education Policy Research." *Environmental Education Research* 22 (3): 319–332. doi:10.1080/13504622.2015. 1108393.

Mayring, P. 2000. "Qualitative Content Analysis." *Forum Qualitative Social Research* 1 (2): 20. http://www.qualitative-research.net/index.php/fqs/article/view/1089/2385.

McKenzie, M., A. Bieler, and R. McNeil. 2015. "Education Policy Mobility: Reimagining Sustainability in Neoliberal Times." *Environmental Education Research* 21 (3): 319–337. doi:10.1080/13504622.2014.993934.

Macedo, B. Y., and C. Salgado. 2007. "Educación Ambiental y Educación Para el Desarrollo Sostenible en América Latina [Environmental Education and Education for Sustainable Development in Latin America]." *Revista Forum de Sostenibilidad* 1: 29–37. http://www.ehu.eus/cdsea/web/revista/numero_1/01_03macedo.pdf.

Maguire, M., K. Hoskins, S. Ball, and A. Braun. 2011. "Policy Discourses in School Texts." *Discourse: Studies in the Cultural Politics of Education* 32 (4): 597–609. doi:10.1080/01596306.2011.601556.

Mejía Cáceres, M. A., and A. C. Zambrano. 2018. *Ciencia, cultura y educación ambiental. Una propuesta Para los educadores [Science, culture and environmental education. A proposal for educators]*. Cali: Programa Editorial Universidad del Valle.

Ministerio de Educación Nacional. 1994a. *Ley general de educación* [General Education Law]. http://www.mineducacion.gov.co/1621/articles-85906_archivo_pdf.pdf

Ministerio de Educación Nacional 1994b. *Decreto 1743 de 1994. Por el cual se instituye el Proyecto de Educación Ambiental para todos los niveles* [Act 1743 of 1994. By which the environmental education project is instituted for all levels]. http://corponarino.gov.co/expedientes/juridica/1994decreto1743.pdf

Ministerio de Educación Nacional. 2005a. "*Educación ambiental construir educación y país* [Environmental education builds education and country]." *Al tablero*, 36. Agosto-Setiembre. Colombia: Bogotá, Ministerio de Educación Nacional http://www.mineducacion.gov.co/1621/article-90891.html.

Ministerio de Educación Nacional. 2005b. *Educar Para el desarrollo sostenible [Educating for sustainable development]*. Al tablero, 36. Agosto-Setiembre. Colombia: Bogotá. http://www.mineducacion.gov.co/1621/article-908931.html.

Ministerio de Educación Nacional 2010. *Programa de Educación Ambiental: Colombia Aprende [Environmental Education Program: Colombia Learns]*. http://aprende.colombiaaprende.edu.co/en/node/86542

Ministerio de Educación Nacional. 2016. *Objetivos PRAE [Objectives of the School Environmental Program]*. http://aprende.colombiaaprende.edu.co/es/node/90638

Ministerio de Medio Ambiente y Ministerio de Educación Nacional. 2002. Política Nacional de Educación Ambiental (National Environmental Education Policy). Gobierno de Colombia: Bogotá.

Ministerio de Ambiente y Desarrollo Sostenible. 2016. *Los proyectos ambientales escolares-PRAE en Colombia [School environmental projects-PRAE in Colombia]*. Bogotá, Colombia: Ministerio de Ambiente y Desarrollon Sostenible. https://www.minambiente.gov.co/images/OrdenamientoAmbientalTerritorialyCoordinaciondelSIN/pdf/VII_Encuentro_Nacional_de_Educación_Ambiental/PRAE.pdf.

Mora Ortiz, J. R. 2016. "Los Proyectos Ambientales Escolares. Herramientas de gGestión Ambiental [School Environmental Projects. Environmental Management Tools]." *Bitácora Urbano Territorial* 25 (2): 67–74. doi:10.15446/bitacora.v2n25.39975.

Noguera, A. 1998. "Hacia una ética del respesto ambiental [towards an ethic of environmental respect]." *Ánfora: Revista Científica de la Universidad Autónoma de Manizales* 1 (2): 23–33. doi:10.30854/anf.v1.n2.1993.467.

Noguera, A. 2002. *El reencantamiento del mundo [The re-enchantment of the world]*. Manizales, Colombia: PNUMA-UNCIDEA. [*Mismatch*]

Noguera, A. 2006. *Pensamiento ambiental complejo y gestión del riesgo: Una propuesta epistémico-ético-estética. Taller internacional sobre gestión del riesgo a nivel local [Complex environmental thinking and risk management: An epistemic-ethical-aesthetic proposal. International workshop on risk management at the local level]*. Colombia: El caso de Manizales, http://idea.manizales.unal.edu.co/sitios/gestion_riesgos/descargas/gestion/Propuestaepistemico.pdf.

Novo, M. 2009. "La educación ambiental, una genuina educación Para el desarrollo sostenible [Environmental education, a genuine education for sustainable development]." *Revista de Educación* (Extraordinario 1): 195–217. http://hdl.handle.net/11162/74555.

O'Brien, P. 1995. "Participation and Sustainable Development in Colombia." *Revista Europea De Estudios Latinoamericanos Y Del Caribe/European Review of Latin American and Caribbean Studies* 59: 7–35. https://www.jstor.org/stable/25675674.

Paz, S., Avendaño C, L. W. Parada-Trujillo. and A. 2014. "Desarrollo conceptual de la Educación Ambiental en el contexto colombiano [Conceptual development of Environmental Education in the Colombian context]." *Luna Azul* 39: 250–270. doi:10.17151/luaz.2014.39.15.

Pierce, C. S. 2015. *Policy as Text and Tech: Exploring the Intersection between Policy and Technology Implementation within a Healthcare Organization*. (Unpublished doctoral dissertation), Evanston, IL: Northwestern University.
Reid, A. 2020. "Researching Environmental and Sustainability Education Policy: Slumbers and Awakenings." *Journal of Philosophy of Education*, 1-28. doi:10.1111/1467-9752.12474.
República de Colombia. 1991. *Constitución Política de Colombia [Political Constitution of Colombia]*. República de Colombia: Santa Fé de Bogotá. https://www.ramajudicial.gov.co/documents/10228/1547471/CONSTITUCION-Interiores.pdf.
República de Colombia. 1993. *Ley 99 de 1993. Sistema Nacional Ambiental [Law 99 of 1993. National Environment System]*. República de Colombia: Diario Oficial No. 41.146, de 22 de diciembre de 1993. Santa Fé de Bogotá. https://www.cvc.gov.co/sites/default/files/Sistema_Gestion_de_Calidad/Procesos%20y%20procedimientos%20Vigente/Normatividad_Gnl/Ley%2099%20DE%201993-Dic-22.pdf.
República de Colombia. 1994. *Ley 115 de 1994. Ley General de Educación* [Law 115 of 1994. General education law]. de febrero 8 de 1994. Santa Fé de Bogotá: República de Colombia. http://www.suin-juriscol.gov.co/viewDocument.asp?ruta=Leyes/1645150
República de Colombia. 2012. *Ley N° 1549. Educación Ambiental.* [Law 1549. National Environmental Education Policy.] Gobierno de Colombia: Bogotá http://www.sic.gov.co/recursos_user/documentos/normatividad/Leyes/2012/Ley_1549_2012.pdf
Rizvi, F., and B. Lingard. 2010. *Globalising Education Policy*. London: Routledge.
Rodriguez Becerra, M. 1994. *Crisis Ambiental y Relaciones Internacionales - hacia un estrategia colombiana [Environmental Crisis and International Relations - towards a Colombian strategy]*. Bogota: Fescol.
Sauvé, L. 2005. "Currents in Environmental Education: Mapping a Complex and Evolving Pedagogical Field." *Canadian Journal of Environmental Education* 10: 11–37.
Sauvé, L., R. Brunelle, and T. Berryman. 2005. "Influence of the Globalized and Globalizing Sustainable Development Framework on National Policies Related to Environmental Education." *Policy Futures in Education* 3 (3): 271–283. doi:10.2304/pfie.2005.3.3.5.
Scott, W. 2010. "La investigación y la educación ambiental: La necesidad de apuestas multidimensionales [Environmental education and research: The need for multidimensional approaches]." In *Investigacion y educacion ambiental: apuestas investigativas pertinentes a los campos de reflexion e intervencion en educacion ambiental [Environmental education and research: research approaches pertinent to the fields of reflection and intervention in environmental education]*, edited by M. Torres Carrasco, 23–36. Medellín: Corantioquia.
Spratt, J. 2017. *Wellbeing, Equity and Education: A Critical Analysis of Policy Discourses of Wellbeing in Schools*. Cham, Switzerland: Springer International Publishing, doi:10.1007/978-3-319-50066-9.
Stevenson, R. B. 2007. "Schooling and Environmental/Sustainability Education: From Discourses of Policy and Practice to Discourses of Professional Learning." *Environmental Education Research* 13 (2): 265–285. doi:10.1080/13504620701295650.
Stevenson, R. B. 2013. "Researching Tensions and Pretensions in Environmental/Sustainability Education Policies: From Critical to Civically Engaged Policy Scholarship." In *International Handbook of Research on Environmental Education*, edited by R. B. Stevenson, M. Brody, J. Dillon, and A.E.J. Wals, 147–155. New York: Routledge.
Talero de Husain, E., and G. Humaña de Gauthier. 1993. *Educación Ambiental – Capacitación de Docentes de Basica Primaria [Environmental Education: A Primary School Teacher Training Program]*. Bogota (Colombia): Ministerio de Agricultura, Instituto Nacional de los Recursos Naturales Renovables y Del Ambiente.
Teitelbaum, A. 1978. *El Papel de la Educación Ambiental en América Latina [the Role of Environmental Education in Latin America]*. Paris: UNESCO.
Thompson, J. B. 2004. *Ideología y Cultura Moderna [Ideology and Modern Culture]*. (G. Fantinati Caviedes, Org.). Coyoacán, México: Universidad Autonónoma Metropolitana, Unidad Xochimilco.
Torres Carrasco, M. 1996. *La dimensión ambiental: Un reto para la educación de la nueva sociedad. Proyectos Ambientales Escolares. PRAE. [The environmental dimension: A challenge for the education of the new society. School Environmental Projects]*. Santa Fe de Bogotá: Ministerio de Educación Nacional. https://www.guao.org/sites/default/files/biblioteca/Dimensión%20ambiental.%20%20Un%20reto%20para%20la%20educación%20de%20la%20nueva%20sociedad.pdf
Torres Carrasco, M. 1998. "La educación ambiental: Una estrategia flexible, un proceso y unos propósitos en permanente construcción. La experiencia de Colombia [Environmental education: A flexible strategy, a process and purposes in permanent construction. The Colombian experience]."*Revista Iberoamericana de Educación* 16: 23–48. doi:10.35362/rie1601110.
Torres Carrasco, M. 2009. "Los Proyectos Ambientales Escolares – PRAE hoy: Retos y proyecciones en el marco del proceso de institucionalización de la educación ambiental en Colombia [School Educational Projects – SEPs today: Challenges and projections in the process of institutionalizing environmental education in Colombia]." *Revista Cuadernos Pedagógicos* 342: 43–47.
Torres Carrasco, M. (ed.). 2010a. *Investigacion y eEducacion ambiental: apuestas investigativas pertinentes a los campos de reflexion e intervencion en educacion ambiental [Environmental education and research: research approaches pertinent to the fields of reflection and intervention in environmental education]*. Medellín: Corantioquia.

Torres Carrasco, M. 2010b. "La política nacional de educación ambiental en Colombia: un marco Para la exploración y la reflexión, sobre las necesidades investigativas en educación ambiental [The national environmental education policy in Colombia: A framework for exploration and reflection on research needs in environmental education]." In *Investigacion y educacion ambiental: apuestas investigativas pertinentes a los campos de reflexion e intervencion en educacion ambiental [Environmental education and research: research approaches pertinent to the fields of reflection and intervention in environmental education]*, edited by M. Torres Carrasco, 113–126. Medellín: Corantioquia.

Torres López, E. 2011. *Medio ambiente y Proyecto Ambiental Escolar (PRAE) en el Colegio Nicolás Esguerra [Environment and School Environmental Project (PRAE) at the Nicolás Esguerra School]*. Masters Thesis, Universidad Nacional. http://www.bdigital.unal.edu.co/4633/.

Torres Palacios, S. C., and A. Rodriguez Bolanos. 2013. *Educación Ambiental Para La Participación En La Gestión Integral Del Riesgo*. Colombia: Kencer Impresores. https://www.cortolima.gov.co/sites/default/files/images/stories/gestion_riesgos/Gestion_del_Riesgo/Modulos/Modulo_I_260913_baja.pdf.

United Nations Educational, Scientific and Cultural Organization (UNESCO). 1978. *Intergovernmental Conference on Environmental Education: Final Report* (Tbilisi, Georgia, USSR). Paris, France: UNESCO.

UNESCO. 1980. *Environmental Education in the Light of Tbilisi Conference*. Paris: UNESCO. http://unesdoc.unesco.org/Ulis/cgiin/ulis.pl?catno=38550&gp=0&lin=1&ll=1.

UNESCO. 1997. *Educating for a Sustainable Future: A Transdisciplinary Vision for a Concerted Action*. EPD-97/Conf.401. /CLD.1. Paris: UNESCO. http://unesdoc.unesco.org/images/0011/001106/110686eo.pdf.

UNESCO. 2016. *Education for People and Planet: Creating Sustainable Futures for All, Global Education Monitoring Report*, 2016. 2nd ed. Paris: UNESCO.

Van Dijk, T. A. 1997. *Discourse as Structure and Process*. London, Thousand Oaks & New Delhi: Sage Publications.

Van Dijk, T. A. 2007. *Racismo y discurso en América Latina [Racism and discourse in Latin America]*. Barcelona: Gedisa.

Van Dijk, T. A. 2016. "Discurso cognição sociedade: estado atual e perspectivas da abordagem sociocognitiva do discurso [Discourse cognition society: current state and perspectives of the sociocognitive approach to discourse]." *Revista Digital do Programa de Pós Graduação em Letras da PUCRS* 9: 8–29.

Vélez Rojas, Óscar Alonso, and Abraham Allec Londoño Pineda. 2016. "De la Educación Ambiental Hacia la Configuración de Redes de Sostenibilidad en Colombia [from Environmental Education to the Configuration of Sustainability Networks in Colombia]." *Perfiles Educativos* 38 (151): 175–187. [online]. http://www.scielo.org.mx/pdf/peredu/v38n151/0185-2698-peredu-38-151-00175.pdf. doi:10.22201/iisue.24486167e.2016.151.54923.

Ventura, G. 2017. *Da Dissimulação Das Relações de Dominação às Possibilidades de Superação da Crise Socioambiental: uma Análise Discursiva Das Finalidades da Educação em Ciências (Tese de Doutorado). [from Dissimulation of Relationships of Domination to the Possibilities for Overcoming the Socio-Environmental Crisis: A Discursive Analysis of the Purposes of Education in Sciences (Doctoral Thesis)]*. Rio de Janeiro: Universidade Federal Do Rio De Janeiro

Wodak, R., and B. Matouschek. 1993. "'We Are Dealing with People Whose Origins One Can Clearly Tell Just by Looking': Critical Discourse Analysis and the Study of Neo-Racism in Contemporary Austria." *Discourse & Society* 4 (2): 225–248. doi:10.1177/0957926593004002005.

Youkhana, E., C. Leifkes, and T. León-Sicard. 2018. "Epistemic Marginality, Higher and Environmental Education in Colombia." *Gestión y Ambiente* 21 (2Supl): 15–29. 2), doi:10.15446/ga.v21n2supl.77752.

Zuluaga, O. L., and A. Echeverri. 2003. "Campo intelectual de la educación y campo pedagógico. Posibilidades, complementos y diferencias [The intellectual fields of education and pedagogy. Possibilities, complementarities and differences]." In *Pedagogía y epistemología [Pedagogy and epistemology]*, edited by O. L. Zuluaga, A. Echeverri, A. Martínez, H. Quiceno, J. Sáenz O and A. Álvarez, 111–125. Bogotá: Cooperativa Editorial Magisterio, Grupo Historia de la Práctica Educativa.

Improving policy through research-practice partnerships: Reflections and analysis from New York City

Oren Pizmony-Levy ⓘ, Meredith McDermott and Thaddeus T. Copeland

ABSTRACT
Although interest in ESE policy studies is on the rise, we argue there is a gap in scholarship about the nature and extent of interactions between policymakers and researchers in the ESE field. This paper addresses this gap by discussing one example of such interaction – an ongoing research-practice partnership (RPP) between the New York City Department of Education Office of Sustainability and Teachers College, Columbia University. Using qualitative document analysis, we – a researcher and two policymakers – make two contributions to the literature. First, we analyze the emergence of the partnership and point to the importance of trust, social relationships, and production of local and relevant knowledge. Second, we demonstrate how policymakers use knowledge produced in the RPP to inform specific programmatic decisions (instrumental use) and to clarify assumptions about the system (conceptual use). We also show how engagement with research informs participants' views towards improving school engagement with ESE. Implications for furthering research-policy relationships in ESE include: supporting comparative and longitudinal research designs, giving more attention to the socio-political context shaping partnerships, investigating other forms of knowledge use in RPPs, and reflecting on the politics and priorities given to conducting research with policymakers that demonstrate contributions to the collective good.

Introduction

Interest in environmental and sustainability education (ESE) policy is on the rise (Aikens, McKenzie, and Vaughter 2016), with scholars increasingly calling for a strengthening of this important line of research (Laessøe, Feinstein, and Blum 2013; Stevenson and Robottom 2013). This trend is evident in research at different levels of policymaking, including global, national and sub-national (Bromley, Meyer, and Ramirez 2011; Huckle and Wals 2015; Iyengar and Bajaj 2011; Pizmony-Levy 2011; Sadan and Alkaher 2020; Stahelin 2017; Verschueren, forthcoming). The growth of research on ESE policy is important for at least two reasons. First, the broader field of educational policy tends to focus on issues of access, quality, and finance—with limited attention paid to ESE (e.g. Cho 2017; Park et al. 2020). Second, the emergence of research on ESE policy is a sign of further institutionalization of ESE policy in education systems. Although research on ESE policy has progressed over the past two decades, knowledge about the relationship between research and policy is still emerging within ESE, which is the focus of this special issue (for a broad discussion on the relationship between research and policy in education, see: Lingard 2013).

This article contributes to the literature about the relationship between research and policy by exploring a research-practice partnership (RPP) in the ESE field. RPPs are part of a larger family of collaborative approaches to education research (Penuel et al. 2020). They are long term relationships between researchers and education system leaders who "share an open-ended commitment to build and sustain a working collaboration over multiple projects" (Coburn and Penuel 2016, 48). They focus on problems of practice that policymakers and/or practitioners face, and they involve original research. RPPs are currently proliferating in the United States thanks to support and investment from foundations and other funders. To our knowledge, however, RPPs are not as common in ESE as in other educational domains.

In a recent review of empirical research on RPPs, Coburn and Penuel (2016) demonstrate that the current knowledge base in education on this topic is limited. They propose a research agenda on the process and outcomes of RPPs, and call for studies on the emergence and design of partnerships in different contexts and educational domains. They argue that research on the impact of RPPs in education is focused on interventions that were developed in the context of a partnership. Thus, they call for investigations of additional outcomes, such as research use, spread and scale of innovation. We respond to this call by analyzing our experiences of establishing the New York City Partnership for Sustainability Education (NPSE), which is a RPP between the Office of Sustainability at the New York City Department of Education (DOE) and Teachers College, Columbia University (TC). Team members from both organizations jointly wrote this article. In other words, this article does not only focus on analyzing the DOE–TC partnership, but it is also an example of an output produced by the partnership.

The DOE–TC RPP brings together teams from both organizations to conduct research in an effort to better understand and improve the role of schools in supporting New York City's sustainability goals. Working together, the two teams identify research questions to guide their inquiry. The two teams work together on crafting research design and data collection efforts, including surveys, interviews, focus groups, observations, and document analysis. The TC team standardizes school-level responses across sources and over time to create longitudinal data on ESE engagement. The TC team then conducts data analysis and supports the DOE team in understanding research findings and implications. This collaborative process enables the DOE to make data-driven policy and programmatic decisions with regard to its sustainability efforts.

In this paper we explore the role of the relationships between researchers and policymakers in this RPP, and the research and impact it facilitates. More specifically, through qualitative document analysis of relevant artefacts from the partnership (e.g. meeting minutes, PowerPoint presentations, and email exchanges between the DOE and TC teams), in this paper we address the following research questions:

RQ 1: What is the process by which researchers and policymakers co-create an RPP to improve ESE in public schools?

RQ 2: How do policymakers use the research outcomes from an RPP to improve ESE in public schools?

To respond to these questions, the first section of the paper presents a literature review detailing the primary lines of inquiry that informed our analysis. We then present the data and methods, including a discussion of our positionality. The next section provides further background on the partnership as regards policy context in New York City and the specific needs of the DOE and TC teams. This is followed by discussion of the analysis of the partnership, focusing on the process (i.e. co-creating an RPP) and the outcome (i.e. research use of RPP products). The paper concludes with key takeaways and an examination of potential future scholarship on RPPs in the field of ESE.

Background

Existing scholarship offers insight into the relationships between research and policy, and informs the focus of this paper on a particular kind of relationship, that of an RPP. In this section, we review three areas of prior literature related to this topic. The first line of work is research on RPP in education (Coburn and Penuel 2016; Henrick et al. 2017; Penual et al. 2020). The second is the application of improvement science in education (Bryk et al. 2015; Langley et al. 2009; Lewis 2015), which informed the design of the DOE–TC RPP. The third line of work is research use studies (Davies and Nutley 2008; DuMont 2015). We draw on the latter as frameworks with which to analyze process and outcomes in the context of the DOE–TC RPP.

Research on Research-Practice partnership in education

The relationship between research and policy has received much attention over the years in the literature beyond ESE, which has resulted in various and conceptualizations. Gordon, Lewis and Young (1977), for example, distinguish between *research of policy* and *research for policy*, with the former being more independent (or academic) and the latter being commissioned or sponsored. Lingard (2013) argues that research of policy has a greater impact potential than research for policy because the former is broader and open (rather than narrower with a focus on a specific problem of practice). More specifically, in the context of ESE, Rickinson and McKenzie (2020) call for more engagement by researchers with policymakers; engagement that is oriented towards problem-solving and that seeks to broaden public dialogue and action. Another common terminology that is often used in the context of the relationship between research and policy is *translation* of research findings into forms useful for educational practice (National Research Council 1999). This terminology suggests the "directionality of learning is one-way, and the goal is for knowledge to travel unchanged" (Penuel et al. 2015, p. 185).

RPPs offer a different framework for the relationship between research and policy. Scholars define RPPs as long-term collaborations between researchers and practitioners that leverage research to address persistent problems of practice (Coburn, Penuel, and Geil 2013). Indeed, RPPs are part of a larger family of collaborative approaches to education research, which includes design-based implementation research, networked improvement communities, and community-based design research (for review and comparison, see Penuel et al. 2020). In other words, RPPs represent a different type of relationship: *research with policymakers*.

The relationship between research and policy that is embodied in RPPs aligns well with the vision of the science of sustainability (SOS). A branch of the broad sustainability science that emerged over the past two decades, SOS is characterized by reflexivity and applicability (Spangenberg 2011). SOS recognizes there are multiple ways of knowing and that empirical research is but "one component of an extensive process of knowledge production" (Spangenberg 2011, 279). That is, SOS invites collaborations from the extended community and not only from academic peers (i.e. in other disciplines or fields). Broader collaborations between academic research institutes and other sectors (government, industry, and civil society) are seen as facilitating "co-creation for sustainability" that could further advance sustainable urban transformations (Trencher, Yarime, and Kharrazi 2013, p. 40). Thus, both RPP and SOS follow a relational logic and pay attention to discursive processes among stakeholders (e.g. researchers, policymakers, teachers, parents, and students). In other words, we posit that RPP is especially important in the context of sustainability and ESE.

Following the proliferation of RPPs in education in the past decade, scholars began to explore the factors associated with effective partnerships (Henrick et al. 2017). For example, based on review of the literature and interviews with scholars, Henrick et al. (2017) developed a framework for assessing RPPs. Their framework includes five dimensions: (a) building trust and cultivating partnership relationships, (b) conducting rigorous research to inform action, (c) supporting the partner practice organization in achieving its goals, (d) producing knowledge that can inform educational improvements efforts more broadly, and (e) building the capacity of all participants to engage in partnership work. The framework stresses the importance of producing knowledge that could inform actions in terms of policy and practice. In our analysis, we focus on the first two dimensions as they directly relate to the aforementioned research questions. The three remaining dimensions, while present, are still emerging in the ongoing partnership between the DOE and TC. In the next section, we offer important insights on how to produce such knowledge through the application of improvement science framework.

Application of improvement science in education

A second body of literature framing this study is that of improvement science in education. Although research and evidence-based interventions are abundant in the field of education, policymakers and scholars are increasingly worried about the ability of this research-based knowledge to spur broad-scale improvements in schools (Bryk, Gomez, and Grunow 2011). Improvement science seeks to address this problem by developing the necessary *know-how* to allow reform ideas to spread faster and more effectively (Langley et al. 2009). While the ideas underlying improvement science are not new to education researchers (e.g. action research and formative evaluation), this framework can nonetheless contribute new tools, processes, and approaches that have proven useful outside the realm of education (Lewis 2015).

Scholars writing within this framework theorize that two types of knowledge are needed in the pursuit of educational improvement (Langley et al. 2009; Lewis 2015). The first type is basic knowledge from the field of education, which for the ESE field might include effective ways to teach sustainability concepts or effective strategies to encourage schools to address sustainability goals. The second type is systematic knowledge regarding *how* to enact that basic knowledge within organizations; for example, knowledge about educators' motivation, knowledge about organizational routines that promote or prevent collaboration, and understanding of variations in inputs and outcome (e.g. what works for whom?). This type of knowledge is drawn from academic disciplines and from practical experience in a specific organizational context. Improvement science relies on "rapid tests of change to guide the development, revision and continued fine-tuning of new tools, processes, work roles and relationships" (Carnegie Foundation for the Advancement of Teaching, n.d., para. 1). These rapid tests are also known as Plan-Do-Study-Act cycles.

Improvement science literature is particularly useful for developing RPPs because it offers a profound shift in the traditional roles of researchers and practitioners (Bryk, Gomez, and Grunow 2011). A common division of labor sees researchers perform the intellectual work at the front end of an idea pipeline, with practitioners subsequently implementing and adapting the researchers' efforts. This common approach, however, overlooks practitioners' vital first-hand knowledge and experience with local problem-solving. By contrast, improvement science argues that complex problems demand collaboration between different stakeholders, including researchers, policymakers, and practitioners. This collaborative effort brings together different perspectives and skills, while simultaneously fostering necessary buy-in from key stakeholders.

Research use studies

A third body of literature informing our analysis is that of research use studies. Although high-quality research has the potential to improve policy and practice, it often does not (National Research Council 2012). Research use studies therefore strive to understand when, how, and under what conditions research-based knowledge is taken up within policy and practice (Davies and Nutley 2008). This field of study, therefore, informs our analysis of the DOE-TC RPP' outcomes by providing a framework to understand how and why and when policymakers and practitioners may use the research created through the RPP.

Classic typologies from the literature are used in the research use field for further specification of research utilization categories (Davies and Nutley 2008; Lavis et al. 2003; Weiss 1979). *Instrumental* use occurs when policymakers use research to address a particular problem. *Conceptual* use concerns the influence of research on the way actors think about issues and frame problems and solutions. *Strategic/Tactical/Symbolic* use involves employing research evidence to support or challenge a particular action (e.g. a program or reform effort) or a predetermined position. *Process* use occurs when engagement in the process of producing research shape participants' views towards the topics/issues covered in the research. In the analysis to follow, we draw on this typology to evaluate how policymakers use evidence produced in the context of am RPP.

Past research in this field draws on diverse methodologies, including qualitative, quantitative, and social network analysis (Gitomer and Crouse 2019). Notably, according to these prior studies, research use is influenced by norms and values. When organizations value research, individuals within the organizations are more likely to use it in their work (Fitzsimons and Cooper 2012; Spillane and Miele 2007). In turn, a key finding across studies of different systems and levels of policy suggests that relationships between researchers and stakeholders matter (DuMont 2015; Finnigan, Daly, and Che 2013). Another important driver of research use is the ability of organizations and individuals to "localize" knowledge (Honig and Coburn 2008), which also proved true in the partnership. Finally, scholars have pointed to the role of intermediary organizations – such as think tanks and advocacy organizations – in shaping research use in school districts (Honig, Venkateswaran, and McNeil 2017; Scott et al. 2017).

Insights from these three literatures highlight important considerations for our current study of the DOE-TC RPP. The literature on RPPs in education offers a conceptual framework to study the process of emergence of the DOE-TC RPP (first research question). The literature on improvement science articulates the nature of the partnership where the DOE and TC took part in multiple Plan-Do-Study-Act cycles intended to conduct rigorous and actionable research. Finally, the emerging literature on research use informs our analysis of how policymakers use research produced in the context of a RPP, or in other words, the outcomes of the RPP (second research question).

Study setting: New York City

Similar to other major cities around the world, New York City (NYC) has initiated several efforts to address the long-term challenges the city faces relating to climate change and sustainability (C40 Cities Climate Leadership Group 2019; Portney 2017). In 2007, Mayor Michael Bloomberg announced the city's first strategic plan for sustainability (City of New York 2007) that was later expanded by Mayor Bill de Blasio (City of New York 2015). In its most recent iteration, the plan presented a vision for the city that is organized around principles of growth, equity, sustainability, and resiliency.

NYC has the largest school system in the United States. More than 1.1 million students and over 1,850 schools fall within the DOE's jurisdiction—meaning the agency's actions significantly affects the city's ecological footprint. Given this, and the fact that schools have the potential to serve as meaningful change agents within their communities, both strategic plans for sustainability addressed the city's education system as part of their sustainability efforts. For example, Chancellor's Regulation A-850, which was first published in 2009, established the DOE Office of Sustainability to address city priorities, create an overall vision, and set goals for sustainability initiatives at the DOE. Positioned within the DOE's Division of School Facilities and given overarching waste and emissions goals to oversee, the Office of Sustainability initially approached sustainability from a purely facilities-based standpoint. Over time, however, the Office's approach evolved beyond facilities to engage directly with faculty and students in an attempt to meet city sustainability goals.

Following changes in the city's strategic plans, Chancellor's Regulation A-850 was expanded in 2013, emphasizing "the importance of sustainability, to create a culture that accepts fiscal

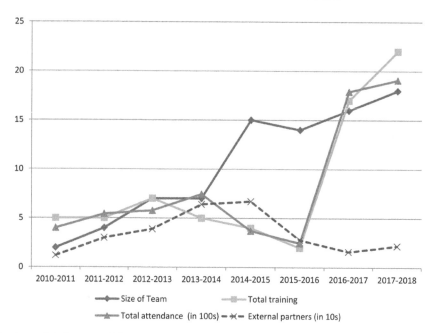

Figure 1. Annual indicators of four sustainability education activities in New York City Department of Education.

responsibility for sustainability goals, to enhance building performance, and to foster a sense of citizenship [...] encouraging students to focus on sustainability" (City of New York 2013, 1). The updated regulation required every public and private school in the city to designate a school-based Sustainability Coordinator, mandated new timelines for reporting progress, and required schools to complete and submit an extensive school sustainability plan and annual sustainability survey.

As the city's policies and regulations for school sustainability have evolved, so has the Office of Sustainability. Figure 1 illustrates the Office's development over the past decade in four key areas: (1) office size, (2) number of external partners, (3) number of training sessions, and (4) number of participants in training (e.g. non-governmental organizations and higher education institutions).

All four areas show growth over the past decade, with a particularly notable increase in office size. The Office of Sustainability formed in 2009 with just a single employee, but is now a team of 18 full-time employees. The Office of Sustainability has dedicated Energy and Zero Waste Teams to provide customized educational and operational support to match facility needs and school stakeholder interests. This growth was necessary to help implement city sustainability goals and oversee priorities from the Mayor and the DOE's Chancellor.

In conclusion, the DOE established its Office of Sustainability, in part, to administer the Sustainability Plan and the Annual Sustainability Survey. Yet early on, the Office lacked sufficient capacity to utilize these instruments and the data they collected in a meaningful, strategic manner. The Office therefore needed to develop its research capacity and data infrastructure to inform its policy and programming activities. The DOE–TC RPP emerged within this context.

Data and methods

The current study explores the emergence of the TC-DOE RPP and analyzes the ways in which the DOE used the evidence produced by the RPP. While there are multiple ways to examine these issues (e.g. interviews and observations), we opted to rely on analysis of documents and artefacts. Following Gitomer and Crouse (2019) and Mahoney (2004), we posit that these data are particularly well suited to a study that focuses on processes. Documents and artefacts memorialized what we – co-leaders of the partnership – did and produced over the years (Bowen 2009; Hodder 2000). Further, these data include justifications and reasons for actions we took in the context of the partnership. Because we originally created these materials and we know the social context in which we produced them, we have the ability to interpret the meaning of them (Wildemuth 2009).

The corpus of materials include memos summarizing results from Plan-Do-Study-Act cycles, PowerPoint presentations, abstracts for conferences (e.g. Comparative and International Education Society and Green Schools Conference and Expo), meetings minutes, email communications, transcripts of professional development sessions, and research instruments. We assembled all the artefacts in one shared virtual folder. To ease data management and analysis, we also listed all items in a worksheet with a unique identification code.

Data analysis began with a careful reading of all the materials. We followed the methodological literature on artefacts and documents analysis (Hodder 2000; O'Leary 2004) and proceeded in two sequential phases. First, we created a timeline for the development of the RPP. We coded different types of interactions between members of the DOE and TC, including conference calls and in-person meetings. Working through the data, we noticed a series of exchanges where the DOE team presented at the TC and vice versa. Data fitting this pattern became a category in our analysis.

Second, we identified the use of research evidence produced as part of the relationship between the DOE and TC. We read together the working paper "Learning More about How Research-Based Knowledge Gets Used: Guidance in the Development of New Empirical Research" (Davies and Nutley 2008). We spent two meetings discussing Davies and Nutley (2008) to ensure that we have a shared understanding of the different types of research use. We then developed a system of categories to code the artefacts and documents based on types of research use derived from Davies and Nutley (2008).

For quality control of the coding process, we employed team–based data analysis (MacQueen et al. 1998) as suggested by Drezner and Garvey (2016). Revising their strategies for our study, each team member coded the artefacts independently, taking notes on general impressions and themes. We compared our coding and discussed differences to develop a common understanding of the category system. Once we achieved agreement on the coding, we synthesized the findings into a coherent narrative.

Every study has limitations and our study is no different. Readers should consider two limitations. First, this study involves retrospective analysis, making it subject to hindsight bias. This approach, however, is very common in RPP scholarship as it can reveal critical turning points in the development processes and identify principles for guiding future efforts (Coburn and Penuel 2016). Second, this study is an insider account of the RPP. Outside researchers may have a greater ability to probe and report on additional perspectives. In contrast to the vast majority of previous RPP scholarship that is written solely by researchers (Coburn and Penuel 2016), the authors of this article are researchers and policymakers.

Positionality statement

Acknowledging researchers' positionality is important in all studies. However, perhaps it is even more important here in that we wrote a first-person analysis and reflection on a RPP that we designed. We approached our work through our current and previous professional roles and educational backgrounds. Throughout this process, as a research-team, we acknowledged our professional identities and the intimacy we have with this work. By directly engaging our professional identities within the partnership, we learned that all three co-authors have a personal passion for ESE. This passion and commitment continue to be an aspect that strengthens the RPP.

Oren Pizmony-Levy is Associate Professor and Director of the Center for Sustainable Futures at Teachers College, Columbia University in New York. Trained in both sociology and education policy studies, he has worked on issues related to social movements and schools. Prior to graduate school, Oren 1 worked at the Society for the Protection of Nature in Israel (NGO). Specifically, he was involved in the development of new environmental education curriculum and professional development for K-12 schools.

Meredith McDermott is the Director of Sustainability for the NYC DOE, overseeing programs such as NYC Solar Schools, Zero Waste Schools, NYC Demand Response Program, and extensive training/professional learning programs for technical staff, teachers, administration, and students. Prior to this position, Meredith directed sustainability efforts for Chicago Public Schools as well managed an immersive science program for elementary through college students in San Diego. Having earned Masters' degrees in Environmental Management and Marine Biology, Meredith has designed, conducted, and reported on research using both quantitative and qualitative methods.

Thaddeus T. Copeland is the Deputy Director of Sustainability for NYC DOE, overseeing the implementation of a number of school sustainability programs that support Sustainability Coordinators and strengthens the relationship between school facilities and education. Previously, Thad managed an environmental education program that worked with K-12 NYC students on recycling and zero waste programs. Having earned a Masters' degree in Sustainable Development and a Post Graduate Certificate in Sustainability Strategies, Thad has designed and implemented monitoring and evaluation projects.

Collectively, we discussed how our professional experiences shaped all aspects of this study and larger partnership. This included the development of the partnership's work, the research design of this study, and the ways in which we interpret the DOE-TC RPP. These perspectives strengthened our ability to engage in critical analysis of the RPP.

Findings

In engaging our research questions that look at how researchers and policymakers co-create an RPP and how policymakers use research outcomes from an RPP, we present the results of our analysis through discussion of key dimensions in the framework proposed by Henrick et al. (2017). Recall that their framework included five dimensions or factors associated with effective partnerships. For the purpose of this article, we focus on two dimensions: (a) building trust and cultivating partnership relationships, and (b) conducting rigorous research to inform action. In this paper, we advance the literature by documenting not only the research outputs from the RPP, but also the ways in which policymakers use this research to inform their work. Thus, we show that the DOE-TC RPP functions as a form of a practice-research relationship.

Building trust and cultivating partnership relationships

Research on effective education RPPs highlights the role of strong interpersonal relationships grounded in transparency and trust (Henrick et al. 2017). This was also reflected in our analysis of the study data. The DOE and TC established the RPP in effort to meet the complimentary needs of the two partners. On the one hand, the DOE needed to develop its research capacity and data infrastructure to inform its strategy and support the work of Sustainability Coordinators in schools. On the other hand, TC sought to provide real-world learning opportunities for students and faculty. Email exchanges and meetings minutes show that both partners articulated their needs in a transparent way and early on.

Creating lasting RPPs, which takes strong interpersonal relationships, takes significant time and resources, yet the critical early stages of this process are often overlooked. Drawing on qualitative analysis of documents and artefacts, we constructed the timeline and activities for

Table 1. Timeline and activities for DOE–TC research-practice partnership.

Year	Quarter	DOE presentation at TC	TC presentation at DOE	DOE–TC share work with others	Research activity	Ad-hoc meetings	Regular meetings
2014	1st	+			+	+	
	2nd				+		
	3rd						
	4th						
2015	1st	+			++	+	
	2nd			+	+	+	
	3rd						
	4th						
2016	1st					+	
	2nd						
	3rd				++	+	
	4th				++		
2017	1st	+	+		+	+	
	2nd		+	+	++	+	+
	3rd				+++		+
	4th				+++		++
2018	1st	+	++	++	+	+	++
	2nd				++		++
	3rd				+++	+	++
	4th				+++		++

Note: Quarters (1st January–March; 2nd April–June; 3rd July–September; 4th October–December); activity level (+ low; ++ medium; +++ high).

the DOE-TC RPP. As illustrated in Table 1, the initial contact between the DOE and TC teams came in February 2014. A campus presentation by the former Director of the Office of Sustainability (Dr. Sharon Jaye) inspired several students to explore ESE in NYC public schools in their work. One of these papers analyzed collaborations between schools and community-based organizations (CBOs) and was ultimately developed into a larger study (Pizmony-Levy and Fernandez 2015). The DOE incorporated descriptive patterns from this study in their 2013–2014 Annual Report (New York City Office of Sustainability 2014); this was an early sign for the emergence of a mutual relationship between the partners.

Successful early interactions like this led to the first official collaboration between the DOE and TC in early 2015 where a TC-based team analyzed DOE administrative data and conducted interviews with Sustainability Coordinators and CBOs to understand the actualization of the Chancellor's Regulation. Email exchanges between the partners show the growing trust between them. In April 2015, a year after the first contact between the partners, for example, the then Director of the Office of Sustainability sent this note to local NGOs and DOE staff:

We have partnered with Teachers College, Columbia University to conduct research on environmental and sustainability education programs in our schools […] Our ultimate goal is to create a report to inform and shape policies that would create more access to educational programs in this area. […] On a personal note, I would like to say thank you for participating in the research. Teachers College's holistic approach to this project and the level of their analysis will provide us incredible information that will enable us to improve our programs and make national-level impacts in the green schools movement.

By building trust and transparent working relationships, these engagements helped create the foundation for the long-term success of the RPP. This research led the DOE to engage TC in the redesign and administration of subsequent sustainability plans and annual sustainability surveys. Findings from this collaborative work helped generate new research questions and inform DOE policy and programing.

Although the overall experience was positive and productive for both the DOE and TC teams, RPPs can be challenging. Our qualitative analysis point to two constant, but productive, tensions. The first tension exists due to the differing principles and priorities that guide each organization. For example, the TC team generally wanted to keep the surveys similar across the years to better measure change, while the DOE team sought to update and revise different measures to better capture what was happening in the field. The dialog between the partners produced a compromise in the shape of surveys with constant and of rotating modules.

The second tension concerns the definition of ESE. At first, the TC team relied and advocated for an expansive definition of sustainability, which includes the three pillars of environment, society, and economics. The DOE team, however, focused more on the environmental pillar (e.g. waste and energy). The dialog between the partners led to a working definition of ESE as an approach that provide students and their communities with opportunities to learn about and participate in addressing sustainability challenges. That is, ESE is defined here in terms that echo the whole-school approach with attention to organizational culture, facilities, and educational program (Barr, Cross, and Dunbar 2014; Henderson and Tilbury 2004).

The DOE and TC settled these tensions through conversations and dialog. Both partners made efforts to balance input and mutually respect each other's expertise (as reported above). This dynamic is a useful indictor of the strong interpersonal relationships between the partners, which is a critical factor in effective education RPPs (Henrick et al. 2017).

Conducting research to inform action: Research use analysis

A central theme in the framework for assessing RPPs (Henrick et al. 2017) is concerned with the production of knowledge that *could* inform action. This also emerged as a central consideration of the RPP in our analysis of the project artefacts. Indeed, as illustrated in Table 2, the DOE-TC RPP implemented several research projects to improve school engagement with ESE. In this section, we assess how policymakers actually used the research conducted by the partnership; we focus on instrumental use, conceptual use, and process benefits from engagement (Davies and Nutley 2008).

Instrumental use. Much of the work exploring research use has focused on instrumental use where policymakers and practitioners use research-based knowledge to inform and direct specific actions and programmatic decisions (Davies and Nutley 2008). This kind of relationship between research and policy aligns with Trowler's (2003) "engineering model," in which research informs policymakers about the facts and, in turn, proposes solutions to problems. In the case of the RPP, the DOE often uses evidence produced by the partnership in an instrumental fashion. This makes sense given the rationale behind the Plan-Do-Study-Act cycles. The following three examples illustrate this pattern.

The first example of how the DOE uses evidence in an instrumental fashion relates to the way Sustainability Coordinators are supported and compensated. Although current policy requires every public school to appoint a Sustainability Coordinator, the policy does not stipulate any funding. For the most part, therefore, the position of Sustainability Coordinator is unpaid. Critics of the policy point to the lack of compensation as a critical weakness and call for public investment in hiring full-time Coordinators.[1] As a preliminary step to addressing this critique, the partnership launched an inquiry into existing school supports that are available to Coordinators and the extent to which these supports are associated with stronger engagement. Through interviews and focus groups with principals and Coordinators, it became apparent that certain principals employ creative solutions to better support the work of their Coordinators.[2] Data from the 2017 Sustainability Plan Survey established that about half (47.0%) of the Coordinators receive at least one type of school support. In addition, a link exists between school supports and stronger engagement with sustainability practices. Coordinators receiving at least one type of school support were more likely to engage with energy conservation and waste management. Findings from this inquiry, in turn, informed the design of communication

Table 2. Selected projects of the DOE–TC research-practice partnership 2014–2018.

Project	Guiding question	Partnership structure	Action / Use
1	Who are the Sustainability Coordinators? What is their professional background? What motivate them to work on ESE projects?	* Quantitative analysis of DOE data.	DOE use information in conversations with policymakers and partners to debunk misconceptions.
2	How do Sustainability Coordinators define the terms sustainability and sustainable development? Is there a shared understanding of the term?	* Qualitative study of open-ended data collected through a survey. Social network analysis of co-mentioned themes. * Quantitative analysis of DOE data.	DOE use information in strategic planning and in professional development.
3	What barriers prevent Sustainability Coordinators from attending ESE-related professional development?	* Quantitative analysis of DOE data.	DOE revamped professional development offerings, and introduced a basic training for new Coordinators. DOE and TC piloted a webinar, and TC submitted a grant for piloting a series of webinars.
4	To what extent Sustainability Coordinators are known or visible to the school community?	* Quantitative analysis of DOE data.	DOE created a reusable poster that indicates the name of the school sustainability Coordinator and several sustainability goals.
5	To what extent schools support their Sustainability Coordinators in order to do enhance their engagement with ESE?	* Qualitative study using interviews and focus groups. * Quantitative analysis of DOE data, including descriptive statistics and cross-tabulations.	DOE prepared a principal checklist and handouts for Sustainability Coordinators.
6	To what extent Sustainability Coordinators engage students through green teams? What are the common practices for working green teams?	* Quantitative analysis of DOE data. * Action research in four schools that offer a green team.	DOE and TC piloted a webinar on how to work with school green team. DOE and TC implemented a mentoring program for schools interested in establishing a student green team.
7	What types of school engagement with ESE exists in the system? How these types of engagement vary across individual and school characteristics?	* Latent Class Analysis to identify underlining types of school engagement with ESE. * Quantitative analysis of DOE data.	DOE use information in conversations with policymakers and partners to advocate for policy revisions.
8	How (do) Sustainability Coordinators learn from each other?	* Social network analysis of DOE data. * Qualitative study using interviews.	DOE use information in strategic planning and in professional development.

materials. The DOE prepared a checklist for principals outlining different ways to provide time/support for Coordinators (Artefact ID D-17-05). The DOE also prepared handouts for teacher Coordinators detailing the options available for them to allocate more time to this role (Artefact ID D-17-06). Both documents are intended to raise awareness to the availability of school supports.

The second example of how the DOE uses evidence in an instrumental fashion centers on professional development. Education scholars agree that active participation in continuing, high-quality professional development is critical for new policies to be successfully implemented and for the overall professionalization of the field (Darling-Hammond, Hyler, and Gardner 2017; Garet et al. 2001; Opfer 2016). The partnership's research, however, repeatedly revealed that only a small portion of Sustainability Coordinators has participated in training offered by the DOE or other CBOs. In AY 2017/2018, only one-quarter of Coordinators (24.5%) attended at least one workshop organized by the DOE. The discovery of this low figure led to an exploration of the kinds of barriers that prevent Coordinators from attending training

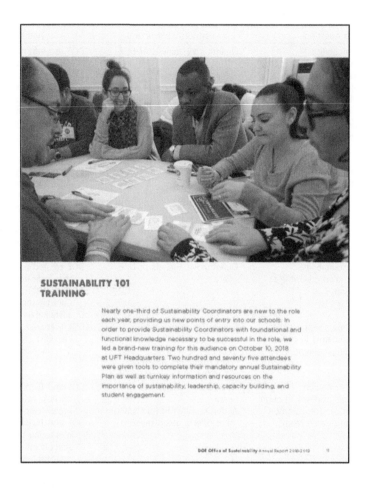

Figure 2. Advertisement for professional development showing the instrumental use of research.

Source: NYC DOE Office of Sustainability, Annual Report 2018–2019 Source: NYC DOE Office of Sustainability, July 2018

and the topics/issues they find interesting or important. Survey data and qualitative data analysis revealed that time and participation in prior trainings are the two main reasons for Coordinators not attending training sessions. These results also showed, however, that Coordinators are generally interested in learning about green spaces (e.g. school gardens and living roofs) and a full two-thirds are interested in attending short, web-based training. Using this evidence, the DOE changed its training offering for AY 2018/2019, creating a completely revised training opportunity for newly designated Coordinators, titled "Sustainability 101 Training." Figure 2 shows advertisement for this training, which includes a direct quote from the research.

The third, and final, example of how the DOE uses evidence in an instrumental fashion focuses on engaging students through green teams. Scholars have documented the positive impact of environmental clubs on student engagement with ESE (McDuff 2000; Said, Yahaya, and Ahmadun 2007). The partnership's research shows that one-third (36.0%) of all Coordinators are working with a student green team, and 62.0% are planning to establish a green team in the future. To support these efforts, the DOE and TC organized a webinar explaining how to work with green teams.[3] TC, in coordination with the DOE, allocated three fellowships (one in AY 2017/2018, and two in AY 2018/2019) for students to assist Title I schools (those that, because they have a large concentration of low-income students, receive supplemental funds to assist in meeting students' educational goals) with developing a school green team (Kessler 2018). Preliminary feedback suggests that this model is working, but more development is required to better equip the fellows with knowledge on mentoring and organizational change.

Conceptual use. Decision-making can be complex and is often not a linear process. In such instances, there is not a direct link to decisions, but rather a gradual diffusion of theory and data into the sphere of organizational decision-making (Weiss 1980). Theory and data may also be absorbed into professional or tacit knowledge of practitioners (Davies and Nutley 2008). Research-based knowledge serves to promote general "enlightenment" (Trowler 2003) by clarifying policymakers' assumptions about organizations and the system as a whole. Research-based knowledge also contributes to enriching public discussion. This pattern can be seen in the following two examples.

The first example of how the DOE uses evidence in a conceptual fashion relates to the misconceptions regarding Sustainability Coordinators and the implementation of the Chancellor's Regulation. Prior to the RPP, the DOE lacked key information about the population of Sustainability Coordinators, such as their professional background, experience, and motivation. Given this lack of information, two common assumptions were often made: (1) Coordinators are mostly science teachers, and (2) the position experiences significant turnover and instability. The partnership's research analysis, however, debunked these assumptions. In reality, less than half of Coordinators (44.0%) are teachers, while approximately one-third (30.0%) are assistant principals and the rest (26.0%) have other roles in their schools (e.g. secretary or librarian). Among teacher Coordinators, about half (49.0%) are science teachers. Notably, only one-third (33.0%) of Coordinators are newly designated to their role. To help process this information, the DOE shared these findings with partners and stakeholders to consider new ways to engage the diverse population of Coordinators (see Figure 3).

The second example of how the DOE uses evidence in a conceptual fashion relates to the meaning of sustainability and sustainable development. Recognizing that these terms are vague and contested (Little 2014; Wals and Jickling 2002), the RPP initiated a study to assess how Sustainability Coordinators make sense of the term "sustainability." Using the 2016 Sustainability Plan Survey platform, Coordinators were asked to define the term "sustainability" in their own words. A qualitative coding of close to 1,400 open-ended definitions was then conducted to identify main themes and co-mentioning patterns. Findings from this study suggest that Coordinators tend to focus on the environmental pillar of sustainability while overlooking the economic and social pillars. In turn, Coordinators view sustainability as related to waste management, pollution, and energy conservation. Importantly, almost no variation based on professional background or other characteristics was found. The environmental and recourse management foci echo the legacy of the Office of Sustainability and its strong connections to

Figure 3. Excerpt from NYC DOE Annual Report showing the conceptual use of research.
Source: NYC DOE Office of Sustainability, Annual Report 2017–2018

the city's sustainability goals (e.g. reduction in greenhouse gas emissions). The DOE used these findings to redesign professional development activities (Artefact ID D-18-10) and to reframe the discussion on ESE in city schools.

Process benefits from engagement with research. Although evidence plays a significant role in informing decision-making, engagement in the process of producing research-based knowledge can also have an impact on policymakers and practitioners (Davies and Nutley 2008). Through participation in the process of production of knowledge, participants can begin to change their ways of thinking about social problems and solutions. This type of use identified in the literature was also affirmed by analysis of the project artefacts. For example, when asked to comment about any of the topics discussed in the Sustainability Plan or Annual Sustainability Survey, several Coordinators mentioned the instruments helped them to better understand their role, the expectations of the DOE, and the possibilities for engagement. The following Coordinator quotes illustrate this point:

"The survey offered me a list of ideas for which to start with! Thank you!"

"I am very interested in pursuing a collaboration with different non-profits and city agencies that were listed on this survey to help in implementing sustainability programs at my school.

I was not familiar will all of the organizations on the list, and am willing to reach out for outside support."

In addition to informing Coordinators of the scope of their role, the research instruments also have the capacity to create greater awareness of the importance of the Sustainability Coordinator role for principals. This is important because principals are solely responsible for designating the Coordinator role to a member of their staff on an annual basis. A better organized and accessible Sustainability Plan can result in a more informed principal who, in turn, will be more likely to select a Sustainability Coordinator properly suited for the role. This idea is reflected in the following quote:

"I'm quite embarrass[ed] by this survey. I didn't have any idea what was involve[d] [in] being a sustainability coordinator. Not sure if my principal does either because I don't think she would have chosen me to for this position."

Discussion and conclusion

This study was motivated by the growing interest in ESE policy and the call for more attention to the relationship between research and policy. RPP is one promising framework to establish productive relationships between policy and research. Advocates argue that RPPs can increase research use in policymaking, address persistent problems of practice, and improve educational outcomes (Coburn and Penuel 2016). Indeed, over the past decade, scholars and foundations have encouraged the creation of education RPPs (Coburn and Penuel 2016). A review of recent grantees from the US-based Spencer Foundation and the William T. Grant Foundation, however, show that funded RPPs pursue improvement efforts in many domains but not in the field of ESE. In this paper, we presented a study of DOE-TC RPP that seeks to improve ESE in NYC, which is the largest school system in the United States. We now revisit our research questions to summarize what we have learned.

First, *what is the process by which researchers and policymakers co-create an RPP to improve ESE in public schools?* Generally, and consistent with previous research, our analysis highlights the importance of strong relationships, transparency, and trust in order to build effective and long-lasting RPP. Our analysis demonstrates the gradual process that led to the creation of the DOE-TC RPP. In other words, the organizations did not join forces to establish an RPP; rather the decision to establish an RPP emerged from a series of interactions between the two organizations. These prior interactions built the necessary trust between the organizations. The fact that both organizations are co-located in New York City allowed for regular in-person meetings, opportunities for socializing, and shared understanding of the locale. A partnership with separate locales would present fewer opportunities for team members to develop strong working relationships.

Second, *how do policymakers use the research outcomes from an RPP to improve ESE in public schools?* The findings from our analysis of the DOE-TC RPP bear out claims about the potential benefits of RPPs. Drawing on a qualitative analysis of documents and artefacts, we show that research-based knowledge co-produced by both organizations has been—and continues to be—used to inform policy and practice. In certain cases, the use is more instrumental, while in others it is more conceptual or diffuse. Although Davies and Nutley (2008) point to other types of evidence use or misuse (e.g. strategic, political, and tactical), no misuse of the data was identified. This finding could be related to the high level of trust between the DOE and TC, or the fact that the knowledge produced was local and relevant (Honig and Coburn 2008). Additionally, the DOE and other key stakeholders did not need to "translate" the research in order to apply it to their own context and experience. Another possible explanation of this finding is that we are too close to the RPP and cannot objectively observe all types of use or misuse.

So, what comes next for the partnership and ESE in New York City? The city's current ESE policy relies on programs that are either made available to schools by CBOs and/or driven by the DOE (i.e. Office of Sustainability, STEM, Service Learning, etc.). To make sure the public school system is making a sustained improvement in terms of engagement with ESE, there is a need for strong collaboration across all agencies and CBOs. Strong collaboration across all agencies and CBOs is necessary to make sure the public school system continues to improve ESE engagement. In line with ideas from Bryk et al. (2015), the DOE–TC RPP is a potential foundation for establishing a networked improvement community (NIC) dedicated to ESE. NICs are scientific learning communities encompassing a diverse set of stakeholders—such as local school districts, colleges and universities, local businesses, CBOs/NGOs, and foundations—committed to using improvement science to solve problems of practice. The main difference between RPPs and NICs is that the former usually bring together two organizations whereas the latter connect multiple organizations and agencies. Because the organizational field of ESE in New York City includes a diverse set of actors, an ESE-focused NIC would go a long way towards advancing sustainability goals.

Going forward, further research on the relationship between research and policy in the field of ESE could develop in several different ways. Formal qualitative studies could document and explore additional cases of RPPs. A comparative study of partnerships could shed light on the role of the socio-political context in shaping partnerships. Drawing on interviews and observations, scholars could analyze whether or not having a local sustainability strategic plan affect the work of RPPs. Another possible direction could be to investigate whether RPPs promote the use of other types of knowledge in the design of ESE policies. Applying social network analysis to policy documents produced before and after the RPP, for example, could point to changes in citation patterns (see for example: Baek et al. 2018).

The study also has implications for the development of relationships between researchers and policymakers in the broader ESE field. First, more of these relationships could be mutually beneficial. Past research on RPPs emphasizes the importance of supporting policymakers and practice organizations in achieving their goals. Our findings suggest that it is important to pay attention to the needs of both sides. Second, conducting *research with policymakers* and establishing on-going conversation about the meaning of the research results help ensure the efficient use of knowledge in policy. While, our findings clearly demonstrate how policymakers used the research-based knowledge that was produced in the context of the DOE–TC RPP, we found that it goes beyond 'just' research use. It is efficient use in the sense that since the research and analysis were done within the RPP, by both the researchers and policymakers, there was no misinterpretation of findings, nor was there any misappropriation of external research that was not appropriate for the context of the NYC DOE.

In conclusion, as evidenced above, university-based teams can successfully partner with governmental agencies to support and enrich ESE policy and practice on a wide scale. In time when public discourse can be critical of higher education institutions (Brown 2018; Drezner, Pizmony-Levy, and Pallas 2018) and societies face serious sustainability challenges, it is all the more important for researchers to work closely with policymakers to demonstrate their contribution to the collective good. Drawing on our partnership in New York City, we are cautiously optimistic that RPPs are a viable and effective way for advancing relationships between research and policy in ESE.

Notes

1. An estimated cost for hiring fulltime Sustainability Coordinators in every public school in New York City is close to 100 million USD per year.
2. For example, some principals use preparation periods or school-based options, which allow schools to modify the collective bargaining agreement to meet the needs and philosophy of their school community (UFT, n.d.).

3. A recording of the webinar is available here: https://www.tc.columbia.edu/sustainability/resources/pulled-content-2/how-to-build-a-school-green-team/. At minute fifteen, the presenters share research from the DOE-TC RPP.

Acknowledgements

We are especially thankful for the thoughtful feedback we received from Noah Drezner, Nancy Green Saraisky, Erika Kessler, and Carine Verschueren. We thank the Special Issue Co-Editors Marcia Mckenzie and Mark Rickinson and the anonymous reviewers for their detailed and constructive comments that improved this article.

Disclosure statement

No potential conflict of interest was reported by the authors.

ORCID

Oren Pizmony-Levy http://orcid.org/0000-0002-4095-6571

References

Aikens, K., M. McKenzie, and P. Vaughter. 2016. "Environmental and Sustainability Education Policy Research: A Systematic Review of Methodological and Thematic Trends." *Environmental Education Research* 22 (3): 333–359. doi:10.1080/13504622.2015.1135418.

Baek, C., B. Hörmann, B. Karseth, O. Pizmony-Levy, K. Sivesind, and G. Steiner-Khamsi. 2018. "Policy Learning in Norwegian School Reform: A Social Network Analysis of the 2020 Incremental Reform." *Nordic Journal of Studies in Educational Policy* 4 (1): 24–37. doi:10.1080/20020317.2017.1412747.

Barr, S. K., J. E. Cross, and B. H. Dunbar. 2014. *The Whole-School Sustainability Framework*. Colorado: Center for Green Schools, U.S. Green Building Council

Bowen, G. A. 2009. "Document Analysis as a Qualitative Research Method." *Qualitative Research Journal* 9 (2): 27–41. doi:10.3316/QRJ0902027.

Bromley, P., J. W. Meyer, and F. O. Ramirez. 2011. "The Worldwide Spread of Environmental Discourse in Social Studies, History, and Civics Textbooks, 1970–2008." *Comparative Education Review* 55 (4): 517–545. doi:10.1086/660797.

Brown, A. 2018. *Most Americans Say Higher Ed Is Heading in Wrong Direction, But Partisans Disagree on Why*. Pew Research Center. http://www.pewresearch.org/fact-tank/2018/07/26/most-americans-say-higher-ed-is-heading-in-wrong-direction-but-partisans-disagree-on-why/

Bryk, A. S., L. M. Gomez, and A. Grunow. 2011. "Getting Ideas into Action: Building Networked Improvement Communities in Education." In *Frontiers in Sociology of Education*, edited by M.T. Hallinan. New York: Springer. (pp. 127-162).

Bryk, A. S., L.M. Gomez, A. Grunow, and P. G. LeMahieu. 2015. *Learning to Improve: How America's Schools Can Get Better at Getting Better*. Massachusetts: Harvard Education Press.

C40 Cities Climate Leadership Group. 2019. About C40. https://www.c40.org/research

Carnegie Foundation for the Advancement of Teaching. 2006. *Higher Education: Civic Mission and Civic Effects*. Stanford, CA: Carnegie Foundation for the Advancement of Teaching.

Carnegie Foundation for the Advancement of Teaching. n.d. "Our Ideas." https://www.carnegiefoundation.org/our-ideas/

Cho, H. 2017. "The Effects of Summer Heat on Academic Achievement: A Cohort Analysis." *Journal of Environmental Economics and Management* 83: 185–196. doi:10.1016/j.jeem.2017.03.005.

City of New York. 2007. *PlaNYC: A Greener, Greater New York*.

City of New York. 2013. *Chancellor's Regulation A-850 Sustainability*. https://www.schools.nyc.gov/docs/default-source/default-document-library/a-850-sustainability_english

City of New York. 2015. *One New York: The Plan for a Strong and Just City*.

Coburn, C. E., and W. R. Penuel. 2016. "Research–Practice Partnerships in Education: Outcomes, Dynamics, and Open Questions." *Educational Researcher* 45 (1): 48–54. doi:10.3102/0013189X16631750.

Coburn, C. E., W. R. Penuel, and K. E. Geil. 2013. *Practice Partnerships: A Strategy for Leveraging Research for Educational Improvement in School Districts*. New York: William T. Grant Foundation.

Darling-Hammond, L., M. E. Hyler, and M. Gardner. 2017. *Effective Teacher Professional Development*. Palo Alto, CA: Learning Policy Institute.

Davies, H. T., and S. Nutley. 2008. "Learning More about How Research-Based Knowledge Gets Used." Unpublished Working Paper. William T. Grant Foundation.

Drezner, N. D., and J. C. Garvey. 2016. "LGBTQ Alumni Philanthropy: Exploring (Un) Conscious Motivations for Giving Related to Identity and Experiences." *Nonprofit and Voluntary Sector Quarterly* 45 (1_suppl): 52S–71S. doi:10.1177/0899764015597780.

Drezner, N. D., O. Pizmony-Levy, and A. Pallas. 2018. *Americans Views of Higher Education as a Public and Private Good*. New York: Teachers College, Columbia University.

DuMont, K. 2015. *Leveraging Knowledge: Taking Stock of the William T. Grant Foundation's Use of Research Evidence Grants Portfolio*. New York: William T. Grant Foundation.

Finnigan, K. S., A. J. Daly, and J. Che. 2013. "Systemwide Reform in Districts under Pressure: The Role of Social Networks in Defining, Acquiring, Using, and Diffusing Research Evidence." *Journal of Educational Administration* 51 (4): 476–497. doi:10.1108/09578231311325668.

Fitzsimons, E. and Cooper, J. 2012. Embedding a culture of evidence-based practice. *Nursing Management – UK* 19(7): 14-19.

Garet, M. S., A.C. Porter, L. Desimone, B. F. Birman, and K. S. Yoon. 2001. "What Makes Professional Development Effective? Results from a National Sample of Teachers." *American Educational Research Journal* 38 (4): 915–945. doi:10.3102/00028312038004915.

Gitomer, D. H., and K. Crouse. 2019. *Studying the Use of Research Evidence: A Review of Methods*. New York: William T. Grant Foundation.

Gordon, I., J. Lewis, and K. Young. 1977. "Perspectives on Policy Analysis." *Public Administration Bulletin* 25: 26–35.

Henderson, K., and D. Tilbury. 2004. *Whole-School Approaches to Sustainability: An International Review of Sustainable School Programs*. New South Wales, Australia: Australian Research Institute in Education for Sustainability.

Henrick, E. C., P. Cobb, W. R. Penuel, K. Jackson, and T. Clark. 2017. *Assessing Research-Practice Partnerships*. New York: William T. Grant Foundation.

Hodder, I. 2000. "The Interpretation of Documents and Material Culture." In *Handbook of Qualitative Research*, edited by N. K. Denzin and Y. S. Lincoln, 393–402. Thousand Oaks, California: Sage Publications, Inc.

Honig, M. I., and C. Coburn. 2008. "Evidence-Based Decision Making in School District Central Offices: Toward a Policy and Research Agenda." *Educational Policy* 22 (4): 578–608. doi:10.1177/0895904807307067.

Honig, M. I., N. Venkateswaran, and P. McNeil. 2017. "Research Use as Learning: The Case of Fundamental Change in School District Central Offices." *American Educational Research Journal* 54 (5): 938–971. doi:10.3102/0002831217712466.

Huckle, J., and A. E. Wals. 2015. "The UN Decade of Education for Sustainable Development: Business as Usual in the End." *Environmental Education Research* 21 (3): 491–505. doi:10.1080/13504622.2015.1011084.

Iyengar, R., and M. Bajaj. 2011. "After the Smoke Clears: Toward Education for Sustainable Development in Bhopal, India." *Comparative Education Review* 55 (3): 424–456. doi:10.1086/660680.

Kessler, E. 2018. *Sustainability Coordinators in New York City Public Schools: Change Makers in Action*. Unpublished Integrative Project. New York: Teachers College, Columbia University.

Laessøe, J., N. W. Feinstein, and N. Blum. 2013. "Environmental Education Policy Research–Challenges and Ways Research Might Cope with Them." *Environmental Education Research* 19 (2): 231–242. doi:10.1080/13504622.2013.778230.

Langley, G. J., R. D. Moen, K. M. Nolan, T. W. Nolan, C. L. Norman, and L. P. Provost. 2009. *The Improvement Guide*. San Francisco, CA: Jossey-Bass.

Lavis, J. N., D. Robertson, J. M. Woodside, C. B. McLeod, and J. Abelson. 2003. "How Can Research Organizations More Effectively Transfer Research Knowledge to Decision Makers?" *The Milbank Quarterly* 81 (2): 221–248. doi:10.1111/1468-0009.t01-1-00052.

Lewis, C. 2015. "What is Improvement Science?" *Educational Researcher* 44 (1): 54–61. doi:10.3102/0013189X15570388.

Lingard, B. 2013. "The Impact of Research on Education Policy in an Era of Evidence-Based Policy." *Critical Studies in Education* 54 (2): 113–131. doi:10.1080/17508487.2013.781515.

Little, D. 2014. "Defining Sustainability in Meaningful Ways for Educators." *Journal of Sustainability Education* 7: 1–18.

MacQueen, K. M., E. McLellan, K. Kay, and B. Milstein. 1998. "Codebook Development for Team-Based Qualitative Analysis." *Cam Journal* 10 (2): 31–36. doi:10.1177/1525822X980100020301.

Mahoney, J. 2004. "Comparative-Historical Methodology." *Annual Review of Sociology* 30 (1): 81–101. doi:10.1146/annurev.soc.30.012703.110507.

McDuff, M. 2000. "Thirty Years of Environmental Education in Africa: The Role of the Wildlife Clubs of Kenya." *Environmental Education Research* 6 (4): 383–396. doi:10.1080/713664697.

National Research Council. 1999. *Improving Student Learning: A Strategic Plan for Education Research and Its Utilization*. Washington, DC: National Academies Press.

New York City Office of Sustainability. 2014. Annual Report 2013-2014 New York.

National Research Council. 2012. *Using Science as Evidence in Public Policy*. Washington, DC: National Academies Press.

O'Leary, Z. 2004. *The Essential Guide to Doing Research*. Thousand Oaks, California: Sage.

Opfer, D. 2016. "Conditions and Practices Associated with Teacher Professional Development and Its Impact on Instruction in TALIS 2013." OECD Education Working Papers, No. 138. Paris: OECD Publishing. doi:10.1787/5jlss4r0lrg5-en.
Park, R. J., J. Goodman, M. Hurwitz, and J. Smith. 2020. "Heat and Learning." *American Economic Journal: Economic Policy* 12 (2): 306–339.
Penuel, W. R., A. R. Allen, C. E. Coburn, and C. Farrell. 2015. "Conceptualizing Research–Practice Partnerships as Joint Work at Boundaries." *Journal of Education for Students Placed at Risk (JESPAR)*, 20 (1–2): 182–197. doi:10.1080/10824669.2014.988334.
Penuel, W. R., R. Riedy, M. S. Barber, D. J. Peurach, W. A. LeBouef, and T. Clark. 2020. "Principles of Collaborative Education Research with Stakeholders: Toward Requirements for a New Research and Development Infrastructure." *Review of Educational Research* 90 (5): 627–674. doi:10.3102/0034654320938126.
Pizmony-Levy, O. 2011. "Bridging the Global and Local in Understanding Curricula Scripts: The Case of Environmental Education." *Comparative Education Review* 55 (4): 600–633. doi:10.1086/661632.
Pizmony-Levy, O., and R. Fernandez. 2015. "How Green is the Big Apple? Social Inequality and School Engagement with Environmental and Sustainability Education." Paper Presented at the Annual Meeting of the American Educational Research Association (AERA), Chicago, IL.
Portney, K. E. 2017. "Taking Sustainable Cities Seriously: What Cities Are Doing." In *Environmental Policy: New Directions for the Twenty-First Century*. 10th ed., edited by N. J. Vig and M. E. Kraft ,297–319. Thousand Oaks, California: Sage. Chapter 12.
Rickinson, M., and M. McKenzie. 2020. "Understanding the Research-Policy Relationship in ESE: Insights from the Critical Policy and Evidence Use Literatures." *Environmental Education Research*: 1–18.
Sadan, N., and I. Alkaher. 2020. "Development and Formation of ESE Policy: Learning from Teachers and Local Authorities." *Environmental Education Research* 27(2): 192-216.
Said, A. M., N. Yahaya, and F. L. R. Ahmadun. 2007. "Environmental Comprehension and Participation of Malaysian Secondary School Students." *Environmental Education Research* 13 (1): 17–31. doi:10.1080/13504620601122616.
Scott, J., E. DeBray, C. Lubienski, P. G. La Londe, E. Castillo, and S. Owens. 2017. "Urban Regimes, Intermediary Organization Networks, and Research Use: Patterns across Three School Districts." *Peabody Journal of Education* 92 (1): 16–28. doi:10.1080/0161956X.2016.1264800.
Spangenberg, J. H. 2011. "Sustainability Science: A Review, an Analysis and Some Empirical Lessons." *Environmental Conservation* 38 (3): 275–287. doi:10.1017/S0376892911000270.
Spillane, J. P., and D. B. Miele. 2007. "Chapter 3 Evidence in Practice: A Framing of the Terrain." *Yearbook of the National Society for the Study of Education* 106 (1): 46–73. doi:10.1111/j.1744-7984.2007.00097.x.
Stahelin, N. 2017. "The Political Ecology of Environmental and Sustainability Education Policy across Global-National Divides." Doctoral diss., Teachers College, Columbia University.
Stevenson, R. B., and I. Robottom. 2013. "Critical Action Research and Environmental Education." In Stevenson, R. B., Brody, M., Dillon, J., & Wals, A. E. (Eds.). (2013). International handbook of research on environmental education. New York: Routledge., 469–479.
Trencher, G. P., M. Yarime, and A. Kharrazi. 2013. "Co-Creating Sustainability: Cross-Sector University Collaborations for Driving Sustainable Urban Transformations." *Journal of Cleaner Production* 50: 40–55. doi:10.1016/j.jclepro.2012.11.047.
Trowler, P. 2003. *Education Policy*. London: Routledge.
Verschueren, C. forthcoming. "Local and Global (F)Actors in Environmental and Sustainability Education Policies: The Case of New York City Public Schools." *Environmental Education Research*
Wals, A. E., and B. Jickling. 2002. "Sustainability" in Higher Education: From Doublethink and Newspeak to Critical Thinking and Meaningful Learning." *International Journal of Sustainability in Higher Education* 3 (3): 221–232. doi:10.1108/14676370210434688.
Weiss, C. H. 1979. "The Many Meanings of Research Utilization." *Public Administration Review* 39 (5): 426–431. doi:10.2307/3109916.
Weiss, C. H. 1980. "Knowledge Creep and Decision Accretion." *Knowledge* 1 (3): 381–404. doi:10.1177/107554708000100303.
Wildemuth, B. M. 2009. "Existing Documents and Artifacts as Data." In Wildemuth, B. M. (Ed.) (2009). Applications of social research methods to questions in information and library science. California: ABC-CLIO., 158–165.

Sustainability education research and policy in Cyprus: an investigation into their roles and relationships

Aravella Zachariou and Konstantinos Korfiatis

ABSTRACT
This paper is motivated by the idea that the study of the interplay of research and policy related to Education for Sustainable Development (ESD) in specific national contexts can contribute to global conversations about the relationships between education research and policy-making. It is written by two individuals who have been involved in various roles within the development of ESD research and policy in Cyprus. The study involved thematic analysis of all ESD policy and research documents in Cyprus from 1998 and 2017, in order to examine interactions between research and policy. Findings suggest that ESD research and policy in Cyprus empower each other, with researchers participating to on-going policy development and policy processes highlighting new directions for research. Based on these findings, we discuss the effectiveness of a participatory model for ESD research and policy processes, and the importance of situations where education policy interrupts established research traditions. Further, we highlight the danger of research being suppressed under the power of politics. We conclude that the study of the development of ESD research and policy in specific national contexts, especially beyond Western Europe and North America, can reveal the varied possibilities in the interplay of policy and research, and therefore can inform understandings of the relationships between them.

Introduction

In this paper we discuss the development of education policy and research in relation to Education for Sustainable Development (ESD) in Cyprus as a case study for the exploration of, and insights into, the characteristics of ESD research-policy relationships internationally. Prior papers have highlighted the need to study and analyse aspects of the relation between research and policy in ESD. Laessøe, Feinstein, and Blum (2013), for example, suggested that the intertwined fields of Environmental Education (EE) and ESD need more empirical research on policy-practice relations, including 'examining the struggles, negotiations, constructions, and re-contextualizations through which policy informs education practices' (p. 235). Aikens, McKenzie, and Vaughter (2016) also called for strengthening research on ESD policy, arguing, amongst other things, for 'increased empirical engagement (of policy research) with policy origins and enactment' (p. 352) and 'greater considerations of how policy research engages research users, including policy makers (p. 353).

It is noteworthy that claims about gaps in research have been made in relation to research on education policy more generally, and not just in relation to ESD. Sebba (2007), for example, indicated that even when prior research addressed education policy issues, it was often based on a rather superficial knowledge of existing policies and offered policy-makers few recommendations for policy change. Other authors have suggested that research on policy-research relationships often fails to capture the actual characteristics and complexities of these relationships. Oliver, Lorenc, and Innvaer (2014), for example, found, after a critical analysis of the literature on evidence use in health policy, that research on policy-research relationships typically draws simplistic conclusions, such as criticising policy-makers for limited use of research evidence, or suggesting that policy improvement requires more scientific data. Similarly, Laessøe, Feinstein, and Blum (2013) argued that the use of research in policy had been disconnected from a broader perspective on policy-making; they called for clarity of definitions of 'evidence' and 'policy' and their use in improving decision-making. Furthermore, Laessøe, Feinstein, and Blum (2013) recommended widening the scope of research on policy-research relationships, in order to include studies of knowledge production practices and policy implementation, as well as studies on how scientific research is impacted by the interactions between policy and research.

In an attempt to further explore the nature of interactions between research and policy, Oliver, Lorenc, and Innvaer (2014), as well as Wehrens (2014), proposed that the study of research-policy relationships could focus on processes of co-creation and co-production of policy and research, rather than expecting a linear, unidirectional relationship between knowledge production (research) and knowledge implementation (education policy and practice). Wehrens (2014) claimed that it is more suitable to consider the co-production of knowledge by researchers and policy-makers rather than treat them as separate communities. He reported three models of research-policy interactions, describing them all as ultimately unsuccessful: (1) rationalistic linear models presuming a one-way process from research to policy or practice; (2) interactive and incremental models presuming dialogue (relationship models); (3) system or network models trying to incorporate the more complex interactions between policy and research. Wehrens (2014) argued that the main reason for all the above models being unsuccessful is that they encapsulate researchers and policy makers as two distinct worlds which communicate either in more linear or in more interactive ways. Instead of these models, he (echoing Jasanoff's 2004 co-production framework) suggested an alternative view of science-policy relations, focusing on how science and policy are being produced simultaneously and intertwine with each other. The co-production model reflects the constant intertwining of the cognitive, material, social and normative aspects of research and policy processes. This perspective challenges the traditional distinction between scientific research and policy, according to which the cognitive domain (the facts) is usually associated with research, whilst the social and normative domain (the social practices and values) is linked with policy. The co-production model recognises that there are not key distinctions between research and policy processes, and implies that both are cognitive and social or normative.

It should be pointed out that, according to Wehrens (2014), the co-production perspective does not imply that there is only a consensus between collaborating research and policy actors. In contrast, it examines how and what boundaries are formed, and what strategies of inclusion/exclusion of policy actors into research and research actors into policy are developed. Related to this within ESE, Laessøe, Feinstein, and Blum (2013) recommended that researchers serve as 'critical friends' in an interactive network of researchers, politicians and stakeholders. In doing so, they can use expertise to address situations and challenges whilst also reserving the right to question actions and discourses of stakeholders. Laessøe, Feinstein, and Blum (2013) admitted that this model of the researchers as 'critical friends', or as 'engaged researchers', contains the risk of research losing its autonomy, but they also provided fruitful international examples where it has worked, thus highlighting the potential improvement it could bring to ESD policy research.

Different methods can be used to study the research-policy relationships: Oliver, Lorenc, and Innvaer (2014), for example, in their review of evidence-based policy research in the health sector, reported that most of the studies use only interviews or surveys to ask researchers and policy-makers about their perceptions of evidence use. According to Oliver, Lorenc, and Innvaer

(2014), this method of research leads to findings which emphasise certain aspects of the research-policy relationship alone, such as the restricted access to proper information and the poor relationships between researchers and policy-makers as the reasons for problematic use of evidence in education policy. However, other studies used methods, such as participant observation, or attempt to find documentary proof of research use. For example, Asen et al. (2013) used field notes and audio recordings in order to study the use of research evidence in the context of education board members' arguments in support of or opposition to district policies. Rickinson et al. (2017) combined interviews with policy-makers, documentary analysis, and observations and feedback from policy staff in order to study the use of evidence in education policy and practice.

In the present study we investigate the policy-research relationships in ESD in Cyprus through the examination of: a) the governmental education policy documents regarding ESD in Cyprus; and b) research papers on ESD policy and practice in Cyprus. The study of policy documents allows us to extract conclusions on how ESD policies were framed in Cyprus, what priorities were set and when and how they changed (for a discussion of the usefulness of policy documents analysis see Bowen 2009). The simultaneous study of research documents allows us to draw conclusions about ESD research priorities, their correspondence with policy needs and priorities, as well as to examine relations, synergies and interactions between ESD research and policy (Cardno 2018). We analysed all of the policy and research documents produced during the relatively short history of ESD in Cyprus (from the late 1990s onwards). It is perhaps worthwhile mentioning here that both authors are personally highly involved in the process of policy and policy research production in Cyprus. Specifically, the first author has served as an ESD civil servant since 2001 and is a part-time academic who has long participated in the development and implementation of national ESD policies. The second author has been an academic in the field of EE and ESD since 2005, and is a member of various state advisory committees for ESD development and/or reform in Cyprus. Therefore, we claim to possess well-developed knowledge of the processes that were involved in the development of policy and research in ESD in Cyprus.

Our aim is, through the examination of the policy and research interaction in a national context, to reach conclusions that could contribute to the discussion of the 'how, what, when and why' (expression borrowed from Oliver, Lorenc, and Innvaer 2014 and Rickinson et al. 2017) of interactions between research and policy in ESD internationally. Actually, this point of view is in accordance with Hankivsky et al. (2014) and Pizmony-Levy (2011), who argued that the international context is enriched and transformed via interplay with different local contexts.

In order to achieve our aim, we set the following questions to guide the research reported in this paper:

a. How did researchers, policy-makers and stakeholders interact to produce ESD research and policy in Cyprus?
b. When and how did research and policy in Cyprus exchange information (i.e. data, ideas, suggestions)?

In order to situate the subsequent discussion on research and policy in its historical context, a brief outline of the development and status of ESD in Cyprus is presented before we continue with the methodology of the paper and the presentation of results and the discussion.

ESD in Cyprus

Conditions for the development of ESD in Cyprus were influenced by the fact that Cyprus became an independent state for the first time in its history in 1960. Before that it was always part of large empires, such as the Roman, Byzantine and Ottoman empires. In more recent years,

Cyprus was an English colony until 1960. After its independence in 1960, the state's education system initially focused on national identity development with an emphasis on religious ideals rather than creating citizens who could confront global community challenges (Kasoulledis 2012; Zachariou 2007). Furthermore, the education system was (and in many aspects still is) characterised by traditional school practices focused on discipline-based, transmissive and teacher-directed pedagogies to learn predetermined content. Another characteristic of Cyprus' education system is that it is centralised nationally in terms of school curriculum, timetable and funding (Pashiardis 2004). Dominant purposes and pedagogical practices of schooling focus on reproducing rather than transforming ideological, social and economic structures of society. This situation diverges from the philosophy and practice of ESD, which aims to re-orient education and society towards an ecologically, socially and economically sustainable way of living. Additionally, this situation acted as a barrier to the introduction, implementation and development of ESD in education (Zachariou 2005).

The first attempt to introduce ESD in Cyprus' education system occurred in the 1990s (MoEC (Ministry of Education and Culture) 1998). As explained by Zachariou and Valanides (2006), this mostly took the form of outdoor nature-based activities and environmental education programmes, which were in accordance with international approaches to EE in the 1990s (see also UNESCO and IIEP 1997). It was an attempt to introduce ESD without questioning the main characteristics of Cyprus' education system, such as the teacher-centered approaches and the limited environmental content of the curriculum (Zachariou 2005). Despite limitations, those introductory steps paved the way for the implementation of ESD in Cypriot education.

The first decade of the 21st century welcomed important international documents, such as the United Nations Millennium Declaration (UN (United Nations Millennium Declaration) 2005), the Rio Declaration on Environment and Development (UNESCO (United Nations Educational and Scientific and Cultural Organization) 2002), the UN Decade for ESD (UNESCO (United Nations Educational and Scientific and Cultural Organization) 2004)], the United Nations Economic Commission for Europe (UNECE) Strategy for ESD (UNECE (United Nations Economic Commission for Europe) 2005), and the Mediterranean Strategy for Sustainable Development (MIO (Mediterranean Information Office) 2014). These documents influenced the enactment of policy regulations and action plans for the implementation of ESD in Cyprus (MB (Ministerial Board) 2007; MoEC (Ministry of Education and Culture) 2009; MoEC (Ministry of Education and Culture) 2012). The resulting legislations established between 2004 and 2013 are the ones which still frame current ESD policy in Cyprus. This policy is characterised by: a 'whole-school' approach with an emphasis on the development of ESD programmes that involve the whole school community in collaborative action; the development of a plan for informal ESD education through a network of Governmental Environmental Education Centers (EECs); and a programme for educators' professional development in ESD.

It is also noteworthy that according to current ESD policy in Cyprus, special emphasis is placed on the transition from environmental education programmes, which mainly focused on nature conservation and outdoor activities, to community action programmes. In the latter, schools and communities are considered legitimate places for action towards sustainability, and all interested parties (students, parents, community members) can participate (Zachariou, Symeou, and Katsikis 2005).

In contrast to the ESD policies pursued within Cyprus' Kindergarten-Grade 12 (K-12) education system, we cannot claim the same for higher education. The delayed establishment of academic institutions in Cyprus resulted in the slow development of ESD research in Cyprus' universities. In a report on the implementation of the UNECE ESD Strategy in Cyprus, the limited presence of ESD in higher education stands out when compared to ESD policy and implementation in the K-12 education system (MoEC (Ministry of Education and Culture) 2014). This lack of focus in higher education, including in terms of research, means that ESD policy had to develop without support from pre-existing academic research, as research had not had the opportunity to 'pilot test' and suggest possible improvements for a policy act before it was implemented in the education system.

Due to the country's small size, it is common for the same person to be responsible for various roles in the education system. An ESD policy maker can also be a researcher, and a researcher can also be a member of an ESD policy committee, or a civil servant at the Ministry of Education and Culture, or a primary school teacher. Indeed, this paper is itself a result of these interchangeable roles amongst people involved in ESD policy and research in Cyprus. As we have already mentioned, both authors have participated under various conditions and roles in the development of ESD policy and research in Cyprus. Therefore, researchers of education policies in Cyprus have the characteristics proposed by Laessøe, Feinstein, and Blum (2013) in that they are neither detached from policy processes, nor naively involved. Instead, they can be participants in networks of agents, of which academic researchers are also members, as is the case with ESD policy research in Cyprus.

Methodology of the study

Documents

The documentary evidence drawn on in this study consisted of all of the official governmental documents concerning ESD in Cyprus between 1998 and 2017, as well as all of the research documents concerning ESD policy in Cyprus over the same time period. The selection of those documents was an easy task, since both authors of this article participated in the development of ESD in Cyprus from the beginning, and both official policy documents and research documents are kept in their personal archives.

The selected documents included: sixteen national education policy documents, reports and circulars; three international documents with direct reference to Cypriot ESD issues; seven research papers published in academic journals; four chapters published in edited volumes; four papers published in conference proceedings, and two master's theses (for a full list of selected documents, see Appendix 1).

Analysis procedure and thematic categories

A thematic analysis approach was adopted to process the selected corpus of documents. Thematic analysis is a qualitative analysis method that focuses on identifying patterned meaning across a dataset (Braun and Clarke 2006; Bryman 2016). It is suggested that thematic analysis, as a flexible research tool, provides a rich and detailed, yet complex, account of the data (Braun and Clarke 2006; Guest, MacQueen, and Namey 2012). This approach has been used in various fields, including environmental and sustainability education (Russ et al. 2015; Rogan, O'Connor, and Horwitz 2005), health studies (Vaismoradi, Turunen, and Bondas 2013) and gender studies (Farvid and Braun 2006).

For the purpose of the present article we first familiarised ourselves with the selected documents by reading them and keeping initial notes about possible themes that referred to ESD policy and research relationships in Cyprus. We then discussed and refined these initial themes by drawing on our readings of the documents, and reflecting on the two overarching research questions noted earlier. Specifically, we noticed that a number of research publications and official documents provided evidence for synergies in the production of ESD research and policy between policy-makers, researchers and stakeholders. Therefore, we created a thematic category in order to discuss the details, the results and the importance of those connections, which we called: 'Synergies between researchers, policy-makers, and stakeholders in ESD policy and research in Cyprus' (Appendix 2). We also noticed that there were many cases amongst the selected documents showing the impact of research on policy. Therefore, we created a second thematic category, in order to discuss the ways and the instances where research had impacted

ESD policy in Cyprus. The name of the second thematic category is: 'ESD research informs ESD policy'. Finally, the analysis of the textual corpus revealed a policy document focusing on directions that research should have taken (GENE (Global Education Network in Europe) 2017), as well as cases of research work that were repetitions of older works. We decided to create a third theme named 'ESD policy illuminates gaps in ESD research', in order to discuss these findings (see Appendix 2 for the classification of the selected documents in the corresponding theme).

In conclusion, the three themes that resulted from the thematic analysis are:

I. Synergies between researchers, policy-makers, and stakeholders in ESD policy and research in Cyprus
II. ESD research informs ESD policy
III. ESD policy illuminates gaps in ESD research

As shown in Appendix 2 we also classified the selected documents according to their field of analysis. For example, the documents included in the thematic category 'synergies between researchers, policy-makers, and stakeholders in ESD policy and research in Cyprus' focused on a specific topic (i.e. field of analysis): that of 'ESD and schools leadership'. Therefore, the 'field of analysis' presents the specific topics that attract the interest of research and/or policy during the period we study.

It should be noted that the importance of a theme in thematic analysis was not necessarily dependent on quantity of content, but rather on whether it captured something important in relation to our research question. Furthermore, in thematic analysis, we conceived of coding reliability as a matter of consensus between ourselves as co-authors (Braun and Clarke 2013; Sandelowski and Leeman 2012).

Results of thematic analysis

In the following sub-sections, we present the results for each of the thematic categories.

Synergies between researchers, policy-makers, and stakeholders in ESD policy and research in Cyprus

The analysis of research and policy documents revealed evidence for a pattern of participation of multiple agents in the production of ESD policy and research in Cyprus. We elaborate on this pattern in the following paragraphs, by discussing the participation of schools' principals in ESD research, and the way it changed the educators' professional development policy in Cyprus.

ESD policy in Cyprus attributes an important role to school principals. Specifically, official circulars from the Ministry of Education and Culture state that school principals are important for (a) supporting and encouraging teachers to undertake initiatives for ESD curriculum implementation; (b) encouraging cooperation for the integration of School Environmental Education Policy (SEEP) in schools and communities; (c) promoting non-formal ESD education and outdoor learning; and (d) supervising and leading effective SEEP implementation (CPI (Cyprus Pedagogical Institute) 2011).

The role of principals for the successful development of ESD in schools has also been the focus of attention for researchers in the field of ESD in Cyprus. Our analysis revealed a number of studies by Cypriot researchers who had conducted investigations into principals' roles in primary schools (Kadji-Beltran, Zachariou, and Stevenson 2013; Zachariou and Kadji-Beltran 2009; Zachariou, Savvides, and Skordi 2015; Zachariou, Kadji-Beltran, and Manoli 2013). Data included in these studies were gathered through interviews, focus group discussions and questionnaires answered by principals across Cyprus, giving them an opportunity to evaluate the ESD curriculum and to participate in the improvement of ESD policies. The findings of these studies indicated that whilst principals played a positive role in enabling factors for ESD implementation, there were also several constraining factors. Principals reported a lack of confidence in administrative skills for sustainable schools, limited willingness to challenge the status quo, and limited engagement in actions supporting ESD activities. The studies also identified specific areas for ESD-related professional development, such as empowering staff, encouraging critiques of current approaches, and exploring alternative possibilities in curricula, pedagogies and policies.

As a response to these kinds of studies, the Cyprus Ministry of Education and Culture reorganised its ESD professional development courses in order to emphasise principals' roles in incorporating all stakeholders (teachers, students, parents) in the development of a sustainable school. Other topics that were added into the professional development courses were the development of leadership styles which are compatible with quality education, and the role of principals in promoting a whole-school approach in ESD (Kadji-Beltran, Zachariou, and Stevenson 2013; Zachariou and Kadji-Beltran 2009; Zachariou, Savvides, and Skordi 2015; see also CPI (Cyprus Pedagogical Institute) 2015, 2016, 2017).

In conclusion, it was the opinions expressed by a large number of principals during their participation as interviewees or/and narrators in research studies that triggered and guided the formation of policies to develop a cycle of professional development courses. Therefore, it could be argued that the formation of ESD policy in Cyprus was not an un-reflexive discourse with unchallenged experts (researchers or policy makers). Policy structuring included numerous stages for negotiation and communication, engaging all interested parties. As Zachariou, Kadji-Beltran, and Manoli (2013) commented, principals became co-modifiers of ESD policies.

Furthermore, it should be noted that the authors of the particular research studies that are referred to in this section (specifically: Zachariou and Kadji-Beltran 2009; Zachariou, Savvides, and Skordi 2015; Zachariou, Kadji-Beltran, and Manoli 2013) have multiple professional identities (e.g. that of researcher and policy-maker, or that of researcher and school teacher or principal). The paradox of one person with several roles, which was described in the 'ESD in Cyprus' section as a national particularity, helped bridge the gap between practitioners, policy makers, and researchers, uniting them to work cohesively towards common tasks.

ESD research informs ESD policy

In this section we present two cases from the analysed literature where ESD research informed and transformed ESD policy in Cyprus. The first case concerned the development of informal ESD structures in Cyprus, and the second the professional development of teachers.

Specifically, in 2007, the Cypriot National Action Plan for ESD implemented the gradual development of a network of Environmental Education Centers (EECs) as structures for introducing and implementing informal education into the education system of Cyprus (CPI (Cyprus Pedagogical Institute) 2007; MB (Ministerial Board) 2007). Research published in works such as Petrou (2011), Amyrotou (2013) and Hadjiachilleos and Zachariou (2013) showed that programmes implemented in EECs are not effective in their education goals if they are not aligned with the school curriculum. The conclusion of this research was that informal types of ESD should act in tandem with formal education to support and expand on work by schools concerned with environmental and sustainability issues. More specifically, it was proposed that EECs should not only provide optional complementary ESD activities, but instead should be connected to schools and integrated into the official education process.

The above-mentioned research works even suggested specific topics that EECs could facilitate the better implementation of ESD in formal curriculum, such as the exploration of sustainability issues within the community (e.g. water, biodiversity, local communities, local agriculture, etc.). The implementation of diverse pedagogical methods (e.g. field studies, experimental inquiries, social surveys) in both formal and informal ESD curricula was also part of the suggestions made by the researchers (Hadjichilleos and Zachariou 2013).

The aforementioned suggestions were used as guidance for the development of EECs programmes in close connection with the formal education curriculum and were embedded in a policy frame to justify informal ESD in Cyprus (CPI (Cyprus Pedagogical Institute) 2013). They were also included in the Cyprus Pedagogical Institution circular for ESD curriculum implementation (CPI (Cyprus Pedagogical Institute) 2012; CPI (Cyprus Pedagogical Institute) 2013).

In another instance of research-informed policy, research has highlighted teachers' inability to deliver ESD in Cyprus due to insufficient training. Specifically, in Zachariou (2013) it was shown that teacher training courses, organised by the Ministry of Education, failed those skills and competences that render an educator capable of implementing ESD issues in schools.

One of the ideas, successfully tested by research, for filling the gap between policy and practice was the value of mentoring as a means of building professional capacity in ESD (Kadji-Beltran, Zachariou, and Stevenson 2013; Kadji-Beltran et al. 2014). Another research focus was the evaluation of professional development seminars and experiential workshops in Environmental Education Centers (EECs). Indeed, it transpired that the participatory and experiential nature of these seminars was very successful in improving participating educators' self-efficacy for implementing ESD in their schools (Zachariou and Kadji-Beltran 2009; Zachariou, Kadji-Beltran, and Manoli 2013). Both research-tested ideas (i.e. mentoring and participatory and experiential seminars) have become parts of the national professional training framework (CPI (Cyprus Pedagogical Institute) 2016; MoEC (Ministry of Education and Culture) 2015).

It should be noted that research on professional development impacted not only ESD policies, but also shaped the formation of a national strategy for teachers' professional learning more generally. This national strategy suggested that teachers should develop pedagogical and education practices that contribute to improving schools and the education system through an action research approach (MoEC (Ministry of Education and Culture) 2015).

ESD policy illuminates gaps in research

Studies of the research-policy interface often focus on whether and how policy makers adapt instructions and guidelines provided by research findings (Oliver, Lorenc, and Innvaer 2014). However, an interesting, albeit largely neglected, aspect of research/policy relationships is when policy sets priorities and necessities for research and the latter has difficulties in responding. This kind of interaction became evident within the analysis for this paper.

Specifically, the National Report on Global Education in Cyprus (GENE (Global Education Network in Europe) 2017) highlighted aspects of ESD that were important for its development in policy and practice, but that had not been investigated by the research community in Cyprus. These unexplored topics included: instances where ESD had been implemented in practice through the Cyprus school curriculum; techniques for integrating Sustainable Environmental Education Policy (SEEP) in school contexts; how the tripartite 'environment-society-economy' is interpreted pedagogically in school practice; and what kinds of pedagogical approaches are used in ESD. Therefore, in theses specific cases, the policy sector revealed gaps that it would be helpful for research to address.

In addition, the examination of research publications in Cyprus exposed instances where research simply repeats itself, through overlapping studies that confirm pre-existing studies. Examples include studies by Zachariou, Symeou, and Katsikis (2005), Symeou, Zachariou, and Valanides (2007), Zachariou and Symeou (2009), all of which investigated the same subject (the role of the local community in ESD school projects), using the same methodology.

Discussion

As suggested at the outset of the paper, the study of the development of ESD policy and research in specific contexts allows for the possibility of insights into the modes of communication between policy and research which may be of wider interest. ESD research and policy in Cyprus can be seen to empower each other, enabling researchers to contribute to on-going policy development and providing opportunities for policy to support empirical research. Findings from the analysis of research papers and policy documents suggest that research and policy in Cyprus constitute aspects of the same endeavor that co-exist and co-evolve in a dynamic manner. As Van Poeck and Lysgaard (2016) declared, 'what comes to the fore then, is that in order to take care of an issue, one cannot ignore the effects this has on the other actors caught up in it' (p. 311). In a similar line of reasoning, Edwards, Sebba, and Rickinson (2007) argued that when considering policy 'users' as 'co-researchers', all relevant education parties should also be treated as policy makers. This creates a bottom-up process in developing ESD policy. The role of in-service teachers and principals is essential for the success of the bottom-up approach since they contribute to both policy makers' and researchers' collection of evidence regarding a policy's effectiveness. Therefore, they should be considered as key players in the formation of policies, and be provided with opportunities to shape and revise curriculum policies through critique, strategic appropriation, and the suggestion of alternatives (Singh 1998; Stevenson 2013).

Within our analysis, it was found that stakeholders' participation in various phases of ESD policy and research, as well as the involvement of policy-makers in research and of researchers in policy processes, were key elements that supported a viable participatory model of ESD research and policy development in Cyprus. Notably, one aspect of specific actors' participation in many roles is that, in Cyprus, researchers are linked to governmental and other formal institutions which co-produce knowledge and policy. Under these conditions there is a risk that researchers can lose their emancipatory, reflective, and critical roles of contributing constructively to the development and integration of the ESD policies (for a discussion about this issue within and beyond ESD, see Hard and Jamison 2005; Laessøe, Feinstein, and Blum 2013; Nowothy, Scott, and Gibbons 2001). Within education more generally, Biesta (2009) noted that in situations where researchers serve as experts with a technical role, they can become a 'cover' for politicians, allowing them to hide behind expert advice to avoid making decisions by or for themselves. Therefore, the danger of research being suppressed under the power of politics and taking on a totally instrumental role should not be underestimated. Special attention should be paid not only to the patterns of co-operation and integration of policy and practice, but also to the conditions under which the independence of research is guaranteed.

Evidence presented in the 'ESD research informs ESD policy' section showed that ESD research in Cyprus influenced policy in various ways, including the transformation of informal ESD and of professional development seminars. In the case of informal ESD, research shaped policy by highlighting the need to directly connect the programmes run by Environmental Education Centers (EECs) with the formal education curriculum. In the case of professional development seminars, research informed policy by revealing the insufficiency of the current in-service teacher training. The same insufficiency has been pinpointed as a main problem for the implementation of ESD internationally (McKeown and Hopkins 2005; Powers 2004; Van Petegem et al. 2005). Consequently, these findings can be seen to support claims by Sebba (2007), Oliver, Lorenc, and Innvaer (2014) and Laessøe, Feinstein, and Blum (2013) that the use of research in policy should be seen from a perspective which takes into account the multiple ways in which research acts on policy-making. Furthermore, the cases analysed in this paper show that policy processes should be understood as complex concepts, with research intervening in ways that influence which issues are identified as policy problems, what solutions are available, and how these policy solutions are championed in practice (see also Aikens, McKenzie, and Vaughter 2016 for similar argumentation).

Interesting findings also included instances where policy revealed gaps in research, or research practices that were rendered trivial and repetitive. A suggested remedy could be to view the development of ESD (policy) research within the contexts of adjacent scientific fields. A review report of the Global Education Network of Europe on Global Education (GE) in Cyprus (GENE (Global Education Network in Europe) 2017) stated that researchers and academics who were active in different strands of GE seldom joined forces to explore commonalities and opportunities. The integration of different strands and disciplines of GE is a parameter that can be considered missing from ESD policy research in Cyprus. It would be interesting to examine if this lack of inter- and transdisciplinarity in research is one of the reasons that research in Cyprus has not yet addressed important elements of ESD pedagogical practice. There is a need for an 'osmosis' of scientific fields and their transitions towards a transdisciplinary policy and research dialogue 'which can open up new entry points for discussion of ESD policy research' (Van Poeck and Lysgaard 2016, 315; also Hankivsky et al. 2014). As pointed out in the UNESCO report (2009), a synergy of ESD with other adjectival educations will result in a mutual enrichment to solve tensions and contribute to their improved conceptualisation (UNESCO (United Nations Educational and Scientific and Cultural Organization) 2009 , 72). According to Rice (2013), transdisciplinary research integrates academic knowledge in order to be able to study real world problems and create new knowledge and theories on sustainability.

In conclusion, the study of the development of ESD research and policy in specific national contexts reveals the varied possibilities in their interplay, and therefore can contribute to global conversations about their relationship. For example, in this paper we showed how a collaborative and participatory approach to research and policy development was implemented in practice. We explained that this was the result of specific conditions that applied in the development of ESD research and policy in Cyprus, such as the small size of the country, which allowed for interchangeable roles and cooperation between multiple stakeholders.

Another insight that this study could offer to the international literature on education research and policy relationships is the focus on the instances where the policy sector highlighted the priorities that ESD research should set. These instances problematize approaches in research-policy relationships which see only unidirectional linear relationships where research affects policy. Overall, we suggest that our findings are in support of approaches focusing on how education research and policy are being produced collaboratively and can be intertwined with each other. We also consider the case study of the development of ESD research and policy in Cyprus as supportive of the argument that the representation of more varied geographical, cultural or political domains within the ESD literature can expand scientific dialogue and help research progress (Canaparo 2009; Lotz-Sisitka 2016). We support an expanded focus on the interplay of ESD research and policy in national contexts beyond Western Europe and North America. We thus look forward to further research from diverse countries and regions that can help inform understandings of the relationships between research and policy.

Disclosure statement

No potential conflict of interest was reported by the authors.

References

Aikens, K., M. McKenzie, and P. Vaughter. 2016. "Environmental and Sustainability Education Policy Research: A Systematic Review of Methodological and Thematic Trends." *Environmental Education Research* 22 (3): 333–359. doi:10.1080/13504622.2015.1135418.

Amyrotou, G. 2013. "Σύγκριση αποτελεσματικότητας εκπαιδευτικών παρεμβάσεων για την Περιβαλλον τική εκπαίδευση σε τυπικά και μη τυπικά πλαίσια εεκπαίδευσης." Comparing the Effectiveness of Environmental Education Interventions for Biodiversity in Formal and non-Formal Settings." Unpublished Master thes., Nicosia: Frederick University.

Asen, R., D. Gurke, P. Conners, R. Solomon, and E. Gumm. 2013. "Research Evidence and School-Board Deliberations: Lessons from Three Wisconsin School Districts." *Educational Policy* 27 (1): 33–63. doi:10.1177/0895904811429291.

Biesta, G. 2009. *Educational Research, Democracy and TLRP. Methodological Development, Future Challenges*. London: TLRP.

Bowen, G. A. 2009. "Document Analysis as a Qualitative Research Method." *Qualitative Research Journal* 9 (2): 27–40. doi:10.3316/QRJ0902027.

Braun, V., and V. Clarke. 2006. "Using Thematic Analysis in Psychology." *Qualitative Research in Psychology* 3 (2): 77–101. doi:10.1191/1478088706qp063oa.

Braun, V., and V. Clarke. 2013. *Successful Qualitative Research: A Practical Guide for Beginners*. London: Sage

Bryman, A. 2016. *Social Research Methods*. Oxford: Oxford University Press.

Canaparo, C. 2009. *Geo-Epistemology: Latin America and the Location of Knowledge*. Oxford, UK: Peter Lang.

Cardno, C. 2018. "Policy Document Analysis: A Practical Educational Leadership Tool and a Qualitative Research Method." *Educational Administration Theory and Practice* 24 (4): 623–640.

CPI (Cyprus Pedagogical Institute). 2007. Εθνικό Σχέδιο Δράσης για την Περιβαλλοντική Εκπαίδευση για την Αειφό ρο Ανάπτυξη *[National Action Plan for Environmental Education and Education for Sustainable Development]*. Nicosia: CPI/MoEC.

CPI (Cyprus Pedagogical Institute). 2011. "Διευκρινιστικές οδηγίες στους Διευθυντές/τριες της Δημοτικής Εκπαί δευσης για την εφαρμογή του Αναλυτικού Προγράμματος της ΕΑΑ" [Directives to the Primary Pchool principals for ESD Curriculum Implementation] (Circular no. 7.7.09.16/8/6/2011). Nicosia.

CPI (Cyprus Pedagogical Institute). 2012. Εφαρμογή του Προγράμματος Σπουδών Περιβαλλοντική ς Εκπαί δευσης/Εκπαίδευσης για την Αειφόρο Ανάπτυξη για τους Εκπαιδευτικούς της Δημοτικής

Εκπαίδευσης.». *[Guide for Primary Teachers for Implementing the Curriculum for Environmental Education/ Education for Sustainable Development]*. Nicosia: MoEC/CPI/CDU.

CPI (Cyprus Pedagogical Institute). 2013. Οδηγός Προγραμμάτων Δικτύου Κέντρων Περιβαλλοντικής Εκπαίδευσης: ΚΠΕ Κοινότητας Πεδυλά. *[Programmes Guide of Network of Environmental Education Centers: EEC of Pedoulas Community]*. Nicosia: CPI/MoEC.

CPI (Cyprus Pedagogical Institute). 2015. Πρόγραμμα επιμόρφωσης των νεοπροαχθέντων Διευθυντών και των Βοηθών Διευθυντών της Μέσης Εκπαίδευσης. *[Program for in-Service Training of Novice School Principals and Assistant School Principals in Secondary Education]*. Nicosia: MoEC/CPI.

CPI (Cyprus Pedagogical Institute). 2016. Πρόγραμμα επιμόρφωσης των νεοπροαχθέντων Διευθυντών Δημοτικής Εκπαίδευσης. *[Program for in-Service Training of Novice School Principals]*. Nicosia: MoEC/CPI.

CPI (Cyprus Pedagogical Institute). 2017. Πρόγραμμα επιμόρφωσης των νεοπροαχθέντων Διευθυντών Δημοτικής και Μέσης Εκπαίδευσης. *[Program for in-Service Training of Novice School Principals in Primary and Secondary Education]*. Nicosia: MoEC/CPI.

Edwards, A., J. Sebba, and M. Rickinson. 2007. "Working with Users: Some Implications for Educational Research." *British Educational Research Journal* 33 (5): 647–661. doi:10.1080/01411920701582199.

Farvid, P., and V. Braun. 2006. "Most of us Guys Are Raring to Go Anytime, Anyplace, Anywhere: Male and Female Sexuality in Cleo and Cosmo." *Sex Roles* 55 (5-6): 295–310. doi:10.1007/s11199-006-9084-1.

GENE (Global Education Network in Europe). 2017. "The European Global Education Peer Review Process: National Report on Global Education in Cyprus." http://gene.eu/wp-content/uploads/2017-10-10-Cyprus-Peer-Review.pdf

Guest, G., K. M. MacQueen, and E. E. Namey. 2012. *Applied Thematic Analysis*. Thousand Oaks, CA: Sage.

Hadjiachilleos, S., and A. Zachariou. 2013. "The Impact of Non-Formal Learning Environment in Developing Scientific Investigation Skills in Students of pre-Primary Education in Cyprus." In *Concepts for Nature and Environment in pre-Primary Education: Research Data, Methodological Approaches and Educational Applications*, edited by A. Dimitriou, 264–279. Thessaloniki: Epikentro.

Hankivsky, Olena, Daniel Grace, Gemma Hunting, Melissa Giesbrecht, Alycia Fridkin, Sarah Rudrum, Olivier Ferlatte, and Natalie Clark. 2014. "An Intersectionality-Based Policy Analysis Framework: Critical Reflections on a Methodology for Advancing Equity." *International Journal for Equity in Health* 13 (119): 119. doi:10.1186/s12939-014-0119-x.

Hard, M., and A. Jamison. 2005. *Hubris and Hybrids*. New York, NY: Routledge.

Kadji-Beltran, C., and A. Zachariou. 2004. "Experiential and Active Learning as a Means of Environmental Cognition Enhancement: The Contribution of the Environmental Education Centres in the Development of Environmentally Responsible Citizens." In *International Perspectives in Environmental Education* edited by W. L. Filho & M. Littledyke, 167–182. Frankfurt: Peter Lang.

Kadji-Beltran, C., A. Zachariou, and R. B. Stevenson. 2013. "Leading Sustainable Schools: Exploring the Role of Primary Pchool Principals." *Environmental Education Research* 19 (3): 303–323. doi:10.1080/13504622.2012.692770.

Kadji-Beltran, C., A. Zachariou, G. Liarakou, and E. Flogaiti. 2014. "Empowering Education for Sustainable Development in Schools through Mentoring." *Professional Development in Education* 40 (5): 717–739. doi:10.1080/19415257.2013.835276.

Kasoulledis, A. 2012. "Πολιτική, Εκπαιδευτική Πολιτική και Διδασκαλικός Συνδικαλισμός στην Κύπρο: Το Παράδειγμα της ΠΟΕΔ (1960-1974). [Policy, Educational Policy and Teacher Syndicalism in Cyprus: The Example of POED (1960-1974)." PhD diss., Thesalloniki: Aristotele's University.

Laessøe, J., N. W. Feinstein, and N. Blum. 2013. "Environmental Education Policy Research – Challenges and Ways Research Might Cope with Them." *Environmental Education Research* 19 (2): 231–242. doi:10.1080/13504622.2013.778230.

Lotz-Sisitka, H. 2016. "Reviewing Strategies in/for ESD Policy Engagement: Agency Reclaimed." *The Journal of Environmental Education* 47 (2): 91–103. doi:10.1080/00958964.2015.1113915.

McKeown, R., and C. Hopkins. 2005. "EE and ESD: Two Paradigms, One Crucial Goal." *Applied Environmental Education & Communication* 4 (3): 221–224. doi:10.1080/15330150591004616.

MB (Ministerial Board). 2007. "Απόσπασμα από τα πρακτικά της συνεδρία του Υπουργικού Συμβουλίου, Στρατηγικό Σχέδιο για την Περιβαλλοντική Εκπαίδευση με επίκεντρο την Αειφόρο Ανάπτυξη." [Extract from the Proceedings of the Ministerial Board Meeting "National Action Plan for Environmental Education Focus on Sustainable Development"] (No. of Decision 66/145/4/10/2007). Nicosia.

MIO (Mediterranean Information Office). 2014. *The Mediterranean Strategy on Education for Sustainable Development*. Athens: UNESCO/MIO-ECSDE/MEDIES.

MoEC (Ministry of Education and Culture). 1998. "Οι απόψεις της Επιθεώρησης για την Πολιτική του Υπουργείου Παιδείας και Πολιτισμού για το Περιβάλλον" [Inspectorate Opinion, Ministry of Education and Culture Policy for the Environment] (MoEC Circular no. 115/9/9/1998). Nicosia.

MoEC (Ministry of Education and Culture). 2009. Αναλυτικό Πρόγραμμα για τα Δημόσια Σχολεία της Κυπριακής Δημοκρατίας. [*Curriculum for Public Schools of Cyprus Republic*]. Nicosia: MoEC.

MoEC (Ministry of Education and Culture). 2012. "Έκθεση για τη σύσταση Μόνιμης Μονάδας για την Εκπαίδευση το Περιβάλλον και την Αειφόρο Ανάπτυξη" [Report for the Institution of a Permanent Unit of Education for Environment and Sustainable Development]. (no of doc. MoEC5.25.05/12). Nicosia.

MoEC (Ministry of Education and Culture). 2014. *Informal Country Reporting on the Implementation of the Priority Action Areas on ESD UNECE Strategy*. Nicosia: CPI.

MoEC (Ministry of Education and Culture). 2015. Διαμόρφωση Ενιαίας Πολιτικής για την Επαγγελματική Μάθηση των Εκπαιδευτικών Λειτουργών [*Framing a Unified Policy for Teachers Professional Development*]. Nicosia: MoEC.

Nowothy, H., P. Scott, and M. Gibbons. 2001. *Re-Thinking Science: Knowledge and the Public in an Age of Uncertainty*. Oxford: Policy Press.

Oliver, K., T. Lorenc, and S. Innvaer. 2014. "New Directions in Evidence-Based Policy Research: A Critical Analysis of the Literature." *Health Research Policy and Systems* 12 (1): 1–11. doi:10.1186/1478-4505-12-34.

Pashiardis, P. 2004. "Democracy and Leadership in the Educational System of Cyprus." *Journal of Educational Administration* 42 (6): 656–668. doi:10.1108/09578230410563656.

Petrou, M. 2011. "Τα Κέντρα Περιβαλλοντικής Εκπαίδευσης ως χώροι μη-τυπικής Εκπαίδευσης στην Κύπρο: Ο ρόλος τους στη διαμόρφωση των περιβαλλοντικών στάσεων και δράσεων των μαθητών/τριών του δημοτικού σχολείου." [Environmental Education Centers in Cyprus as Places of non-Formal Education: Their Role in Promoting Primary School Students Environmental Attitudes and Actions]." Unpublished master thes., Nicosia: Frederick University.

Pizmony-Levy, O. 2011. "Bridging the Global and Local in Understanding Curricula Scripts: The Case of Environmental Education." *Comparative Education Review* 55 (4): 600–633. doi:10.1086/661632.

Powers, A. 2004. "Teacher Preparation for Environmental Education: Faculty Perspectives on the Infusion of Environmental Education into pre-Service Methods Programs." *The Journal of Environmental Education* 35 (3): 3–11.

Rice, M. 2013. "Spanning Disciplinary Sectoral and International Boundaries: A Sea Change towards Transdisciplinary Global Environmental Change Research?" *Current Opinion in Environmental Sustainability* 5 (3-4): 409–418. doi:10.1016/j.cosust.2013.06.007.

Rickinson, M., K. de Bruin, L. Walsh, and M. Hall. 2017. "What Can Evidence-Use in Practice Learn from Evidence-Use in Policy?" *Educational Research* 59 (2): 173–189. doi:10.1080/00131881.2017.1304306.

Rogan, R., M. O'Connor, and P. Horwitz. 2005. "Nowhere to Hide: Awareness and Perceptions of Environmental Change, and Their Influence on Relationships with Place." *Journal of Environmental Psychology* 25 (2): 147–158. doi:10.1016/j.jenvp.2005.03.001.

Russ, A., S. J. Peters, M. Krasny, and R. C. Stedman. 2015. "Development of Ecological Place Meaning in New York City." *The Journal of Environmental Education* 46 (2): 73–93. doi:10.1080/00958964.2014.999743.

Sandelowski, M., and J. Leeman. 2012. "Writing Usable Qualitative Health Research Findings." *Qualitative Health Research* 22 (10): 1404–1413. doi:10.1177/1049732312450368.

Sebba, J. 2007. "Enhancing Impact on Policy-Making through Increasing User Engagement in Research." In: *Educational Research and Policy-Making: Exploring the Border Country between Research and Policy* edited by L. Saunders, 127–143. London: Routledge.

Singh, M. 1998. "Critical Literacy Strategies for Environmental Educators." *Environmental Education Research* 4 (3): 341–354. doi:10.1080/1350462980040308.

Stevenson, R. D. 2013. "Researching Tensions and Pretensions in Environmental/Sustainability Education Policies: From Critical to Civically Engaged Policy Scholarship." In *International Handbook of Research on Environmental Education*, edited by R. B. Stevenson, M. Brody, J. Dillon, and A. E. J. Wals, 147–155. New York: Routledge.

Symeou, L., A. Zachariou, and N. Valanides. 2007. "Συμμετοχή των γονέων σε περιβαλλοντικά προγράμματα δράσης στην κοινότητα: Η εμπειρία των γονέων της Κύπρου." [Parental Involvement in Action Community Environmental Education Programs: The Experience of Cypriot Parents." *Educational Sciences* 4: 197–2011.

UN (United Nations Millennium Declaration). 2005. "The General Assembly, 8th plenary meeting (A/RES/55/2)." http://www.un.org/millennium/declaration/ares552e.pdf

UNECE (United Nations Economic Commission for Europe). 2005. "Unece Strategy for Education for Sustainable Development (CEP/AC. 13/2005/3/Rev.1)." http://www.unece.org/fileadmin/DAM/env/documents/2005/cep/ac.13/cep.ac.13.2005.3.rev.1.e.pdf.

UNESCO (United Nations Educational, Scientific and Cultural Organization). 2002. *Education, Public Awareness and Training for Sustainability: Input to the Report of the Secretary General to the Second Preparatory Session for the World Summit on Sustainable Development*. Paris: UNESCO.

UNESCO (United Nations Educational, Scientific and Cultural Organization). 2004. "United Nations Decade of Education for Sustainable Development 2005-2014. Draft Implementation Scheme." http://portal.unesco.org/education/en/filedownload.php/03f375b07798a2a55dcdc39db7aa8211Final+IIS.pdf

UNESCO (United Nations Educational, Scientific and Cultural Organization). 2009. *Review of Contexts and Structures for Education for Sustainable Development*. Paris: UNESCO.

UNESCO (United Nations Educational, Scientific and Cultural Organization) and IIEP (Institute of Educational Planning). 1997. *Appraisal Study of the Cyprus Education System*. Paris: UNESCO.

Vaismoradi, Mojtaba, Hannele Turunen, and Terese Bondas. 2013. "Content Analysis and Thematic Analysis: Implications for Conducting a Qualitative Descriptive study." *Nursing & Health Sciences* 15 (3): 398–405. doi:10.1111/nhs.12048.

Van Petegem, P., A. Blieck, I. Imbrecht, and T. Van Hout. 2005. "Implementing Environmental Education in pre-Service Teacher Training." *Environmental Education Research* 11 (2): 161–171. doi:10.1080/1350462042000338333.

Van Poeck, K., and J. A. Lysgaard. 2016. "The Roots and Routes of Environmental and Sustainability Education Policy Research." *Environmental Education Research* 22 (3): 305–318. doi:10.1080/13504622.2015.1108393.

Wehrens, R. 2014. "Beyond Two Communities – From Research Utilization and Knowledge Translation to Co-Production?" *Public Health* 128 (6): 545–551. doi:10.1016/j.puhe.2014.02.004.

Zachariou, A. 2005. Περιβαλλοντική Εκπαίδευση και Αναλυτικό Πρόγραμμα: Θεωρητικό Πλαίσιο κα ι Αρχές στη Δημοτική Εκπαίδευση της Κύπρου. [*Environmental Education and National Curriculum: Theoretical Framework and Principles in National Curriculum of Cyprus Primary Education*]. Athens: Hellin Publications.

Zachariou, A. 2007. "Περιβαλλοντική Εκπαίδευση και Αναλυτικό Πρόγραμμα: Ζήτημα «Οικολογικ ποίησης» ή ζήτημα «περιθωριοποίησης" [Environmental Education and National Curriculum. "Ecolozisation" or Issue of "Marginalization"?" In *Themes of Educational Design*, edited by F. Kalavasis and A. Kontakos, 211–239. Athens: Atrapos.

Zachariou, A. 2013. "Teacher Professional Development and Education for Sustainable Development: Focal Points for Reorientation [Επαγγελματική Ανάπτυξη των Εκπαιδευτικών και Εκπαίδευση για την Αειφόρο Ανάπτυξη: Σημεία επικέντρωσης και προσανατολισμού]." In *Education for Sustainable Development as an Education Framework for Primary and Pre-Primary Education*, edited by C. Kadji-Beltran and A. Zachariou. Nicosia: Teachers' guide. Frederick Research Center.

Zachariou, A., and C. Kadji-Beltran. 2009. "Cypriot Primary Chool Principals" Understanding of Education for Sustainable Development Key Terms and Their Opinions about Factors Affecting Its Implementation." *Environmental Education Research* 15 (3): 315–342. doi:10.1080/13504620902862902.

Zachariou, A., C. Kadji-Beltran, and C. Manoli. 2013. "School Principals Professional Development in the Framework of Sustainable Schools in Cyprus: A Matter of Refocusing." *Professional Development in Education* 39 (5): 712–731. doi:10.1080/19415257.2012.736085.

Zachariou, A., and L. Symeou. 2009. "The Local Community as a Means for Promoting Education for Sustainable Development." *Applied Environmental Education & Communication* 7 (4): 129–143. doi:10.1080/15330150902744152.

Zachariou, A., I. Savvides, and A. Skordi. 2015. "Σχολική Ηγεσία και Αειφόρο Σχολείο" [School Leadership and Sustainable School." In *Environment, Education and Geography*, edited by E. Flogaiti and N. Lambrinos, 193–216. Athens: Pedio.

Zachariou, A., L. Symeou, and A. Katsikis. 2005. "Action Community Programs: An Alternative Proposal for Promoting the Sociocritical Orientation of Environmental Education in School." In Proceedings of the 1st Pan-

Hellenic Conference "Environmental Education School Programs", edited by T. D. Lekkas, 162–171. Lesvos, Greece, University of Aegean.

Zachariou, A., and N. Valanides. 2006. "Education for Sustainable Development: The Impact of an Outdoor Program on Student-Teachers." *Science Education International* 17 (3): 187–203.

Appendix 1: List of sources included in the analysis of policy and research documents

Policy documents	Research documents
CPI (Cyprus Pedagogical Institute)) 2007.	Amyrotou, G. 2013.
CPI (Cyprus Pedagogical Institute)) 2011.	Hadjiachilleos, S., and A. Zachariou. 2013.
CPI (Cyprus Pedagogical Institute)) 2012.	Kadji-Beltran, C. and A. Zachariou. 2004.
CPI (Cyprus Pedagogical Institute)) 2013.	Kadji-Beltran, C., A. Zachariou, and R.B. Stevenson 2013.
CPI (Cyprus Pedagogical Institute)) 2015.	Kadji-Beltran, C., A. Zachariou, G. Liarakou and E. Flogaiti. 2014.
CPI (Cyprus Pedagogical Institute)) 2016.	Petrou, M. 2011.
CPI (Cyprus Pedagogical Institute)) 2017.	Symeou, L., A. Zachariou, and N. Valanides. 2007.
GENE (Global Education Network in Europe)) 2017.	Zachariou, A., and C. Kadji-Beltran 2009.
MB (Ministerial Board) 2007.	Zachariou, A., C. Kadji-Beltran, and C. Manoli. 2013.
MoEC (Ministry of Education and Culture)) 1998.	Zachariou, A., and L. Symeou 2009.
MoEC (Ministry of Education and Culture)) 2009.	Zachariou A., L. Symeou, and A. Katsikis. 2005.
MoEC (Ministry of Education and Culture)) 2012.	Zachariou, A. and N. Valanides. 2006.
MoEC (Ministry of Education and Culture)) 2014.	Zachariou, A., I. Savvides, and A. Skordi. 2015.
MoEC (Ministry of Education and Culture)) 2015.	

Appendix 2: Classification of documents according to corresponding theme, field of analysis, and document type

Theme	Field of analysis	Document Type	Documents
Synergies between policy makers, researchers and stakeholders	ESD and school leadership	Research papers	Leading sustainable schools (Kadji-Beltran, Zachariou, and Stevenson 2013) School principals' opinions for ESD (Zachariou and Kadji-Beltran 2009) School principals' professional development and Sustainable Schools (Zachariou, Kadji-Beltran, and Manoli 2013)
		Papers published in edited volumes	School leadership and sustainable school (Zachariou, Savvides, and Skordi 2015)
ESD research impact on policy		National policy documents	Curriculum for environmental education/education for sustainable development (MoEC (Ministry of Education and Culture) 2009) Programs for in-service training of novice school principals and assistant school principals in secondary education (CPI (Cyprus Pedagogical Institute) 2015) Programs for in-service training of novice principals in primary education (CPI (Cyprus Pedagogical Institute) 2016) Programs for in-service training of novice school principals in secondary and primary education (CPI 2017)
		Circulars	Directives to primary school principals for ESD curriculum implementation (CPI Circular no. 7.7.09.16/8/6/2011)
	Informal education and ESD	Papers published in edited volumes	Environmental education centers, active learning and environmental literate citizens (Kadji-Beltran and Zachariou 2004) The impact of informal learning environments in developing scientific investigations (Hadjiachilleos and Zachariou 2013)
		National Policy documents/reports	National Action Plan for environmental education and education for sustainable development (CPI (Cyprus Pedagogical Institute) 2007) Proceedings of the Ministerial Board meeting National Action Plan for Environmental Education focus on Sustainable Development (Ministerial Board decision 66/145/4/10/2007) Primary Teachers guiding tool for implementing the Curriculum for Environmental Education/Education for Sustainable Development (MoEC/CPI/CDU 2012) Programmes guide of Network of Environmental Education Centres: EEC of Pedoulas Community (CPI (Cyprus Pedagogical Institute) 2013) Report for Governmental Network of Environmental Education Centers (CPI 2017)
		Circulars	Ministry of Education and Culture Policy for the Environment (MoEC Circular no. 115/9/9/1998)
		Master theses	interventions for biodiversity in formal and non-formal settings (Amyrotou 2013)

(continued)

Continued.

Theme	Field of analysis	Document Type	Documents
	Professional Development and ESD	Proceedings	Environmental education centers in Cyprus as places of non-formal education *(Petrou 2011)* Environmental Education and environmental education goals *(Zachariou and Kadji-Beltran 2009)*
		Research papers	School principals opinions for ESD *(Zachariou and Kadji-Beltran 2009)* School principals professional development and Sustainable Schools *(Zachariou, Kadji-Beltran, and Manoli 2013)* Education for Sustainable Development and Mentoring *(Kadji-Beltran et al. 2014)*
		National Policy documents/ reports	Framing a Unified Policy for Teachers Professional Development (MoEC (Ministry of Education and Culture) 2015)
Policy illuminates gaps in research	ESD research and other educational fields	Research Papers	Parental Involvement in Action Community Environmental Education Programs *(Symeou, Zachariou, and Valanides 2007)* Local Community and ESD *(Zachariou and Symeou 2009)*
		Proceedings	Action Community programs and social-critical orientation of EE in school *(Zachariou, Symeou, and Katsikis 2005)* ESD and action community programs *(Zachariou & Symeou 2009)*
		Papers published in edited volumes	Action Programmes for ESD School and Community Collaboration *(Zachariou, Kadji-Beltran and Symeou 2014)*
		National Policy Documents/ reports	National Report on Global Education in Cyprus *(GENE (Global Education Network in Europe) 2017)*

Index

Note: **Bold** page numbers refer to tables; *italic* page numbers refer to figures and page numbers followed by "n" denote endnotes.

academics: analysis 20; journals, research communication in 42; research 43; structures for 42
AdTAT 115, 117
African National Congress (ANC) 62, 65
Ahmed, S. 12–13, 40
Aikens, K. 17, 62, 64
algorithmic governance 36
analytic autoethnography 8, 95, 97, 103
ANC *see* African National Congress (ANC)
Ángel Maya, A. 115, 117, 120, 122–123
Anthropocene 43
Appadurai, A. 37–38
audit culture 19
Australia 20, 23, 36, 38, 40, 46; bushfires in 43; Morrison government in 44
authoritarian populism 112–113

Bakhtin, M. 114
Ball, S. 37–38, 112–114
Barreras, R. 24
Bhaskar, R. 72
Bieler, A. 64
Biesta, G. 158
big data 19; to determine policy 40; in policy production 36; in school systems 46
Blum, N. 4, 54–55, 103, 151, 153
Boaz, A. 9–10, 23
Bourdieu, P. 37
Braun, A. 113
Brock, A. 9, 11
Brown, A. D. 23–24
Bryk, A. S. 146
Burns, T. 40

Cairney, P. 55
Calderón, J. J. 111–112
capacity building 7, 64, 71, 94
Carrizosa, J. 115, 121

CBOs *see* community-based organizations (CBOs)
CCE *see* Climate Change Education (CCE)
Cerón, P. D. 111–112
Chaiklin, S. 52
Chaux, G. W. 115, 119–120, 123
Cheeseman, A. 17, 27
children: protection 4; welfare 52
Chouliaraki, L. 125n1
citizenship education policy 43
civically-engaged policy research 28
civically-engaged scholarship 4
civil society organisations (CSOs) 94
classroom 19–20, 37
climate: action 9, 29; crisis 38; emergency 46; policy 38–39; science 36
climate change 12, 34–36, 40; contribution of 44; education 4; role of evidence in 3–4
Climate Change Education (CCE) 4
co-creation 102, 133, 151
Colombia: bioregional pedagogical model in 110; collaborative policy development in 11; conceptualisation and practice development in 108; critical discourse analysis 113–114; culture 117–120; Decree 1743 in Law 114 of 1994 111; dominant ideology in 113; education of 109; environmental education in 108; environmental protections 110; ethics 121–122; findings and interpretation 116–117; global educational policies 113; intertextuality in NPEEC 123–124; legislative provisions 109; National Constitution of 1991 110; national environmental education policy in 11; National Environmental System of 121; policy 108, 111–113; problem category 120–121; public education system 107–108; research/researchers (*see* research/researchers); resource management 113; schooling for children 109; seeds of

disidentification 122–123; state and regional levels 109; system 121; tense coalition of forces in 113; territory 121
common knowledge 10; description of 51; models 52
communication differences 42
community-based organizations (CBOs) 139, 141, 146
complex policy processes 19, 21, 27; critical policy studies 21–22; evidence use studies 22–23
conceptualisation 73–74, 108, 159
contemporary policy: agenda 44; education 35, 38; processes 39; production 9; realities of 37
Coole, D. 72
Copeland, T. 7–8, 138
co-production model 151
cosmopolitanization of policy actors 37
critical discourse analysis (CDA) 7, 113–114
critical education policy 20–23
critical policy studies 7, 17–18, 21, 23, 26, 28; analysis 36; approaches 45; 'evidence' governing decision-making 19–20; perspective of 28; research 23–24, 45; work in 27
Crouse, K. 136–137
CSOs *see* civil society organisations (CSOs)
cultural disjunction, evidence of 42
cultural-historical activity theory 7
Cyprus, Education for Sustainable Development (ESD) 157; analysis procedure and thematic categories 154–155; curriculum 153; description of 150–154; documents 154; education 153–154; Environmental Education Centers 156; environmental education programmes 153; ESD in 12; global community challenges 153; Kindergarten-Grade 12 (K-12) education system 153; policy 152, 154, 156; professional development courses 156; research/researchers 151, 156–157; school principals 155–156; synergies between researchers, policy-makers, and stakeholders in 155–156; thematic analysis approach 154–155
Cyprus Pedagogical Institution 157
Cyriot study 6

data infrastructures 21
Davies, H. T. 43, 137, 145
Decade for Education for Sustainable Development 5
decision-making 18, 20, 49; evidence base for 21; nuances of 23; policy making in 20; research in 24
dedicated journals 3
deep mediatization 40–41
democratic socialism 112–113

democratising policy processes 4
Densmore, K. 37
Department of Education and Teachers College (DOE-TC): education scholars 141–142; instrumental fashion 143; partnership 132; research-practice partnership **141**; RPPs 136, **141**
De Sousa Santos, B. 72
Dialnet platform 125n2
digital education governance 20
discourses: codes 115; of dominance 116; ideological strategies, modes of operation and features 116, **116**; symbolic construction in 116, **116**
disembedding 117, 120
disidentification 107, 117, 123–125
district policies, opposition to 152
document analysis 55–56, 132
documentary artifacts, qualitative analysis of 11
DOE-TC *see* Department of Education and Teachers College (DOE-TC)
Donoghue, R. 72
Drezner, N. D. 137
Dussel, E. 65–66, 74
Dye, T. R. 18

Easton, D. 37
ecological wealth 109
economic policy 108
Eco-Schools policy 70
edu-businesses 39
education 4, 11, 29, 34–36; bureaucracy, layers of 39; citizenship education policy 43; climate change 4; contemporary policy 35, 38; contexts 43–46; critical education policy 20–23; defining policy in 39; digital education governance 20; evidence-informed 11; formal and informal 26; global citizenship 45; higher 12, 17, 25–26, 111, 126, 146, 153; improvement science in 134; initiatives, financing of 22; international organisations in 38; marketization, privatization and commercialization in 35; orientations to 22; policy (*see* policy); policymakers 55–56; politics of 9; research/researchers 9, 41–43, 52, 114; research-practice partnership in 133–134; sustainability 4, 11–12, 49–50
Education for Sustainable Development (ESD) 4, 108, 159; conceptualisation 159; curriculum policies 158; development of 159; education research and policy relationships 159; GAP, Germany 91–93; nationwide monitoring, Germany 93–94, *94*; policy and research 157–159; science-policy interfaces within 9; SPIs (*see* science-policy

interfaces (SPIs)); stakeholders' participation 158; transdisciplinary research 159; *see also* Cyprus, Education for Sustainable Development (ESD)
education for the environment (EfE) 26
Edwards, A. 9, 157
EE *see* Environmental Education (EE)
EECI *see* Environmental Education Curriculum Initiative (EECI)
EECs *see* Environmental Education Centers (EECs)
EEPI *see* Environmental Education Policy Initiative (EEPI)
emissions reduction 40
empirical investigation 3
entanglements 34–35
environmental and sustainability education policy 1, 16, 90, 131; developments 5, 16–17; growth of research on 131; institutionalization of 131–132
environmental and sustainability education research 1, 10, 34–35, 52–53; advance research and policy in 9; complexity, sources of 6–7; content and contribution of special issue 2, *2*; contributions to special issue 9–12; definition of 139; developments within 25; distinctiveness of 6; empirical insights 6; engaging, ways of 7; and ESE policy making 2; future needs and opportunities 8–9; global influences 6–7; implications for 25–29; investigating, ways of 8; meta-review of 83–89; partnership and 146; personal passion for 137; policy 3–5, 146; potential implications for 19; prioritisation and resources 2; reflecting, ways of 8; research/researchers (*see* research/researchers); special issue and contribution 5–6; theoretical perspectives 7
environmental degradation 36
Environmental Education (EE) 4, 11–12, 26, 150; in Colombia 108; goal of 27; internationalized conception of 108; national policy of 116–117; policy 6, 25, 107; principles of 27; research 1, 49–50
Environmental Education Centers (EECs) 157–158
Environmental Education Curriculum Initiative (EECI) 71
Environmental Education Policy Initiative (EEPI) 71
environmental policy 3–4
Environmental Sector Skills Plan, 2010 70
environment and sustainability education (ESE): critical incident periods 63–64; intersectionality 64; meta-review 65, 67–74, 83–89; as policy engagement (*see* policy engagement); policy realism and politics as potential 65–66; policy studies, complex conditions 64
epistemological: innocence 44; relativism 44
ESD *see* Education for Sustainable Development (ESD)
evidence: forms of 21; by health-related policy makers 4; narratives 10, 58; oversaturation of 20; in policy 9–10, 19, 21–22; quality 57; types of 20, 56–57; varieties of 20–21
evidence-based approaches 18–19
evidence-based policy 5, 35–36, 39; concept of 35–36; making 41
evidence-driven policy making 17
evidence-informed decision-making 55
evidence-informed education 11
evidence use 26; course of 22–23; nature and dynamics of 23; perceptions of 151; in policy 10; and policy development as practices 22–23; research 18; studies 7, 17–18, 21, 28

Fairclough, N. 114, 125n1
Fakir, S. 64, 75n1
Farley-Ripple, E. 22
Feinstein, N. W. 4, 54–55, 61, 103, 151, 153
fidelity to science 10, 57
Fine, M. 24
fossil fuel industry backers 42
Foucault, M. 37, 113–114
Freeman, R. 23
Freire, L. M. 6, 9
Frost, S. 72

Gale, T. 37
GAP *see* Global Action Programme (GAP)
Garvey, J. C. 137
Geden, O. 100
Germany: Education for Sustainable Development (ESD) implementation 6–7, 90; ESE research-policy relationship in 6
Giddens, A. 52
Gitomer, D. H. 136–137
Global Action Programme (GAP): National Action Plan, ESD 92–93; scientific advisor 93
global agreements 37
global citizenship education 45
global climate change 12
global education policy 39
Global Financial Crisis 38
globalization 45; conditions of 41; contemporary conditions of 37; contemporary processes of 37–38; context of 35–36; of economy 38; multiple processes of 38
global meta-policies 45
global policy model 41–42
global warming 44–45
González-Gaudiano, E. 68, 74

Gordon, I. 133
governance: contemporary modes of 42–43; implications for 38; modes of 42
Griggs, S. 23
Grund, J. 9, 11

Haan, G. de 9, 11
Hankivsky, Olena 152
Head, B. 39–40
Henrick, E. C. 133, 138
higher education 12, 17, 25–26, 111, 126, 146, 153
Hogan, D. 42
Huérfano, A. 6, 9
Humaña de Gauthier, G. 110
Huntley, R. 40

illicit drug policy 4
immigration policy, knowledge in 4
improvement science in education 134
Indigenous knowledge laws 22
individual policy areas 25
information policymakers 21
informed knowledge flows 51
inform policy, research and seeking to 41
initial policy failure, 2000-2010 63
Innvær, Simon 55, 151–152
instrumental use of research *142*
intellectual enterprise 41
interdiscursivity 114, 116
interfaces: knowledge exchange at 52–53; relational approach knowledge exchange 52–53; relational aspects of 49–50; relational expertise for knowledge exchange 50–51; relational work at 51–52
intergovernmental agencies 25
international empirical studies 26–27
international large scale assessments (ILSAs) 19, 38
international organisations 25
international policy: discourses 11; programs 25–26
interprofessional collaboration 10, 50
intertextuality 114, 116

Jacobi, P. R. 61
Janse van Rensburg, E. 72
Jickling, B. 113

Kaaronen, Roope 95–97
Kadji-Beltran, C. 156
Katsikis, A. 157
knowledge 21; common 10; exchange 50–53; production 4, 28, 151; translation 42; utilisation 18
Korfiatis, K. 7–8, 12
Kyoto protocol 45

Læssøe, J. 4, 27, 54–55, 64, 103, 151, 153
Lather, P. 42
Latin America 110, 115, 125
Lewis, J. 133
Limpopo Basin Curriculum Innovation Network, Limpopo Province 71
Lingard, B. 6, 9, 18–19, 37, 58, 133
Lomas, J. 23–24
Lorenc, T. 24, 55, 151–152
Lotz-Sisitka, H. 6–10, 61, 72
Luke, A. 42
Lysgaard, J. 5, 27, 35, 43, 54–55, 58, 65, 157

Maguire, M. 113
Mahoney, J. 136–137
Mandela, N. 62
Manoli, C. 156
Maybin, Jo 55–57
Mcdermott, M. 7–8, 11, 138
McIntyre, L. 44
McKenzie, M. 6, 8–9, 17, 40, 43, 62, 64, 74, 133
media coverage 44
Mejía-Cáceres, M. A. 6, 9, 11
mental health workers 50
mobile policy models 41
moral responsibility, neutrality of 52
Morrison, T. 42, 101–102

National Environmental Sector Skills Plan 73
National Environmental Skills Planning Forum (NESPF) 71
national policy agenda 50
National Policy Forum 5
National Policy of Environmental Education in Colombia (NPEEC) 107, 112, 124; aims of 117; discursive practices 115–116; ideology in 112–113; journals and books 115; notion of disidentification 117; textual structure of 115
natural resource management 27
necropolitics 66
neo-conservatism 112–113
neo-liberalism 37, 112–113
neoliberal policy influences 19
neo-positivism 42
NESPF *see* National Environmental Skills Planning Forum (NESPF)
networked improvement community (NIC) 146
network governance 35, 38
new public management 37
New York City 131–132; application of improvement science in education 134; artefacts and documents analysis 137; Chancellor's Regulation A-850 135–136; coding process 137; conceptual use 143; data analysis 137; data and methods 136–137; DOE Annual Report *144*; DOE-TC 132,

141; improvement science literature 134; long-term challenges 135; organizational decision-making 143; policy context in 132; positionality statement 137–138; process benefits from engagement 144–145; research-practice partnership in education 133–134; research use 134–135, 140–145; school sustainability programs 138; school system 135; strategic plan for sustainability 135; study setting 135–136; sustainability education 136, *136*; Sustainability Plan Survey 2017 140; team–based data analysis 137; trust and cultivating partnership relationships 138–140; use of research evidence 137

New York City Partnership for Sustainability Education (NPSE) 132

New Zealand, education policy and evaluation in 5

Noguera, A. 115, 122

non-decision making 18

NPEEC *see* National Policy of Environmental Education in Colombia (NPEEC)

Nutley, S. 43, 49–50, 137, 145

O'Brien, P. 109

Oliver, Kathryn 55, 151–152

opinion polls 20

organizational policy makers 22

Orland, M. 41–42

oversaturation of evidence 20

Ozga, J. 18

Paris protocol 45

participatory action research (PAR) 24

partnership 'problem-solving' research 23

Peck, J. 39, 41

personalized learning 20

Pineda, Londoño 111–112

Pizmony-Levy, O. 11, 138, 152

Plan-Do-Study-Act 137

pluralism of research types 43

policy 4, 11, 13, 18, 34–35, 37, 39; academic research on 41; actors, cosmopolitanization of 9–10; advocates 22; borrowing 21; change 24, 151; collaboration, structured forms of 7; communities 51; decision-making 19, 21; decisions 55; discourses 9–10, 39; enactments 22, 113; entrepreneurs 22, 27; environments 58; evidence 17; imaginaries, 'debordering' of 36; immobilities of 22; implementation 50; improvement 151; inconsistency, 2010-2019 63; initiatives, evaluations of 20; mediatization of 40; mobility 22, 39; models 42; narratives 7, 10, 58; by numbers and international performativity 26; practices of 18, 23, 27; preparation, 1990-1994 63; problems 158; production 27, 35–36, 38; programs 28; proliferation, 1994-2000 63; realism 65–66; reception, respect of 40; research 8–9, 13, 41, 45, 151; sociology 18; special issues 3; types for 29; 'vehicular idea' in 36

policy and research: co-production of 151; as practices 9

policy development 43; evidence use and 22–23; influences on 21; policies on 22; process 10

policy engagement 66–68; complex conditions, policy flux 62–64; ESE research 62–63; multi-modal nature 72–74; relational and embedded nature 70–71; South Africa 62; theoretical work, expanding and deepening 71–72; wider policy shifts 68–70

policy making/makers 7, 21, 26–27, 41, 43, 56; commitments and realities of 18; daily work practices 56; demands for evidence 58; dispositions of 41; global dispositions of 37; perspectives of 17–18, 57–58; practices of 28, 50; projects to 50; realities and dilemmas of 13; research/researchers 3, 27, 36; specialist practices of 49; spheres 20; structures for 42; work practices 58

policy processes 7, 17, 24, 36; analyses of 24; empirical research on 3; focus on 9; investigation of 17; qualitative and conceptual insights into 21; research evidence in 4

policyscapes 39

politics: and policy, centrality of 3; political complexity 6; political theory 7

politics as potential: description 66; (re)invigoration 65–66; outcomes 67–70

post-truth 44; context 45–46; political environment 36; politics of 36, 40–41, 44–45

power 66, 71

practical development 3

practice-based inquiries 23

PRAES 111–112, 120–121, 123

private sector involvement 39

problem-solving actions 50

professional learning processes 7

Programme for International Student Assessment (PISA) 19–20

provincial health policy makers 23

public policies 1, 42, 125; aspect of 37; definition of 37; discourse 113–114

public scholarship 28

qualitative documentary analysis 8

quality of life 109

queer uses 12

questions of power 11

Ramsarup, P. 6–10
real-time policy instruments 20
Reconstruction and Development Programme (RDP) 62
regional agreements 37
Reid, A. 6, 9, 27, 54–55, 58
relational: agency 10, 51–52; concepts 51–52; engagements 10; expertise 50–52; processes 6
Renshaw, P. 42
research-policy interface 5, 8, 10, 17, 19, 28, 50, 157
research-policy relationships 2–4, 9, 11–12, 16–17, 25, 28–29, 40, 54–55, 151; complex policy processes 21; critical policy studies 17–24; department-wide systems and processes 57–58; disclosure statement 29; evidence and policy 55–56; evidence in decision-making 19; evidence to shape policy narratives 56–57; evidence use studies 17–25; features of 17; interpretation of 58; nature of 58; policymakers perspectives on evidence use 58; roles of research 23
research-practice partnership (RPP) 8, 131–132; application of improvement science in education 134; classic typologies 135; conceptual use 135; creation of education 145; data and methods 136–137; DOE–TC 135–136, 138–139, **139, 141**; in education 133–134; empirical research on 132; formal qualitative studies 146; framework for assessing 133–134, 140; instrumental use 135, 140; and policy 133; policymakers and practitioners 134; positionality statement 137–138; potential benefits of 145; process 132, 135; proliferation of 133; research/researchers 132, 134–135, 140–146; scholarship 137; strategic/tactical/symbolic use 135; study setting 135–136; trust and cultivating partnership relationships 138–140; working relationships 139
research/researchers 21; accountability 42; assessment processes 3; cultural-historical approach to 50; discourses 7, 11, **118**; disjunctive cultures between 41; evidence 21, 24–25; features of 42; foundational figure in 41; impact, construction of 43; inductive categories for **119**; informed policy 40, 45; informed strikes 12; and policy interactions 7–8; policy relationships 21, 36; and public interfaces 49–50; reductive definition of 43; relationships 35–36, 42; use, complexity of 24–25; utilisation 41
Rice, M. 159
Rickinson, M. 6, 8–9, 23, 55–57, 133, 152, 157
Rizvi, F. 37
Rojas, Vélez 111–112
Rosenberg, H. 6–10
RPP *see* research-practice partnership (RPP)

Sauvé, L. 110
Sayer, A. 73
schools 19–20, 39; autonomy 40; diversity of social practices in 124; planning 25; practices 37
Schuller, T. 40
science-based domains 26
science denial 36
science of sustainability (SOS) 133
science-policy interfaces (SPIs) 7, 9, 11; definition 90; evidence base 99–101; expectations of measuring, ESD 98–99; insights, ESD 97; methodological background, analyses 95, 97; models of 95; power dynamics 101–102; typology 96, **96**
science-policy relations 151
Scott, Bill 1
SDGs *see* Sustainable Development Goals (SDGs)
Sebba, J. 150–151, 157
SEEP *see* Sustainable Environmental Education Policy (SEEP)
separate orbits 42
service users, daily interactions with 50
SGBs *see* Standards Generating Bodies (SGBs)
Shaxson, L. 9–10, 57
Singer-Brodowski, M. 6–9, 11
social: inequality 18; mediatization of policy 40–41; policy development 20; practice, concept of 125n1; researchers, neutrality of 52; structure 18; work/workers 17, 50
social science 1, 4; application of 18; researchers 17
soft governance 20
South Africa 7; ESE 10, 64, 66–68, 70–71; multimodal nature of ESE research and evaluation 72–74; policy engagement 8, 62–64; policy realism and (re) invigoration of 'politics as potentia' 65–66; policy shifts 68–70; research paper 61–62; theoretical work over time 71–72
special issues: contributions to 9–12; on ESE policy research 5
specific edited collections 3
SPIs *see* science-policy interfaces (SPIs)
stakeholders 9, 57
Standards Generating Bodies (SGBs) 71
state policy production 37
state restructuring 40
Stevens, A. 20
Stevenson, R. B. 4, 17, 25–27
Stratford, R. 5

sustainability 4, 6, 29, 34–36, **136,** 143; education 4, 11–12, 49–50; policies 3–4, 25–26
Sustainability and Education Policy Network (SEPN) 5
sustainable development 3–4, 109
Sustainable Development Goals (SDGs) 2, 26
Sustainable Environmental Education Policy (SEEP) 157
Symeou, L. 157

Talero de Husain, E. 110
technological and social mobility 18
textual analysis, form of 3
Theodore, N. 39, 41
theoretical inquiry 3
Think Tanks 43–44
Thompson, J. B. 112
Toomey, A. 50
Torres Carrasco, M. 110, 115, 123
transnationalization 37
Trellez, F. 123
Trowler, P. 140
Trump, Donald 38, 44
Tuck, E. 24

UK: Health Alliance on Climate Change 51; Research Excellence Framework 2014 51
undemocratic technocracy 40
UNESCO-UNEP International Environmental Education Program 27
United Nations (UN): Conference on the Human Environment 108; Decade for ESD 36; Intergovernmental Panel on Climate Change (IPCC) 35; Millennium Declaration 153

Valanides, N. 157
Van Poeck, K. 5, 27, 44, 54–58, 65, 157
Vaughter, P. 17, 62

Wals, A. E. J. 5, 113
Walter, Isabel 43
Wehrens, R. 151
Weiss, C. H. 41
White Paper on Education and Training 70
Williams, Raymond 40
work: practices 56; trajectories of 3

Yale Program on Climate Change Communication 40
Young, K. 133

Zachariou, A. 7–8, 12, 156–157

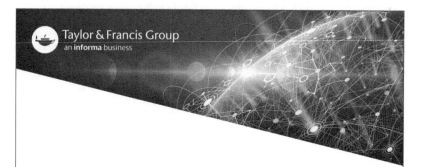